Ageing with Smartphones in Urban Brazil

Ageing with Smartphones in Urban Brazil
A work in progress

Marília Duque

First published in 2022 by
UCL Press
University College London
Gower Street
London WC1E 6BT

Available to download free: www.uclpress.co.uk

Text © Author, 2022
Images © Author, 2022

The author has asserted her rights under the Copyright, Designs and Patents Act 1988 to be identified as the author of this work.

A CIP catalogue record for this book is available from the British Library.

This book is published under a Creative Commons Attribution Non-commercial Non-derivative 4.0 International licence (CC BY-NC-ND 4.0). This licence allows you to share, copy, distribute and transmit the work for personal and non-commercial use provided author and publisher attribution is clearly stated. Attribution should include the following information:

Duque, M. 2022. *Ageing with Smartphones in Urban Brazil: A work in progress*. London: UCL Press. https://doi.org/10.14324/111.9781787359963

Further details about Creative Commons licences are available at http://creativecommons.org/licenses/

Any third-party material in this book is published under the book's Creative Commons licence unless indicated otherwise in the credit line to the material. If you would like to reuse any third-party material not covered by the book's Creative Commons licence, you will need to obtain permission directly from the copyright holder.

ISBNS:
Hardback 978-1-78735-998-7
Paperback 978-1-78735-997-0
ePDF 978-1-78735-996-3
ePub 978-1-78735-999-4
Mobi – 978-1-80008-338-7
DOI 10.14324/111.9781787359963

Contents

List of figures	vii
Series foreword	xi
Acknowledgements	xiii
Abbreviations	xv
1. Introduction	1
2. Life after retirement	35
3. The art of being busy	61
4. Family gathering	98
5. Unlocking the smartphone	126
6. Crafting health	152
7. Challenging sexuality at the best age	181
8. Seeking a purpose in life	208
9. Conclusions	233
Bibliography	252
Index	269

List of figures

1.1	Map of Brazil showing regions and states. Brazil Map © Pixabay. Graphic © Marília Duque.	7
1.2	The 'Monumento às Bandeiras' (monument to the flags) celebrates the 400th anniversary of São Paulo. © Marília Duque.	9
1.3	Map of the 96 districts in São Paulo city. © Rede Nossa São Paulo. Mapa da Desigualdade 2020.	10
1.4	Houses and buildings juxtaposed in Bento. © Marília Duque.	12
1.5	The oldest grocery shop in Bento, where the owner may recount the histories of the neighbourhood. © Marilia Duque.	13
1.6	A modern grocery shop in Bento. © Marília Duque.	14
1.7	An outdoor gym in a public square in Bento. © Marília Duque.	14
1.8	Entrance to one of the public hospitals in Bento. © Marília Duque.	15
1.9	The waiting room of one of the public hospitals in Bento. © Marília Duque.	16
1.10	Entrance to the shopping centre. The stairs lead to the underground railway and the bus station. © Marília Duque.	16
1.11	An underground station in Bento. © Marília Duque.	17
1.12	The main street in Bento, with the silhouette of the Catholic church at the end. © Marília Duque.	17
1.13	Items used in an Umbanda ritual are placed in the square that lies in front of one of the Catholic churches in Bento, showcasing the neighbourhood's religious diversity. © Marília Duque.	19

1.14	Teaching WhatsApp in the Catholic church hall. Photograph by one of the students in the class.	21
1.15	Backstage at the fashion show with the models in the background. © Marília Duque.	22
1.16	At the gym. © Marília Duque.	23
1.17	At a meeting of the group that discusses alternative forms of work for older people in Bento. © Marília Duque.	25
1.18	People worshipping inside the church at the festival of the patron saint. © Marília Duque.	26
1.19	The party outside the church. The roses symbolise the miracle performed by the church's patron saint. © Marília Duque.	27
1.20	My referral at the public hospital at Bento, where I was sent to the orthopaedic unit. © Marília Duque.	28
2.1	Post from digital influencer: 'creative women, curious, sensitive, learners and entrepreneurs. Grandmothers!' © @It-Avo.	37
2.2	Official image currently used to indicate spaces and facilities reserved for older people (on the left), and the proposed new one on the right. © senado.leg.br.	41
3.1	*Active Ageing: A Policy Framework* eBook cover. © WHO.	66
3.2	Brazilian version of *Active Ageing: A Policy Framework* eBook cover. © WHO.	67
3.3	Longevity Playground sign. © Marília Duque.	68
3.4	Older people using the Longevity Playground in Bento. © Marília Duque.	69
3.5 and 3.6	Photos of a rose and orchids cultivated by older people and shared on WhatsApp. Screenshot taken by Marília Duque.	81
3.7	A typical Facebook post shared by older people in Bento. Attributed to Millôr Fernandes. Screenshot taken by Marília Duque.	83
3.8	Facebook post shared by an older person in Bento. Screenshot taken by Marília Duque.	84
3.9	Facebook post shared by an over-60s group: 'Stop ageing. Keep moving. Happy 2019 to the Active Older People'. Screenshot taken by Marília Duque.	85
3.10	A Facebook post shared by a retired couple preparing for a motorcycle trip. © @lilianacenturine.	86

3.11	Facebook post: 'Sometimes we have to admit it is time to retire.' Screenshot taken by Marília Duque.	87
3.12	Facebook post shared by an older person in Bento: 'What's on TV?' 'Some shit … every channel is showing the same old man.' Screenshot taken by Marília Duque.	88
3.13	Image shared by a participant in a WhatsApp group for people of 60 and over. Screenshot taken by Marília Duque.	90
3.14	Dialogue between members of a WhatsApp group for over-60s in Bento. Screenshot taken by Marília Duque.	
4.1 and 4.2	Traditional roast chicken sold every Sunday in Bento's bakeries. © Marília Duque.	102
4.3	Family leaving Sunday Mass. The elderly mother is assisted by her older daughter. © Marília Duque.	103
4.4	A Doriana TV advert from 1990. Frame captured by Marília Duque at 0:20. See the video at https://youtu.be/rpdsSusd4rE.	104
4.5	Set of stickers shared by a participant to quickly inform her family when she is at the gym, taking a shower, going to meet them, meditating, doing yoga and going to sleep. © anonymised participant.	116
4.6	Post shared on a WhatsApp family group. 'There are a lot of hugs waiting for an opportunity to hug.'	118
4.7	Post shared on a WhatsApp family group. 'For today: a grateful mind and a happy heart. Have a good day.' Messages like this are shared throughout the day.	119
5.1 and 5.2	Messages containing alerts about new scams are constantly shared among WhatsApp groups. Screenshots taken by © Marília Duque.	132
5.3	Students taking notes during a WhatsApp course in Bento. © Daniel Miller.	134
5.4	Older people in Bento have become intense users of social media, like the younger generations they criticise. Photograph taken during a social event in Bento. © Marília Duque.	138
5.5	Saturday evening in a dance club in Bento. The lady at the table brought both her smartphone and her charger to the event. © Marília Duque.	140

5.6	Example of *gambiarra*. © Hélvio Romero.	145
5.7	Example of 'desire line'. © wetwebwork. CC BY 2.0.	147
6.1	Example of a message shared on a WhatsApp group of people over 60. The message consists of guidelines attributed to a 'doctor friend' for preventing Alzheimer's. Screenshot taken by Marília Duque.	154
6.2	Example of nutrition tips being shared in a WhatsApp group. Screenshot taken by Marília Duque.	157
6.3 and 6.4	Figure 6.3 shows 'Feijoada', a typical heavy Brazilian dish made with black beans and pork. Figure 6.4 shows jelly, often made from collagen and commonly served as a free dessert in low-cost restaurants in Bento. © Pixabay.com.	159
6.5	'Point of light': mini ikebana arrangement offered as a gift at the Church of World Messianity in Bento. © Marília Duque.	161
6.6	Rice and salt enriched with special properties which they acquired during worship at the Church of World Messianity and offered to visitors with the instruction that they should be mixed into food prepared at home. © Marília Duque.	162
6.7 and 6.8	Low-cost clinics operating in Bento, including Dr Consulta (6.8). They look like shops and one of them (6.7) is indeed inside the biggest shopping mall in Bento. © Marília Duque.	169
6.9 and 6.10	Screenshots from the 'Agenda Fácil' app, in which users are advised to ask for a code at their nearest UBS. Screenshots taken by Marília Duque.	171

Series foreword

This book series is based on a project called ASSA – the Anthropology of Smartphones and Smart Ageing. It was primarily funded by the European Research Council (ERC) and located at the Department of Anthropology, UCL. The project had three main goals. The first was to study ageing. Our premise was that most studies of ageing focus on those defined by age, that is youth and the elderly. This project would focus upon people who did not regard themselves as either young or elderly. We anticipated that their sense of ageing would also be impacted by the recent spread of smartphone use. Smartphones were thereby transformed from a youth technology to a device used by anyone. This also meant that, for the first time, we could make a general assessment of the use and consequences of smartphones as a global technology, beyond those connotations of youth. The third element was more practical. We wanted to consider how the smartphone has impacted upon the health of people in this age group and whether we could contribute to this field. More specifically, this would be the arena of mHealth, that is, smartphone apps designed for health purposes.

The project consists of 11 researchers working in 10 fieldsites across nine countries, as follows: Al-Quds (East Jerusalem) studied by Laila Abed Rabho and Maya de Vries; Bento, in São Paulo city, Brazil studied by Marília Duque; Cuan in Ireland studied by Daniel Miller; Godown in Kampala, Uganda studied by Charlotte Hawkins; Kochi and Kyoto in Japan studied by Laura Haapio-Kirk; NoLo in Milan, Italy studied by Shireen Walton; Santiago in Chile studied by Alfonso Otaegui; Shanghai in China studied by Xinyuan Wang; Thornhill in Ireland studied by Pauline Garvey; and Yaoundé in Cameroon studied by Patrick Awondo. Several of the fieldsite names are pseudonyms.

Most of the researchers are funded by the European Research Council. The exceptions are Alfonso Otaegui, who is funded by the

Pontificia Universidad Católica de Chile, and Marília Duque, Laila Abed Rabho and Maya de Vries, who are mainly self-funded. Pauline Garvey is based at Maynooth University. The research was simultaneous, except for the research in Al-Quds, which is extended since the researchers are also working while researching.

The project has published a comparative book about the use and consequences of smartphones, called *The Global Smartphone*. In addition, we intend to publish an edited collection presenting our work in the area of mHealth. There will also be nine monographs representing our ethnographic research, the two fieldsites in Ireland being combined in a single volume. These ethnographic monographs will mostly have the same chapter headings. This will enable readers to consider our work comparatively. The project has been highly collaborative and comparative from the beginning. We have been blogging since its inception at https://blogs.ucl.ac.uk/assa/. Further information about the project may be found on our project's main website, at https://www.ucl.ac.uk/anthropology/assa/. The core of this website is translated into the languages of our fieldsites and we hope that the comparative book and the monographs will also appear in translation. As far as possible, all our work is available without cost, under a creative commons licence.

Acknowledgements

This book wouldn't have been possible without the collaboration of my research participants. On the one hand, I became their 'mascot' and the 'guardian angel' who helped them with some technological issues during my fieldwork. On the other hand, they became my mentors, my parents and my friends, and this friendship lasts to this day, thanks to our connection on WhatsApp.

I also want to thank Mariana and Nikki. And, above all, I must thank my son for his patience regarding my absence during those years.

I would like to thank ESPM São Paulo and Coordination for the Improvement of Higher Education Personnel (CAPES-PDSE) for providing me with scholarships for my PhD. I wouldn't have been able to be part of this project without the support of Luiz Peres-Neto, Mari Mitsuru Nishimura and Cristina Helena Pinto de Mello.

Finally, thanks to the ASSA team, Georgiana Murariu and the anonymous reviewers for commenting on this book and Glynis Baguley for copy-editing it.

This project was funded by the European Research Grant ERC-2016-ADG – SmartPhoneSmartAging – 740472.

Abbreviations

ADL	activities of daily living
ANS	Agência Nacional de Saúde Suplementar (Brazilian national regulatory agency for health insurance plans)
ASSA	Anthropology of Smartphones and Smart Ageing
CAAE	certificado de apresentação de apreciação ética (ethics approval certificate)
CAP	Caixa de Aposentadoria e Pensões (pension and retirement fund)
CAPES	Coordenação de Aperfeiçoamento de Pessoal de Nível Superior (coordination for the improvement of higher education personnel)
DRC	Democratic Republic of Congo
ERC	European Research Council
ET	essential tremor
GDP	gross domestic product
HCor	Hospital do Coração (heart hospital)
HIV	human immunodeficiency virus
HRT	hormone replacement therapy
IADL	instrumental activities of daily living
IAP	Institutos de Aposentadoria e Pensões (retirement and pension institutes)

IBGE	Instituto Brasileiro de Geografia e Estatística (Brazilian Institute of Geography and Statistics)	
ICF	informed consent form	
ICI	intracavernosal injection therapy (a treatment for erectile dysfunction)	
INPS	Instituto Nacional de Previdência Social (Brazil's national institute for pension security)	
INSS	Instituto Nacional de Seguro Social (Brazil's national pension system)	
LBV	Legião da Boa Vontade (Legion of Goodwill)	
OADR	old-age dependency ratio	
PAISM	Programa de Assistência Integral à Saúde Mulher (women's integral health assistance programme)	
PDSE	Programa de Doutorado Sanduíche no Exterior (Brazilian doctoral sandwich programme)	
QoL	quality of life	
Sebrae	Serviço Brasileiro de Apoio às Micro e Pequenas Empresas (Brazilian service for the support of micro and small businesses)	
SESC	Serviço Social de Comércio (trade social service)	
SUS	Sistema Único de Saúde (the Brazilian public health system, which is free to all citizens of Brazil)	
UBS	Unidade Básica de Saúde (basic healthcare unit).	
WHI	Women's Health Initiative	
WHO	World Health Organization	

1
Introduction

Summary of conclusions

It is not a surprise that in a country known as the cradle of outstanding football players, like Pelé, Neymar and Marta, the expression *pendurar as chuteiras* (to hang up one's boots) is synonymous with retirement. The metaphor is convenient for addressing the role retirement plays in the experience of ageing in Bento, the middle-class neighbourhood in São Paulo city where this ethnography took place. A wise football player could choose to *pendurar as chuteiras* and end her career while she is at her peak, leaving the field on a high note, or she could stay on the pitch and watch her performance decline with age. The younger players might not have her experience, but they could make up for this by being faster and stronger. Gradually, compared with the other players, the 'legend' comes to be seen as 'old'. And thus the experienced football player ends up being considered obsolete. A celebration might be held in her honour to mark her compulsory retirement or, in the worst scenario, people might just forget her. Whatever happens, the fact is that her occupation has defined who she has been for most of her life so far. It is not easy to decide when to leave the pitch, but a former player (like anyone who has retired) can follow other avenues to reinvent herself and age with purpose and dignity. The good news is that she still feels young inside. Moreover, she is finally free from the strict training routine and has proved her value through her past conquests. She can now start the second half of the game, which is life between retirement and death.

My main argument is that retirement is not the end of working life, at least not in Bento. Instead, I argue that research participants will enter new fields in which new and old rules sit alongside each other. On the one hand, they still live in the same work-oriented community, where inactivity is a moral failure. On the other hand, they have to comply with health and ageing policies that require them to stay productive to avoid becoming a burden to the state or society. Retirement is still, therefore, a field of duties and moral expectations. However, it is also a space for freedoms and pleasures postponed to this stage of life. Smartphones can be a game-changer in this match. As we will see, they empower older people to stay active, productive and autonomous, while at the same time finding ways to meet their desires and pursue new occupations that can provide them with a sense of usefulness, dignity and purpose. Yet this balance is not easy to achieve, and it results in multiple and diverse experiences of ageing in Bento. We can only understand this complexity through a holistic approach, and by considering how research participants manage their bodies, time, finances, health, family, friends and reputations.

Their decisions will also be influenced by local values that associate work with character. This morality reflects the essence of the city of which Bento is a part. As we will see in chapter 2, the identity of São Paulo was historically built on the glorification of workers who arrived from different parts of the world and from other parts of Brazil, motivated by the promise of prosperity through hard work. Thus, inactivity, extended to retirement, is not welcomed in Bento. Even so, a whole generation did retire, and at early ages. Some based their decision on rumours of a reform to the national pension system. Others were made redundant because of ageism in the labour market.[1] For both, retirement was not the end of their busy lives but a problem they had to solve, as they now have to find new forms of work to fit social expectations and local moralities. Some will pursue new occupations in order to balance free time, productivity, pleasure and purpose, while some are still worried about the financial losses of retirement. Others live in limbo, as they are 'old' but neither employed nor retired. However, research participants are more likely to keep silent about these negative aspects, as I argue in the final chapter. Rather than complaining, older people in Bento use their smartphones to endorse positive images of ageing. By doing so, they contribute to the normativity of old age as 'the best age', as a time to be independent, extremely social, busy, healthy and happy.

Chapter 3 addresses how this normativity brings about an awareness of the importance of taking care of oneself and remaining active. On top of their daily activities, older people in Bento prioritise physical activities, and exercises to improve their memory, cognition and autonomy. As we will see, they are more likely to approach these activities as an obligation once they are expected to remain independent and productive for reasons other than the ones posed by health policies focused on prevention. At the same time, however, these activities provide pleasure, promote socialisation and help them to prove that they are still active even after retirement. As well as exercising, any activity can be regarded as an opportunity to develop a busy schedule. A full diary allows research participants to say 'I'm busy. I don't have time,' while enjoying the status they had while they were working. Thus, managing their social life online can become an activity in itself. They start working as content curators, sharing on WhatsApp groups the opportunities for activities aimed at the third age in Bento, which their peers value highly. In addition, as content producers they work to produce evidence that they are healthy and busy. By giving visibility to their moments of activity, they cope with global and local demands, blurring the borders between obligation and self-realisation in the third age.

These borders are more rigid when research participants prioritise care for elderly parents, children and grandchildren over the time they spend having fun with friends. As discussed in chapter 4, WhatsApp brings efficiency to their family interactions, helping them to manage expectations and conflicts between generations. It also brings the extended family into their daily communication. Once restricted to annual family events, this conversation has turned into a co-presence embedded in everyday life, which is facilitated by visual resources that keep the conversation flowing. A key finding reveals that frequency is more important than content within family WhatsApp groups, as the priority is to keep the connection (and bonds) active.

WhatsApp is responsible for expanding older people's sociability in Bento, including engagement with friends, and friends of friends, whom they meet at local activities aimed at the third age. WhatsApp creates a feedback mechanism. WhatsApp groups are the place in which they share opportunities for new encounters and activities that result in the creation of new WhatsApp groups to support the activity or group in question. WhatsApp is also the app that promotes digital inclusion among older people in Bento, who are likely to look to expert assistance or ask friends for help, as children don't have the time or patience to teach them. In chapter 5, I address their learning process, how they overcome their low self-esteem, and how they try other apps like Uber and Google Maps in order to gain mobility in the city, which adds to their independence and socialisation even more. However, the key finding in this chapter is that research participants combine multiple apps and strategies to bypass their lack of digital skills and get things done.

In chapter 6, I observe how this 'smartness' is applied to seeking medical help. In preference to bespoke apps, WhatsApp is where older people in Bento share health information and receive medical guidance. Although they search for information on Google and follow specialists on YouTube, they are more likely to trust medical authorities when they have a problem. Only a few doctors in Bento share their contact details with patients. However, even when research participants have them, they reserve them for genuine emergencies. Thus, they are more likely to rely on friends, and friends of friends, who work in healthcare for guidance on everyday health issues. This assistance, mediated through WhatsApp, is informal (being based on their personal connections) and professional (the connections are with qualified people) at the same time. This arrangement is not exclusive to health, and it results in a network of favours and solidarity based on friendship and reciprocity.

Beyond WhatsApp groups and social media, smartphones are a space for intimacy. In chapter 7, I look at participants' smartphones to meet them in that private space, where they consume pornography or try apps for casual sex. Although the representation of old age as 'the best age' is reinforced by dating websites and apps aimed at the third age in Brazil, older people in Bento complain that their ageing bodies are not at their best. Menopause and impotence bring new challenges to their sexuality, resulting in possible mismatches, as men are likely to search for younger women. Among married people, some have lost their admiration of and desire for their long-time partners, while others focus on partnership, accepting a decline in sexual life. This chapter explores possible happy endings that go beyond penetration (the matches and marriages observed were all heterosexual).

But what would be a happy ending from a broader perspective? Chapter 8 tries to understand the purpose of life, which is replaced, in Bento, by the desire to live in the present with purpose. Some might retire. Yet they still live in a society in which work is seen as a virtue, providing integrity, dignity and citizenship. Consequently, research participants try to find ways to return to work and re-establish the professional credentials they lost, and achieve a sense of belonging. Entrepreneurship, self-development and volunteering are alternative forms of work chosen by them, with the advantage that these activities allow them to work for themselves, rather than others, which is a frequently expressed desire after retirement. Working for and on themselves enables them to meet their own needs and expand their possibilities in old age as a kind of activism, building a legacy for the next generations of older people in Bento.

However, before settling down in Bento, I propose a quick zoom out, so that you can understand the big picture that reveals Brazil as an ageing nation and São Paulo as a city historically associated with work. After this brief contextualisation, I introduce Bento and the methodology used in this project.

Welcome to Brazil

Brazil is a democratic federal republic of 26 states and a federal district. Located in South America, its official language is Portuguese, inherited from Portuguese colonisation. Brazil is the world's fifth-largest country by area[2] and the sixth most populous,[3] with a population of around 211,755,692 inhabitants in 2020.[4] To understand where this ethnography took place, we first must account for the *demographic changes* that have turned Brazil into an ageing nation. Following that, we should address its impacts on *inequality* and *diversity* as experienced in the country. According to the Instituto Brasileiro de Geografia e Estatística (IBGE; Brazilian institute of geography and statistics),[5] by 2060 25.5 per cent of Brazilians will be over 65, representing 58.2 million people. The ageing population brings new challenges to public resources and finances, especially regarding healthcare and pension systems.

As in other developing countries, ageing results in an epidemiological transition in which morbidity caused by infectious and transmissible diseases is replaced by or overlaps with non-transmissive chronic diseases related to the later stages of life.[6] In Brazil, this shift means that the already overstretched Sistema Único de Saúde (SUS; public health system),[7] which provides unlimited healthcare assistance to all Brazilian citizens[8] at no cost, becomes subject to even greater demand. As a consequence, health and ageing policies in the country start to focus on prevention and individual autonomy. The anthropologist Guita Grin Debert called this process the 're-privatisation of ageing', as the primary responsibility for older people is placed on the family and on older people themselves.[9] The role played by the state and society in ageing policies[10] was mainly redefined by the National Policy for the Elderly implemented in 1996,[11] by the Brazilian Statute for Elderly People[12] in 2003 and by the WHO's Active Ageing framework.[13] The latter was then incorporated into the National Health Policy for Elderly Persons in 2006.[14] As the WHO's guidelines suggest, states and societies should develop opportunities to 'keep, recover and promote the autonomy and independence of older people'.[15] Consequently, as I argue throughout this book, research participants are not supposed to become a burden on any of these institutions, including their families.

The expectation surrounding the extension of autonomy into old age is expanded to financial autonomy, as older people are the age group targeted as responsible for the deficit experienced by the Instituto Nacional do Seguro Social (INSS; national institute for social security).[16] The dependency ratio in the country was 44 per cent in 2018 and is projected to be 51.5 per cent in 2039.[17] Considering only the proportion of old-age dependants (people aged 65 and over) per 100 persons of working age, 20–64, Brazil is predicted to have the fourth-highest old-age dependency ratio (OADR) in Latin America by 2030, behind Uruguay, Chile and Argentina. However, the Brazilian OADR is predicted to be the second in growth (compared with 2019), just behind Chile.[18] Since the 1980s, projections like these have frequently been discussed in the media,[19] helping to cast ageing as an economic problem and a burden to society. The need to balance the effect of the old-age dependency ratio on finances resulted in a reform to the Brazilian pension system in 2019. A new pension scheme was approved, establishing a minimum age for retirement (statutory retirement age). Before that, Brazilians could retire if they had contributed to the pension system for enough years. On the other hand, in 2018, older people provided 69.8 per cent of the income in Brazilian households that had at least one resident aged 60 or above (33.9 per cent of the households in the country). The state pension represented 56.3 per cent of older people's incomes.[20] These pensions can provide a certain stability during recessionary years.[21] However, they can also result in different experiences of ageing, depending on how many people rely on retired people and other factors such as house ownership or additional incomes. As we will see, retirement is just another arena for inequality in Brazil.

The country is one of the most unequal in the world when it comes to income distribution. In 2019,[22] half of the Brazilian population received 15.6 per cent of the total income. The 10 per cent of the population with the lowest incomes received 0.8 per cent of the total income. At the opposite end of the spectrum, the 10 per cent of the population with the highest incomes received 42.9 per cent of the total income. These inequalities should also be considered within the frame of the macro-regions of Brazil. For example, in the same year, the *per capita* household income in the Southeast and the South was almost twice that in the North and the Northeast.[23] This imbalance means Brazil can be a very different country, depending on where one lives and ages. And it is not just about income. Even considering basic infrastructure, we can see the contrast between the country's best and worst conditions. The population living in households

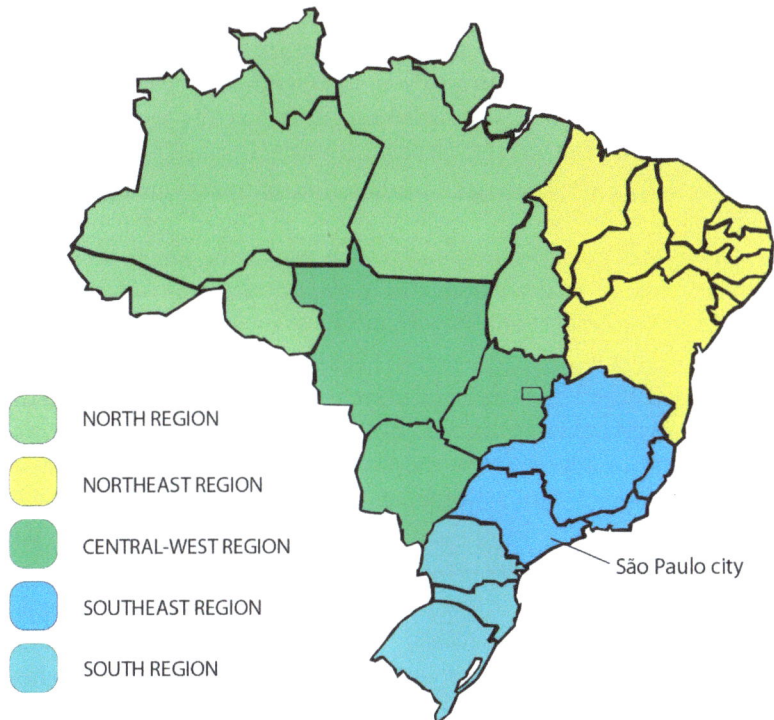

Figure 1.1 Map of Brazil showing regions and states. Brazil Map © Pixabay. Graphic © Marília Duque.

that has a public water supply is 92.1 per cent in the Southeast and 58.3 per cent in the North. In comparison, the proportion that has sanitary sewers is 88.3 per cent and 26.1 per cent respectively.[24] Those numbers highlight that this book is not about Brazil but about São Paulo, a city in the Southeast of Brazil that is the capital of the federal state (also called São Paulo) with the highest gross domestic product (GDP) in the country (figure 1.1).[25]

Inequality in Brazil is a consequence of multiple historical processes[26] that also brought about its cultural diversity. Besides being colonised by the Portuguese, over the course of more than three centuries, Brazil received 4.9 million enslaved Africans.[27] It was the main destination for slaves in the New World.[28] The end of slavery in Brazil, in 1888, was followed by the arrival of immigrants who came to work on the coffee plantations and later in industry. By the 1890s, 3.8 million immigrants were living in Brazil. Portuguese, Spanish, Italian and Japanese were the ones in the most significant numbers.[29] By 1930, the country had received immigrants from more than 60 countries.[30] Their destinations influenced the multiple and diverse cultural backgrounds observed across Brazil. São Paulo received a massive number of these immigrants. Between 1872 and 1914, for example, the city population rose from 23,000 to 400,000.[31] As we will see in the next section, this fast growth resulted in a plurality of cultures in the city and the consolidation of São Paulo as a work-oriented society.

But first, to understand what this plurality means and its consequences for the experience of ageing addressed in this book, the reader should consider two things. The first is the image that many foreigners hold of the country as a tropical paradise where festive Brazilians celebrate Carnival or enjoy life on picture-perfect beaches.[32] This imaginary is not representative of São Paulo. The second is the idea that work is experienced as a kind of punishment in Brazil, something the anthropologist DaMatta[33] attributed to the Roman Catholic foundation of the country in opposition to the Calvinist tradition that would have transformed work into salvation. In addition, he argues, there is no glorification of the figure of the Brazilian worker, and no belief that it is possible to prosper or achieve dignity through honest work. It is true that DaMatta's work was done before Protestantism became widespread in the country. As a Pew Study shows,[34] one in five Brazilians is a former Catholic, while 54 per cent of current Protestants say they were raised Catholic. Even so, São Paulo never fitted DaMatta's description. Instead, the city was historically built as a place where people succeed and where work can show character and provide citizenship. That is the image that Brazilians share when they think about São Paulo[35] and it is also the imaginary that bonds research participants together.

A citizen of São Paulo

The identity of São Paulo as a place for work was built on the figure of the *Bandeirantes*, the romanticised heroic conquerors responsible for expanding Brazilian territories in colonial times.[36] At first, the local elite linked to the coffee culture used this imaginary to distinguish them as real *paulistas* (born in São Paulo) and highlight their ancestral vocation to entrepreneurship and hard work. Later, the *Bandeirantes* were replaced by the Bandeirantes' spirit, or *espírito das Bandeiras* ('spirit of the flags'). This shift was an effort to unify the multiple waves of migrants living in the city and ideologically consolidate the old and new *paulistas* as the labour force that would lead Brazil to industrialisation, development and progress.[37] Some of these 'new *paulistas*' were, as mentioned earlier, immigrants. However, in 1941, a new internal flow started, now

Figure 1.2 The 'Monumento às Bandeiras' (monument to the flags) celebrates the 400th anniversary of São Paulo. One of the icons of the city, the monument is a tribute to the workers of São Paulo. © Marília Duque.

comprised of Brazilians who moved to the city to pursue the same opportunities for work and prosperity as the foreigners before them. During the 1960s, 128,000 Brazilians arrived in São Paulo per year.[38]

The 400th anniversary of the city, in 1954, can be seen as a mark of the unification of São Paulo as a work-oriented society. The 'Monumento às Bandeiras' (monument to the flags; see figure 1.2) embodies the old and new *paulistas* as the dauntless workers who made São Paulo the economic power of the country.[39] At this time, São Paulo had already become the biggest city in Brazil, responsible for 30 per cent of the industrial production in the country. The exaltation of work and workers was also expressed in advertisements and articles published in the local newspapers to honour the city's anniversary. As Moura[40] noted, work was the element that bonded people while they fully experienced the status of being a citizen of São Paulo.

Nowadays, with a population of just over 12 million, São Paulo is the most populous city in Brazil[41] and the fourth-largest urban agglomeration in the world, behind Tokyo, New Delhi and Shanghai.[42] São Paulo is a hub for business and one of the largest centres of innovation in Latin America. The city is planning to become a smart city[43] as well as an age-friendly city.[44] It has already been designated a pet-friendly[45] city and a gay-friendly[46] city, and has the status of being the cultural capital of Latin America. The

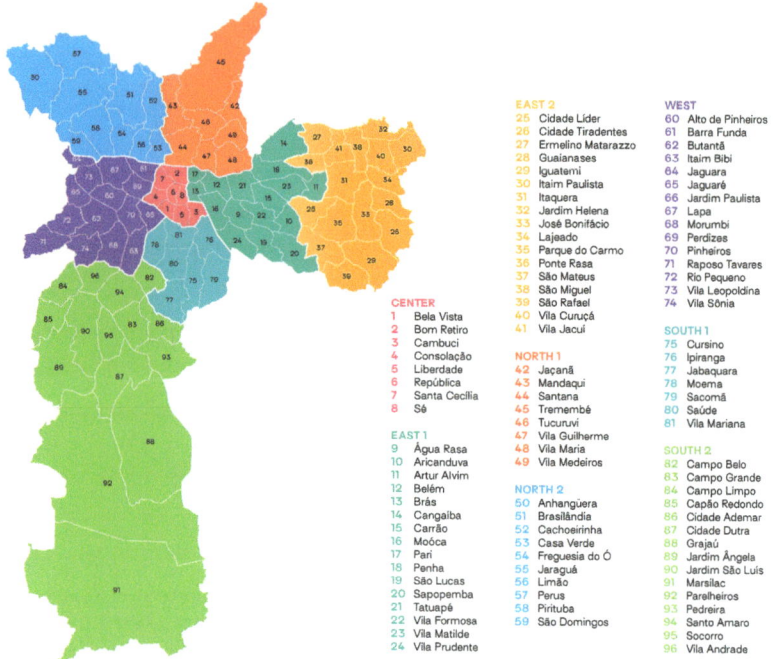

Figure 1.3 Map of the 96 districts in São Paulo city. © Rede Nossa São Paulo. Mapa da Desigualdade 2020.

number of museums in the city rivals Milan's, for example.[47] However, São Paulo is not a golden land for everybody. The inequalities observed in Brazil are reproduced in the 96 districts of the city (figure 1.3).

São Paulo provides very different experiences depending on which district one lives in. Among them, the number of households in '*favelas*' varies from 0 to 69.5 per cent.[48] The waiting time for a primary care consultation in the SUS can be from 5 to 43 days,[49] while proximity to public transport[50] is available to 0 to 88 per cent of the population in the districts with the worst and best rates. Contrasts like these are also observed in access to sports, culture and leisure.[51] Inequalities also impact the quality of life in old age. In 2018, there were 1.73 million people aged 60 or over in São Paulo, that is, 14.7 per cent of the population. In 2030, this age group will comprise 20 per cent. The inequalities between districts and between ageing experiences in the city can be illustrated by income and age at death. At the extremes, the income of older people can vary by a multiple of 20 and the age at death varies by 23.2 years.[52] The following section will focus on Bento, the site where this ethnography took place, which is one of the most privileged districts in which to age in São Paulo.

Age-friendly Bento

Bento is the fictional name given to a neighbourhood in an upper-middle-class district in São Paulo city. In 2019, the proportion of residents aged 60 and over in the district was 25.1 per cent, and the number of people aged 60 and over for every 100 people younger than 15 years old was 195.2 (both higher than the average in São Paulo).[53] The district has the second-best indices of income, life expectancy and education according to São Paulo's Human Development Index.[54] As for São Paulo as a whole, work and migration define Bento's identity. Historically, the area developed around the municipal slaughterhouse built in the area in 1887.[55] The area became the destination for many Italian and Japanese immigrants, who came to work also in industry and commerce, both of which were flourishing at the time.[56] The development of the Medical School of São Paulo,[57] founded in 1933, is another milestone that helps us understand Bento's particularities. Nowadays, the Medical School occupies many houses in the neighbourhood, which has turned the area into a hub for health services across both public and private sectors. Consequently, the concentration of hospitals and clinics, including low-cost clinics, results in a distinct flow of people to the area, who come and go every day for medical purposes.

Living in Bento means combining all the facilities of a big city like São Paulo with the atmosphere of a small neighbourhood. Single houses are now side by side with some apartment buildings (see figure 1.4). There are plenty of trees and birds, and local amenities such as grocery shops (see figure 1.5) whose owners know the history of the families in the area and why there are so many abandoned properties nearby. One of these owners explains that these properties were inherited by children living abroad or too busy to manage their parents' house sales.

Even so, the neighbourhood is going through a gentrification process, with organic bakeries and fancy restaurants opening gradually. Two big grocery shops opened in 2018 and 2019 (see figure 1.6), but the old ones are still there, as is the traditional supermarket. The latter is more like a convenience store on three floors, selling everything from food to clothes. On one of the higher floors, there is a restaurant where older people can have a good and affordable lunch after doing their morning activities. Despite its central location, the price also matters, as most of the research participants make adjustments in their finances after retirement. Thus, even within an upper-middle-class district, they are likely to perceive Bento as a middle-class neighbourhood. Shopping locally is also part of

Figure 1.4 Houses and buildings juxtaposed in Bento. © Marília Duque.

their routine. As old customers, they are greeted by name in the traditional grocery shops and supermarkets. It is common to see them carrying their bags on the streets and, if they bump into a neighbour or a colleague from one of the activities and courses that they regularly go to, they will probably stop for a chat. Although it doesn't stop them from walking a lot, research participants periodically complain about the local pavements. Just recently, these were redesigned and now include access for those with disabilities. However, this was not a coincidence.

Figure 1.5 The oldest grocery shop in Bento, where the owner may recount the histories of the neighbourhood. © Marilia Duque.

Bento has also been chosen for the roll-out of a pilot project that aims to implement age-friendly neighbourhoods in São Paulo (see figure 1.7).[58] The project was developed in partnership with the Medical School, which also maintains an Ageing Studies Sector in Bento, where residents older than 60 can access an outpatient service. The unit also offers activities and courses focused on prevention, and contributes to ongoing studies of ageing. A consequence of its proximity to the Medical School is that many students and doctors live in the area. A local paper noticed this

Figure 1.6 A modern grocery shop in Bento. © Marília Duque.

Figure 1.7 An outdoor gym in a public square in Bento. © Marília Duque.

particularity. 'Who doesn't have a neighbour dressed in a white coat?' was a question raised in one article.[59]

The region is well served by public transport, including two underground railway lines and a bus station, handy for research participants, who are more likely to use public transport after retirement. The availability of public transport also increases the flow of people from many areas of São Paulo to receive medical treatment during the week, as mentioned above (see figures 1.8 and 1.9). Most hospitals and clinics are concentrated in two streets, where it is common to see many people going up and down, carrying envelopes containing their medical tests and images. Most of them arrive there via the oldest underground station or the bus station, which are directly connected to a shopping centre (see figures 1.10 and 1.11). Together with the giant Catholic church on the other side of the street, this centre can be considered the heart of my fieldsite (see figure 1.12).

The area offers many courses aimed at the third age. In addition, there are plenty of museums, parks and institutes providing a vast portfolio of activities aligned with the Active Ageing framework. Even public hospitals in the area offer special programmes for this purpose. One of them, created in 2002, offers exercise, choir, dance classes, and English, French and Spanish language courses, among other activities. Because of that, Bento

Figure 1.8 Entrance to one of the public hospitals in Bento. © Marília Duque.

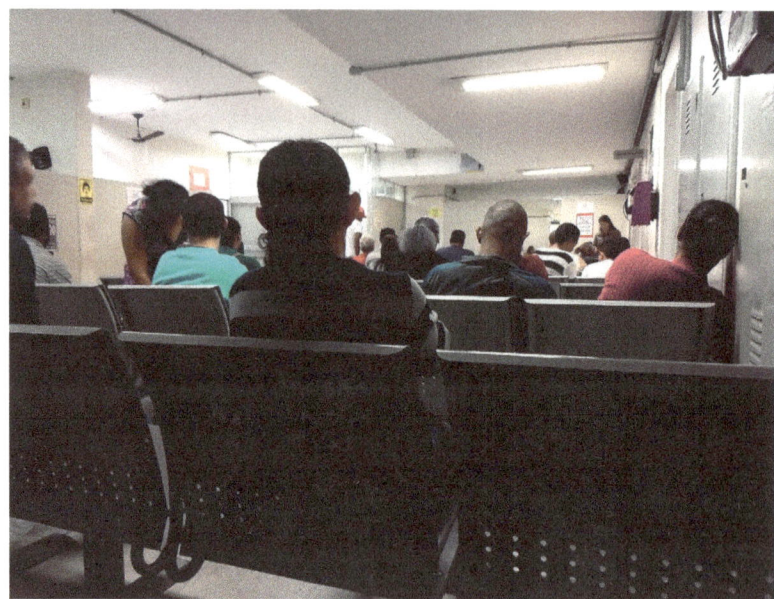

Figure 1.9 The waiting room of one of the public hospitals in Bento. © Marília Duque.

Figure 1.10 Entrance to the shopping centre. The stairs lead to the underground railway and the bus station. © Marília Duque.

Figure 1.11 An underground station in Bento. © Marília Duque.

Figure 1.12 The main street in Bento, with the silhouette of the Catholic church at the end. © Marília Duque.

has become a hub for healthy ageing, attracting older people from other areas of São Paulo. Throughout this book, I show how these activities become crucial to the experience of ageing, as they provide opportunities for older people to exercise, learn and socialise. Those who participate in these activities become connected on WhatsApp groups created to support the activities, which expand their networks in both number and diversity, creating a powerful resource for information, solidarity and care.

Bento celebrates diversity when it comes to religion.[60] Despite the three huge Catholic churches located in the area, different Christian denominations, such as Adventists, Baptists and Evangelicals, are well represented. For example, within 500 metres of each other, it is possible to find a Baptist church, a Catholic church, a Church of World Messianity centre (see chapter 6), and one Kardecist-Umbanda (an Afro-Brazilian religion) centre (figure 1.13). There is no conflict, as people are likely to combine elements of these different religions depending on the kind of guidance they want. As chapter 8 shows, research participants seek spiritual advice, but sometimes they are just looking for opportunities to socialise and to feel busy and valuable again.

Religious institutions help to expand the portfolio of activities aimed at the third age in Bento. I started my fieldwork by taking part in some of them, as explained in the next section, on methodology. By doing that, I got to know research participants' routines and eventually followed them to their homes and the intimacy of their smartphones to understand how they experience ageing. Through topics such as retirement, everyday life, family, friends, health and sexuality, this book argues that ageing in Bento is a matter of balancing freedoms, pleasure and obligations while coping with new and old social expectations. On the one hand, research participants are still living in São Paulo, where unproductivity is unacceptable. On the other hand, this cultural background adds a special meaning to retirement and to the policies on ageing that expect them to remain active. As we will see, research participants live the paradoxes of the third age with great help from their smartphones, which can be used as allies and alibis in their pursuit of a meaningful life.

Empathy as methodology

Considering empathy to be the primary ethnography method,[61] I tried to be where older people were, doing the things they do. Thus, I engaged in some activities aimed at the third age in Bento from February 2018 to June 2019. This long commitment allowed me to observe and take part

Figure 1.13 Items used in an Umbanda ritual are placed in the square that lies in front of one of the Catholic churches in Bento, showcasing the neighbourhood's religious diversity. © Marília Duque.

in their everyday lives, sharing their joys, sorrows and frustrations, and the strategies they adopt to deal with their ageing bodies, young spirits, obligations, needs and desires. From the beginning of my fieldwork, I volunteered as an instructor to teach them how to use WhatsApp. WhatsApp is why research participants are motivated to adopt smartphones, as the platform now mediates Brazilians' communication with family and friends.⁶² The course took place in the most prominent Catholic church in Bento as part of a portfolio of over 50 courses aimed at the third age. These courses are taught by volunteers, most of them retired. I worked with four different classes; a few students attended the course more than once. The classes were for beginners. But, in one term, I conducted two classes, one for beginners, the other for former students who wanted to learn how to use apps other than WhatsApp. Classes always took place on Tuesday mornings. Technological resources were scarce in the church. The WhatsApp classes took place in a room generally used for adult literacy classes,⁶³ with individual desks and a large blackboard (figure 1.14). While the blackboard was a limitation (a multimedia screen would have allowed me to project the screen of a smartphone, for example), it was an element familiar to older people, along with their notebooks and pens. Most of them had decided to seek assistance because their children didn't have the time or patience to help them. My experience as an instructor allowed me to map their learning processes and how they experienced the stigma surrounding older people and technology adoption.

However, and more importantly, this experience revealed how far these students could go and how their smartphones impacted their lives as they became more confident. In Bento, as will become clear throughout this book, WhatsApp plays a crucial role in health and sociability, resulting in a support network that goes beyond blood ties. WhatsApp groups are also where research participants share helpful information with their peers, including health tips and the opportunities for activities that are the basis of the Active Ageing framework adopted in São Paulo. Usually, one WhatsApp group is created to support each activity. That was also the case with my students, who quickly appropriated the spaces to share their own topics of interest (a behaviour observed among older people in Bento in general). As it was for research participants, WhatsApp was a powerful tool for me to expand my connections and sociability during my fieldwork. For example, at this church, I was included in the WhatsApp group for instructors, and in three others. One was created to manage sales of second-hand items; one focused on organising cultural programmes during the weekends. The last one aimed to plan a fashion show for a charity event (figure 1.15).

A second programme complemented my observation of how older people adopt smartphones. This time I volunteered as a teaching assistant. The classes took place in a hospital that holds a preventive health programme aimed at the third age. These classes were always on Thursday afternoons. Among the physical and other activities, the

Figure 1.14 Teaching WhatsApp in the Catholic church hall. Photograph by one of the students in the class.

Figure 1.15 Backstage at the fashion show with the models in the background. © Marília Duque.

smartphone classes most promoted older people's digital inclusion. For many of these students, as for 65 per cent of Brazilians aged 60 and over, the smartphone was their exclusive means of access to the internet.[64] Chapter 5 addresses this learning process and how older people in Bento engage in WhatsApp groups.

As part of my activities, I attended a gym that has a programme exclusively designed for seniors. These classes take place in the afternoons. However, this programme was not popular among research participants (the programme is for the 'real old', as they argued later). Instead, they attend the gym classes open to everyone, especially in the mornings, including dance, yoga, Pilates and weight-training classes. For 12 months, I attended the yoga classes on Tuesday and Thursday mornings and the Pilates classes on Wednesday and Friday mornings, and tried the Zumba twice (see figure 1.16). I also followed the gym unofficial Facebook group. Updated by a gym-goer in her sixties, this group was far more effective than the official communication channels provided by the gym. The gym was the place where most of the gender-related issues emerged. After 'the work was done', women allowed themselves to spend time talking and engaging in extracurricular activities such as birthday parties and themed classes. On the other hand, men remained in the gym strictly for exercising, mainly because they still felt guilty about being seen as unproductive during working hours.

Even with different routines, men and women in Bento commit to keeping their bodies in good health. But they are also concerned about their minds. Because an eventual decline in mental faculties is one of their great fears, some take part in courses where they can learn new things,

Figure 1.16   At the gym. © Marília Duque.

while others play memory games on their smartphones to 'exercise the brain'. Some will dedicate themselves to mindfulness and meditation practices to manage stress, avoid psychosomatic illness and keep their minds in the present. Focusing too much on the past is associated with depression, and focusing too much on the future with anxiety. The unit dedicated to studying ageing at the local Medical School offers meditation classes once a week on Tuesday afternoons. The activities are coordinated by a doctor and validated by positive results achieved by the same practice at a public hospital on the outskirts of São Paulo. The study found that practising meditation led to an improvement in vitality, posture and immunity. The meditation classes are among the initiatives conducted in this unit to stimulate cognitive and physical activity. I was accepted in the meditation group and added to the WhatsApp group they use. Many participants had been referred to the meditation classes by doctors to help them deal with retirement and the free time most of them were experiencing for the first time in their life.

Life after retirement and the challenges of spending this free time with purpose were what brought together a group that discusses work alternatives for the third age. Its members met every Monday morning (figure 1.17). At the beginning of every meeting, they recap the purpose of the group: 'An empathetic and collaborative approach for the reintegration of older people into the labour market, seeking fair remuneration and physical, mental, spiritual and financial health.' This purpose backs up the main argument of this book, namely that, for research participants, remaining in work is a condition of staying healthy in old age. I attended the group's meetings for eight months (from November 2018 to June 2019). The group also invited me to talk about design thinking and prototyping because of my background in advertising. Although members distinguish between themselves and 'the others', meaning younger people, the group recognise the importance of intergenerational dialogue and collaboration. Thus, they adopted me as their 'mascot' and included me in all their social activities and online platforms. They have a WhatsApp group, a WhatsApp Broadcast list and a Facebook group (where the meetings were live-streamed before they migrated to Zoom because of the Covid-19 pandemic). I had access to all of these.

At another Catholic church in Bento, in 2018 and 2019 I volunteered to help to organise the annual festival dedicated to the church's patron saint. The week-long event takes place in the square in front of the church, where the community comes to eat and have fun together (see figures 1.18 and 1.19). All the money raised is donated to the church. Most of these activities are coordinated through WhatsApp groups by volunteers.

Figure 1.17 At a meeting of the group that discusses alternative forms of work for older people in Bento. © Marília Duque.

The busiest day is the day of the patronal feast, when people bring flowers to share with other worshippers. This church was also where I attended Mass, usually on Sundays, during the morning or in the afternoon. One of the priests is recovering from cancer. Many of his sermons addressed the ageing body, frailties, dependence and dignity, all concepts vital to an understanding of the experience of ageing in Bento.

Combining these activities, I ended up having the same busy schedule as research participants. Like them, I divided my time between activities associated with self-care, learning and volunteering. By doing these things, they can feel, and be seen as, busy, and so to be making amends for having so much free time after retirement. As argued above, in Bento work produces proof of character, shapes identity and provides a sense of belonging for the citizens of São Paulo. In addition, these activities show that they are coping with active ageing while working to maintain their autonomy and avoid being a burden to others.

Figure 1.18 People worshipping inside the church at the festival of the patron saint. © Marília Duque.

However, there is a methodological problem in this. My participation in the activities described so far could not represent the local experience of ageing. What about those who do not take part in the Active Ageing agenda in Bento? Thanks to the long-term ethnography, I could build strong bonds with community members in such a way that our relationship was extended to their homes, their families and their friends. These connections allowed me to access the outsiders and observe that although they share the same concern about ageing well, some are not yet turning

Figure 1.19 The party outside the church. The roses symbolise the miracle performed by the church's patron saint. © Marília Duque.

this concern into healthy habits, at least not in terms of active ageing. In addition, because older people from other regions of São Paulo come to Bento to attend the same activities as I did, I was able to meet those who don't share the financial stability most of Bento's residents enjoy. For example, 'limbo' was the expression used by those who are neither retired nor employed. In a sense, because of that mobility, Bento became a kind of fieldwork with dynamic borders, as WhatsApp allowed me to connect with some research participants while they were at their homes in other districts of São Paulo, facing different challenges and constraints. These connections are still active, and so are the WhatsApp groups I followed during my fieldwork, even with in-person activities suspended because of the Covid-19 pandemic. Incidentally, these ongoing connections enable me to make comments on what might have changed since then.

While the Active Ageing agenda focuses on prevention, I was also interested in how research participants manage health issues. Their tactics are likely to combine different approaches, even if they seem to be inconsistent. Instead, as Laplantine[65] argues, people can combine knowledge from the fields of traditional medicine, alternative medicine, spirituality and popular healing, including magical and religious treatments. That was the case among research participants. Thus, to reproduce their approaches, I tried different health practices available in

Bento. A pain in my shoulder led me to the casualty department of a local hospital managed by the SUS (figure 1.20) and to Dr Consulta, a clinic that offers low-cost consultations and medical tests, both services used by research participants. I also had an appointment with the spiritual healer Dr Spanish at the Umbanda Centre (Umbanda means 'the art of healing', and is a syncretic Afro-Brazilian religion that blends elements from indigenous culture, Catholicism and Kardecism). He referred me for six sessions of chromotherapy and three 'disobsession' sessions (spiritual therapy to release oneself from the influence of spirits). In addition to this, I received vital energy applied through a practitioner holding their hands over my body at the Church of World Messianity more than twice. This energy aims to bring balance to the spirit, and it is also applied for healing. Finally, I attended the Bible study meetings of the International Church of Christ of São Paulo. These meetings allowed me to observe the relationship between faith and healing. Lastly, to understand how older people in Bento use WhatsApp to seek medical guidance, I followed doctors and nurses in their daily practices. They showed me how they use WhatsApp for communicating with patients, and highlighted the pros and cons of using the platform. Chapter 6 addresses this discussion and the perspective of these different actors.

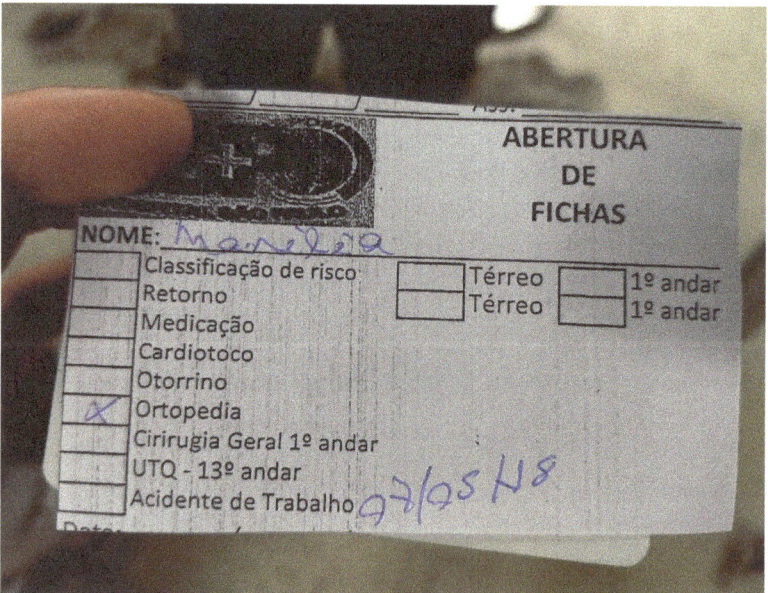

Figure 1.20 My referral at the public hospital at Bento, where I was sent to the orthopaedic unit. © Marília Duque.

During my fieldwork, I conducted in-depth interviews with people aged 50 to 76 who owned a smartphone. I interviewed participants who lived or worked in Bento, or used services aimed at the third age that were available there. They referred me to family and friends, who participated in further interviews according to the same eligibility criteria. These in-depth interviews created a space for dialogue in which I could access the meanings attributed by participants to their own experience of ageing, from a present and a place of belonging, which is physical but also historical, shaped by culture and within a community.[66] These encounters were an opportunity to observe how interviewees adjust their narratives[67] to comply with the habits they believe they are expected to adopt in order to age well. However, these were safe environments, in which participants could talk about the indulgences and extravagances they enjoy when they are alone. In these moments of privacy, they feel safe from moral judgements that may frame their pleasures as inappropriate or unhealthy. In addition to this, during interviews they could relax, as they were away from the classificatory look that defines who is old and who is not, once the relationship with the other person imposes the awareness of age itself.[68] As ethnography has shown, this look can result in a kind of self-surveillance as an effort to hide the natural decline of ageing from others. By doing this, older people can avoid the stigma of age (of being incapable or dependent) or even exclusion from social groups.[69] In addition, research participants are likely to hide any frailty from their children. On the one hand, they don't want to burden their children, whose time should be dedicated exclusively to working. On the other, they don't want to risk being put under their children's control. These concerns turned the private context of the interview into a space in which research participants could 'lower their guard' and express themselves freely about the difficulties and challenges of ageing.

The interviews addressed the three main topics of this research. There were three sets of questions, regarding ageing, health and smartphones. At the end of the last session, I asked participants to unlock their smartphones and show all the installed apps. I then asked how they use each app and who had installed it. Together, these sessions were designed to take from 90 to 120 minutes. However, many of my interviews lasted for more than three hours. This long duration was no burden to the participants interviewed. Indeed, many of them explicitly complained about the lack of opportunities to be listened to as they got older. Some explained that they had started to see a psychologist for precisely this reason – to have a guaranteed amount of time when they would be able to talk and be listened to. I chose not to interrupt their narratives, which often strayed far away from the questions I had asked them. In a sense, they talked about what they wanted, which revealed much more than I could have anticipated. However, although the participants were glad they had had time to speak, they became tired during the last part of the interview, when I asked them to show me their apps. They were surprised when they realised how many apps they had installed on their smartphones. They got excited when describing the apps they used but bored when it came to talking about those they didn't use or recognise. This behaviour became one of the critical findings of the research. As we will see in chapter 5, research participants are not focused on apps. What matters to them is how apps can be appropriated and combined to meet everyday needs. My observation of their smartphones also provided a timeline representing present, past and future interests. With regard to the future, interviewees often installed an app to signify an intention, for example that they mean to eat better. As we will see in chapter 6, many of these apps are related to adjustments older people intend to make in order to age well, including improvements in their diets and strategies to postpone dependence upon others.

A total of 38 participants were interviewed, 22 women and 16 men, between 50 and 76 years old. Among them were five couples (all in heterosexual relationships). Taking into consideration the waves of migration considered earlier in this chapter, it was not surprising that research participants were not interested in defining themselves according to the ethnic categories used in Brazil.[70] They were more likely to present themselves as a mix of their family ancestry, highlighting their African, Asian and European descent. Throughout this book, when I give quantitative data, the total number of participants interviewed may vary depending on the topic addressed: some opted out of answering specific questions while others used a question as a starting point to discuss another topic or issue. This practice corroborates my previous argument, that older people miss having opportunities to talk openly about the challenges of ageing in Bento.

The concluding chapter, chapter 9, develops this idea by arguing that the 'silence' surrounding ageing, as denounced by Simone de Beauvoir,[71] has changed. In Brazil, São Paulo and Bento, ageing is discussed everywhere as a social and economic problem, as chapter 2 will explore. However, older people's perspectives remain silenced. As they are supposed to be healthy, independent and productive, there is no room for frailties and decline, which are likely to be framed as moral failures[72] by discourses on healthy and successful ageing. That is the most significant commitment of this writing. Having walked in older people's shoes for 16 months, I hope to give visibility to the experience of ageing as lived by them, by considering what they do, what they say they do, and what they keep silent about. To understand the reasons for this silence, we must address how ageing actively is constructed as morality and what it means in the cultural context of work-oriented Bento. The following are the final questions this book aims to answer. Is Active Ageing a healthy policy for older people in Bento? Does it make them happy? As we will see, culture shapes happiness and, for research participants, this means finding new forms of work in order to remain busy and useful after retirement. By doing this, they can achieve dignity and purpose in life while remaining citizens of São Paulo. But what does this 'work' look like? How will they find it? This is a work in progress.

Ethical protocols

All of the research, including the in-depth interviews, followed the ethics protocols regarding privacy and data processing adopted in Brazil (certificate CAAE 90142318.2.0000.5511). From the beginning of the fieldwork, research participants were informed of the reasons for my presence, and I made myself available for further explanation about the nature of the research. The invitation to participate in the in-depth interviews required participants to fill in and accept the conditions set out in the Informed Consent Form (ICF). The form acknowledges that digital spaces will be observed for the study as well as the interviews. That was relevant, as the face-to-face interactions usually migrated to social networks such as Facebook and WhatsApp but also to Instagram, Facebook Messenger and, less often, LinkedIn. By making them aware that my observation would be expanded to social networks, I adhered to the principle that all consent must be contextualised and restricted to the spheres for which participants have given specific consent.[73]

The ICF was read out to the participant interviewed by the researcher, who provided them with a copy of the document. The researcher emphasised that there was no payment for participation and participants were informed that, at any moment, they could decide to pull out of the research. To do so, they should communicate this directly to the researcher so that the data held could be destroyed. The researcher also explained that the interview, which was audio-recorded, would be transcribed and that the data that identified the participant would be changed to protect their anonymity and privacy. Because of this, all research participants quoted in this book have had their names changed.

The transcriptions were saved on a protected device. In chapter 2, I address the reasons older people in Bento share information they consider helpful to their peers, and their criteria for selection. As we will see, research participants base their judgement not only on the piece of information itself but on the reputation of, and the emotional connection they have with, those who shared the information with them in the first place. The same thing happened when I tried to follow ethical protocols during the interviews. Because some participants had known me for a long time or because they had been referred to me by relatives and friends who could vouch for me, they felt embarrassed about going through the ICF, and most tended to say, 'It's okay, I trust you.' The same behaviour will be addressed when we discuss trust and fake news dissemination among older people in Bento.

Notes

1. Ageism is discrimination based on age. As Lamb (2019, p. 7) explains, it is not restricted to individuals and it entails a 'pervasive aversion to and embarrassment about the condition of old age in general'.
2. Agência IBGE Notícias 2018.
3. PopulationPyramid.net 2019.
4. Agência IBGE Notícias 2018.
5. Agência IBGE Notícias 2018.
6. Batista et al. 2011.
7. Souza et al. 2016.
8. 71.5 per cent of Brazilians rely on the public health system (Tajra 2020).
9. Debert 2012.
10. Brazil was a member of the first and second UN World Assemblies on Ageing. The first Assembly met in 1982, and resulted in the Vienna International Plan of Action on Ageing. The instrument provided recommendations for the development of policies and programmes on ageing, addressing health and nutrition, the protection of elderly consumers, housing and environment, family, social welfare, income security, and employment and education (United Nations 2021). The second Assembly met in 2002, and resulted in the Madrid International Plan of Action on Ageing. The instrument highlighted three themes: 'older persons and development; advancing health and well-being into old age; and ensuring enabling and supportive environments' (United Nations 2021).
11. One of the main contributions of the Política Nacional do Idoso (National Policy for the Elderly; PNI) was to create mechanisms to allow civil society to participate in the elaboration of public policies addressing old age (Dias & Pais-Ribeiro 2018).
12. In 2003, the Statute for Elderly People established that the family, society and the state all share legal and social responsibility for older people (Brasil, Ministério da Saúde 2013). However, as Küchemann (2012) observes, state participation in elderly care is perfunctory compared with that of the family, which remains the primary provider for older people, including of their nourishment, living conditions and routine care.
13. In 2002, the World Health Organization launched the Active Ageing framework. The policy proposed that states and societies provide the environment and opportunities to allow every person to live a 'long and healthy life'. The document also emphasised the concept of autonomy, highlighting that older people should engage with these opportunities to prevent, correct and postpone frailties. In other words, they need to become responsible for their ageing by maintaining their health and, consequently, their participation in society (World Health Organization 2002).

14 The National Health Policy for Elderly Persons focuses on the promotion of Active Ageing, addressing disease prevention and the maintenance of functional capacities in old age, which will allow older people to remain in their communities with autonomy (Dias & Pais-Ribeiro 2018).
15 Batista et al. 2011.
16 The Brazilian Federal Constitution introduced social security in 1988. Social security comprises an integrated set of initiatives by public authorities and society to ensure citizens' rights to health, assistance and social security in Brazil. Created in 1990, the INSS is responsible for the recognition and operationalisation of the rights established by the Regime Geral de Previdência Social (RGPS; the general social security regime) (Instituto Nacional do Seguro Social 2017). Since then, and especially given the worrying projections regarding the ageing of Brazil's population, social security has been framed as an economic problem (FecomercioSP 2016).
17 The dependency ratio is the proportion of dependants (those under 15 or over 64) per 100 persons of working age (from 15 to 64 years old) (Agência IBGE Notícias 2018).
18 United Nations, Department of Economic and Social Affairs 2019, pp. 36–7.
19 Correa 2009.
20 The ethnography that resulted in this book was conducted before the Covid-19 pandemic. However, this scenario should consider the effects of the pandemic in Brazil. Indeed, this data was used by a study (Camarano 2020) that aimed to answer the question 'What would happen if, because of limited resources, young people were the ones selected to receive care?' The question's relevance is demonstrated by the fact that 73.8 per cent of deaths caused by Covid-19 up to 1 July 2020 in Brazil were among people aged 60 or above. Exploring the high dependency of households on older people's incomes, the study made a projection considering households in which older people's incomes represented at least 50 per cent of total family income (20.6 per cent of Brazilian households) and households in which an older person's income is the only one in the family (18.1 per cent of Brazilian households). In the first category, the death of an older person would reduce by 75 per cent these households' income per capita, which would affect 11.6 million people. In the second category, the death of an older person would leave 5 million people with no income.
21 In 2018, the year this ethnography started in São Paulo, Brazil's gross domestic product (GDP) had grown by only 1.1 per cent compared with the year before. In January 2019, the unemployment rate was 12 per cent (International Monetary Fund 2019). That impacted the healthcare system, as 3 million people abandoned their private health insurance plans, migrating to the public health system (SUS) (Exame Invest 2018).
22 IBGE 2020b.
23 Agência IBGE 2020.
24 Agência IBGE 2020.
25 IBGE 2021.
26 For example, the consequences of slavery and immigration (mainly White European and Asian) in the country are expressed in the income distribution on the country. In 2019, for example, White Brazilians earned an average of 73.4 per cent more than Blacks and Browns did (IBGE 2020b, p. 33).
27 Rossi 2018.
28 Brazilian Report 2020.
29 Arquivo Público do Estado de São Paulo 2009.
30 Wejsa & Lesser 2018.
31 Hall 1969.
32 Goldenberg 2010.
33 DaMatta 1986.
34 Pew Research Center 2014.
35 Queiroz 1992, p. 78.
36 The city was founded in 1554. São Paulo was the port from which the colonial expeditions called the 'Bandeiras' departed. Their members, known as 'Bandeirantes', were responsible for expanding the Brazilian territories into the southern and south-west parts of the continent. But that was a consequence of their main goals: to capture indigenous people (to work as slaves) and search for minerals (such as gold) (IBGE 2017a).
37 Queiroz 1992; Moura 1994; Marins 1999; Tassara & Rabinovich 2007.
38 In the same decade, the city population increased by 56.6 per cent (Governo do Estado de São Paulo 2021).
39 Marins 1999.

40 Moura 1994.
41 IBGE 2017b.
42 United Nations, Department of Economic and Social Affairs 2018.
43 Câmara Municipal de São Paulo 2019.
44 Cidade de São Paulo Direitos Humanos e Cidadania 2019.
45 G1 2015.
46 Cidade de São Paulo 2021.
47 Statista Research Department 2021a.
48 Percentages in Jardim Paulista and Jardim São Luís districts respectively (Rede Nossa Cidade 2020).
49 Days in Cambuci and Água Rasa districts respectively (Rede Nossa São Paulo 2020).
50 Percentage of the population living 1,000 metres or less from public transport in the Pedreira and República districts respectively (Rede Nossa São Paulo 2020).
51 Rede Nossa São Paulo 2020.
52 Prefeitura de São Paulo Desenvolvimento Urbano 2019.
53 Secretaria Municipal de Direitos Humanos e Cidadania, Coordenadoria de Políticas para Pessoa Idosa 2019.
54 Gonçalves & Maeda 2017.
55 *Folha de S. Paulo* 2008.
56 Cidade de São Paulo Subprefeitura Vila Mariana 2019.
57 Escola Paulista de Medicina 2019.
58 This project follows the WHO's protocol *Global Age-Friendly Cities: A guide* (World Health Organization 2007).
59 Freitas 2017.
60 Nogueira 2016.
61 Miller et al. 2016.
62 According to a Mobile Time Opinion Box (2021) survey, WhatsApp is installed on 98 per cent of smartphones in Brazil.
63 In 2019, 18 per cent of Brazilians aged 60 or over were illiterate (IBGE 2020a).
64 Cetic.br 2020.
65 Laplantine 2010.
66 Moré 2015.
67 As Amossy (2011) argues, in an interaction, subjects adjust their performance to take into account the image they craft for themselves, the image they make of the other and the image they believe the other makes of them.
68 Caradec 2014; Featherstone & Hepworth 1991.
69 Degnen 2007.
70 The ethnic categories officially used in Brazil are Indigenous, Yellow, Black, Brown and White (Petruccelli & Saboia 2013).
71 Beauvoir 1972.
72 Lamb 2019.
73 Nissenbaum 2011.

2
Life after retirement

How old are you?

At any point in life, ageing is both a subjective experience and a social construct. Every life stage implies a set of permissions and obligations. But these change with time. This chapter shows how the images associated with ageing are changing and reshaping social expectations after retirement in the world and in Brazil. Retirees are now expected to remain productive and independent. While they retain their autonomy, they can enjoy the freedom associated with the third age. In Bento, however, there are specific expectations about how they fill their free time. Even after retirement, work is still the element that provides a sense of belonging and shapes identity and character. That is why retirees take part in as many activities as possible, so that they can continue to enjoy the social status of being busy even while devoting some time to themselves. But what about those who age without becoming eligible for retirement? What are the particular challenges reserved for them? These are the final questions addressed by this chapter. As we will see, ageing in Bento can be a place of inequality.

Mirror, mirror: the images of ageing

The experience of ageing is a negotiation between the image I face in the mirror, the experience of my inner self and the classificatory look of the other. As Featherstone and Hepworth[1] argue, our embodied identity emerges from what we see as subjects and how others see us. You can't see my inner self. In other words, you can't imagine how I feel inside my body. The only thing you see is the surface: my hair, skin, wrinkles, clothes and posture. These elements, combined, give you an image of me. This image will be compared with the images you are familiar with as representatives of categories of people in the culture in which you live.[2] On the grounds of similarity or contrast, you will quickly classify me as old, young, beautiful or ugly, frail or out of date. I might complain that you are reducing me to a stereotype. But I can't blame you. Looking and classifying are what we do most of the time to adjust to and live in society. As a result, I have to recognise that I may feel younger than I am, but my age is defined by the other and the culture that shapes our frame of reference and our values.

In Bento, it is usual for research participants to say that their chronological age[3] doesn't reflect their real self. They feel younger than ever. They refuse to see themselves as the aged body they see in the mirror, and also refuse to identify with their memories of their parents and grandparents, who lived in a time when 'being older was being really, really old', as they say. They feel they have aged better than previous generations. They expect to live much longer than them and are preparing themselves to do so. They are right. Since 1940, life expectancy at birth has increased by 31.1 years in Brazil, reaching 76.6 years in 2019.[4] São Paulo city has a similar figure, 76.8 years, while the district in which Bento is situated has a higher life expectancy at birth, 80.83 years.[5] Thus, research participants say pretty often that they are a healthier and more energetic generation. Even if they recognise that their bodies and memory are not the same as they used to be, they feel they are more active than ever.

If you call them (the research participants) 'old' you will be told 'Your grandmother is the one who's old.'[6] On the other hand, to say that someone does not look their age sounds like the highest praise. It is not true of everyone, however. There is a class divide in Bento when it comes to appearance. Among older people of lower social status, the stressful aspects of living in the city, combined with financial constraints and physical demands throughout their working life, seem to leave their scars.[7] But among the fortunate ones, people are more likely to look ageless. Especially among the women in this group, it is difficult to tell whether they are sixty or seventy.

It is not just about aesthetics, skincare and hair. Ageing is also about an attitude reflected in clothing, consumption and relationship to family, friends and society. Women start to feel comfortable with their grey hair, but, invariably, they will choose a short and asymmetrical cut. Their clothing also gains new shapes and fabrics that combine comfort and fashion. The way one dresses is a controversial topic, since older women in Bento don't want to fit the image suggested by the clothes designed for their age group.[8] This mismatch characterises fashion and other consumer sectors like study programmes, food and tourism.[9] Not being able to identify with the fashion industry and the clothing it creates for their age group has driven these 'mature' women, as they call themselves, to create their own trends, spelt out in their profiles on Instagram. Some profiles reach thousands of followers, and their creators enjoy the status of digital influencers.[10] This position helps older people in Bento craft and disseminate new images for their age group, now presented as an entrepreneurial, empowered and anything-goes group. The Instagram profile 'It_Avó' ('it grandmother', by analogy with the English 'it girl', a trendsetting young woman) is one of these cases. The woman behind it considers it an honour to contribute to what she calls 'the reinvention of ageing'. In giving visibility to positive images of women of her age, her purpose is to guarantee that the next generations of older people will be able, as she says, to 'age without having to become old, enjoying freedom and respect from society' (figure 2.1).

Figure 2.1 Post from digital influencer: 'creative women, curious, sensitive, learners and entrepreneurs. Grandmothers!' © @It-Avo.

This twist on how ageing is represented through images is not a particularity of Bento. The anthropologists Guita Grin Debert[11] and Annette Leibing[12] observed the same shift in Brazil as Featherstone and Hepworth[13] did in North American society. Until the 1970s, older people were represented by images of frailty, decline, senility and dependence. They were the object of mockery and pity.[14] But, since then, the ageist caricature of older people has been replaced by positive images, which present healthy ageing as a lifestyle anyone could (and should) achieve. Old age has, then, become a time free from frailties, dedicated to exploring new projects, possibilities, identities, pleasures and consumption. Research participants refer to this life stage as one in which they are free to assume an idealised version of the self, in contrast to the previous one, which conformed to career, family and community obligations. As a woman puts it, 'At our age, we can be the person we should have been.' She referred to youth, when the future was full of possibilities, and people could afford to take the riskier path in life. Participants are more confident in saying what they think because, they argue, 'We are older, so we can.' This status has released them from the obligation to adhere to social expectations, as they can now live according to their own preferences.

They may say what they want, but that doesn't mean people will listen to them. One man argues that he can say anything, because 'It will not make a difference, nobody cares,' meaning that no one cares what older people say. But research participants will find their ways of making their statements, including remaining silent or refusing to consume products and services that don't take into account their needs and desires. One woman decided to stop shopping at her favourite supermarket in Bento because she just couldn't read the price labels or use their discount app. Another woman quit her Pilates classes. The instructor wanted her to do exercises that she considered to be beyond her bodily limits. 'At my age, I don't have to prove anything to anybody,' she explains. By avoiding direct conflict, they may succeed in doing what they want. But how were older people in Bento influenced to want the things they want? Are they really free from social obligations and expectations at this stage of their life? The answer is no.

The idealisation of ageing as a space in which to exercise freedom happens at the same time as ageing is constructed as a contemporary social problem. Since the 1970s, statistics and reports have warned of the increase in life expectancy, a drop in birth rates and how the balance between workers and retirees will pose a risk to economic and social development in the future.[15] In addition, older segments of the population are framed as demanding more from already overwhelmed public healthcare systems. Since then, and as a consequence of the development of gerontology, discourses associated with ageing have started to promote a desirable and responsible way of ageing, which corresponds to ageing paradigms and policies based on the principle of autonomy, with a focus on prevention and healthy habits.[16] The Successful Ageing paradigm is an example. Success here is measured by the individual's ability to maintain and recover physical and cognitive functionalities, postponing dependence and participating actively in society.[17] Conceived within the North American culture, where self-preservation and independence are more likely to be seen as virtues,[18] this hegemonic paradigm has received significant criticism from scholars who stress its impacts on other cultures, in which interdependence and ageing have different meanings.[19] Even so, the paradigm answers to a global challenge: to make older people remain for as long as possible a bonus to society.

Placing this discussion into the Brazilian context, Debert calls this process the 'reprivatisation of ageing', in which responsibility for older people is renegotiated between the state and the individual.[20] The call for older people to age 'well' brought about a shift in the representations of ageing as discussed so far, through the dissemination of new images that are at the same time normative, educational and aspirational. In Brazil, since the institutionalisation of retirement (the country's first pensions were in 1923[21]), older people have been stigmatised as unable to work, inactive and useless. Gradually, this representation has been replaced by ones of older people enjoying healthy and productive lifestyles. This change creates a new morality, as Debert argues. This morality is not restricted to Brazil. The stigma of 'old' is now attributed to the irresponsible citizen who failed to adopt a healthy lifestyle that could have postponed the natural declines of ageing, creating unnecessary costs for healthcare services.[22] In Bento, positive images of ageing are everywhere, as a reminder that 'you are free to do anything, but you mustn't become a burden'. Older people themselves are the ones sharing these images on social media.[23] By doing that, they show awareness of and compliance with this new set of expectations imposed on ageing.

The film *Envelhescência*[24] (parallel with the word *adolescência*, 'adolescence') is an example of how images operate this paradigm shift and how they work as moralities. With the participation of authorities (a doctor, an anthropologist and a philosopher), the documentary shows six older people who have redefined the limits of their bodies to explore all the possibilities of healthy ageing. All the 'new' stereotypes of older people are there: the tattooed woman, the parachute jumper, the surfer, the marathon runner, the aikido instructor and the recently graduated student. They represent older people who are physically, mentally and financially independent, active, living freely and making this the best time of their lives. 'We only age if we want to,' 'Happy is the one who can be busy all day,' 'You don't have to be a hero, you just have to be dedicated' are among their testimonials. From time to time, this documentary popped up in the social media and WhatsApp groups observed during this ethnography. Laís, a woman in her fifties, watched the film. Those life stories were a true inspiration to her. They were models she wants to follow. However, as for many other research participants, these images also made her feel guilty about the way she had been managing her health until then.[25]

> 'A friend of mine shared this movie called *Envelhescência*. I love it. There are six characters. They are six people who challenge the way we expect someone older should be or live. One started surfing at 58. One graduated from university at 82. And another had her first tattoo at 72, and now her body is completely covered in tattoos. They are an inspiration to me. When I watched them, I thought, this is it! That is what I want to do. I want to disseminate this [at the time, she planned to start working with information and educational programmes for older people]. ... And I haven't realised this until now, but that is true. It will help me too, as I am also ageing. I am already thinking differently. Now I see everything older people do and everything I don't. I can tell I am late. I should have adopted these habits a long time ago.'

If the new images of ageing offer lifestyles older people in Bento might aspire to, a name for the 'new old' has not been settled on yet. As Bourdieu[26] argues, 'youth is just a word', and so is 'old'. However, both terms are a sphere for social disputes, as each implies a code of permissions and expectations. In the past, older people in Bento might have accepted and complied with the term *velho* ('old'), associated with retirement and culturally linked with inactivity.[27] Many would have dedicated themselves to the lives of their grandchildren, to watching television or to spending time on the park bench or in the marathon of medical consultations, dealing with the chronic diseases and frailties related to ageing. However, as argued above, that is the image older people in Bento ascribe to their parents. In these portraits they see a stigma they refuse to carry. The term *velho* ('old') is too old for them. The term *idoso* ('elderly') is only welcome when they want to access benefits guaranteed by law, such as free passes for public transport, half-price admission into cultural events, and priority seats. Yet this creates controversy. I call this the 'priority seat paradox'.

By law, in Bento, people aged 60 or above are eligible for priority seats on public transport. However, research participants experience this status in different ways. Some of them consider the priority seat a right they have earned by working throughout their lives. The priority seat is a sign of respect, for them, even if the icon used to identify priority seats on public transport is considered disrespectful[28] (the icon is a severely stooping humanoid with a walking stick; see figure 2.2).

If someone offers them the priority seat, some will accept it as deference. Others will feel offended and stigmatised by this. They argue that older people are always seen as tired or unhealthy. 'It is not because I am older that I have to be seated. I am healthy. I can stand,' one woman complained. Research participants can also redefine the right to a priority seat. For example, if a younger person occupying the priority seat is coming from work, older people might prioritise her. This attitude illustrates the centrality of work as a moral value in Bento. As one woman explains, if this person has been working, she must be tired, and so deserves the seat. The priority seat brings back the disputes between the worker and the unproductive retiree, and those who aged well and those who did not. In this last case, the priority seat is used, even among research participants, to define who they call 'old, old', meaning the person who shows the decline of ageing. One man explains, 'Younger

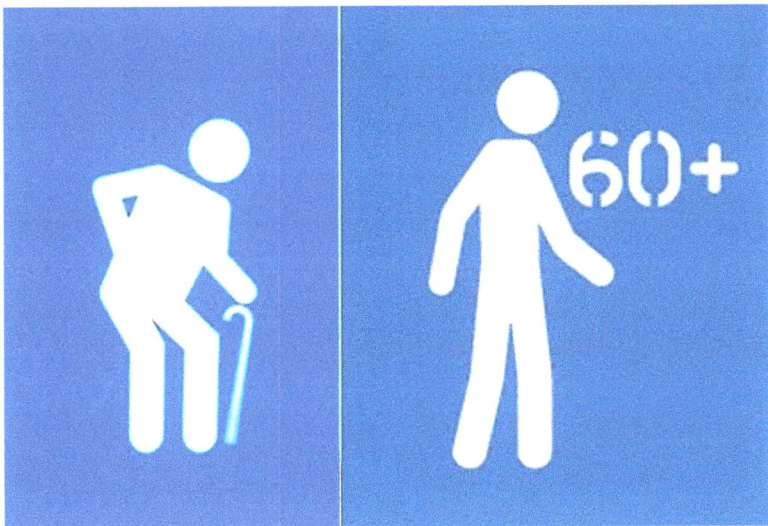

Figure 2.2 Official image currently used to indicate spaces and facilities reserved for older people (on the left), and the proposed new one on the right. © senado.leg.br.

people take the priority seats and ignore the needs of older people. But I am not talking about myself, because I am a cool older person. I have aged healthily. I am talking about those old ladies.' The priority-seat dynamic brings into view how ageing is seen by the state, society, and older people themselves. Its tension reflects the complexity with which the experience of ageing can be lived, perceived and represented in Bento.

This tension results in other terms which aim to frame old age. 'Third age' was and is the term used in public policies and private projects focused on occupational and preventive interventions.[29] The 'third age' is a stage of life after retirement reserved for self-realisation and free from dependence (I will discuss the term further in chapter 6). In Bento, the 'third age' is also called the 'best age' or the 'happy age', representing everything that older people can achieve when they choose to do the right thing and age well. Yet those terms receive criticism for not taking into account the frailties and limitations that are a natural part of the process of ageing.[30] Finally, in Bento, the words that define older age have been condensed in the term '60-plus', which means going back to chronological age (those aged 60 and above). However, the plus sign can be seen as positive, referring to those older people who remain active, productive and healthy.[31] Under the '60-plus' umbrella, people prefer to be called 'mature' or 'senior'. 'Mature' emphasises their experience, which has gained in value over the years. The term 'senior' also has a double connotation. Seniority can mean maturity, but it can also describe a position achieved through a professional career, which is why the 'senior' status can be very convenient, particularly in work-oriented Bento. 'Old', 'older', 'elderly', 'third age', 'best age', happy age', 'mature' or 'senior': there are many terms, but then, there are many experiences of ageing. Older people in Bento will choose the word they most identify with while still feeling misrepresented by discourses of ageing. One man summed this up as 'neither using a stick nor being a marathon runner: we want to be protagonists'.

Ageing as protagonists

For research participants, ageing as protagonists means reshaping their lives, rights, and participation in society according to their own needs and projects. Smartphones empower them to do so by expanding their options. They can now date on Tinder, rekindle old friendships on Facebook, start a blog, learn a language on Duolingo, shop for items made in China on Wish, explore the city with the help of Google Maps and Moovit or stay out late at night and then call a Uber. These are all possibilities taken up according to each person's goals and digital skills. Sandra is a good example. In her seventies, she is pursuing an old dream with the help of her smartphone. She has finally started repairing a van to go on a road trip through Brazil. As she plans to drive alone, she wants to be able to send videos to her children. This way they will see she is okay. While she is considering buying a new smartphone with a better camera, she has already downloaded some apps for editing videos and creating gifs. In addition, she has learned how to use her banking app as well as Google Drive and email to manage the accounts and documentation of the properties she lets to supplement her pension wherever she is. By combining these resources, Sandra will enjoy full autonomy, as she will be able to show her children that she is healthy and safe. At the same time, she won't become a burden, as all financial arrangements have already been made. Sandra is planning each tiny detail to ensure that, in the end, she can be free to do what she has dreamt of for so long.

As in Sandra's case, as long as older people in Bento maintain their autonomy, their families generally won't intervene. Consequently, research participants are not afraid of getting older and eventually dying, but they worry about their physical, mental and financial state. To show fragility or become a burden implies submitting to someone else's rules, which is the 'death' they want to postpone. From their perspective, 'death' should be expanded from the 'death of personhood' approach conceptualised during the early accounts of Alzheimer's disease,[32] as the loss of agency over oneself can be triggered equally by physical decline or financial dependence. Thus, any sign of vulnerability can be used to put research participants under family administration. In addition to this, as this book will demonstrate, participants don't want to burden their children (whose work is seen as sacred in Bento), or they don't expect they will take care of them after all. This explains both why they fear dependence, and the tactics they adopt to remain healthy and keep silent about their frailties.

Dependence is a fear shared by Brazilians in general. In a survey of people aged 60–79 in Brazil, 82 per cent said they feared physical dependence, 81 per cent said they feared mental dependence, and 69 per cent said they feared financial dependence.[33] Only 20 per cent said they feared death. Retired for a few years, Juliana, aged 66, illustrates how it feels. She cannot bear the idea that her children might use her possible weaknesses to determine what she can and cannot do in the future. That is why she thinks 80 might be a nice age to die, as she believes she will be independent until then. But if she doesn't maintain her autonomy, Juliana has already told her family that she wants to go into a nursing home, which she sees as a place where she does not have to submit herself to her children's wishes. Not everyone is as practical as Juliana. Older people in Bento are more likely to hide any frailties or conditions they develop, corroborating one of the arguments of this book, that ageing is experienced in silence. That is why Tzu, aged 83, covers the bruises caused by her constant falls with make-up. She says she panics whenever she imagines herself living with her children. She says, 'I will do whatever I can to stay in my house for as long I can.'

However, most of the time, older people in Bento do not pretend they are fine but work hard to achieve and maintain a state of good health. With a large portfolio of activities aimed at the third age, Bento is a supportive environment for those who want to stay fit after retirement. Consequently, while retirement provides them with financial autonomy and free time, these activities support their efforts to prolong physical and cognitive autonomy. These resources, combined, sound like everything participants might need to guarantee their roles as protagonists. But what does 'stay fit after retirement' really mean for them? To answer this question, we first have to address how retirement is experienced in Brazil and Bento. Luborsky and Le Blanc[34] challenge the hegemonic concept of retirement as conceived in Western cultures by presenting examples of retirement-like practices in non-Western and non-industrial societies.

On the one hand, they argue, within the Western paradigm retirement is a relationship between citizens and the state. It is also a social category associated with chronological age, which defines when someone can stop working and start receiving state-supported income without the stigma of dependence and without losing their social identity as a member of society. They highlight that retirement has nothing to do with unemployment, as retirees are not supposed to be labelled as lazy or dependent. On the contrary, retirement brings a right to a period of leisure, invested with freedom and responsibility for managing one's own life.

On the other hand, Luborsky and Le Blanc's work gives plenty of examples of cultures in which retirement is an entirely different experience. Retirement may be defined not by age but by children's marriage, which leads to exclusion from effective participation in society. Retirement may mean not the end of but a decrease in labour activities and social responsibilities. And retirement can also be inconceivable, as in societies in which, without labour, an adult has no social identity or role. Considering these cross-cultural perspectives, I might argue that retiring in Bento can be a complex experience. Brazil has a Western model of retirement. The right is given to every citizen in the country. Chronological age indexes it. It marks the end of working life (although there is no restriction on taking paid work after retirement). The state-supported income doesn't imply dependence but an earned right to a time of leisure. However, in Bento, retirement is more likely to be seen as unacceptable, as social identity and citizenship are strongly based on work.

As argued in the introduction, the identity of São Paulo was historically built on the figures of strong and romanticised workers, first represented by the Bandeirantes. They were tireless conquerors from colonial times. Subsequent generations of workers linked to the city were immigrants who were attracted here by the opportunity to prosper through hard work. After the end of slavery in Brazil in 1888, São Paulo received many waves of immigrants, who first came to work on the coffee plantations as part of a programme, subsidised by the Brazilian government, that lasted until 1927. A new wave of immigration began after World War II, with labourers finding jobs during the rapid industrialisation of the city.[35] Driven by the same promise of work and prosperity, an internal flow of migration started. Between 1941 and 1949, for example, almost 400,000 Brazilians migrated to São Paulo state, mainly from the North and Northeast regions and Minas Gerais state. For most of them their destination was São Paulo city.[36]

These migration flows are part of research participants' stories. Paulo and Bia are the grandchildren of Italians. Romulo was born in Japan and came to Bento with his parents as a child. Fernanda came from Minas Gerais to study pharmacology and was followed by her sister, who came to try life in the city after a period in Rio de Janeiro. Fernanda married Cesar, born in Bahia state, who arrived in Bento two years before her to try his luck as a musician. Sonia came from Natal, without her family, to study and work in the city. Bete came from Sergipe state. Mauro is from Maceió. João and Amelia came from Santos. Luisa came from Americana. Nelson came from Paraná. Rita came from Rio de Janeiro to accompany her son, who was pursuing a new job opportunity. Bento is the sum of the histories of these people and their families, who came to the city to work and prosper. As they say, 'I came to work and make a living.' The calling to work is, still today, the foundation of what Bento is. For example, even among younger generations, the question 'How are you?' is commonly understood as 'What do you do?' The answer typically includes information about work, professional credentials and achievements.[37]

Inactivity and unproductivity are both culturally unacceptable in work-oriented Bento. Even among older people the call to return to work is strong, highlighting that having an occupation is a way of rescuing the identity and sense of belonging lost with retirement. In other words, keeping busy and productive is what 'stay fit after retirement' really means in Bento. Chapter 8 discusses, for example, how companies and initiatives support older people to find a way to get back in the game. The text below reproduces one of these initiatives' emails, in which the association between identity and work is explicitly addressed.

> One very important aspect that shapes our identity is our work, our professional life. Sometimes, we identify so much with our careers and the company we work for that it becomes our surname. When we introduce ourselves to someone, we say: 'Hello, I am (our names) from the company (name of the company).' Now, what happens when our careers significantly change, and we don't carry our 'corporative surname' with us any more? What happens to our identity then?
>
> (Part of email received by the author on 21 July 2020)

The need to feel 'busy again' in old age and restore one's identity as a citizen of São Paulo is crucial also because many of the research participants ended their careers prematurely. Their premature retirement was possible because, until 2019, Brazilians could retire if they had contributed to the pension system for long enough, with no minimum age required. And this generation started working very young. Among participants, the earliest retirement was at 49. But what is the point in retiring so young if, in the end, what they pursue in life is how to get back to work? The answer is that participants didn't want to retire. They were driven to retirement by two factors: ageism[38] in the corporate environment and the fear that the benefits they were already eligible to enjoy would become extinct as a result of a pension system reform.[39]

Suddenly retired

Retirement may be a recognition of a lifetime dedicated to working. It may also be seen as a celebration of one's commitment, as, in the past, careers developed within a single institution where employees would learn to share the same values. Work would shape character and identity and help organise the narrative of people's lives.[40] Retirement would be, from that perspective, the symbol of a mission accomplished, when people finally get some well-deserved time for themselves and leisure. This recognition does not mean that retirement will be a fair reward. The way the social security system is set up in Brazil means that retirement can compound existing inequality,[41] even if there is a consensus between research participants from different social classes that retirement always means downgrading. However, even if the financial benefit was not always ideal or fair, retirees used to exit their working life through the front door as virtuous individuals who had contributed to their institutions and to society. This picture has changed, and not only in Brazil.

From the 1980s onwards, a new flexible production model led to a reconfiguration of work in various institutions. Markets and the workforce became globalised while technology aided the interconnection of processes and helped make decisions faster.[42] Productivity replaced loyalty. Thus, workers were supposed to comply with the new culture of corporations while developing new skills to engage with technologies. Lúcio, now aged 76, remembers this time. From 1989 to 1990, he was officially declared a public enemy of computers by his colleagues. He resisted any collaboration with the brand-new computer department, essentially created to digitise the memos and proposals his team had the task of writing. He complained about mistakes made in the newly digitised documents and said that things would only work if one of his engineers managed the inputs. He won his battle with a bonus: a 386 computer (developed by Compaq in 1986) was placed on his desk. 'For three months, we faced each other, with "him" still not having been switched on. Then I thought, I needed to tame this beast. Then I started, I got excited. I even bought a computer for my personal use.' However, once you have developed a reputation at work, it is hard to get away from it.

Older people have come to be seen as the most resistant to adapting to these changes. In a PwC study conducted with Brazilian companies,[43] employers list factors such as 'a lack of flexibility, difficulties in dealing with technology and an inability to keep up to date' as barriers to retaining older employees in organisations. In Bento, research participants experience this stigma as a kind of bullying, which resulted, in the best scenario, in them taking compulsory retirement. For example, Flávio retired 20 years ago at the age of 52 when another bank bought out the bank he worked at. The company's culture changed, new technologies were adopted, and his experience was no longer valued. He did not understand the new bank's decision to hire a whole team to perform the same function he used to carry out on his own and without all the technological support. He also lost his autonomy and suffered bullying from his younger colleagues. He had paid into the pension system for enough years to be able to retire, and so he did, but he left by the back door. Flávio ended his career without laurels.[44] He worked for a few more years as a consultant, but was rejected for a job he applied for because he had 'too much experience'.

As well as changes in work models and ageism, retirement in Bento has been motivated by uncertainties surrounding changes to the Brazilian pension system. Over the past 30 years, the Brazilian media has regularly warned of an imminent reform to the system, motivated by the need to balance Brazil's budgetary deficit, as the ratio between working-age people and pensioners shifts because of the country's rapidly ageing population.[45] In one of the two most widely read newspapers in Bento, a total of 13,724 articles containing the term 'pension reform' were published between 1990 and 2019,[46] which is the year the pension reform was finally approved.[47] Informally, as the research participants report, there was a rumour that the new criteria for retirement would bring them fewer benefits. For that reason, those who were already eligible to retire opted to do so, not because they no longer wanted to work but because they were anxious and insecure about the future. For example, Rita, aged 70, loved her job as a civil servant. She speaks with pride of how she was an exemplary employee, arriving early and working at weekends without even receiving overtime pay because it was the right thing to do. She was so competent at her job that she missed two opportunities to move into a new field of work, because her boss did not want to lose her. When she was eligible to retire, she was strongly advised to do so. 'I was scared,' she says, because her manager warned her that things were about to change and she had better move quickly to guarantee the benefits she was entitled to. Rita retired when she was only 51.

The requirement to look busy

For one reason or another, among research participants, retirement had nothing to do with a desire to end their working life. In addition to this, it didn't matter whether they ended their careers with financial stability. Being seen as unproductive would still be embarrassing in Bento. Therefore, the euphoria about retirement vanishes, and they take up activities in order to feel and look busy again. Although research participants recognise that their bodies are no longer the same and that working eight to ten hours a day can be exhausting, they feel too fit and motivated to give up their potential. Actually, with age, they feel more prepared than ever. They have accumulated a wealth of professional as well as life experience. They acknowledge that there may be no jobs available for them, at least not the kind of jobs they were used to. So they adapt their speech. They do not talk about jobs any more. They talk about working, about having an occupation or an activity that gives their time a purpose. For them, retirement represents a milestone in life, but with a twist. Retirement is no longer an end but the beginning of a new productive life. Especially among those with financial stability, this desire to return to work comes a year or two after retirement. During this time, research participants do everything they couldn't do before because they were stuck in their working routine. Tourism becomes one of the main activities in this period, as retirees are motivated to explore new places and visit old friends or relatives. However, after the feeling of freedom passes, they experience a sense of incompleteness that brings back the desire to work. The ideal new occupation would provide purpose in life and a new identity, which complies with the desired sense of utility in Bento.[48]

Trying a new occupation was what Fernanda did. Aged 63, she retired two years ago. Although she loved her job at a multinational food factory, the pace of work was stressful, and she started to have health issues. Her company offered her an excellent redundancy package, and she took the opportunity. Her husband was worried about how she would adapt, as she had always been very active. He suggested she join a Pilates class. She did this and now enjoys the fact that her instructor broadcasts her classes on Instagram as an example of what someone her age can achieve. But Pilates was just the beginning. The following two years, she remembers, were 'all about having fun'. She and her husband (a professional musician) took advantage of her freedom to travel,[49] experience new places and visit one of her children, who lives abroad. She could also, finally, follow him to music shows and events without having to worry about waking up at five in the morning. But then, 'there was a void'. She felt incomplete, with plenty of energy and idle time. She never considered going back to her old routine at the factory, but she began to wonder what the years ahead would be like. That was when she decided to join her friend in launching a start-up that aims to provide care at a distance. 'I didn't know anything about it,' she says. The new challenge motivated her to do extensive online research on the topic, which she used to make a business plan, all using applications on her smartphone. She now feels alive again.

Some research participants distinguish between 'working' and 'having an occupation' after retirement. While work is connected to maintaining their financial situation and a series of obligations, 'occupation' refers to feeling productive and useful. For these, work becomes an occupation related to the pursuit of pleasure and self-realisation, which may or may not result in financial gain. Sonia, aged 59, is an example of this. She retired a few years ago, and her income is sufficient for her to live comfortably. However, she did not feel like an 'old,

old lady'. Therefore, she decided to transform one of her passions into her future occupation. She was interested in exploring other cultures, and she loves to travel. This passion led her to complete a course offered by the Brazilian Ministry of Tourism, making her an official tour guide. Since she gained her certificate, she organises her schedule to balance the time she devotes to reading the books she loves and her activities as a tour guide. She does this because she makes a distinction between work and her occupation. Her activity as a tour guide is an occupation with no pressure, a commitment she has just to herself and her desire not to waste her capacity to be productive.

Having an occupation after retirement does not always imply a drastic change in career. In some cases, research participants remain in their professions but work fewer hours so that they can enjoy other activities and pleasures. That was what Bete did. She raised her daughter alone, working hard as a hairdresser in her own salon. At the age of 66, she drew up a sort of balance sheet of her life. She asked herself what her material needs were and concluded that she had enough to live comfortably on. However, she is a very reserved person, and doesn't make friends that easily. Continuing to work as a hairdresser allows her to socialise and maintain the sense that she is useful. That is why she doesn't think about stopping work. Instead, she has made some adjustments to make her routine easier. She sold her own salon and now works a few days a week in her sister's. She has thereby made room for other pleasurable activities, such as yoga and bodybuilding. With less responsibility, she can afford to spend long periods abroad visiting her daughter and grandson.

Another way retirees find to continue in their original career paths after retirement is by offering consultancy in their area of expertise, as they see themselves as 'seniors', older but with professional seniority. That was the case with Lúcio, who we have met before. He retired as an electrical engineer, owning his apartment and benefiting from a private pension. Since then, he has worked in a few more jobs, and then started working as a consultant. Although he says he was concerned about maintaining his income level, an essential aspect of his work as a consultant was keeping his professional status. And it doesn't matter if his friends keep asking him whether it is time to stop working. He still feels ashamed of being free during working hours, especially now that he realises that contract offers are becoming rarer and rarer:

'The fact I have no occupation makes me anxious. I could never ever accept myself as idle during working hours. At night, for example, it is not a problem to know I have nothing to do. But to do what I did today? To do Pilates and play tennis on an ordinary Monday morning? That is a mortal sin.'

As we have seen so far, working after retirement has a personal component. People can discover new passions and abilities that reflect their interests and personalities, or they can reorganise their time and working models. However, a social component also emerges from the cultural context in Bento, where work provides a sense of belonging as citizens of São Paulo.[50] That is causing Lúcio anxiety, as he feels embarrassed to be seen out of work during working hours. He is not alone, as he found out when he joined a weekly meeting organised by a group of older people which focused on developing new work alternatives for their age group. At the beginning of these meetings, new members like Lúcio are invited to introduce themselves to the group briefly. It is common for them to associate retirement with loneliness or an identity crisis. Invariably, their presentations are based on their past professional experience, highlighting their higher education, positions in multinational companies and the distinctions achieved throughout their careers. When they recount the moment they left their last formal job, it is not rare for them to feel a lump in the throat. A new member summarised it thus: 'It's hard to lose the company badge,' referring to the professional credential that shaped his identity for most of his life.

A positive discourse quickly replaces the nostalgia. New members say they are happy to be there, and most of them emphasise that they still feel motivated to work and that they still believe they can make a difference, and conclude by saying that their expertise and skills are available to help the group. That means engaging in any project that could result in an opportunity for them to get out of the house and feel useful again. The projects offered by this collective are ideas brought to the group by members themselves. The person bringing the idea acquires the status of project manager and recruits other people to work together in a subgroup. A project requires regular meetings, which will take place in parallel with the main one. The subgroup periodically report their progress and what they plan to do next to the leading group. Usually, besides the collective official WhatsApp group and transmission list, each subgroup ends up with its own dedicated WhatsApp group, whose members collaborate to expand their social lives even more. These routines combined give group members the feeling that they are working just as they used to, and with a bonus. Through their participation in these activities, they are no longer either retirees or unproductive people.

They have a new status. They have reinvented themselves as *entrepreneurs* with a purpose in life, which is the main topic of chapter 8.

However, the desire to fill idle time, feel productive, and restore their identity by achieving a new 'professional badge' is not the only reason that drives research participants to look for an occupation in old age. For some, this occupation is still associated with everyday needs, as they have grown older but are not retired yet. As one man puts it, 'There is no reinvention, there is survival.'

A plan B for ageing

The ageing experience in Bento is not only represented by retired people who have achieved financial stability. Some simply haven't prepared themselves or haven't accrued the means for this kind of ageing. This implies an entirely different relationship to work in the later years. For them, it is not just about being judged for their unproductivity. It is about trying to adapt in order to continue to make a living. That means shifting to informal employment, accepting lower-skilled jobs or resigning themselves to the possibility that they may have to work until they die.

That is the case with Laís, whom we have met before. She is a freelance translator. Her husband is also a freelancer, who maintains his practice as a physiotherapist. In her fifties, she says she and her husband have done everything wrong throughout their lives. They have misused their money. Thus they have no prospects of retiring. They'll have to work as long as they can, and after that she does not know what's going to happen. Bianca feels the same. Working at a public hospital in Bento, she explains that she went through many informal jobs at the beginning of her professional life. At the time, her salary was never enough to contribute to the pension system as a self-employed person. Thus, Bianca knows she will retire some day, but she has no idea when, even though she realises she has an exhausting routine. She works with HIV-positive older people from low-income populations. As a psychologist, she manages cases of misinformation, abandonment and violence. She confesses that when she arrives home after work, she does not have the energy to do much but listen to music and watch movies on YouTube. She thinks about retirement with fortitude. She knows she will still have to work for many years.

Bianca and Laís are almost the same age and share the same concerns about the future. However, their perspectives are very different. Although she might feel tired, Bianca has stability at work. Laís doesn't.

She has to figure out how to manage her ageing body with the productivity she might have to make a living as a freelancer. In addition to this, she may have to compete with people younger than herself. Companies are likely to associate ageing with a possible loss of productivity. The older contingent is also seen as a potential source of increased expenses for companies because of their increased health needs.[51] As Laís is a freelancer, her health needs wouldn't be a problem. However, she might end up living in limbo anyway. Participants call 'limbo' the period in which they are considered too old to work by employers or clients, but are still too young to be eligible for retirement or to enjoy the benefits of being officially older. Beto, aged 58, explains how limbo works:

> 'At fifty, you have two options: you are either the director or the owner. If not, you're out. You're old, but you still do not have the benefits of old age. You are a nobody, and no one is talking about it. People will only remember that you exist when you turn 60. Today it is nice to talk about older people. It's cute.'

One alternative for those who are 'off the market' and have not retired yet is to enter the informal market as a self-employed person, with no guarantees. Especially for men, three opportunities stand out: working as estate agents, insurance brokers, or drivers for ride-hailing companies (such as Uber). Those who want to work as estate agents or insurance brokers must take a training course and an exam to get the licence required to start this type of work, which they have to pay for themselves. The exam requires a significant commitment in terms of time and money. João, aged 64, and Felipe, aged 63, had tried to work as estate agents when they were made redundant. Both have higher education, and although the two have similar stories, they have had different experiences. Weighing up the costs of the licence, Felipe concluded that he would end up paying to work. He therefore gave up the estate agent course and tried to work as a salesperson, but still without any of the benefits of employment (paid holidays, dental care, etc.). One day he made a big sale. The customer received the goods but never sent the payment. Felipe was held responsible for the loss, even though it was the company's responsibility to check the customer's references. He was then dismissed. With no prospect of retiring, he is a member of the collective that discusses work opportunities for older people. He is still trying to find a plan B, and his need is urgent. He can't rely on his adult children, even though they live with his ex-wife in a luxury apartment the couple bought together when they were married.

João, on the other hand, went through the whole preparation process and became an estate agent. But he had no reason to celebrate. He had to wait a long time before it was his turn to try to make a sale. His colleagues were unimpressive, the work environment was highly competitive, and the job offered no guarantees. Sometimes, all he had to eat during the day was the packet of biscuits he had brought from home. He was embarrassed to be there. The money wasn't good, but he could pay the bills and contribute to the national pension system until he was able to retire in a few years' time. When he finally retired, he decided he would keep working to supplement his income. At that time, he started working as an Uber driver. He also kept his work as an estate agent. The reason for this is that he can now make his sales using his smartphone. By 2017, 5 per cent of drivers who worked for Uber-like apps in São Paulo were over 60. Besides the extra money, the desire to stay active and to get out of the house are the main grounds for older people to start working as drivers.[52] That is João's case, as his wife retired two years ago. He loves her, and they text each other throughout the day. But, he explains, 'Being at home together for the whole day? That wouldn't work.'

Among research participants, men find it harder than women to accept that there is no place for them in their area of expertise. And not everyone will take any job, as João did. Olívio is an example. At 56, he refuses to consider an alternative career. He is not retired, but he inherited some money from his parents, and the house they used to live in, which will give him a few years of financial stability. Like Don Draper on the American television series *Mad Men*, Olívio can be defined as an 'old-fashioned' advertising man. He worked for large agencies with inflated structures, managing big accounts at a time when salaries were high and the business's revenue was based on traditional media such as television, newspapers and magazines. However, the advertising industry is more and more driven by digital media, and Olívio has not kept up with these changes. Nevertheless, he keeps looking for the same type of job he had always had. His smartphone plays a crucial role in his search. He works using Google Drive, Dropbox, Facebook, WhatsApp, LinkedIn and Gmail. He receives job offers from his LinkedIn, WhatsApp and Facebook groups. He uses Google Drive and Dropbox to store his CV, and email to check whether his job application was submitted successfully. This routine consumes most of his days, so he feels he is actually working. In this way, as will be shown in the next chapter, managing a digital life can become an occupation in itself.

On the other hand, women seem to be more comfortable choosing a plan B and moving on. They can afford to take alternative jobs because their identities are generally not defined only by their careers.[53] Their jobs were just part of the work they did, combined with the demands of their houses, their marriages and their children. They are more practical and more optimistic about the opportunity to get out of the house and earn extra income.

Magali, aged 67, thinks that way. She retired when she was 60, motivated by the rumours about the imminent reform of the national pension system. She had been an executive secretary for decades. She enjoyed her retirement for a few months, but then she got depressed. She used to put on make-up, and she always liked her high heels, but she no longer has any motivation for that. Moreover, she saw her monthly income decrease from R$7,000 (about £967) to R$2,800 (about £387), something experienced earlier by her retired husband. One day, someone asked her to recommend a carer for an older lady. Without consulting anyone, she applied for the job, and got it. Since then, she has divided her time between her family and her new job, which requires her to spend the night at the client's a few times a week. She confesses that sometimes she returns home exhausted, but she prefers to focus on the positives. As she has plenty of free time when her older lady is sleeping, she uses her smartphone to watch TV and Netflix and learn French. The extra income allows her to keep up her family's standard of living and indulge herself, enjoying rewards for her hard work, such as travelling.

Neither/nors

As we have seen, some research participants retired early, motivated by the rumours of pension system reform or pushed by ageism in the corporate market. Besides them, some left the labour market without retiring. Camarano and Carvalho[54] call attention to a third group, those who are neither working, nor retired, nor looking for a job. They call them 'neither/nors', emphasising that this status is increasing among Brazilian men. On the one hand, their premature exit from the labour market is associated with barriers to technology adoption, absences from work due to morbidity, decrease in physical strength, and levels of education. On the other hand, the conditions for survival while not retired are provided by children, parents (when these men go back to their parents' houses, for example), or spouses whose incomes come from working or pensions. As the authors argue, the 'neither/nor' status may challenge gender relations, as men leave their traditional role as providers. As observed earlier, this change in gender relations can be facilitated among research participants because women quickly adapt to other jobs and activities while men are more attached to their previous careers.

There is, however, a particularity in Bento. As a community in which work shapes character and identity, there are no declared 'neither/nors' among the research participants. Among those who are neither employed nor retired, it is unacceptable not to be searching for a job. In such cases, research participants are likely to say they are 'not working at the moment', stressing that this status is temporary. Usually, they follow this disclosure by outlining what they are doing to find a job or become productive again. As Olívio, who we met earlier, illustrates, managing multiple social media to find a job can become an occupation that works as a proof of character. While waiting for an opportunity, unemployed and not yet retired research participants choose to fill their 'limbo' by attending the portfolio of activities aimed at the third age. These activities bring a double gain. As long as people can fill their time with them, they can reproduce their working routines and feel busy while the new job doesn't come. In addition, they can choose the activities they believe will help them return to work by improving their skills and knowledge. This is not a behaviour restricted to those living in 'limbo'. As this book argues, inactivity in work-oriented Bento is embarrassing even after retirement. That is why retirees join in the same activities as those who are 'not working at the moment'. Some will invest in skills to start a new occupation, while others will invest in self-development and self-care, as discussed in chapter 8. What matters in the end is that they will be able to say proudly, 'I don't have time,' just as one woman did before describing all the activities she has engaged in since she retired. By doing this, she can claim a workaholic-like status, which is seen as a virtue in São Paulo.[55]

> 'I have Mondays available. Actually, I am also busy on Mondays. I stay at home. I do the laundry. I go to the market. I cook. I may go to the doctor's or have medical tests scheduled that day. I squeeze everything into Mondays. On Tuesdays and Thursdays, I go to a programme for older people run by the state. I go to the gym, take English classes and attend all the social events they organise there. On Wednesdays, I do Pilates and attend two courses where I learn more about using the computer and WhatsApp. On Fridays, I learn French at an open course at one of the Catholic churches near here, and I also like to have my hair done.'

A new working life

As this chapter argues, retirement remains a milestone in the experience of ageing in Bento. It works as a social label that comes attached to a set of expectations and permissions that define a place for older people in society. However, as ageing populations have emerged as a social and economic problem in the last few decades, what society expects from older people after retirement has changed. Older people are supposed to postpone dependence (physical, mental, financial) and to remain active. The dissemination of positive images of ageing contributes to this new normativity, presented as a celebration of freedom. Marc Augé argues that while age can be a social cage, the experience of time is a space for reinvention and freedom, leading to a feeling of youth.[56] This book argues that this space for reinvention has turned into a cage in which pleasure, freedom and the obligation to remain healthy and busy are connected. In Bento, this call for action is more than welcome, as the desire to stay productive conforms with local moral standards. The next chapter develops the idea that, thanks to the Active Ageing framework as adopted in Brazil,[57] participants will be able to fill their timetables with 'appointments' that attest to their productivity and autonomy. That is how retirement becomes not an end but the beginning of a new working life. For some, as discussed in this chapter, work in later life is still attached to material needs. For others, as will be shown in chapter 8, work is a way to achieve self-realisation and respect. For both groups, and with great help from their smartphones, ageing will become an occupation in itself.

Notes

1. Featherstone & Hepworth 2005.
2. Lippmann 2010.
3. Chronological age is the number of years a person has been alive (Mitnitski et al. 2002).
4. IBGE 2020c, p. 8.
5. Life expectancy at birth in 2017 (Cidade de São Paulo, Direitos Humanos e Cidadania 2020, p. 46).
6. To research participants, being seen as 'old' can be offensive and even an embarrassment. Lamb (2019) observed that this may be the case among Americans, but not among Indians, who are more likely to welcome ageing.
7. As observed by Lamb (2019) in the US and Lassen and Jespersen (2017) in Denmark, socioeconomic inequalities can result in different experiences of ageing. It is not just about the material conditions that affect one's ability to adopt a healthy lifestyle. These inequalities also influence the physical conditions in which one reaches old age.
8. In the urban middle-class families researched by the anthropologist Goldenberg (2010) in Rio de Janeiro, she observed that clothes could be shared by three generations of women, daughter, mother and grandmother. That is not the case in Bento. These women are concerned with fashion but also with comfort, and they recognise that some clothes are inappropriate for their

age and bodies. They don't want to wear the miniskirts young people wear, but they don't fit into the looks they identify as for 'old, old ladies'.
9   Mindminers & Hype60+ 2018.
10 Boni 2019.
11 Debert 1997.
12 Leibing 2005.
13 Featherstone & Hepworth 2005.
14 Debert 2003.
15 In 1982, the UN held the World Assembly on Ageing, which resulted in the Vienna International Plan of Action on Ageing. The document established a set of goals and recommendations to manage global ageing. The paper targets the ageing population as a potential risk for societies (United Nations 1983). Brazil was one of the signatories of this plan.
16 Debert 1997; Correa 2009.
17 Rowe & Kahn 1997.
18 Pike 2011; Whyte 2017; Lamb 2019.
19 Lamb 2017.
20 Debert 2012.
21 Westin 2019.
22 Lamb 2019; Lassen & Jespersen 2017.
23 As highlighted by Featherstone and Hepworth (2005), the production and dissemination of positive images of ageing was one of the recommendations of the Madrid International Plan of Action on Ageing (United Nations 2002). In the same year, the WHO launched its Active Ageing framework policy, which calls on older people to become aspirational models for younger generations (World Health Organization 2002).
24 The documentary *Envelhescência* (Martines 2015) got funding from ProacSP (a fund for cultural programmes from the state of São Paulo) and the Secretary of Culture of the State of São Paulo, as well as from Plenitud, a brand that makes incontinence products for older people and whose slogan is 'For those who haven't given up living life to the full'. See the company's website at https://www.plenitud.com.br/ (accessed 5 January 2022).
25 Regarding narratives of ageing in Brazil, Rodrigues and Soares (2006) argue that they materialise new moralities and cultural references. From the individual perspective, comparing oneself with these narratives can result in a negative self-evaluation internalised as guilt or a feeling of inferiority.
26 Bourdieu 1993.
27 Debert 1997.
28 The image was also considered inappropriate by the Comissão de Direitos Humanos e Legislação Participativa (CDH; Commission on Human Rights and Participatory Legislation), in the Brazilian Senate, in 2016 (Senado Federal 2018). The prohibition on using pejorative images to identify older people was turned into a law (PL10282/2018), but is still waiting for approval (Câmara dos Deputados 2018).
29 Although three major initiatives addressing older people date from the 1960s (Serviço Social de Comércio (Sesc; trade social service), Legião da Boa Vontade (LBA; legion of goodwill) and universities of the third age), the boom in private programmes and public policies focused on promoting sociability, activities and education was observed during the 1980s (Debert, 2012). Scholars argued that the state had started to manage older people's free time in a Foucauldian way. Because of this, activities focused on prevention and leisure overlapped in the name of quality of life in old age (Correa 2009; Zago & Silva 2003).
30 Schneider & Irigaray 2008.
31 For example, one private health insurance company that focused on older people created the term 'Adult Plus' to target this sector while highlighting the autonomy and freedom they will enjoy when they adopt healthy habits.
32 Leibing 2017.
33 Collucci & Pinto 2018.
34 Luborsky & LeBlanc 2003.
35 Arquivo Público do Estado de São Paulo 2009.
36 Governo do Estado de São Paulo 2021.
37 In their work with older people in Ireland, Garvey and Miller (2021) address retirees' relationship with their previous work life. While in Bento older people continue to present themselves in terms of what they did before retirement, these authors argue that they could spend a year meeting

38 Like racism for race and sexism for gender, ageism is discrimination based on age (Lamb 2019).
39 The Covid-19 pandemic could be added as a cause of early retirement or leaving the labour force. A comparison between the first quarters of 2019 and 2020 showed that 1.3 million Brazilians aged 60 or over left their jobs or stopped looking for a job (Alegretti 2020).
40 Sennett 2006.
41 In the 1980s, for example, retirees organised themselves into associations and confederations to fight the disparities in monetary adjustments between pensions and salaries. In the early 1990s, their national political mobilisation gained media attention as the '147 per cent movement', which symbolises the deficit among those who earned more than the minimum wage. The movement succeeded, gaining a judicial victory (Veras and Oliveira 2018; Debert 2012).
42 As Harvey (1989) argues, flexibility has become the new operational logic of late capitalism, which reshapes work models. Long-term contracts are replaced by remote, transnational, temporary and flexible work, quickly adapting to capital demands. Consequently, as observed by Luborsky (1994), North American retirees share the perception that family-like business relationships became impersonal and bureaucratic.
43 PricewaterhouseCoopers Brasil & EAESP-FGV 2013.
44 In cases like these, there is no ceremony or celebration which would give participants a validation for the accomplishments of a working life. As rituals, Savishinsky (2000, p. 45) argues, such events would help the transition to the new stage of life defined by retirement.
45 Simson et al. 2003.
46 Acervo Estadão 2020.
47 The pension reform established a minimum pension age of 62 years for women and 65 for men. Before the reform, there was no minimum pension age, as men and women could apply for a proportional pension based on their years of contribution to the pension system (Temóteo et al. 2019).
48 Luborsky (1994) addresses the fact that retirement brings a need for new retirees in America to reorganise their self and their personal and social identities. The transition requires a psychological effort in the face of a dilemma. Having time to relax is balanced by the fear of being labelled by the community as a 'full retiree', which may denote those who have aged and become useless or discarded. Luborsky explores the mechanism adopted by a group of men to transition from work to retirement until they feel ready to present themselves in public and engage in social life. In their case, the brief euphoria about being free from obligations and work routines lasts one or two months. They allow themselves to 'laze around' and take a trip during that time, which marks their rupture with the community. This phase is also when some of them engage in hands-on projects in the domestic space, mainly working in their back gardens. This work can be seen as a continuation of valued practices inherited from their working time, when new retirees remain productive. The choice of the back garden rather than the front denotes that they desire time for reclusion to work on their self-images. The next step is to review conjugal and domestic routines. Finally, retirees reconnect with the community with an identity shaped for post-retirement life. In Bento too, participants struggle with their retiree status. They experience the same phase of euphoria, take trips, and allow themselves pleasure free from work obligations. They then face a 'void'. This feeling drives them to seek new occupations and activities in order to restore the productivity and usefulness that allows them to be seen again as members of the community and as citizens of São Paulo. One particularity is that some participants will try to find the means to return to the work they built their careers on. This means their efforts are not focused on creating new identities but on restoring the identity and credentials they had before retirement.
49 Like Fernanda, many participants chose to take a trip when they retired. As Savishinsky observed among American retirees, travel can work as a ritual to mark the end of the working life and the beginning of a new life. Travelling can help recent retirees to make these transitions, as they can separate themselves from 'work, hometown, the daily life routine and the common flow of social life'. It provides some time and space for evaluating the past and imagining the future. Travelling can also provide a convenient answer when new retirees are asked what they are going to do after retirement (Savishinsky 2000, p. 51).
50 Queiroz 1992; Marins 1999.

51 Saul Levmore (2017) argues that productivity is likely to decrease with age. However, employers can't let go of employees when their performance decreases without being accused of ageism. Assuming most people retire at 68, the author defends the right of the employer to design work contracts that specify a mandatory age of retirement, which, he suggests, should be 65. This retirement age should be applied to all contracts, including those young people sign when they start working for a company. He argues that this would make companies more likely to hire middle-aged employees.
52 Cardoso 2017.
53 As Camarano and Carvalho (2015) argue, work defines men's role in Brazilian society, while marriage and motherhood define women's. They highlight the fact that in the traditional gender contract, men are identified as providers and women as caregivers. Even with greater female participation in the labour market, men's status is based on work.
54 Camarano & Carvalho 2015.
55 Moura 1994.
56 Augé 2016.
57 Dias & Pais-Ribeiro 2018.

3
The art of being busy

How to fit in

'I don't feel guilty for saying that I do nothing. Most people go to a psychiatrist. I have no remorse.' At first, Roger, aged 61, seems to be the antithesis of everything previously said about the experience of ageing in Bento. This chapter shows how Roger ends up fitting the local 'normality' by highlighting how everyday activities that have nothing to do with a previous career or a new job can provide a busy timetable and a sense of usefulness after retirement. It also explains why research participants are more likely to prioritise activities that can help them stay healthy and independent. With that 'mission accomplished', as they say, they can try activities more closely associated with pleasure, like hobbies. A good question to be asked here is how staying healthy became a 'mission' in the first place. We will get there after we get to know Roger better.

Roger retired when he was 55 years old. As with many others in Bento, this was not his own decision. In his case, his private pension policy established that he should retire when he reached 30 years of contributions. Even so, he retired with a privileged status, as he kept the same standard of living he had when he was employed. He acknowledges that he was not expected to stop being productive at that time, being as healthy as he was and still is. However, after living through the exhausting routine of the finance sector for three decades, he needed some time for himself. He didn't become an entrepreneur or an Uber driver. Instead, he walked away from LinkedIn and his work colleagues, who insisted that he should join them as a consultant after retirement. The idea of a man who doesn't want to have any occupation is quickly proved false when Roger presents us with his new routine.[1] It is not that he does nothing. He is extremely busy. He just doesn't want to work for others any more. He says, 'My whole life, I had no time for myself. Now everything is fine. That is something that seems very clear to me. I have no guilt.'

However, Roger is concerned about not being a burden, ageing well, and who will take care of him in the future. He therefore cultivates healthy habits, including exercise. He has always insisted on doing a lot of sporting activities. He used to run, and for a while this was his kind of meditation. He used to track his performance using his Samsung Health app so that he could run against himself. After he was injured, he abandoned both the app and the running. Now he combines spinning classes (a form of exercise on a stationary bicycle) with Pilates, weight training and yoga practice. Yoga helps him deal with the finiteness of life as it makes him conscious that the best things in life are always happening here and now. Since retirement, he has also started to learn music theory. He is passionate about music, and he confesses he is sick of hearing Led Zeppelin's 'Going to California'. While his friends think that good music is defined by the 'classics', he keeps up to date with new bands and artists on Spotify. Music is not just his passion. It was the last thing his father 'forgot' when he developed Alzheimer's. There are other cases of Alzheimer's in his family, and this affective learning also helps Roger to exercise his brain.

Travelling with his wife is another activity he enjoys. He is planning their next trip, to Italy. He is therefore taking Italian classes and exercising his language skills on Duolingo. Roger carefully manages his presence on eight different social networks. This makes him proud, as he claims he never posts the same content across his accounts. He uses Facebook, Instagram, Snapchat, Twitter, Tumblr, Pinterest, Musical.ly and Spotify. Some of them reflect his interests. Others are used to catch up with, but also to expand his surveillance over, his grandchildren and nephews. Being very protective, he uses the Kindle app to read the books he thinks they might like before buying them. If he approves of it, the printed version is sent to them as a gift. Roger enjoys the status of being the official family photographer, editor and archivist. After going through two rounds of editing using two different apps, all of his photos are stored and organised in the Cloud. Recently, he and his wife decided they would take responsibility for the care of her parents, as they are the most financially secure in her family.[2] She has three siblings, and any decision or action is discussed on the WhatsApp group they created for this purpose. Besides supporting his wife, Roger is responsible for looking for information and doctors and buying medication, using his experience of taking care of his own father.

We can say that Roger is an exception among older men in Bento, especially from the perspective of the previous chapter, since his life is detached from his last professional credentials. In his case, even with mandatory retirement, this rupture didn't trigger an identity crisis. Instead, Roger manages a busy schedule that expresses his interests and personality while he retains activities that help his mental and physical health. He doesn't say so, but he could, like others, argue that he doesn't have idle time after retirement, meaning he stays productive, a culturally desirable status in work-oriented São Paulo. However, that is not the only way in which Roger conforms to the local 'norm'. Like him, most research participants reconcile activities associated with pleasure and with self-preservation and care, as they are concerned to keep their autonomy. But what comes first? This chapter argues that older people in Bento engage in activities that help them maintain their physical and mental health first and foremost.[3]

First things first

As we saw in the previous chapter, older people can exercise the freedom associated with youth and stay safe from family interventions and peers' judgements by keeping their autonomy. But that is just one part of the story. Like Roger, research participants share the desire not to become a burden to their children, which is reinforced by the fact that they have no expectation that their children will take care of them in the future. The next chapter will address the shift in the *intergenerational contract* regarding reciprocity between parents and children. However, it is relevant to stress that the moral obligation between generations is being replaced by discourses that regard self-care as a virtue[4] and dependence as a failure.[5] This morality drives older people in Bento to cultivate healthy routines. However, their concerns with the healthy body should be seen in the context of the work-oriented São Paulo too.

Goldenberg argues that the body is social capital in Brazilian culture.[6] Her analysis considers the middle class of Rio de Janeiro, where the youthful sculpted body (*corpo sarado*) is used to attain distinction, functioning as clothing that is never out of fashion. Although this aesthetic is not representative of the 'typical' Brazilian body, she explains, it gains visibility, primarily through Brazilian soap operas, as an ideal to be copied and followed. This normativity contributes to the consolidation of the plastic surgery market in Brazil, the second-largest in the world. As noted by Edmonds in his ethnography, also conducted in Rio de Janeiro,[7] the plastic surgery industry developed with the promise of correcting 'age-related defects' by extending youthfulness and the attractiveness needed to preserve self-esteem and social relations. He argues that plastic procedures become a 'surgery for life', a kind of therapeutic process that celebrates youth as a beauty norm for Brazilian women, but also as a form of capital and lifestyle.

While Goldenberg and Edmonds stress physical appearance, Leibing[8] emphasises that taking up activities and continuing to work have become another way to 'not look old' in Brazilian society, even if, for those with material means, productivity can be combined with interventions to avert the signs of ageing. In addition to this, she cites examples of how media coverage in the 1980s and early 1990s helped to promote work in old age (not just leisure activities) as the 'right attitude' and also as a 'good medicine' to extend the third age. In São Paulo, as discussed so far, that attitude towards working is historically rooted, and has become a key value in the city's identity.[9] Work is the element that allows one to enjoy the status of a citizen of São Paulo at all ages. We could argue that work is the major form of social capital in the city, in opposition to 'the body', as identified in Rio de Janeiro.

That is the case in Bento. What research participants pursue in old age is the functional body, the one that allows them to remain productive. Caradec argues that the ageing body is experienced in three different registers: the organic body, appearance and energy, which are related to health, beauty and vitality (feeling of being in shape) respectively.[10] In that perspective, it is possible to argue that while appearance and beauty play a central role in Goldenberg's analysis in Rio de Janeiro,[11] energy and vitality are the main concerns in Bento. Energy and vitality are not only the factors that allow them to enjoy the third age or postpone dependency. They are also what enable research participants to participate in as many activities as possible to keep them productive after retirement. They consider any activity to be an effort to age well, but as they associate health with productivity most start with physical activities as a logical choice for achieving energy and motivation to put other interests into practice.

This local logic is supported by 'Active ageing: A policy framework', published by the World Health Organization (WHO) in 2002.[12] In the framework, being 'active' means participating actively in society. Although older people's contributions are extended to the care of relatives or volunteering, the main expectation is that this contingent should adopt health habits focused on prevention. By doing this, older people can extend their autonomy and avoid being a burden to society. Ultimately, being active demands energy and motivation, which means older people should first remain healthy. The document was translated into Portuguese in 2005, becoming the guideline for ageing policies in Brazil.[13] However, the translation gave prominence to physical activity.[14] Although the original document published in English highlights the difference between healthy ageing[15] (maintaining good health while ageing) and active ageing[16] (good health, participation and security), the Brazilian document emphasised healthy ageing, with particular attention to physical activities.[17] Even in the foreword,[18] signed by the Secretary of Health Surveillance of the Brazilian Ministry of Health, the text 'Active ageing: A policy framework' is replaced by 'Healthy ageing: A policy framework'. That may be a lapse. However, these different approaches are also expressed on the covers of the publications (see figures 3.1 and 3.2). The English version shows a group of hands applauding the ageing population as a triumph of humanity. In contrast, the guideline published in Brazil shows an ageless human body engaging in physical activity.

The emphasis on physical activity is also observed in São Paulo city. Since 2007, for example, 2000 open-air gyms have been installed in public squares.[19] These spaces are also called 'Longevity Playgrounds'. The signs by these playgrounds (see figure 3.3) explain: 'This space targets the third age, as an alternative solution that can be used for physical activities with a focus on promoting health, sociability, independence, autonomy and leisure.'

As a response to the WHO's Active Ageing policy, age-friendly outdoor spaces like the Longevity Playgrounds offer an alternative to older people for staying physically and socially active (figure 3.4). In China, for example, older people constitute the age group that makes most use of urban parks. As Zhai et al. show in their comparative study of two urban parks in Xi'an,[20] the main reasons older people visit parks are to rest and relax, exercise and socialise. Their work provides a guideline for the development of outdoor spaces to meet the needs of older people. Among their observations, they point out that conflicts between groups occupying the same space can compromise the experience of relaxing. In their study, the conflicts are related to noise and overlapping music. Similarly, in the Longevity Playgrounds in Bento, the outdoor experience is compromised by conflicts with groups occupying the space. Here, older people share the space with homeless people, who they perceive as potential risks. Thus, in the playgrounds, older people can't always relax and fully enjoy the activity, having to keep one eye on their exercise and the other on their surroundings.

In their comparative study of park-based physical activities in urban China and Germany,[21] Wagner et al. argue that security (in addition to the

Figure 3.1 *Active Ageing: A Policy Framework* eBook cover. © WHO.

park's attractiveness and features) is positively associated with older people's park-based physical activities while the time it takes to get there appears as a negative factor. In Bento, this is not a barrier, as there are five Longevity Playgrounds in the area, placed in public squares. Bento also has one of the largest parks in São Paulo, where older people can find the same equipment as in the playgrounds. However, once there, older people are more likely to choose walking or engage in activities offered by volunteers, like the square dance that happens in the morning on working days.

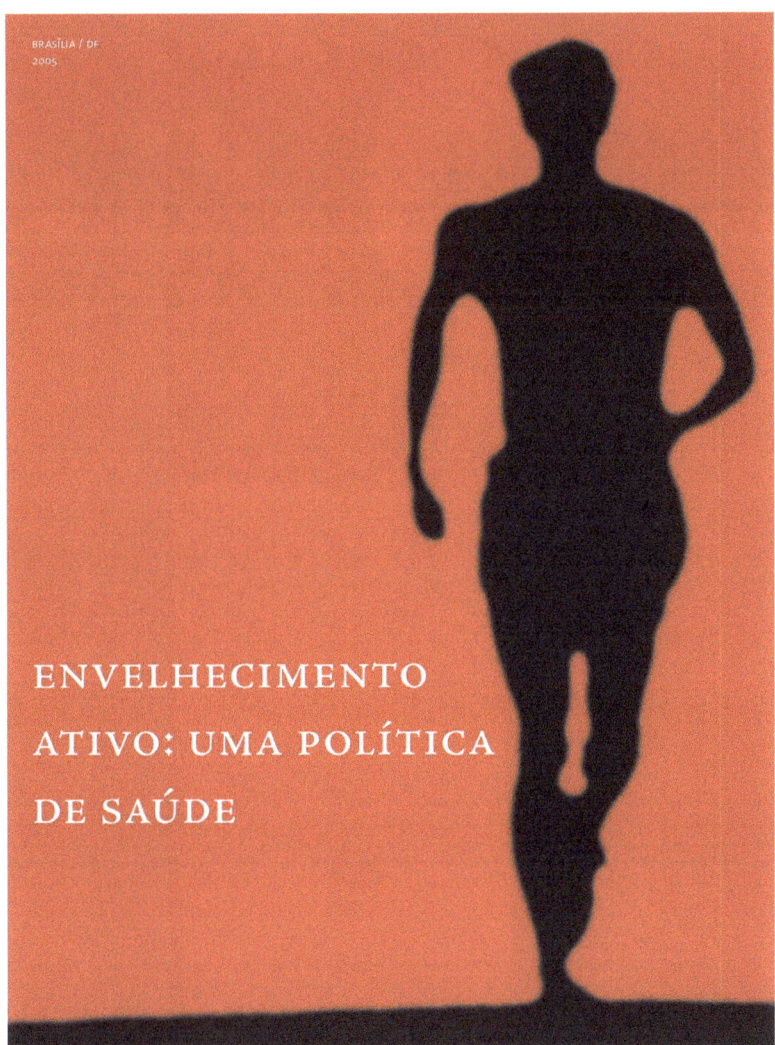

Figure 3.2 Brazilian version of *Active Ageing: A Policy Framework* eBook cover. © WHO.

In Bento, women use the 'Longevity Playgrounds' more than men, coming in the mornings, mostly in pairs, to exercise together. However, as security is a concern, when they go by themselves they avoid bringing bags, wallets and sometimes their smartphones (the use of smartphones in public spaces will be considered further in chapter 5). A safer option is to engage in the indoor programmes offered by public hospitals. But even there, older people can't relax. There is a significant demand for these Active Ageing programmes. That means that if you become a member you

Figure 3.3   Longevity Playground sign. © Marília Duque.

Figure 3.4 Older people using the Longevity Playground in Bento. © Marília Duque.

must make a serious commitment to the rules. There are, for example, attendance lists, and you are only permitted a limited number of absences, which you need to notify the coordinator about in advance.[22] Here, however, obligation is combined with pleasure. Older people enjoy being there. The routine of care is at the same time an opportunity for social inclusion, interaction and freedom, as they can combine exercise with other activities they like. In that sense, as the Longevity Playground illustrates, the duty to maintain healthy habits merges with the right to enjoy freedom and leisure in old age.

In addition to these public initiatives, Bento has a wide range of physical activities aimed at the third age, private or subsidised by the third sector or offered by volunteers. In the private sector, gyms are starting to offer older people special rates in limited daytime hours, mainly during the afternoons. It is common for older people to engage in more than one physical activity in different places to keep themselves busy for the whole week. Many will prioritise free activities as they try to make their schedule fit their budgets after retirement. Others, like Martha, aged 57, will combine paid and free activities. She does yoga classes and weight training weekly for a monthly fee and joins free tai chi classes on Sundays. Few people can afford to pay for all their activities, as Roger, mentioned earlier, could. They are exceptions. Martha and Roger don't know each other, but both attend MyFitness,[23] a private gym that offers activities designed specifically for them.

Mission accomplished

MyFitness is a gym on four floors that offers a programme designed by a gerontologist to match the needs of people who are 60 and above. The programme mixes water aerobics and special gym classes, which happen twice a week. But that programme is not where people over 60 are. They prefer to attend the gym's regular courses (even if the monthly fee is a few reais higher). As seen in the previous chapter, age is a social construction, which defines permissions and privileges for young and older people.[24] In this case, the gym programme developed for the third age constitutes a place designated for older people and defined as where they are supposed to be. Since research participants always feel younger than they are, they consider this space to be reserved for those who are 'really old' and who are always the other. Age is not the only factor that defines the places research participants are supposed to be, the kind of activities they are expected to join, and for how long they should pursue them. As anthropologist Guita Debert observed, gender also plays a significant role in how the third age is experienced in Brazil.[25]

For example, when it comes to the MyFitness gym, men generally do weight training, functional training (training directed at the activities required in everyday life), and spinning, while only a few attend the Pilates and yoga classes. Men typically only stay in the gym for the time needed to practise these activities. They leave with a feeling of 'job done', of being 'released' from their obligation to their body, as they say. Women use a similar expression, 'mission accomplished', but they are not in a hurry to leave. They arrive very early in the morning and usually combine two or three activities. They do weight training, Pilates, yoga, stretching and classes they have more fun at, like ballet and Zumba. They also organise birthday parties for the instructors and attend themed classes, such as one during the Carnival, or in October, when the classes focus on breast cancer awareness. The breaks between classes are when they socialise. They talk about their grandchildren and their latest trips, and exchange health tips and doctors' recommendations. Sometimes they realise they have just been talking rather than exercising. Some use a private joke to leave the group and join an activity: 'I have to go. The only thing I have exercised so far is my tongue.' Even if they allow themselves to stay, it is just until someone comes to check whether they want to go to another class. It is also common for women to check on each other's attendance. If one of them skips one day or one class, her friends will ask her why she was absent. The reason presented is more likely to gain the group's empathy when it is related to health issues or obligations related to children and grandchildren, which will be addressed in the next chapter.

One of the instructors reinforces this kind of surveillance. He condemns women's absences from the gym, considering them to show a lack of commitment to health in old age. He cites a 78-year-old woman who continued to go to the gym even after losing her child and while in mourning. When someone complains that an exercise is challenging, he answers: 'Do you want softness? Stay at home. You will have softness in your bottom, softness in your arms, softness in your whole body.' Women laugh, but, later, they confess they don't like the pressure. They emphasise that one of the good things about getting older is that they don't have to prove anything to anyone. Lourdes, aged 64, explains that she knows and respects the new limits of her body. Besides, she doesn't like people pushing her. 'You know, I am naturally the kind of person who always does things right. And I am not lazy,' she says. To avoid conflict, she left another class taught by an instructor who was pushing her too hard.

Another instructor seems to be more empathetic about the natural declines of the ageing body. One day, he told the story of an older lady, aged 78, who had osteoporosis and used to be his student. He claimed that she could do all of the exercise sequences he gave her, but one day she did the class wearing socks, slipped and broke her femur. Unfortunately, she was never able to come back to the gym. Despite this tragic ending, he used the example to argue that his classes can be done at any age. He claims that people are supposed to be aware of and respect their limits. When he finished telling the sad story, one of the students said, 'Oh! I feel sorry for those people at that age. It is a pity.' She was 51. This kind of comment is just the tip of the iceberg regarding the veiled competitiveness between women of different generations, encouraged by some instructors.

If the instructor praises a woman in her forties or fifties, women in their sixties will comment wryly, 'She is supposed to be able to do this, as she is young.' Meanwhile, women in their seventies and eighties will address this kind of comparison with a sense of humour, as they are more used to living with some pain or a health condition. Thus, when a woman in her sixties complains that a particular exercise is strenuous and that she is in pain, they will comment, 'Wait until you are over seventy, then you will see what pain is.' This last group is also more supportive, and they try to manage their bodies with resilience. One of them explained, 'There are pains that come in your seventies, others will come in your eighties. That's ageing.' While different generations practise the alterity through which one defines how young one is according to one's perception of the limitations of the body and the energy of the other,[26] their concern about physical decline is the same. Even if this kind of comparison can be used for distinction, they are together in the mission to postpone dependence and age well.

Stay fit, adapt or give up

Maria, aged 70, is rigorous about staying in good health. 'Those who don't take care of their health don't deserve to live,' she argues. She takes the statement seriously. For her, taking care of the body is a significant responsibility since, like others in Bento, she wants to avoid being a burden to her children. Thus, she wants to live only as long as her body remains functional.[27] Dying at around the age of 80 would be acceptable for her and for many research participants. She is committed to reaching that age in good health. First, she started running to please her son. He suggested she should join him in going running, so they could do something together when she visits him abroad. She then joined a running club in Bento and has already run a series of marathons. She transformed her story into a motivational speech which she gives at events aimed at the third age in Bento. Recently, she has been considering stopping the marathons, but it won't interfere with her discipline. Her smartwatch sets her daily fitness goals (among 22 women interviewed, she was the only one wearing a smartwatch). The 'Connect app' is in charge of her training, while at the same time being a source of pleasure and satisfaction. She argues, for example, that one of the highlights of her day is when her goal is accomplished, even if she has to take the stairs, rather than the lift, to her flat in order to complete the right number of steps.

At the other end of the spectrum is Amelia, aged 61. She is embarrassed about the fact that she doesn't do any physical activity. She has tried everything throughout her life, but she confesses she is now sedentary. She tries to balance this with the fact that she is, and has always been, thin.[28] But she argues that she is about to 'fall in line'. If Amelia's excuses make her an exception in Bento, she fits the norm when, like others, she shows awareness of the importance of exercising to age healthily. Eduardo shares this awareness. Aged 59, he retired only a few weeks before our interview. Adopting healthy habits is one of his plans. He knows he must include physical exercise in his routine, and he plans to make this change with his wife. 'Eating well doesn't make sense if you are sedentary. We will make a resolution in this area. We haven't made a decision yet, but we will soon,' he explains. Amelia and Eduardo had not been used to exercising. In their case, ageing pushes them towards adopting new health habits, and physical activity is among their priorities.

In some cases, however, this process can happen the other way round. Ageing can make people lose interest in physical activity. Injuries may interrupt the activities they used to carry out, but there is also the frustration experienced by those whose bodies can no longer attain the physical performance of their youth. Flávio, aged 72, has experienced both injuries and frustration. Although he never became a professional, he used to play football when he was young. He kept up the activity as a hobby. A few years ago, during a holiday with his family, his wife insisted that he join the football match played daily on the beach. Finally, after three days, he did. However, he pushed his body beyond its limits and ended up with a knee tissue injury. The holiday was interrupted as he had to go straight to hospital. 'When you are playing, you think you are the same person you were 20 years ago, but your muscles are not,' he explains. He tried swimming for a while, but has wholly given up taking part in any physical activity. An exception among research participants, Flávio refused to adapt to his new limits.[29] Instead, he believes that, after a certain age, sports no longer benefit one's health (or one's self-esteem, as he resents the fact that his body can't achieve the athletic performance he was used to).

Adapting is crucial when one faces ageing. Smartphones can give older people extra help to compensate for some losses. Cesar, for example, suffers from tendonitis and a hernia, a consequence of his long career as a professional musician (he composes, sings and plays the guitar). His religion taught him to take good care of his body and to take responsibility for his actions. 'If people don't have healthy habits and get sick, who are they going to blame? God? That is not fair,' he says. Thus, he does his bit and is very disciplined about going to physiotherapy and doing Pilates and weight training. He is also obedient. He does what doctors tell him to do, and he feels proud when they say that he is a model patient. He also recognises that his voice has changed, but his attitude is the opposite of Flávio's. He just chose to adapt the way he sang as he couldn't reach the notes he used to.[30] Combined with the physical exercises, this change allowed him to go back to work. Now, at 68, he is getting ready to release his twelfth album and no longer thinks about retiring. His memory was the only issue he couldn't resolve. He used to remember all of the melodies he had composed, but this was getting harder and harder. His wife came up with a solution, teaching him how to use his smartphone's recorder. 'Now I'm composing and recording at the same time, and I can share it directly with my colleagues through WhatsApp. It couldn't be easier.'

Exercising the brain

The feeling that their memory is not what it used to be is a constant complaint among older people in Bento. Moreover, losing mental autonomy is one of their biggest fears.[31] Many have already experienced Alzheimer's or another form of dementia in the family, and there are always concerns about inheritance. Although scholars say that regular physical activity improves cognitive function,[32] research participants engage in 'extra' mental stimulation activities that they consider help them to give their memory a work-out. Thus, after exercising the body, exercising the brain is the next priority on their to-do list. Although some classes and workshops specifically address memory, every learning activity is seen as an opportunity for a double gain. While they learn something new, they also exercise their brain. Language classes are one of the places they get both benefits. English language classes are the ones most frequently offered by third age programmes in Bento. But older people have plenty of options. For example, in the most prominent Catholic church they can take French, Spanish, Italian, German and Japanese classes. Duolingo is very popular among research participants, who have incorporated the app's daily exercises into their routines. They usually use the app to complement face-to-face classes or to learn a third language on their own. It is common to take English classes in person and use Duolingo for French, for example. The choice of which language they learn is usually shaped by ancestry or by travel interests. Travelling is one of the great pleasures enjoyed by older people in Bento and is often combined with the opportunity to visit children who live abroad.[33] Learning other languages is also used for distinction. Students will therefore take all the chances they get to show off their knowledge. Ask them a question in Portuguese, and you might be answered in English, with the excuse that they are practising so that they don't forget.

The relationship between smartphones and memory is essentially ambiguous. On the one hand, older people acknowledge the usefulness of smartphones when they organise their list of contacts or use Google Maps or Waze. Yet remembering dozens of telephone numbers, memorising city maps before travelling somewhere or knowing every street of the city they live in are abilities some of them are proud of. In such cases, they will refuse to delegate that particular task to the smartphone, for example refusing to use Waze if they consider that they know the city like the back of their hand. But that is not what typically happens. Most of the time, research participants feel comfortable relying on the smartphone as 'a second brain'. The smartphone is used to help them remember but also to help them not to forget. It means they will use it for the things they see no sense in making an effort to remember. At the same time, smartphones are used as an ally to keep them mentally active and autonomous. To achieve this, besides learning activities, many choose to play brain-training games, which are perceived as a preventive routine and as entertainment. Take Fernanda's case, for example. She considers herself to be in the best stage of her life. Aged 63, she likes her body even more now that she has time for Pilates. She is happy with her husband and children, and she feels challenged by the new business that she runs. The only thing that seems to be ageing is her mind. She recognises that her thoughts are slowing down, but her short-term memory worries her the most. It is hard for her to remember what she did a few days ago, and sometimes the day before. That is why she fills the time between one activity and the next with the brain-training games she has installed on her smartphone.

'With my short-term memory ... it's complicated. For example, I am talking to you today. Tomorrow, I will ask myself, "What did she say? ... I know she mentioned a business on that street, but what did she say about it?" I just can't remember any more – neither that nor what I ate yesterday. When my English teacher asks me what I did at the weekend, I start guessing, and sometimes I remember. I also used to be good at doing maths in my head, but not any more.'

To compensate for this, in addition to using the calculator and her contacts and to-do lists on her smartphone, Fernanda uses 'Lumosity'. She found out about the app on the internet in her research on ageing. As discussed in the previous chapter, her interest in this came after retirement, when she accepted a friend's invitation to start a telemedicine company focused on older people. She found online that older people need to exercise their brains in order to maintain their cognitive function, and then came across the 'Lumosity' app.

'The app has different games for memory and logical reasoning. Every day, it gives you three different games which improve maths, memory and attention skills. This one, for example, takes place at the bottom of the sea. The stickers come in, and you have to select the right ones. You cannot repeat any of them. You have to remember which ones you marked by heart. I'm playing the free version, which gives me three games every day, and you can play as many times as you want. Then the next day there are three more. It is superb and designed for older people to focus on reasoning and work it out. I use it a lot.'

Like Fernanda, Laís, aged 51, researches ageing on the internet and attends events that address the topic. At one of these events, she learned that physical activity is associated with cognitive maintenance. Since then, whenever she needs to go somewhere, she walks. 'There is no bus? I will walk, and I will not complain,' she says. Memory in old age is one of her main interests at the moment. She dreams of designing an activity for older people that will exercise their memories through music. Laís pays extra attention when she does that for herself. According to her, in apps like 'Spotify' you can end up listening to the same stuff, so she disciplines herself by listening to a different radio station every day, even if she doesn't like it. She feels stimulated by new things. Laís is committed to adopting healthy habits to age well. Although she believes that she should already be making a list of things that will help her to age well, like most research participants she has started to focus on the body and memory by exercising both. Usually, after accomplishing this mission, older people in Bento will engage in other activities associated with purpose and pleasure and defined by their interests. As noted previously, they have a whole week to fill, as they want to be, and be seen as, busy after retirement. As we will see in the next chapter, obligations towards family will take up some of their 'free slots'. But, even so, there will be plenty of time to revisit projects they left in the past or try new adventures. For men, the unknown can appear in an unexpected place, like the kitchen.

Men in charge: the discovery of domestic life

The gendered division of domestic labour is revised after retirement. In Bento, married women have been the ones to take responsibility for the home and the children, often represented as a double work shift that combined the hours dedicated to the family and the hours devoted to their careers.[34] Men, conversely, were devoted only to work, with routines that might start early in the morning and end late at night. Thus, many of them now experience for the first time having lunch at home on a weekday. Their house is a safe space in which to figure out what to do with their lives after retirement. This time at home will allow them to realise that there is an entire domestic universe they were never aware of. Very conveniently, housework will be the first work they do after retirement, helping them fill the day with tasks that make them feel busy and useful.

That the house was a safe space for men to make their transition as new retirees was observed also among Americans. Luborsky noticed that men choose the domestic sphere to reorganise their identities and adapt to life after retirement.[35] He observed men engage in projects like improving their back gardens at the same time as husband and wife renegotiate their domestic affairs. However, he maintained, the 'fledgling egalitarianism' soon fails when they engage in other activities and return to their social lives. That is not the case in Bento. And the reorganisation of tasks at home helps husband and wife adapt to each other's presence during working hours. They embrace it as an ongoing effort to renew their commitment to their marriage.

Let's take Eduardo's example. Aged 59, he is a new retiree. His first challenge was to adapt to his new schedule. Or, as he says, the lack of a schedule. He has worked in a factory all his life and used to wake up very early. On retirement he stopped using his smartphone's alarm. But at the very beginning his body insisted on waking up at four in the morning. His second strategy was to stop looking at the clock. Even though he was planning to build a church in the countryside in order to follow his vocation to be a pastor, he hasn't committed to anything yet. So he became more aware of the routine of the house, and he let it dictate his time with his wife. 'I started washing dishes, cooking and learning things about the house I didn't even know existed.'

Similarly, Paulo, aged 56, decided to take the redundancy package his company offered him. He used to work until late at night and at least a day at weekends. Now, he spends his weekends travelling with his wife on his motorcycle. However, other than going to the gym three times a week, he spends most of his time at home. His wife has done the opposite. After retirement, she started a new career in which she has become very successful. Therefore, even with a flexible schedule, she now spends more time out at work. Paulo then became familiar with the routine of the house and took on more responsibilities. He believes that it is the right thing to do, since he never had time to share the housework before. He explains, 'For a retiree, time is never a problem.'

Besides the fact that they have just started their lives as house husbands, Eduardo and Paulo have another thing in common. If they could, they would remarry their wives. They believe they made the right choice, and if right now they are discovering new forms of affection, the household brings them concrete opportunities to demonstrate to their spouse how much they care for them. However, that is not always the case. Sometimes, housework can help couples remain 'just functional', as both had already rebuilt their schedules with activities that might not include each other. In these cases, each of them has a specific obligation, and after the work is done, they are free to go. Beto, aged 58, is not retired, and neither is his wife. They have no prospect of retiring, and they are both trying to adapt their routines to their new lives as entrepreneurs. Married for over 20 years, they recognise that being together is a challenge sometimes. This happens when he is at home or being ignored by her or when they are having an argument about their daughter. Thus he prefers to work in a co-working space instead of being at home. He is allowed to. But first he must meet his new obligations at home. If he doesn't do the housework, 'My wife kills me,' he explains.

Among the household activities that older men discover in retirement, cooking seems to provide the most genuine enjoyment. However, men will pursue the status of a chef.[36] Playing the role of chef gives them a sense of utility combined with the feeling that they can still be good at something. The kitchen as a place for competition and recognition has become a phenomenon in Bento since the massive success of the 'MasterChef' TV show, whose local version first aired in 2014.[37] For retired men, the kitchen may be the place where they will be able to feel like a boss again, while differentiating themselves from the 'housewife', who is still simply 'the cook'. In Portuguese, the word 'chef' sounds similar to *chefe* (chief, boss). They can therefore feel like a boss again in the kitchen. Being a 'chef' in these cases provides men with a new type of professional credential. Their smartphones help them on this journey. They search for tutorials on YouTube and save recipes they see on Facebook. Some of them will use social networks to share pictures of their recipes and to seek recognition. Others, like Eduardo, prefer to aim for their wives' approval.

> 'Yesterday, I learned how to prepare a chicken in the clay pot. I saw the guy cooking it. Do this, do that. I did it by following the video. I managed to do it. There is so much for you to learn. You don't know everything. These basic things are all there. You can learn, and you can do it yourself. You can imitate, right? Today, we imitate a lot. You search on the internet. You can do anything. It helps you, right? And if my wife liked it, it was because it worked.'

Ricardo, aged 64, couldn't count on his wife's approval even if he wanted to. They are going through a crisis, and he has moved to his late parents' house, where his siblings already live. Cooking has been one of his greatest pleasures in these turbulent moments. He has got into the habit of saving the recipes he finds on his social networks, and he talks about the ones he has already tried with pride. He is becoming more and more confident at improving his dinners with what he calls 'a chef's touch'. Even though he is retired, Ricardo is still applying for the same kinds of position he had in the past. It is not just that he needs to supplement his pension. He also wants to recover his past professional credentials. He has been searching for a job for two years, without success. That is how he started having problems with his wife, as he is struggling to keep up the kind of life they were used to. Playing the 'chef' can be a valuable means of restoring men's self-esteem, especially for new retirees. Even when they leave the house and engage in other activities, they are likely to keep up the hobby. As I have argued so far, they have a five-day timetable to fill before they can feel busy, just as they were before retirement. Thus, they will reconcile the 'chef' status with new daily opportunities to feel challenged and satisfied.

Hobbies 2.0: connected and improved

Especially among those who have achieved some financial stability, retirement can be an opportunity to revive interests abandoned earlier in life because of obligations relating to work and family. This time, their hobbies will be tuned by the information they find online and by apps that support their passions. Tutorials found on YouTube will help older people improve their skills as well as learn new ones, making available to them a seemingly unlimited portfolio of DIY (do-it-yourself) possibilities. If they struggle, Google will guide them. Social media, in turn, will make their creations visible. After all, what is the point of cultivating the most beautiful orchids and roses ever seen by humankind if they are restricted to one's garden? It makes much more sense to let them bloom on WhatsApp, Facebook or Instagram, where they can be 'picked' and offered to someone else (figures 3.5 and 3.6).

Sharing this kind of content can bring multiple benefits to research participants in Bento. First, their hobbies prove they are busy and productive. Secondly, if their work used to define who they were, their new activity can partially replace their previous professional credentials while it communicates their values, tastes, new skills and talents. Thus the hobby is used to craft new identities and to build a new reputation. Older people can then be seen to be good at something again, like the former journalist who is now admired for her handworked embroidery, or the IT expert who became an adviser to people who want to make a motorcycle trip.

That was the case with Paulo. As we have seen, he now shares the household chores with his wife. But that is not everything he does while he is at home. Retirement allowed him to revisit a lifelong passion of his – motorcycles. But that is just part of the story. Paulo is also passionate about planning motorcycle trips, which involves choosing the places to go, mapping the routes, calculating how much petrol he will need and determining which rest stops to take, including which hotels to stay at when the itinerary demands that they travel overnight. He uses various apps and websites to do this, ranging from weather apps to Google Maps' Street View through to TripAdvisor and Hotels.com. He started doing this as a way of going on holiday with his wife.

Thanks to Facebook, he got in touch with some old friends who share his passion, and they have started travelling together, all following the trip schedules he planned. His wife has nothing to do while she sits in the back seat, so she has started taking photos and sharing them on her Facebook and Instagram. People showed an interest in these, which

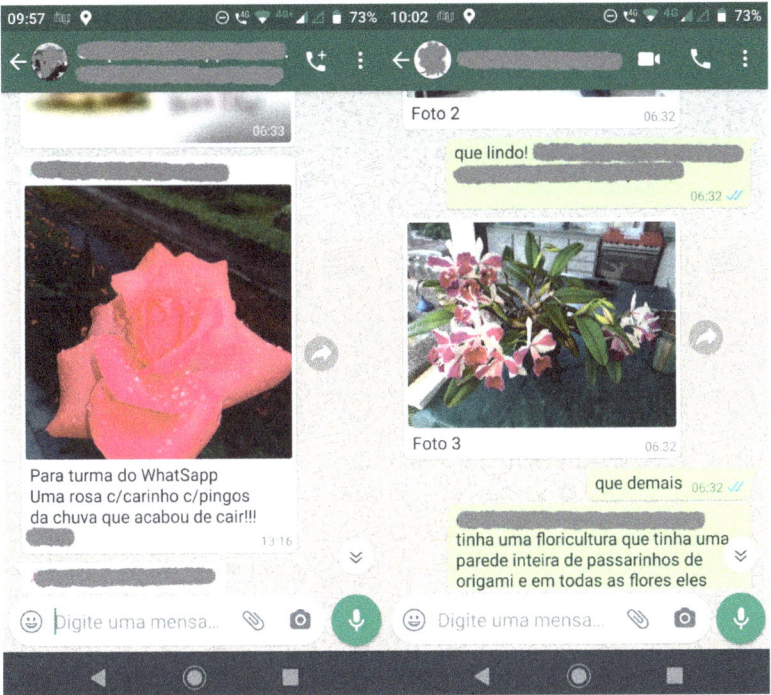

Figures 3.5 and **3.6** Photos of a rose and orchids cultivated by older people and shared on WhatsApp. Screenshot taken by Marília Duque.

motivated her to open an account for her husband on both social networks. She is in charge of keeping the accounts updated. When he retired, she was worried that he would have problems managing his free time, which could, in turn, compromise her own free time. She was afraid he would become dependent on her. However, planning their trips is keeping him busy and makes him feel useful again. 'Your final destination is always your home. You have to plan your way back, too. People want to travel, but they don't want to have to do this kind of work. I do it for them,' he explains. As people started looking to him to help them tailor their trips, his wife suggested turning this new occupation into a business, but he is not ready for that kind of commitment. He considers himself to have been overworked for over 20 years and doesn't want to turn this activity into formal work, although he thinks he might do so in the future. For now, he just wants to keep his rides free from any kind of pressure while enjoying his new reputation.

Pablo, aged 69, has no problem combining his hobby with work, but this is because, in his case, they share the same space. He was made redundant by the university where he worked. His PhD in psychology turned him into an expensive teacher, as the institution was supposed to pay more for someone with his degree. In the end, when he retired his pension was only equivalent to the minimum wage. At that time, his second wife had just inherited a big house in a very central location in Bento. They decided to transform the house into a place for courses, events and co-working. He is responsible for managing the space, including handling reception duties, providing customer support by email or WhatsApp, and updating the place's website and social media accounts. As the house has many rooms, he keeps one for his psychology practice, as he still sees a few patients during the week. But his day is not just about managing his business or working as a psychologist. He has built a carpentry studio in the basement of this house and uses Pinterest to save interesting carpentry links and YouTube to learn new techniques while he buys his tools on eBay. He is as excited as Paulo about his hobby, but he is not interested in replacing his previous work. He laughs at the fact that he can turn himself into a carpenter every time he disappears from the reception front desk. He believes he has already lived three lives in one and doesn't care that he is now a doorkeeper/carpenter. Deep inside, Pablo knows he holds a PhD and his identity is still based on this credential, which explains why he doesn't publicise his hobby even though he knows he is good at it.

In contrast, most retirees in Bento are looking for something new they can identify with, some activity that can provide them with pleasure and reputation. That something can be anything, even working on a playlist for their Sunday lunches with their families. Creating playlists is one of the things Luisa does. Aged 72, she has always had an eclectic musical taste, which later became a hobby. She shares Spotify playlists with her friends, who know they can find a playlist for every mood and occasion on her profile. At the same time, she crafts a new reputation for herself, as she has become the person to consult when her friends think about music. It is impossible to know what may capture people's attention and provide recognition. In Romulo's case it was an origami bird he had made. He shared its picture on one of his WhatsApp groups, and people started asking him for guidance. His friends were so interested in his origami techniques that he promoted an informal face-to-face workshop. Romulo was then recognised as a specialist, gaining his disciples' admiration and gratitude, which helped him gain self-esteem and reputation. In addition to these benefits, hobbies can become an opportunity to form new groups based on affinity and interest. On WhatsApp groups, it means people will experience a sense of belonging while they expand their social circles, which demands extra time and effort from them. Far from being a problem, managing new friends and their demands is a unique opportunity for research participants to feel busy.

Managing a digital life

Together with physical activities, learning and hobbies, managing their social networks is another important pursuit that older people in Bento have integrated into their daily routines. As relatively new users,[38] they still experience a certain excitement while on Facebook, the social media platform on which they are most likely to share personal content.[39] The achievements of their children and grandchildren, and their trips, are excellent opportunities for posts, and so are the courses and events they

9 de junho de 2018

"QUALQUER IDIOTA CONSEGUE SER JOVEM. É PRECISO MUITO TALENTO PRA ENVELHECER."
Millôr Fernandes

3 comentários 4 compartilhamentos

Figure 3.7 A typical Facebook post shared by older people in Bento. The text reads: 'Any idiot can be young. A lot of talent is needed to age.' Attributed to Millôr Fernandes. Screenshot taken by Marília Duque.

attend. They are actively engaged in creating and sharing the images they consider present them at their best, which in Bento means combining freedom, autonomy and productivity. Their testimonials are merged with aspirational life stories of healthy, eccentric, entrepreneurial and creative

Figure 3.8 Facebook post shared by an older person in Bento. The text reads: 'Older people in the 1950s, 1970s, 1990s, and the new generation'. Post published together with the comment 'Much better!'. Screenshot taken by Marília Duque.

older people they identify with – an example of how people can conform to lifestyles seen as examples of successful ageing (see figures 3.7, 3.8 and 3.9).[40] There are also nostalgic posts about how they used to do things in the past. Still, their posts mainly focus on the present and the future by framing old age as a golden age when everything is possible, especially for those who maintain their autonomy (see figure 3.10).[41] When frailties are addressed, they appear as hilarious memes they allow themselves to laugh at, as the 'real old' represented by these images are always the other and never themselves (see figures 3.11 and 3.12).[42]

The use of Facebook serves other functions. The platform enables older people to search for and connect with former colleagues and friends from the past, including those from school or college. It is also the place where they will be reminded of friends' birthdays. In addition, Facebook groups can help research participants get in touch with others on the

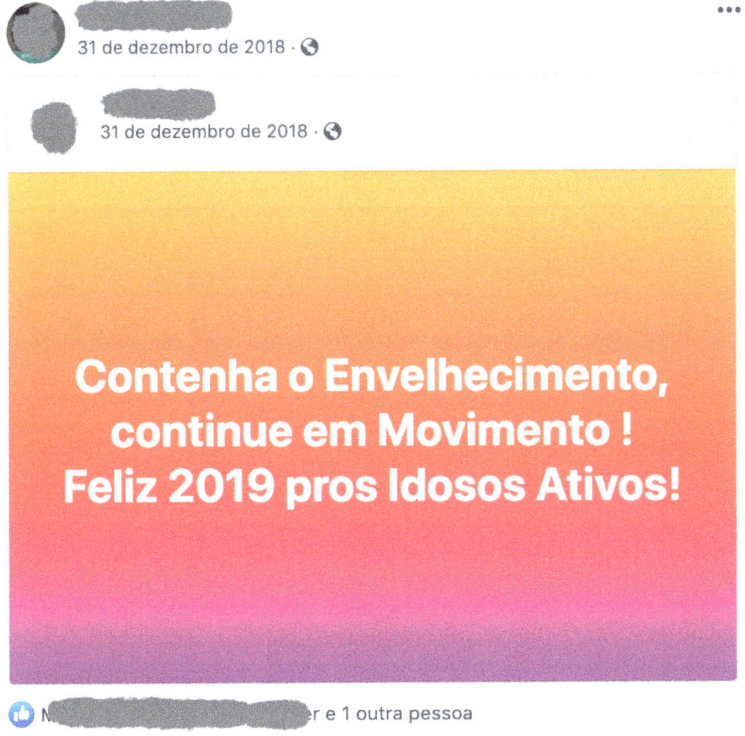

Figure 3.9 Facebook post shared by an over-60s group: 'Stop ageing. Keep moving. Happy 2019 to the Active Older People'. Screenshot taken by Marília Duque.

Figure 3.10 A Facebook post shared by a retired couple preparing for a motorcycle trip. © @lilianacenturine.

basis of common interests. Managing these groups can become an occupation that is carried out with professionalism. For example, at the MyFitness gym, if someone wants information about the timetables of different classes, the best place to find it is the Facebook group's page, which a student informally created. Other profiles are used to turn personal interests into an authoritative source of information, which brings about a sense of utility while enhancing the author's reputation. For example, after retirement, Aloysio, aged 71, started to volunteer with different organisations and causes concerned with environmental

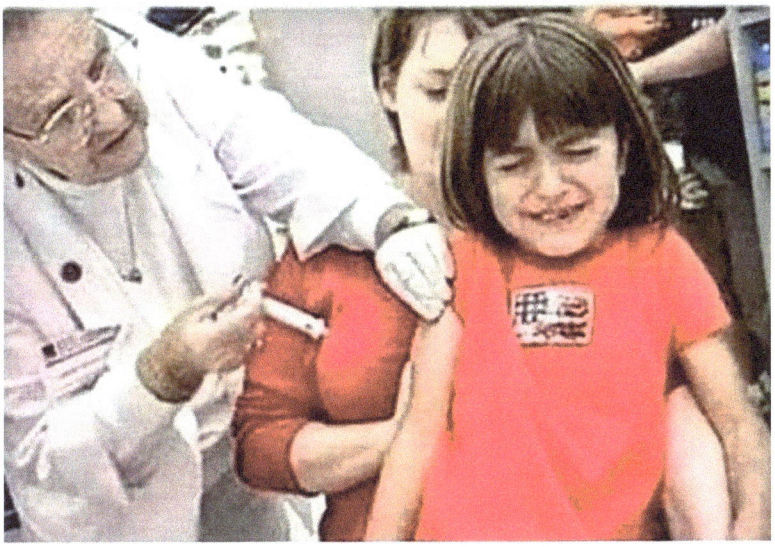

Figure 3.11 Facebook post: 'Sometimes we have to admit it is time to retire.' Screenshot taken by Marília Duque.

sustainability, which provided him with a new 'professional credential'. He presented himself as a digital disseminator. His work is to curate information about sustainability and then share it on his Facebook page. He reads various newspapers and watches different TV channels as part of his working routine. He can't measure how many people he reaches, but the relevance of his work is not based on the size of his audience. He argues that as an agent of social change, raising awareness takes time. Like others, Aloysio works as a micro-influencer in his fields of expertise.

Research participants are starting to use Instagram in order to have more digital clout regarding the things they post, as discussed in the previous chapter in the context of the emergence of mature digital

Figure 3.12 Facebook post shared by an older person in Bento: 'What's on TV?' 'Some shit … every channel is showing the same old man.' Below the dialogue is written: 'Don't laugh, you'll be there soon.' Screenshot taken by Marília Duque.

influencers. However, most of them are not yet familiar with the platform. It is common to find cases like Carla, aged 62, who follows a few friends and relatives, but still doesn't post to Instagram. 'I am there, I see people's stuff, but I don't get it. I don't know how it works yet,' she explains. While Facebook is the platform on which participants are more likely to post personal content, and Instagram is still a social media platform to be explored, WhatsApp is the platform on which they have built an active and powerful community. As Stafford argues, access to information and participation are key factors for age-friendly communities,[43] and are precisely what WhatsApp groups provide. The centrality of WhatsApp as the primary means of communication among Brazilians and its role in older people's digital inclusion will be discussed in chapter 5. This section addresses how research participants act as content curators in WhatsApp groups, how this curation can be seen as a new type of occupation, the improvement in reputation it can bring and its consequences for everyday life in Bento.

WhatsApp is the source of information Brazilians use the most (79 per cent said they used it always as a source of information), followed by television (50 per cent) and YouTube (49 per cent).[44] WhatsApp groups are also where older people in Bento find news about what benefits they may be entitled to, warnings about scams, health tips, interesting facts about ageing, diet-friendly recipes and information about new opportunities of activities aimed at the third age, such as courses, lectures and free events. This kind of information is perceived as a public utility and is the most valued by group members. Participants may access Facebook or YouTube, or multiple websites. Still, most of the time, their starting point will be the WhatsApp group where they first found the link associated with a piece of information. Selecting valuable information and making it accessible to others on WhatsApp groups are curators' main occupations.[45] Their work is motivated by three factors: the desire to help other community members, the opportunity to feel useful and the need for social recognition. Together they place older people in Bento in the participatory culture, as their voluntary work as curators is based on the donation of their cognitive work and their free time to a visible network. The motivation for their voluntary work is the desire for connection and belonging, as well as the demonstration of autonomy or competence.[46]

In the participatory culture, the person that brings fresh news takes the credit and enjoys a reputation as a curator. When the group attributes value to the shared content, other members will comment on it and thank the 'curator' for sending it. Other members will then share the content with other WhatsApp groups. By doing this, they also increase their chances of becoming curators themselves. The problem with this is that many groups have many members in common, as most of these groups are organised around face-to-face activities such as courses or events. For example, the English language class will have a dedicated WhatsApp group, created to support its students. Because many people participate in more than one activity and are in multiple (sometimes overlapping) WhatsApp groups, they often see the same information many times.

Moreover, if information keeps moving from one group to another, the result is that research participants are overwhelmed by the amount of information they have to process. In general, one of the most significant

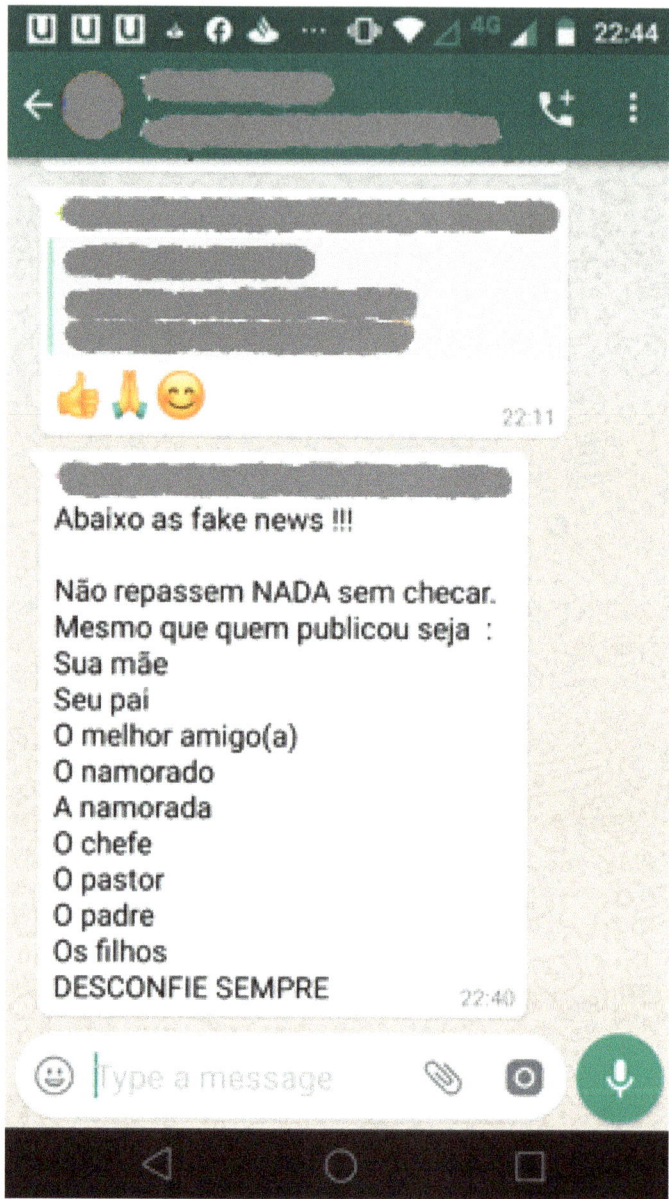

Figure 3.13 Image shared by a participant in a WhatsApp group for people of 60 and over. The text reads: 'Stop Fake News! Don't share ANYTHING without checking. Even if the person who published was Your Mother, Your Father, The Best Friend, The Boyfriend, The Girlfriend, The boss, The pastor, The priest, The children. ALWAYS BE SUSPICIOUS.' Screenshot taken by Marília Duque.

difficulties on WhatsApp groups is that these spaces are created with a single purpose or around a particular interest or activity. However, over time, members circulate content that has no relation to the group's original intent but is associated with what they consider helpful to their peers. This appropriation makes the work of the curator even harder. Besides the rush to get the latest scoop and gain the social capital associated with a valued piece of information, they must manage overlapping audiences and interminable message exchanges between groups. This means things can become stressful and go wrong for curators. Sharing fake news, for example, can profoundly damage the curator's social capital and older people's reputation in general.

A study conducted with Americans has identified older people as the age group that shares fake news most frequently,[47] and this finding has been widely reported by the Brazilian media.[48] Another study showed that older people appear to be less likely than others to identify fake news on social media.[49] In Bento, this means that participants are particularly vigilant about fake news, as they don't want to carry this stigma. According to a DataSenado survey, 30 per cent of Brazilians aged 60 or above claimed that they had never come across a fake news item on their social networks. In comparison, 11 per cent of respondents in the youngest age bracket (16 to 29 years old) claimed the same.[50] In Bento, however, older people constantly rebuke or observe someone being rebuked for sharing fake news on their WhatsApp News. The message containing fake news normally attracts a round of positive comments from other group members until someone reveals that the news is fake. The person who shared the fake news item then apologises. The curator can justify the mistake by saying they forgot or didn't have time to check, or, more frequently, they will say that whoever shared it with them was a trustworthy friend. As the link came from someone they trust, they didn't check whether the news was accurate. It is common among research participants to take into account the reputation of the 'curator' from whom they received the information rather than the source of the data itself (see figure 3.13). They are not alone. The survey described above shows that almost a quarter of Brazilians consider *who shared it* to be the most important factor in their decision of whether or not to trust the content. That means that whether a participant clicks on a link will depend not just on the appeal of the news itself but on who brings it into the WhatsApp group.

Apart from relying on how far they trust the 'curator', research participants create other personal strategies for dealing with fake news. Paulo has decided to wait before sharing anything he receives. 'Usually, the news will come from different people and on different social networks. So I wait to see if anyone is going to contest it. When it turns out to be fake news, someone always comments on it, saying that it is fake news.' This is a job Bianca, aged 51, does often. She uses Google to check everything she receives. In the case of fake news, she has no mercy. She copies the link that shows that it is indeed fake and sends it back to the 'curator' with the message: 'It's fake news. Haven't you checked it?' (figure 3.14).

Fake news can be seen as a side effect of research participants' desire to feel useful by playing the role of 'curators' of content they consider relevant to their peers. Other negative aspects of the amount of information they share and its impacts on anxiety and addiction will be addressed in chapter 5. However, these aspects are outweighed by the positive aspects of WhatsApp groups for research participants. As stated earlier, Bento offers a great diversity of activities aimed at the third age and aligned with the Active Ageing framework as adopted in Brazil.[51] As well as the Longevity Playgrounds, there are two public hospitals and an outpatient care centre, which offer programmes for people aged 60 and over. In addition to clinical follow-ups, members attend courses that get them to take part in physical activity, stimulate their cognitive ability, teach them healthy habits and allow them to socialise. In terms of outdoor options, two parks offer dance classes, tai chi and environmental education workshops. Non-profit and religious institutions complement this portfolio. One institute alone offers 25 workshops, from crochet to digital inclusion, accounting for about 8,500 monthly appointments. In an average term, the prominent Catholic church in the region sees 2,000 students enrol on its dozens of courses. This church maintains an intense schedule of additional activities, including events, parties and lectures, when lawyers, therapists, nutritionists and doctors give free advice to older people.

The 'curators' are responsible for giving visibility to this structure and every opportunity available to older people in Bento. As they engage in these activities, they are added to new WhatsApp groups, which gives them more and more access to information and social contacts. This means that when participants are not busy engaging in face-to-face activities, they are busy interacting in WhatsApp groups. Managing new friends while collaborating actively with WhatsApp groups can be an exhausting, endless job. But they can take it. In some cases, their participation in WhatsApp groups is used to compensate for their absence from a face-to-face activity, which can be extremely useful in work-oriented Bento (the ability to shift to online activities became even more relevant in the Covid-19 context[52]). In one way or another, what matters is that they are seen engaging in activities in both offline and online spheres. By combining them, they can feel busy and productive, just as they were when they had full-time jobs.

Figure 3.14 Dialogue between members of a WhatsApp group for over-60s in Bento. The text reads:
'– This Turkish biscuit, which has two pills inside it that paralyse the body, has already arrived in Brazil, don't buy it and share this message.
– I shared this, but I don't know if it is fake or not.
(Video shared, with the text 'IF YOU DON'T KNOW IT IS TRUE, DON'T SHARE IT'. Link to Google result which demonstrates that the content is fake news.)
– Sorry, I will be more careful.'
Screenshot taken by Marília Duque.

Smartphones can fill any free slot in their timetable.[53] Thus it is usual for participants to go online when they see themselves (and could be seen by others) as idle. That is what Fernanda, aged 63, does to avoid the feeling that she is unproductive:

'If I go somewhere where I have to wait, the smartphone is crucial. Dentist's waiting room, doctor's waiting room, I'm either playing a little game, or I'm doing my English lessons. I'm doing something, right?'

Busy as a bee, free as a bird

The previous chapter addressed the fact that research participants refuse to retire. In Bento, this means that they don't want to be or be seen to be unproductive even if they don't have a formal job. This chapter has explored how participants use every opportunity to build a busy schedule. We observed how smartphones increase their opportunities to remain active and useful. On the one hand, WhatsApp groups have become the place that makes them aware of every new activity aimed at the third age in Bento. On the other, curating and feeding WhatsApp groups with this helpful information has become an occupation in itself, a valued one, which backs up the argument that research participants in Bento are interested not in stopping work but in working for themselves, as addressed in chapter 8. This work includes managing social networks, sometimes as many as eight, as seen with regard to Roger at the beginning of this chapter.

However, we observed that, as research participants' priority is to keep their autonomy, activities that can help them keep their body and mind fit are at the top of their to-do lists. Many will see these activities as missions to be accomplished, as a commitment to age well and not become a burden. With their 'work done', research participants can be free as a bird. In other words, they can spend their time doing more activities, but ones associated with their interests. Everyday life is organised between what they are expected to do (self-care) and what they want to do, the two resulting in a series of activities that allow them to have no idle time. The way they balance duties and pleasures determines how they organise their time to interact with family and friends. As we will see in the next chapter, obligations to the family come first as a mission to be accomplished before they can enjoy the company of their expanded number of friends.

Notes

1. As observed among Americans, developing new projects and hobbies and engaging with new activities play a crucial role in the transition from work to retirement. Scholars argue that these routines give life a purpose and help retirees craft new individual and social identities for this stage of life (Savishinsky 2000; Luborsky 1994). The particularity observed in Bento was the desire to keep the identity associated with past professional credentials. For some research participants, the new projects commonly include new jobs, new occupations or flexible forms of working, as shown in the previous chapter.
2. As Savishinsky (2000) observed within American culture, retirement is a time for negotiation between 'personal freedom' and 'family responsibilities'. In Roger's case, as he and his wife became the primary caregivers for her parents, their travels became more restricted and planned, as their absence must now be negotiated with his wife's siblings. In the next chapter, we explore further the impact of family responsibilities on the experience of ageing after retirement.
3. The ways older people organise their priorities may vary, even when they share the same concern to have a positive attitude towards ageing. For example, in Norfolk, England, Guell et al. (2016) found that there can be a conflict between leading a busy life after retirement and finding time for physical activities. However, that is not the norm in Bento, where people are likely to make space in their diary for physical activities seen as preventive measures that will prolong their autonomy. By doing this, they will achieve a good health status that will allow them to attend other activities. But Guell et al. emphasised that, for their research participants, healthy ageing included awareness of the importance of keeping the mind active, which is associated with the maintenance of cognitive function in old age. Similarly, in Bento, older people make the same association and focus on exercising body and mind, as this chapter will demonstrate.
4. Whyte 2017.
5. Lamb 2019.
6. Goldenberg 2010.
7. Edmonds 2014.
8. Leibing 2005, p. 22.
9. Moura 1994.
10. Caradec 2014.
11. Pereira and Penalva (2014) also worked with middle-class women in Rio de Janeiro. They proposed the term 'madonna-women' to describe the concern of these women with appearance, endorsing Goldenberg's argument that the body is a highly valued form of social capital in the city. However, the authors argue that the body materialised the desire these middle-aged women share for freedom, self-realisation, empowerment and visibility.
12. World Health Organization 2002.
13. World Health Organization 2005.
14. This centrality was also addressed by Lieblich (2014). In line with studies that show a correlation between exercising, health and longevity, she observed how the emphasis on physical activity is reproduced in popular medical advice and the practices of a community of older people in Jaffa in south Tel Aviv. As in Bento, older people in this seaside community showed a strong commitment to daily exercise routines as a strategy for remaining healthy and independent. Many of them did their exercises early in the day, after which they felt they had discharged their obligation.
15. World Health Organization 2002, p. 13.
16. World Health Organization 2002, p. 12.
17. This emphasis is not, however, a particularity of Brazil. Pike (2011) argues that, although Active Ageing focuses on continuing to participate in society, it invariably promotes physical activities, as maintaining high levels of activity is associated with quality of life in old age. She criticises the presentation in the discourses of 'experts' such as the World Health Organization of the maintenance of a high level of activity as a preventive measure all citizens can commit to. In Denmark, Lassen and Jespersen (2017) stress how the Active Ageing policy presents activity as the solution to dependence and decline in old age. However, they show that Danish older people resist adopting the Active Ageing agenda. They are likely to consider a 'health regime' that puts their 'well-earned golden years' of retirement under administration. That is not the case in Bento, where this agenda is welcomed, as it brings opportunities for older people to fill their free time and produce proof of character as busy persons.

18   World Health Organization 2005, p. 3.
19   Natalini 2018.
20   Zhai et al. 2018.
21   Wagner et al. 2020.
22   In these cases, the programme members experience the paradox between care and surveillance explored by Miller et al. (2021) in their discussion of the relationship between citizens and state, relatives and families.
23   The name of the gym has been changed to protect participants' privacy.
24   Bourdieu 1993.
25   According to Debert (2012), the proportion of male participants in third age programmes in Brazil is rarely above 20 per cent. She suggests that the fact that women live longer than men is not enough to explain this disproportion. Instead, she highlights men's participation in associations organised around political interests related to older people's rights and pensions. At the same time, women approach the activities aimed at the third age in order to fight stereotypes and celebrate life in old age. Women can afford to do this as they don't experience retirement in the same way as men. Beyond work, women recognise themselves in the contribution they make to their families, including raising children. Thus they don't feel guilty about having time for themselves and leisure activities. Instead, as they age, they are released from the duties associated with reproduction, and they feel less pressure from society and from their marriages.
26   One of the strategies adopted by older people to minimise the signs of decline they are experiencing, especially concerning their bodies, is to compare themselves with other older people, who they think are in worse condition than they are (Caradec 2014). By doing this, research participants avoid being part of the group that they consider to be 'really old'. As Beaumont and Kenealy (2004) argue, social comparison is a mechanism used to evaluate the experience of ageing and quality of life (QoL) in old age. They call 'downward contrast' the comparison with people with perceived worse conditions, as opposed to 'upward identification', when older people liken themselves to the ones they believe have a better quality of life.
27   The degree of functionality in old age can be measured by two inventories of activities: Activities of Daily Living (ADLs) and Instrumental Activities of Daily Living (IADLs). They range from, for example, the ability to use the bathroom to the management of personal finances (Paula et al. 2014).
28   Other than comparing themselves with other older people, who they think are in worse shape than they are, this is the second strategy older people can adopt to minimise any signs of decline in their ageing bodies. They can neutralise negative aspects by focusing on positive aspects (Caradec 2014). For example, Amelia uses the fact that she is thin to counteract the fact that she is sedentary.
29   The opposite was found among older people living in Norfolk, in the east of England. Even facing physical limitations that could constrain physical activity, those who maintained lifelong activity habits (as Flávio did) were motivated to adapt them in order to remain active in old age (Guell et al. 2016).
30   Barbra Streisand is another singer who successfully developed a technique to compensate for the natural decline in the larynx's performance, which is attributed to ageing (Davidson 2016).
31   Being physically and mentally dependent on others are the two biggest fears among older Brazilians. However, among people who are 80 or older, the number of people afraid of losing their mental faculties and autonomy is higher than the number fearing physical dependence (Collucci & Pinto 2018).
32   McPhee et al. 2016.
33   They use these trips as proof that they are active and having fun while at the same time demonstrating that they are important to their children. Together with photos, details of the trip will be shared widely on Facebook and WhatsApp groups.
34   Of the 22 women interviewed, 14 had children. Of these women, 13 had a formal job when their children were growing up and one was a housewife. The other eight had careers but no children.
35   Luborsky 1994.
36   Dória (2012) argues that there is a gender shift in the division of labour in the kitchen. Women have inherited the responsibility of feeding the family, so their kitchen activity is based on affection. They are also responsible for handling the precarity of everyday life. Men enter the kitchen as professionals, combining the technique and creativity embodied in the figure of the 'chef'.

37 Marquioni & Oliveira 2015.
38 Costa 2018.
39 As reported by Facebook, the practice of sharing personal data is becoming less common among users, who are more likely to act as content curators. According to Facebook's data on the topic, the first significant decrease in the sharing of personal and original content happened between mid-2014 and mid-2015 (when the platform registered a 21 per cent decrease in original, personal content). This was followed by another decrease of 15 per cent by April 2016 (Lorenz 2017).
40 Successful ageing presents old age as an affordable and desired stage of life that celebrates freedom, consumerism and autonomy (Lamb 2017).
41 Lemos 2018.
42 Based on his ethnography in a low-income area in Bahia, Brazil, Spyer (2018) proposes that social media was used in a 'lights-on-lights-off' mode. The 'lights-on' mode is characteristic of the more public online spaces, like Facebook timelines. The content shared there tends to conform to local moral values and is subjected to vigilance and scrutiny. This is also a space for performance, in which people can represent themselves as richer than they are. The 'lights-off' mode represents more private encounters, like Facebook Messenger and WhatsApp conversations, where more sensitive content was shared with trusted peers. That was a space to address sex, humour, gossip, violence and whatever might be classified as 'politically incorrect'. This dynamic has some similarities to the way research participants in Bento manage their digital lives. Their WhatsApp groups are where the lights are on. They share content that conforms to the norms of active ageing. Thus they are also making improvements. But, in their case, they are concerned to show they are healthy and busy. The lights are turned off when they need help or when they present a frailty that could compromise their reputation. In these cases, as argued in chapter 6, their requests will be directed to close friends only and in private messages on WhatsApp. Spyer also observed that his research participants were more likely to address sensitive local issues in private messages to protect the people they know. Local crimes, for example, were handled with the 'lights off'. However, he noted that episodes of violence involving outsiders were more likely to be shared with the 'lights on', as they were not directly connected to locals, who wouldn't feel embarrassed by this kind of content. This shift can be helpful for understanding the memes making fun of old age in Bento. Research participants share them on their social media and WhatsApp groups, which should be seen as spaces for interactions with the 'lights on'. Although they give visibility to the declines and constraints associated with ageing, these memes are not about them. The participants are safe, as this content is about the others, the 'real old' or the 'old, old' ones. So they allow themselves to laugh together at the outsiders, referring to those who no longer belong to the third age.
43 Stafford 2018.
44 DataSenado 2019.
45 Duque 2021.
46 Shirky 2011.
47 Guess et al. (2019) analysed how fake news spread during the 2016 US elections. They say that people over 65 years old were seven times as likely as the youngest age group to share content from fake news websites.
48 Guess et al. (2019)'s findings were published by various media outlets worldwide, including the *New York Times*, the BBC, *The Guardian* and the Brazilian press. In Brazil, the headlines stressed that a scientific study confirmed that it is older people that share fake news the most, without clarifying that the study was conducted among Americans.
49 Brashier & Schacter 2020.
50 DataSenado 2019.
51 Correa 2009; Dias & Pais-Ribeiro 2018.
52 Before Covid-19, WhatsApp groups were used to support face-to-face activities. Some of these activities continued during social isolation, but in WhatsApp groups only, as described in chapter 5.
53 Miller et al. (2021) call 'perpetual opportunism' the intrinsic propriety of smartphones to offer an always-on unlimited number of possibilities of actions. Smartphones can instantly turn into a place to interact with friends, watch movies, read books, learn, and do banking, shopping and so on.

4
Family gathering

Ageing in between

In the previous chapter, we saw how older people in Bento organise their everyday lives between self-care activities and others that they associate with their interests and pleasures. In this chapter, we will consider how they split their time between responsibilities towards their families and self-realisation,[1] challenging the idea that the third age is a stage of life free from family obligations.[2] On the one hand, research participants are responsible for their elderly parents, who require care from them as if they were their children. On the other there are their own children who, although adults, remain their dependants. Smartphones help participants give visibility to this work and gain a reputation as good parents, grandparents or children. However, the main contribution of smartphones is to the management of family affairs, as WhatsApp has become the primary means of communication between relatives, with different outcomes for nuclear and extended families in terms of conviviality, care and reciprocity. Yet, as we will see, research participants may feel they are on their own even when they carry their whole family in their pockets.

Getting older with their parents

It is a mistake to think that ageing itself has the power to soften older people's hearts. Some wounds, especially those from childhood and adolescence, persist over time. They are just too hard to forgive or forget, as in the story of a woman whose mother was forced to marry her father. As she was born with her father's eyes, her mother rejected her and 'never, ever' gave her any love. Stories of cruelty and abandonment are not exceptional among research participants. Thus, the feelings they nourish for their parents, now frail and dependent on them, will define whether taking care of them is seen as a demonstration of affection or as an obligation. There are no miracles to help them balance the two. Children will take care of parents who were loving and devoted to them.[3] In such cases, they will incorporate care routines into their everyday lives as a way of showing gratitude to their fathers and mothers while they are still alive.

Traditionally seen as the natural caregivers within Brazilian families,[4] daughters are more likely than sons to abandon their jobs to make their parents' care a priority. That was the case with Lourdes, aged 64. She was working as a civil servant when her parents began to present some serious health problems. Raised in the upper middle class, she remembers that her parents provided her with everything she needed. Indeed, as she confesses later in the interview, it was not just about her needs. As a spoiled child, she got anything she desired. Thus, when they required full-time care, she decided to retire. 'I had security of employment, but I didn't think it was right to be constantly absent from work, and I also didn't want anyone to think that I was lazy or slacking.'

As some US studies show,[5] taking care of children is not the only reason women give up work. As the population gets older, some women are leaving the workforce to provide unpaid care for the elderly. In Lourdes's case, however, this decision was not seen as a sacrifice. On the contrary, it was a privilege. She could reciprocate all her parents' affection and guarantee that they would be comfortable at the end of their lives. Yet it wasn't an easy task. The care routine was intense, even though the family was able to hire a professional carer. Unexpectedly, this created another problem for Lourdes. As her family could afford this extra help, her brother didn't see why he should take on some caregiving responsibilities. One day, she remembers, her mother was in hospital, and she asked her brother for help. She wanted him to stay there so she could go home, take a shower and get some rest. Her brother said he didn't have time and suggested she should hire an extra professional. 'I took a deep breath and I realised that the decision to be there was mine and mine only. And I don't regret it.'

Rita's parents became ill when she was approaching her fifties. She couldn't afford to leave her work or hire a carer as Lourdes did. Now aged 70, she remembers that everything she did was only possible because she had the unconditional support of her boss.[6] With little money, she moved to a building close to the hospital where her parents were getting treatment. 'I had no money for a taxi, so I got a wheelchair. If my mother needed to go to casualty, I would push the wheelchair round the block until I got to the hospital,' she explains. Like Lourdes, she has a brother, but she was on the frontline when it came to her parents. Although they comprise only 15.7 per cent of those who take care of older relatives in Brazil,[7] men in Bento who take this responsibility are at least as present as women. Their role depends on two factors: their relationship with their parents, as noted above, and the partnerships they establish with their wives. When a couple make a cooperative agreement regarding their parents, care is incorporated into their routine, as if it was one more item in the housework they now share.

That is what happened to Paulo, aged 56. His mother had an argument with her only daughter a long time ago. Since then, he hasn't been able to count on his sister. Now that his mother is at an advanced stage of Alzheimer's disease, he is solely responsible for her, including paying for her stay in a care home. He follows his mother's health status, and if she has an emergency he is notified by WhatsApp. Before he retired, his wife would be the one to help. Nowadays, Paulo visits his mother every week, even if this is painful. Paulo becomes emotional, like others whose parents have Alzheimer's, when he says his mother no longer recognises him. 'It is just that look staring at no one in particular.' But he quickly composes himself and argues that, at this moment, ensuring her quality of life is the most important thing. Besides caring for his mother, he also pays more attention to his mother-in-law's needs. Although she is healthy and independent, she became a widow two years ago and requires his and his wife's presence and support more regularly.[8]

Because of this, the couple have put their plans to move to Portugal on hold. The idea came to them when they realised the financial losses they would face after retirement. 'It is a fact. If you don't prepare yourself for this, you will go crazy,' Paulo says. For this reason, his friends are already leaving Bento and moving to smaller cities with a lower cost of living. The couple were considering moving to Portugal for the same reason. They used Google Maps Street View to see if there were queues at the health centres and clinics, and they compared the results for different cities. This would indicate whether the health system in Portugal was overloaded. That was why they abandoned the idea of moving to Lisbon, the capital, and chose the smaller Monsanto instead. Their next step was to go through the process of proving their citizenship by descent and get their EU passports, and then wait until they both retired. However, Paulo's father-in-law died around the same time, which made the couple realise that they wouldn't be able to take their mothers with them or ensure that they would have access to the same quality of health services as they do in Bento. From these stories, one can see that it is pretty common for the freedom that older people typically associate with retirement to be, in practice, postponed to the moment of their parents' deaths.

Things went easier for Beto, aged 58, whose mother lives in a care home. She herself made the decision to move into the care home, after Beto's father died. She didn't want to be a burden to their children, not even financially. Thus she used her pension to pay her care home fees. Beto's mother was far-sighted: she managed to make the necessary preparations to do what most older women in Bento say would be their wish for when they become frail and lose their autonomy.[9] Moreover, in Beto's case there were 'no hurt feelings' in this process. They all have an excellent relationship, and this arrangement has worked well for more than a decade. Beto visits his mother once a week, as does his sister. Recently, he has started to wonder whether his mother thinks he is boring. He argues that she sometimes pretends to be deaf to avoid talking to him during his visits. But he approaches this with a good deal of humour, as with everything he does. He made a video of one of his visits to show how he was 'snubbed by his mother'. She sits by his side, playing a game on his tablet, while he speaks to the camera. She completely ignores him, even when he says her name. He shared the video on WhatsApp and Instagram as a joke. He is allowed to make fun of this situation because, he explains, 'I loved my father, I have no problems with my mother, and I am absolutely crazy about my sister. There is no crisis. These family issues everyone talks about are not us. We just don't need a therapist.'

The time research participants in Bento spend with their elderly parents is not restricted to care. It includes meetings and pleasant moments together with the family. Although it is common for family members to talk on WhatsApp every day, Sunday is usually the day dedicated to face-to-face encounters. Family lunches take place in restaurants or at home. Those who have lunch at home will often buy the traditional roasted chicken sold by almost all of Bento's bakeries that day (figures 4.1 and 4.2).

At one of the Catholic churches in Bento, it is common to see people leaving Sunday Mass and crossing the square towards the bakery to buy their chicken for lunch. Often, instead of all the family, one of the children will accompany their widowed mother or father to the ceremony (figure 4.3). During the week, it is common to find mothers and daughters frequenting the beauty salons of Bento, where they go to have their hair or nails done together. This kind of meeting, along with the Mass or Sunday lunch, will be thoroughly documented on the children's smartphones and shared on Facebook, WhatsApp and Instagram. By doing these things,

Figures 4.1 and 4.2   Traditional roast chicken sold every Sunday in Bento's bakeries. © Marília Duque.

older people are doing more than simply demonstrating their affection for their elderly parents. Because caring for an older family member is still morally valued by the community, which is a paradox in Bento,[10] they are also producing proof of their character through their work as caregivers, while presenting themselves as busy and useful. Therefore, Sunday is usually the day on which timelines are filled with selfies in which older people honour their parents. The figure of the heroes used by Leibing to address the way caregivers are described can be helpful for understanding the impact of this visibility.[11] She considers the way in which grandchildren emerge in Brazilian media coverage as new heroes playing the role of primary caregivers to grandparents with Alzheimer's. However, before they gained media attention, grandchildren posted this work on social media, where they gave visibility only to their happy moments as caregivers. As a result, Leibing criticises the fact that the difficulties of daily care were absent from their narratives and from the media articles, which contributed to heroic portraits that are more likely to be exceptions than a factual representation of the challenges and conflicts a family might face when taking care of someone with Alzheimer's.

The gap between what is shown in social media and what happens in real life emerges in Bento. As one research participant put it, not every family fits the 'Doriana family' stereotype. Doriana is a traditional Brazilian margarine brand whose advertising campaign has constructed, through the decades, an image of the Brazilian family as one in which all the family

Figure 4.3 Family leaving Sunday Mass. The elderly mother is assisted by her older daughter. © Marília Duque.

members are gathered around the kitchen table, celebrating their love and affection. Since then, 'Doriana family' has become an expression used among Brazilians to describe families that look 'too' perfect. In the past, this perfection was also based on the White heteronormative stereotype of the family.[12] It is only recently that advertisements have changed, becoming more inclusive and representative of Brazilian diversity. Even so, the dynamic of the perfect family that starts the day together has remained the signature of the 'Doriana family'. In one of the TV adverts (see figure 4.4), the grandparents are shown as having arrived for lunch, with the mother quickly setting the table so they can all enjoy a pleasant moment together. Yet, far from the picture painted by the adverts, some research participants reported neglecting or giving only fundamental care to their parents, even though the family is the primary institution held legally responsible for elderly people in Brazil.[13] Abandonment, violence and the perception that parents strongly favour one child over another are among the reasons research participants give to justify their refusal to accept their obligations to their elderly parents.[14]

The feeling that they have been victimised makes some research participants take a secondary role in caring for their elderly parents (delegating most of the care duties to their siblings), or even refuse any responsibility. That is the case with Nelson, aged 58. Later in this chapter we

Figure 4.4 A Doriana TV advert from 1990. The films would commonly feature a couple and their children. This example shows the grandmother, the mother and the children having lunch together. Frame captured by Marília Duque at 0:20. See the video at https://youtu.be/rpdsSusd4rE.

will see him as a devoted grandfather, and in chapter 8 we will see his concerns about being a good husband. However, as a son, he feels released from any obligation to his father, who abandoned his mother when Nelson was very young. With Ricardo, aged 64, it was his marriage that was the problem. Her mother never approved of the fact that his wife had not gone to university. As a devout Catholic and a devoted son, he was convinced he should spend Easter Sunday with his mother. As his wife didn't want to join him, they got into an argument, and he went to his mother's without her. When he arrived at her house, she was away, travelling, without having told him. He swore he would never return to his parents' house, and kept his word. He later had children and, even then, he forbade his mother to contact them. He only saw her again years later, when she already had dementia. At the time, he restricted his participation to the role of a visitor. For Ricardo, the responsibility for taking care of her had naturally been assigned to his brothers, who had lived an everyday family life by her side. Unlike him, Rosangela, aged 68, used to consider her mother her best friend. They lived together for 40 years until Rosangela got married and left home. When her mother became unwell, however, her brothers used the same argument as Ricardo. They suggested she should have the responsibility of taking care of their mother, as she had benefited the most by living under her roof for so many years. According to them, it was her turn to repay her mother for the special treatment she had always received from her.

It is hard for some research participants to forget what they went through with their parents even when they try. Some of them have spent their entire lives waiting for a parent's recognition, which in some cases has never come. It was common for them to start crying during the interviews, just as Cris, aged 63, did when she talked about the day her father passed away. She had taken care of her mother, father and sister before they died. But it was from her father that she wanted some recognition. She got pregnant very young, and her marriage did not work out, so she had lived in her parents' house all her life. Although she had successfully brought up her daughter, she had never felt that her father was proud of her.

> 'He was there, lying on a hospital bed. Sometimes, even today, I remember his eyes. I don't know why his eyes always captured my attention. Then, he stared at me with those eyes. I asked if he was okay. He answered yes. At the time, he treated me kindly and didn't fight with me any more. Then, he stared at my daughter. A doctor came. I think she [the doctor] realised it was the end, so she took my daughter away. As she was leaving, he followed her with that look. I will never forget that look. I think I've been waiting for that look my entire life: that affection, that passion. I was not jealous of my daughter. That was not what happened. With his eyes, he told her that he was leaving, but she would be fine.'

Even if she never got the recognition she wanted, Cris achieved a sense of balance in her relationship with her father while he was still alive. Thus, she misses him a lot, as do those who had a good life with their parents. By remembering the past, they will keep their memories alive. They may do so in a public way, such as by posting tributes to them on Facebook on their birthdays or the anniversaries of their deaths. Or they may express their love by learning something their parents were good at. That is the case with Patricia, aged 65, who is planning to learn to play chess as a kind of tribute to her father. Lourdes, whom we met earlier, is doing the same. She uses YouTube to learn how to sew after inheriting a sewing machine from her mother. In addition, some habits and objects will be kept as a way of materialising the presence of their parents. For example, Olívio, aged 56, has lost both his parents. Since their deaths, he has kept a bowl full of fruit on the kitchen counter because, he recalls, 'That is the way my mother likes it' (in the present tense). While some research participants in Bento find ways of keeping their parents in their lives even after their deaths, they also experience the absence of their living children

– even if, in some cases, they live under the same roof. As we will see, lack of reciprocity can be an intergenerational issue related to both the past and the future.

The absent presence of children

The needs of grown-up children equal the demands of elderly parents. On the one hand, there is financial dependence. The high cost of living in large cities like São Paulo, and the economic recession, which led to high unemployment rates, are reasons used to explain why children return to their parents' homes or postpone their departure from the family home. Retirement turns the parents' house into a safe place, because they have a guaranteed income in times of crisis. In Brazil, for example, 73 per cent of people aged 60 or over receive a state pension. In 2018, the proportion of households in which retirement and pension funds accounted for at least 50 per cent of the family's income was 20.6 per cent.[15]

On the other hand, there is pure convenience. The desire for independence experienced by research participants when they were young finds no resonance among the younger generation. This desire has been replaced by investment in their careers, which have become their top priority. Therefore, they are in no rush to get married or have children. In Brazil, even if they are employed or undertaking some kind of paid activity, one in four people between 25 and 34 years old live with their parents.[16] This can be explained by the fact that, despite earning a certain amount of money, children often feel that this is not enough, as they aspire to higher standards for their independent adult life.[17] That is often the case in middle-class families in Bento.

Children who continue to live in the parental home into adulthood in exchange for material and emotional support are known as the 'kangaroo generation'.[18] Just like the care of elderly parents, the 'kangaroo' presence and demands mean that research participants are not enjoying the free time that should come with the third age.[19] For them, the empty nest is still an abstract idea.[20] However, maintaining the domestic arrangement can prolong their value and utility, and have different gains for mothers and fathers. Most women continue to clean their children's rooms, wash their clothes and cook for them. When a kangaroo's mother misses or is late for an appointment, one of the most acceptable excuses she can come up with is that she was doing something to help her children. No woman questions the dedication of a mother. At the same time, men retain their role as providers. As we saw in the previous chapter, some will join in doing housework, but they are exceptions when children are still living with the couple. In those cases, the gendered division of household labour is likely to be old-fashioned. Children's expenses are incorporated into the family budget by the father. However, as children argue that they are focused on developing their careers, parents do not interpret their dependence as abuse.

That is the case with Rosangela, aged 68. She takes care of her daughter's clothes, room and meals. Her free time is dedicated to English language and WhatsApp classes, which she attends twice a week. Meanwhile, her husband does all the shopping and pays the bills. He prefers to deal with his bank in person by going to the local branch, to have a reason to leave the house. He may go to the supermarket three times a day because it makes him feel busy. When the family eat out together, he pays for his daughter. Before Uber, he was fully available to drive her to or from work. Both support their daughter's decision to invest in her education and career, and proudly stress that she 'works too much'. This is also the perception of Rita, aged 70. She finishes her courses and activities early in the afternoon, so that she can go to the supermarket and buy something fresh to cook for her adult son. 'He works a lot, he is very busy, so I try to make a nice dinner for when he arrives.' She speaks proudly of how he has become a partner in his company and how his colleagues admire him. She does the housework and helps him out with some minor house expenses.

It would be unusual for a parent whose child is working, like Rosangela and Rita, to complain about having to help them, because, as discussed in chapter 2, Bento has this specificity. Any effort associated with work is proof of character. Therefore, career-focused adult children are presented as 'dedicated', 'successful', and as people 'whose life is on track'. If they have a more senior professional position than their parents ever held, or if they achieved a higher level of education, even better. Their children's status is used to claim distinction, as the education of the new generation can be proof that the family has succeeded.[21] Research participants proudly share those achievements in their conversations with friends and on their social networks. Moreover, parents can replace the professional credentials they lost when they retired with their children's credentials. For one reason or another, children's work is seen as sacred; it should not be disturbed by mundane issues.

Mothers are more likely than fathers to feel guilty when they ask for help. For that reason, they try to remain independent. They often hide their psychological and physical needs and weaknesses in order to avoid jeopardising their children's careers. Carla, aged 62, explains: 'In the current economic context, having a child in employment is the most important thing.' Therefore she doesn't tell her daughter when she has to go to hospital to have the cysts removed that periodically appear on her head. 'It's a quick thing, five minutes maximum. I'm not going to disturb my daughter with this. She has to work.' On these occasions, she lied to doctors, saying that someone would come with her. As doctors don't buy her excuse any more, she asks a friend to come with her. Rita's determination not to compromise her child's work was equally impressive. She was depressed for over a year. She argues that the most challenging time was in the morning, when all she wanted was to close the curtains and stay in bed. Instead, she woke up every day and pretended she was fine until her son left the house. At the time, her son was taking some critical steps in his career, and she didn't want to worry him.

The fact that children live with their supportive parents does not imply any reciprocation from them. Mothers are the first to complain that their children, when they are not working or studying, spend their free time at home on their smartphones.[22] This happens especially in relation to daughters, whose mothers resent their having endless chats with their friends on WhatsApp but not sharing anything about their private lives with them. Even when they do talk, mothers feel that their daughters are not listening to them. The lack of dialogue between generations makes some mothers seek out therapy or counselling. They often complain that their children arrive home too tired from work, or that they are just never in the mood. Paying a professional allows them to talk about anything they want, with the guarantee that there will be someone interested in hearing what they have to say.

On the other hand, fathers experience different types of conflict, mainly to do with maintaining their authority. Some children occupy high positions at work and, in addition, are in better physical shape, while their fathers are 'weak' and retired. The idea that the fathers' life experience could be appealing is not realistic, especially for their sons. Instead, ownership of the shared home is the last bastion of fathers' authority, which is challenged as well by their children's digital skills,[23] as addressed in the next chapter. Nelson, whom we met earlier, illustrates how this power bargaining takes place within his family. When he hears his son saying that the younger generation is the smartest, he replies: 'Definitely. But when I was 29, I already had my own house. And you, what do you have?' The house Nelson is so proud of is not that important any more. As observed by Miller et al., smartphones have become the place where people live.[24] This is true of Nelson's son. That is the place where he can be in charge of the remote control, order the dinner he wants, party with friends or listen to loud music. Thus, smartphones allow children to build their own homes inside their parents' houses. It is a kind of upgrade to the teenager's room, with more privacy, more power and free Wi-Fi. This house-within-a-house cohabitation won't necessarily be peaceful, and mothers are likely to end up bearing the brunt of the new domestic tensions. This situation was a cause of stress for one woman until her meditation classes taught her how to keep calm when her husband and son had a row. 'Before, I used to get nervous. Now I understand that it is something that they will have to solve. I stay in my corner. I concentrate on breathing, and I let the dust settle.'

Domestic crises reflect the constant negotiation of boundaries between parents and children. Parents' authority is conditional on their maintaining their physical, mental and financial autonomy, which leads to a kind of self-surveillance and resistance. Children are dependent on their parents, but parents are not supposed to rely on their children, if they want to enjoy their right to decide what to do with their time and money. This independence is something older people in Bento will do anything to keep. Therefore, no matter how overwhelmed they are, they will keep quiet about their frailties and needs in order to preserve their self-determination at home and within their family. These conflicts are, however, kept private. For example, to their friends and on social media, research participants are likely to present only the successful aspects of their children. As stated above, children's achievements are used to attain distinction in work-oriented Bento. Only one living arrangement is more prestigious than children living with their parents in order to invest in their careers, namely children who have left the family home to work abroad. However, in terms of reciprocity and care, there may not be much difference between siblings living apart.[25]

In her work with the transnational families of Syrian Christian nurses in Kerala, South India, Ahlin observed that migration has nothing to do with the idea that elderly parents have been left behind by children living abroad.[26] Instead, parents who benefit from their children's work see migration as a form of care. It is not just about financial support. As the author argues, information and communication technologies (ICTs) allow children to manage their parent's care daily, even from a distance. This care can include friends of the children, who become available to meet everyday needs and emergencies that require physical presence. Thus they can provide care at a distance[27] and navigate new geographies of care.[28] That is not the case in Bento. Nine of the 38 participants interviewed have children working abroad. However, the children do not provide them with either money or care. Instead, the parents are required when the children have a health issue or need some hands-on help with their houses or their newborns. Less frequently, they may help with money when children face an emergency. But, as pointed out above, parents don't complain. Children's demands are a chance for them to feel, and be seen as, useful after retirement. Moreover, their requests can become extra opportunities to travel abroad, supplementing their regular annual visit.

In terms of care, Bete, aged 66, is an exception. When her only daughter moved to Europe, she decided to stay, even though she knows she can't count on her sister, who also lives in Bento. Her daughter then created a care-at-a-distance routine. They agreed that the mother would update the daughter through WhatsApp early in the morning. Bete has until 10 a.m. to send her daughter a message to say she is well. If she doesn't, her daughter will try to contact her. If she can't, she will ask her friends in Bento to check on her. The practice is repeated at night, when Bete confirms she is at home and ready to sleep. Although her daughter is an ocean away, their interaction on WhatsApp makes Bete feel safe. She explains: 'When my only daughter moved to Europe, my friends told me she was abandoning me. But the truth is she is more present in my life than many of their daughters, who live here.' Presence and co-presence (in which people have synchronous communication, even though they are not in the same physical location) are also changing how this generation is grandparenting, as described in the next section.

Grandparenting versus babysitting

Once children's careers become their priority, they are in no rush to start their own families.[29] When they exist, grandchildren are commonly seen as a great joy in life in Bento, especially when they are seen as filling the place of the grown-up children, who once respected their parents' knowledge and experience but now consider them to be outdated. In such cases, grandchildren are seen as inheriting and valuing the legacy of their grandparents. For example, Luisa, aged 72, recently received a letter from her granddaughter, in which she thanked her for turning her into a passionate reader. The granddaughter moved into Luisa's house when her mother got divorced, and they became very close. Indeed, they became accomplices. Together, they cultivate the habit of imagining places they would like to visit. The most important part of this game is to think about everything they would need to organise to make their fictitious trip possible. This type of 'management' is something Luisa is very comfortable with. She works for upper-class families in Bento, helping them to catalogue their artworks and planning their arrangement and organisation. Thus, Luisa is skilled at managing detailed lists, of, for example, different providers, budgets and deadlines. When her granddaughter turned 18, she thought it was time for them to make a real trip, so she took her to Chile as a birthday present. But first, they had fun together preparing every detail.

Apart from the good times spent with their grandchildren, grandmothers are the people children call on when they need hands-on help. Grandmothers are called when their children have to work overtime, when they need a break (they deserve it as they are always working too hard) or when grandchildren are ill. The problem is that sometimes their children confuse grandparenting with babysitting.[30] This misunderstanding can lead to conflict, and grandmothers can find it challenging to set boundaries. Even Luisa, who is crazy about her grandchildren, confesses it was only recently that she was able to set boundaries in terms of what her children could expect from her:

> 'Now, when my daughters call me to ask me if I can look after my grandchildren, they will first ask me if I am free, meaning whether I have any activities scheduled for that day. So when I'm busy, they try the other grandma or rearrange their appointments to fit my diary. I don't mind looking after my grandchildren. They don't give me any trouble. But I have a life, right?'

For Jane, aged 70, it is the opposite. She is fully responsible for the routine of her granddaughter, who aspires to become a professional ballet dancer. Jane picks her up at school and accompanies her to ballet classes at the Municipal Theatre. Her smartphone's calendar merges both routines, hers and her granddaughter's. Jane's timetable is itself pretty full, as she attends many courses and classes. However, as her daughter has a full-time job, her granddaughter's career is her priority. The gallery on her smartphone is full of pictures of her granddaughter, who, socially, is presented as her outstanding achievement. Moreover, her working routine as a grandmother gives her a sense of purpose and provides proof of her utility. However, this kind of full-time dedication is not common in Bento.

Usually, grandmothers will only take responsibility for the care of their grandchildren on days of the week that have been agreed in advance (exceptions are made when their children have an emergency at work, as work is always a priority). As Luisa has argued, they try to reconcile grandparenting with their desire to finally have some time for themselves. Besides this, in some cases the ageing body imposes limits, as grandparenting can be physically exhausting. Lourdes is an example of a grandmother who confesses that, even though she loves her grandchildren, her body can't take too many hours with them. She explains: 'I spend one afternoon a week with my granddaughter. It is delightful, but I have to lie down and rest to replenish my energy as soon as she leaves.' Aiming to tackle this issue, a start-up in Bento offers a portfolio of 'concierge services', which include supporting grandmothers when they are looking after their grandchildren.[31]

While parents rely on grandparents for babysitting, they undervalue their opinions on raising their children, arguing that times have changed.[32] Research participants agree with them, but they believe they succeeded in raising their own children, so their experience should be valued. For them, this means that some of the care routines they followed when they were raising their children should be preserved for the sake of the next generation. Nelson shares this feeling. Having retired from his career job, he now works at the beauty salon he has built for his wife in their garden. They plan to work together until she is eligible to retire, when they plan to travel. At least one of his grandchildren regularly spends the weekend with the couple. He remembers that when his children were kids he used to watch the TV programmes they liked, to check whether they were appropriate and aligned with his religious values. He complains that his children don't do the same. They ignore what their grandchildren watch on television and what they do on the iPad. He admits that the iPad can be very convenient and that his children work hard. Even so, he believes they overuse it as a sort of device that babysits their children. 'When they become teenagers, their parents won't have the right to complain that they don't talk. They no longer talk today because they are always on the iPad,' he argues.

Roger, aged 61, is also concerned about the content his grandchildren consume on the internet, and he is particularly worried about their exposure to social media. However, he has adopted a different tactic. Rather than complaining about his children, his actions address his grandchildren directly (as well as the great-nephews and great-nieces he cares for). They are pretty close, so they accepted Roger's 'friend' requests on all of the social media platforms they use, including those that older people are not expected to use.

> 'One day, my grandson introduced me to his friend. "This is my grandfather," he said. "Can you believe it?", and then he added: "He is on Snapchat." His friend looked at me as if I was from Mars. But I use it because of him.'

By doing this, Roger stays close to his grandchildren and at the same time monitors what they are doing and whether they need any help. When he sees something strange, an inappropriate post or some content that could expose them to danger, he gets in touch with them. He asks if everything is okay and makes his point. However, when he comes across a post that could signify that his grandchildren are in trouble or asking for help, he reports it to their parents. He doesn't believe he is betraying their trust when he does so. He considers that his grandchildren are perfectly aware that he is around on their social media. If they don't want him to see something, they can always change their privacy settings. The transparent relationship Roger enjoys directly with his grandchildren is a better arrangement than the dialogue most participants have with their children when they talk about grandparenting rights and duties. Consequently, it is common for grandparents to be silent or step back to avoid conflict while they form secret alliances with their grandchildren. As Lourdes explains, her daughter-in-law is very annoying, full of rules about what she is not supposed to do with her grandchildren. Thus, she found a way to do what she wants:

> 'They are so cute. I don't care about my children any more. But my grandchildren ... are like a gift. I take care of them, I spoil them, I kiss them, and then I leave. ... I also give them chocolate when their mother is not around. It is our secret.'

Like other domestic matters, what happens in the family stays in the family. For that reason, Facebook is where they show the photos and videos of their great moments together, while WhatsApp is where the negotiations of daily life take place. These arrangements include agreeing which day the grandparents will take the children to school, asking for extra help or criticising something related to education, expectations, behaviour and limits. On the one hand, this type of technology can provide a safe distance when things get tense.[33] On the other, it reduces the barriers imposed by distance when grandchildren live abroad, allowing grandparents to take part in their development and achieve a 'sense of everydayness'.[34] Juliana, aged 66, experiences this feeling. Sometimes, it is hard to know if she is talking about her grandson, who lives in New York, or her granddaughter, who lives two doors away. To her, they are equally present in her life. The presence of one is counterbalanced by the co-presence of the other, which is complemented by the reports, photos and videos she constantly receives from her daughter. By interacting with them, she can express her love and care and ignore the distance. In this way, WhatsApp allows transnational families like Juliana's to effectively put their emotions into circulation in an affective economy in which exchanges bind them together.[35]

In addition, her two grandchildren are given equal space in her smartphone's gallery, which has become the new family album. That is where she keeps her memories of them, including a picture with the first tooth, and videos of the first step, a swimming competition and graduation. Like Juliana, grandparents in Bento keep these cute moments with them, and show them to their friends at every opportunity. As Wilding et al. argue,[36] the images and videos received from family members turn smartphones into 'repositories of emotion'. At the same time these moments can be used as capital to be shared in social interactions as proof of one's family's connection and achievements.

At first glance, grandparenting at a distance may appear to be restricted to the mediated demonstration of affection, but that is not the case, especially when the role played by grandmothers is considered. They are more likely to fit what Nedelcu called 'transnational grandparenting'.[37] Indeed, some grandmothers in Bento are willing to interrupt their routines to be with their children abroad when their grandchildren need help. Some of them travel alone for the first time, as their husbands refuse to retire, or argue that they have an occupation to which they are committed. But these women feel that, at their age, they are released from the social obligation to be always at their husband's side. Thus they allow themselves to extend their stay while their husbands insist that they can't be idle for that long. Smartphones have empowered grandmothers to do this, as they can maintain some control over the routines of their houses and husbands, even at a distance. In these circumstances, their use of WhatsApp changes. The usual intense exchange of messages with their children who live abroad is replaced by chat with their husband. Because of this, women can allow themselves 'to forget' to go home, as they can manage their houses and marriages at a distance.

More efficiency for the nuclear family

As well as for keeping in touch with relatives living abroad,[38] messaging apps are used to organise the practical life of the family,[39] establishing themselves as important communication channels for the nuclear family. In Bento, practical tasks are likely to be coordinated in WhatsApp groups dedicated to everyday issues. As argued above, participants believe their children are busy focusing on their professional development. Thus,

WhatsApp messages are perceived as a way to get things done without interrupting them: there is an informal arrangement that parents can send messages whenever they want, but children will respond when they can. WhatsApp groups organise, for example, the allocation of responsibilities around the house to those still living under the same roof. That is the case with Magali, aged 67. She started working again after retirement and her new job requires her to sleep away from home on some days of the week. She organises the whole routine of the house while she is away at work. She allocates tasks such as shopping and cleaning, and manages emergencies, such as purchasing a new washing machine when the old one broke down. 'My son didn't even know that the washing machine had broken down. He found out from the group because he saw me discussing it with my daughter and my husband, about who would take delivery of the washing machine, which I bought online,' she says. WhatsApp provides excellent efficiency in communication, without the burden of a long phone call and with fewer conflicts. Because people can choose when to reply to a message, they can hide their immediate emotional response and appear objective.

WhatsApp groups are also created as administrative channels for the care of elderly parents. Such a group usually includes only siblings and is used to allocate responsibilities, take decisions, and keep them up to date with their parents' health status. But there are also cases when a WhatsApp group is created as a form of care for healthy parents who want to live independently. That is the case with Bia, aged 55. She and her siblings keep a WhatsApp group to take care of her mother, who wants to continue living in her own house after the death of her husband. In other words, they want to keep an eye on her during the day. As the group is based on reciprocity, everyone is committed to sharing their status and updating the group with information about where they are and what they are doing. The problem is that they don't have much time. Bia is developing a new career after retirement, and her siblings are executives who work hard, so they have opted to use visuals to keep each other informed of what they are doing in a time-efficient way. They have created an avatar for each family member through the Bitmoji app, which generates personalised stickers for routine activities like watching TV or reading (figure 4.5). 'If you are in a hurry, you don't have to write. If I am going to the gym, I just send a sticker of myself on the treadmill. My mother also has her avatar. Everyone in the family has their avatar,' she explains. Among research participants, visual content such as stickers is becoming more popular, as it can summarise information and affection in a single image, requiring minimal effort but being very convenient.[40]

Figure 4.5 Set of stickers shared by a participant to quickly inform her family when she is at the gym, taking a shower, going to meet them, meditating, doing yoga and going to sleep. © anonymised participant.

An exception to the extensive use of WhatsApp groups to manage the everyday life of the nuclear family is Sandra, aged 69, who is very independent. She likes to make her own decisions, and she wants to maintain her privacy and autonomy. In other words, she likes to set boundaries with her three children. On the other hand, she doesn't want to take up their time, which is dedicated to their careers and families. She therefore prefers to contact them individually, and she concentrates on urgent and vital subjects. If the conversation becomes extended and an important decision needs to be made, she phones them or manages to meet them. Rita, aged 70, does it differently. She doesn't keep a group for her nuclear family because she is divorced and has just one child. As she and her son live together, she could manage their practical issues when he is at home. However, as her son is always busy, she uses WhatsApp to coordinate the routines of the house even when he is in the next room. Rita is among the women who complain about the lack of opportunities to talk in general and with children in particular. Paradoxically, WhatsApp is the place where she can fill this need.

Spending more time with the extended family

WhatsApp brings the extended family back into view. The conviviality the extended family experiences online is not limited to the face-to-face rituals and formalities of special occasions such as Easter, Christmas and family birthdays. WhatsApp enables the extended family to become more embedded in everyday life. This shift allows relatives to enjoy trivial conversations and interactions, as they no longer need to be selective in what they talk about. Their time together, previously restricted to a few hours on special dates they have scheduled in the annual festive calendar, is now always-on, as they are all connected on WhatsApp. Therefore it doesn't matter how ordinary a topic of conversation is: it will still be acceptable to discuss it in WhatsApp extended family groups. Whether it is 'good morning' messages, jokes, pictures of the cake someone tried to bake for the first time, a promotion at work, being admitted to a university, taking part in a swimming competition, holiday memories and occasional casual encounters between subgroups of family members, there will always be a relative available to discuss topics like these (figure 4.6).

Cris, aged 63, saw how this transition from the ritual to the ordinary took shape in her WhatsApp family group. The group was created to organise the family's annual Christmas dinner, which involved assigning different tasks and responsibilities concerned with drinks and food. After Christmas, the group remained active under its original name of 'Christmas dinner'. However, the group's function had changed. Now, it keeps the family together, helping them bypass the constraints that make it difficult for them to meet face to face. For Iara, aged 72, this is particularly important. She lives alone and has no children. Her only brother and her nephews live in distant neighbourhoods, but now they can be in touch every day. WhatsApp also enables people to stay in touch with the part of the family left behind when participants have migrated to Bento to work, while reconnecting them to their children who are working abroad. As I argued above, WhatsApp transforms this absence into a co-presence. And this can be pretty intense when we are talking about family.

Carla, aged 62, is amused when she remembers that her husband resisted having a smartphone for as long as he could. Nowadays, the first thing he does when he wakes up is to check his WhatsApp family group. He starts his day by sending a good morning message to the group. At the same time, he can reach the part of the family that lives in Bento, the part that still lives in the city where he was born and his children living abroad.

Figure 4.6 Post shared on a WhatsApp family group. 'There are a lot of hugs waiting for an opportunity to hug.' The 'hug' restricted to face-to-face encounters is what WhatsApp challenges with an always-on connection between relatives.

This message is generally visual, consisting of an image that includes a positive note (figure 4.7).

Everyone complains about the volume of these types of messages, often received in WhatsApp family groups. Known as 'good-morning-good-afternoon-good-night' messages, they can literally be sent every morning, afternoon and night. And they are seen as coming primarily from the older generation. Indeed, keeping the family group active on

Figure 4.7 Post shared on a WhatsApp family group. 'For today: a grateful mind and a happy heart. Have a good day.' Messages like this are shared throughout the day.

WhatsApp has become a new occupation for research participants. There is now an expectation that older people will always use an emoji, gif or sticker to ensure the group's members stay together. These visual messages are the ones they feel most comfortable with. Easy to manage even for WhatsApp beginners, these messages can be received from other groups and shared in the family group (and vice versa), which allows them to express themselves with minimal effort.

Besides the inclusive potential of visual resources, WhatsApp promotes genuine interaction between generations in Bento. Yet each member will find their own way of preserving the group's existence and ensuring its harmony. Thus if older people send messages all day long, the younger generation will often mute the group and check messages a few times a day.[41] Roger, aged 61, notices a generational delay in the content shared in his family group. He claims that the older generation are sharing the same messages he received by email 10 years ago, but he doesn't want to be the spoilsport who criticises the joke his great-aunt found so funny. After all, the content is not important. In the extended family group, what matters is continuing the conversation in order to nurture family ties, and older people have enough free time to keep the messages coming.[42] Much of this conversation has a phatic function, and frequency can be as important as content.[43]

There are, however, some subjects that are taboo in family groups. Generally, football and religious matters should be avoided (it is common for children to choose a different religion from their parents). And there is definitely no room to talk about politics. At the time of writing, the impeachment of the former president Dilma Rousseff (which the Brazilian left sees as a coup that culminated in the arrest of her predecessor, President Lula) and the rise of the far right have led to the election of the current president, Jair Bolsonaro. This process has resulted in acute polarisation on social media, which has been reproduced in WhatsApp groups, including those dedicated to the extended family.[44] Because the maintenance of family bonds is sacred, it was agreed that political content would no longer be welcome in these groups.[45] Less often, a second family group might be created, in which 'everything is allowed'. Joining this second group is optional. Ricardo, aged 64, had a bad experience in his 'official' family group because of politics. While the whole family was busy preparing for a party, the cousin who was going to host the event mentioned Ricardo's political orientation. The cousin joked that he would forget about their disagreement at the event, for the sake of the family. Ricardo was offended and left the WhatsApp group. He considers his cousin's message to be disrespectful, but at the same time he believes his own attitude to be somewhat extreme and regrets his decision.

> 'I was pissed off, because he didn't have to put family and politics together. Then I replied, saying I expect respect when I hear that word [family]. Then we ended up arguing about everything. So what did I do then? I deleted my WhatsApp. I kept thinking that I didn't have to do it this way, just as he didn't need to do what he did the way he did it. We had been getting along well through WhatsApp, but one word can suddenly change everything.'

In a broader context, Ricardo's decision to leave his family group can be considered not only extreme but unusual. For example, Garcia and Vivacqua[46] found that when Brazilians come across messages in their family group that don't conform with their beliefs, 47 per cent ignore the message, 15 per cent complain publicly, and only 10 per cent leave the group. Fear of hurting relatives' feelings is one reason participants give for remaining in the family group. The dynamics of communication in family groups can be as complex as interactions with friends. In both situations, research participants are constantly trying to find the right tone. For example, Ricardo believes writing demands more work, giving people more time to think about and elaborate what they want to say. His experience has led him to believe that time to think (and calm down) can be crucial, so he now prefers written messages in any interaction on WhatsApp. The choice between written messages, audio messages, calls and video calls on WhatsApp does not follow a strict rule but depends on the context and on the intentions of peers. For some, like Olívio, aged 56, the voice is the best way to express genuine affection. On birthdays, for example, when it comes to a person he 'really' likes, he prefers to give them a voice call via WhatsApp. Roger, aged 61, migrates from text messages to stickers to be more affectionate with his daughter who lives abroad (this resource is usually activated to resolve a conflict). Magali, aged 67, prefers to send audio messages because it is more comfortable for her, as she hates typing. But when the message is for her children, she sends them text messages because they are at work, and she knows that they cannot always listen to the audio.

As we can see, participants choose the communication tool that best suits their interactions with friends, relatives, children who work and children living abroad.

WhatsApp rules the house

In this chapter, we have observed how older people in Bento manage the care of three different generations and how WhatsApp is embedded in their everyday life, facilitating their communication as transnational families. The co-presence of children and grandchildren living abroad counterbalances the 'absence' of children who still live at their parents' house. Regarding the latter, participants face the challenge of managing a house-within-a-house cohabitation, as their children seem to live inside their smartphones, where they can set their own rules and preferences. The new domestic dynamic results in conflict for mothers who feel excluded and fathers who feel their authority is at stake. Even though they complain about the effects of smartphones, parents benefit from being online as they can manage practical issues with their nuclear family and expand their sociability with their extended family. WhatsApp reconnects the family and inaugurates a space for brief interactions in which messages are exchanged not necessarily to start a conversation but to nurture family bonds. This is work older people in Bento have time to do, so they will take on that job and cheer up the family on WhatsApp. This might be interpreted as one more job they do for the family. As seen in chapter 3 and in this one, research participants have obligations to meet while finding time for their own interests. For the latter, this time will be shared with friends and friends of friends also connected on WhatsApp. As we will see in the next chapter, friendship makes the third age truly flourish in Bento.

Notes

1. Savishinsky (2000) observed that older people in the US face the same challenge, balancing their freedom after retirement against their obligations to their families.
2. Laslett 1991.
3. Whyte (2017, p. 245) argues that 'some people have alienated their offspring', meaning that some parents who were not diligent in their parenting may find their children have 'little sense of obligation' to become their care providers in their old age.
4. L. T. S. Pereira et al. 2017.
5. Porter 2017.
6. In *Women, Work and Care of the Elderly*, Watson and Mears (2019) address the challenges women face in Australia to reconcile their unpaid work as caregivers with paid work in workplaces where this care doesn't receive formal recognition. The authors found that, in the absence of policies that support women to do this form of unpaid work, they rely on informal arrangements made with supportive colleagues or thoughtful supervisors.
7. L. T. S. Pereira et al. 2017.
8. Women live longer than men, resulting in what Lins & Andrade (2018) called 'the feminization of old age' in Brazil. In 2019, life expectancy at birth was 80.1 years for women and 73.1 years for men (IBGE 2020c).

9. This is not the case in, for example, the West Bengal state of India, where interdependence among generations is experienced as desirable and normal by older people. Lamb (2019) observed that both Hindus and Muslims are likely to consider old age a stage of life in which to receive care and enjoy respect from younger people, even though the latter may accept this reciprocity as part of the local moral code.
10. Reciprocity between generations is lived as a paradox in Bento. With regard to their elderly parents, research participants are likely to comply with the 'intergenerational contract' that places a moral obligation on parents to take care of their children until they need their children to take care of them (Whyte 2017). That is why their care routines gain visibility while cases of abandonment and negligence are hidden. However, when it comes to their children, they are more likely to experience dependence as a burden, as articulated by successful and healthy ageing discourses (Lamb 2019). Thus, research participants reproduce these discourses, which say that they have a moral obligation to take care of themselves. In addition to this, as described later in this chapter, dependence in Bento means intruding on the time one's children dedicate to working, something that is not acceptable in this work-oriented community.
11. Leibing 2017.
12. Oliveira & Iwata 2016.
13. The law enshrined in the 'Estatuto do Idoso' (National Policy for the Elderly) considers the welfare of the elderly to be the responsibility of 'the family, the community, the society and the state'. In other words, the family has become the primary institution legally responsible for people aged 60 and over (Brasil, Ministério da Saúde 2013). For example, people over 60 are expected to live with their families, and the state will only intervene if relatives provide evidence that they cannot afford this responsibility. The same applies to nutrition (Küchemann 2012). The distribution of responsibilities between the family and the state is also addressed by the WHO's Active Ageing framework. For example, one of the questions the policy aims to answer is 'How do we best balance the role of the family and the state when it comes to caring for people who need assistance, as they grow older?' (World Health Organization 2002, p. 5)
14. This kind of abandonment is reflected in the growing number of older people relying on public shelters in Brazil, for day care or as a permanent residence. Between 2012 and 2017, this number increased by 33 per cent (Cancian & Alegretti 2018).
15. The same study shows the possible impacts of Covid-19 on Brazilian households, taking into account that, up to July 2020, 73.8 per cent of the deaths caused by the virus were of people aged 60 or over. Assuming the worst-case scenario, in which everyone in this age group is dead, there are two possible outcomes. For families in which older people's incomes comprise at least 50 per cent of the total income, the per capita income would be reduced by 75 per cent, which would affect 11.6 million people. If an older person's income is the only income in the household, their death would leave 5 million people with no income. As the study suggests, when an older person dies in Brazil, a family falls into poverty (Camarano 2020).
16. Mendonça 2017.
17. Silveira & Wagner 2006.
18. Kublikowski & Rodrigues 2016.
19. Laslett 1991.
20. Empty nest syndrome is the discomfort experienced by parents when their children leave home and they lose their parental function (Sartori & Zilberman 2009).
21. Bourdieu 2010.
22. L. M. Webb (2015) argues there is no evidence that personal communication technologies (PCTs) lead to fewer face-to-face family interactions. Instead, she shows that scholars support the notion that these uses enhance offline relationships in general, including family relations. In addition, multitasking behaviour is presented as a form of interacting online and offline simultaneously. Within the family, this means that relatives can be connected and genuinely together at the same time. Family members can watch and comment on a movie or play a game together while individually connected to their PCTs. That was not the case among research participants in Bento. Parents complain that their children are absent even when they are physically present, as they spend their time at home, on their own, interacting with their smartphones only. Karadağ et al. (2015) described 'phubbing' as the phenomenon of looking at a smartphone during a face-to-face conversation. By doing that, individuals escape from interpersonal communication to interact with their smartphones. Sometimes, in Bento, research participants don't even have the chance to start a conversation. Even so, it is possible to argue that they experience what Miller et al. (2021) call 'the death of proximity', as they feel their children are at home but not actually there.

23 In their work with families in Finland and Slovenia, Taipale et al. (2018) observed that digital skills challenge social roles, especially between children and parents, as children are more likely to retain authority when it comes to a family's technological issues.
24 Miller et al. developed the concept of the 'transportal home' to describe how smartphones provide a space for intimacy and privacy just like the intimacy or privacy one might experience at home, with the added advantages of mobility and comfort, as the smartphone also works as a control hub (Miller et al. 2021).
25 Baldassar et al.'s (2007) work on transnational caregiving addresses how new communication technologies surpass the division of care work between local and non-local kin. Especially in respect of elderly parents, the assumption that those who are geographically close are the ones managing care routines is challenged.
26 Ahlin 2018.
27 Pols 2012.
28 Oudshoorn 2011.
29 Among 22 women interviewed in Bento, only five had grandchildren. Out of 16 men interviewed in Bento, seven had grandchildren.
30 In her work on the voluntary and involuntary nature of the support provided by social networks and its impacts on quality of life in old age in Portuguese society, Paúl (2005) describes how grandparenting can result in happiness or in disappointment. On the one hand, happiness comes with the perception that the support provided for grandchildren is a voluntary occupation, in the grandparents' free time, when they play the role of sharing their legacy with their grandchildren. On the other hand, disappointment is associated with the perception that this support is an obligation, with grandparents playing the role normally filled by the parents.
31 Maele 2021.
32 For example, L. M. Webb (2015) argues that the family elder's wisdom is not being replaced by googling. The author stresses that searches on the internet take place when a face-to-face source can't provide the information needed, or when people share the belief that the most accurate information on a specific topic is available on the internet. As observed in Bento, too, that is the case with new parents, who search on specialised websites for information on raising and caring for their children as they believe their parents can't provide up-to-date information.
33 Baldassar et al. 2007.
34 Nedelcu 2017.
35 Wilding et al. 2020.
36 Wilding et al. 2020, p. 652.
37 In his work on Romanian families living in Canada and Switzerland, Nedelcu (2017) considers how elderly parents gain mobility and cross the border in order to support their grandchildren living abroad, providing care while achieving a sense of utility after retirement. She observes that grandmothers play a crucial role in transnational grandparenting by being the first to help in practical issues, including taking charge of housework or providing support when babies arrive. Grandmothers' work can be seen as a continuation of the role played by women as the main caregiver for the family, which is also the case in Brazil.
38 Plaza & Plaza 2019; Walton 2021; L. M. Webb 2015.
39 L. M. Webb 2015.
40 The same was observed in a cross-cultural study conducted by Miller et al. (2021) in the fieldsites in China, Japan, Italy and Al-Quds.
41 In their work on the dynamics of WhatsApp groups in Brazil, Garcia and Vivacqua (2021) found that 26 per cent of the participants interviewed had silenced at least one WhatsApp group, in order not to be disturbed all the time.
42 Older people are seen as the age group most active in WhatsApp groups in Brazil. Women are more active than men (Garcia & Vivacqua 2021).
43 WhatsApp's role in the extended family, as observed in Bento, supports the main findings of Taipale and Farinosi's (2018) work with Finnish and Italian families. They found that WhatsApp allows members to reach the majority of the family at once, with crucial advantages. As a synchronous and asynchronous conversation, WhatsApp suits individuals' timetables and availability. In addition, the platform offers great adaptability to an individual's skills, needs and preferences. They can choose between texting, audio messages, photos and videos, with visuals facilitating exchanges without a practical purpose between family members. Although other messages may contain important information, these messages are responsible for maintaining bonds between interlocutors and for social coherence. Therefore, the authors

conclude, the family group on WhatsApp has a primarily phatic function. In Bento, one could say, older people use the phatic function to test the channel and who is there, which means checking whom they can count on. As we will see in the next chapter, the same behaviour may be extended to groups of friends on WhatsApp.

44 Trindade 2018.

45 In his book *O que faz o brasil, Brasil?* ('What makes brazil, Brazil?'), the anthropologist Roberto DaMatta (1986, p. 19) argues that the family is the most solid institution in the country and makes a distinction between 'the house' and 'the street'. The street is the external place for movement, leisure and pleasure but also the space for competition, anonymity and survival. The house, on the other hand, is the home, a safe and sacred place, but also a moral unit. DaMatta claims that, once the mundane (business, competition, insecurity) is excluded from the house, the Brazilian family addresses political issues and dissonant political positions in a way that preserves its harmony. Thus political arguments are excluded from the table, the living room and the bedroom and take place in secondary places in the house. The same dynamic was observed in the WhatsApp groups participants maintain with their families. As this space has become the sacred space for family conviviality, political issues should be addressed outside the 'official' WhatsApp family group.

46 Garcia & Vivacqua 2021.

5
Unlocking the smartphone

Smart for what?

This chapter considers how the desire to be included in conversations with friends and family makes older people in Bento want to learn to use WhatsApp. In the end, however, they achieve much more than that, as the platform expands their connections and access to opportunities and activities aimed at the third age. WhatsApp helps research participants to challenge the stigma of retirement in Bento as they find new ways to retain their productive and social lives and share evidence that they remain active and useful. Familiarisation with WhatsApp can be a big step towards digital inclusion for older people. This learning process is full of challenges and anxieties that can result in dependence, but also collaboration, among peers. Participants overcome their constraints with some help from friends and with a lot of creativity to solve their everyday problems. In doing so, they unlock the 'smartness' of their smartphones in ways that were not predicted by the developers, crafting personal strategies to get things done. Before we join them on this journey, Alice, aged 80, will guide you through the development of the telecommunications sector in Brazil to help you understand how WhatsApp has become the primary means of communication between Brazilians.

From 'make a 21' to 'send a zap'

Alice is delighted with her first smartphone. It took her a year and a half to find the courage to open the box she received as a gift from her nephew. At the time, she thought it was too late to catch up with her friends, by which she meant getting in touch with them on WhatsApp. She remembers that before she had a smartphone, she could only talk to her friends who live in the countryside once a year, at Christmas, or on special occasions: call costs together with landline costs were a significant barrier to frequent communication for many decades in Brazil. When Alice was about 50, the first mobile phones arrived in the country.[1] They weighed more than 700 grams and were called 'bricks'. In the 1990s, mobile phones were a potential alternative to landlines, which cost more than the average monthly minimum wage to buy and install. For example, in 1997, a landline cost R$ 1,117.63[2]; in 2021, the monthly minimum wage is R$ 1,100[3]. Applicants had to wait two years or more after enrolling in the state programme that provided the service. At that time, Brazilians had to buy their landline number.

It was only after the privatisation of the telecommunications system in 1998 that landlines became more accessible.[4] There was no need to buy the number any more. Consumers would sign up and only pay for the service. Embratel was one of the first telecom companies to provide these services, launching long-distance call packages promoted across the country. People making the call had to add the prefix '21' before dialling the city code and the local number to choose the company. It didn't take long for the slogan 'Faz um 21' (do a 21) to become famous as a synonym for 'make a call' throughout Brazil. However, the following decade consolidated the expansion of mobile telephony as an alternative way of accessing telephone services. In 2012, 32.2 million Brazilian households were using mobile phones exclusively; mobile telephony helped to reduce the number of households without a telephone service to 8.7 per cent.[5]

Alice had a mobile phone too, but only for emergencies. In 2012, a minute-long mobile call in Brazil was among the most expensive in the world.[6] Calls made to mobile phone networks other than one's own were even more costly, so it was common for Brazilians to carry more than one device, or have more than one SIM card, in order to communicate at a lower cost.[7] Alice was frozen in time along with her landline and her mobile phone. She didn't foresee Steve Jobs introducing the iPhone in 2007,[8] or that WhatsApp would become the most popular messaging app in the world.[9] But she indirectly benefited from these changes. Mobile phone operators understood that, for smartphone users, data had become the top priority. An example of this is the amount of time people spend using the internet on mobile devices. A survey shows that Brazilians spend an average of 4 hours 41 minutes using mobile internet every day, which is more than an hour longer than the global average of 3 hours 22 minutes.[10] As a result, Brazilian mobile network operators offer plans with unlimited calls to landline numbers and mobile numbers, including numbers on other mobile phone networks.[11] Their marketing efforts are focused on data plans, which in some cases include unlimited use of WhatsApp.[12] This shift means that Alice can at last use her mobile phone to call her friends in the countryside and talk for several hours every day if she wants to. The problem is that they probably won't answer the phone. WhatsApp has become the primary means of communication among Brazilians and their first choice even for voice calls, having been installed on 98 per cent of Brazilian smartphones.[13] The motto 'Faz um 21' (make a 21) has been replaced by the popular expression 'Passa um ZAP' (send a ZAP), the nickname of WhatsApp in Brazil.

The desire to be in touch with friends and relatives made Alice join a WhatsApp course offered by one of the Catholic churches in Bento.[14] Among research participants older than 70, like her, familiarising oneself with the smartphone is a big step towards digital inclusion. In addition, 65 per cent of Brazilians access the internet exclusively through their smartphones.[15] Alice explains, 'It is as if I had opened a window and found that there is an entire world out there.' However, there are also those for whom the interface with technology is not new. Running a tech start-up at 58, Beto gets annoyed every time he realises that one of his friends is frozen in time as Alice was. 'If you are older, you created the internet. The problem is that older people are lazy. They forgot about it,' he says. Beto is right. If you take Bob Kahn and Vint Cerf, who developed the TCP/IP protocols which resulted in the creation of the internet,[16] and who are now in their eighties and seventies respectively, then one can undoubtedly say that older people created the internet. However, the 'frozen in time' trait that Beto criticises in other people is not necessarily related to laziness but to an environmental change that has made older people's access to technology difficult in Bento. Technologies are adopted first in the corporate environment, with no cost to the individual. However, as we saw in chapter 2, research participants retired early (mainly to avoid retiring after significant reforms to the national pension system were implemented, but also because of the ageism they faced from employers). It is possible to argue that retirement has, in effect, triggered their distancing from the digital revolution, which started with the internet and is now in progress with smartphones, artificial intelligence and machine learning.

Take Flávio, aged 72, for example. He worked in a bank before he retired. He resents the fact that when he asks his children for help with his computer or his smartphone, they complain, pointing out he used to work with technology at the bank. But Flávio retired 20 years ago, just as internet access providers and free email accounts were starting to spread through Brazil.[17] Carla, aged 62, retired when she was 52, five years after the inception of Facebook and in the same year (2009) as WhatsApp was launched. But this was a decade later than Flávio, so she is far more familiar with smartphones. For example, Flávio still visits his local bank branch to do his banking, while Carla manages all her payments through a banking app. One year older than Carla, Fernanda retired as recently as 2017 from a multinational company where 'technologies always came very fast'. This extra near decade in work made her entirely comfortable with technology, as she lived through the internet's evolution while working, including the mass adoption of smartphones and what became the app culture.[18] Consequently, besides using her bank app for payments, as Carla does, Fernanda uses her smartphone to shop, carry out currency exchanges, send money internationally, study foreign languages, and do many other activities.[19]

Carla would probably be jealous of Fernanda's skills if they knew each other, even if she is more than what we could consider a basic user. Carla considers herself digitally illiterate, especially when she compares her knowledge with her children's and grandchildren's:

> 'I have great difficulty dealing with the smartphone, computer and all this latest technology. But we are trying, right? Today you can't live without it. But we have a lot of difficulties. I even envy someone older who deals with the smartphone in a good way, who blows his own trumpet. Perhaps it was not my focus of interest in the past. Or maybe it wasn't a market requirement while I was working. Already the younger generation, they look like they are born tuned in. They deal with it as if it were an ordinary thing, a natural thing. They do not accept our ignorance. "I'll tell you, but you pay attention because, otherwise, next time you won't know." Children sometimes talk like that. Or when you ask them something, they tell us to go to Google, as though to say, "Don't bother me".'

In order not to disturb their children, who are often too busy or lack the patience to help them with their technological needs, older people in Bento are likely to seek the help of experts. Vania, aged 69, who attends a WhatsApp course in Bento, explains, 'Using your smartphone is like learning to drive. It's best to look for a school because a relative doesn't have the patience to teach you.' Grandchildren are also criticised. 'They solve the problem, but they don't explain how to do it. They take your smartphone and click, click, click … it's done. You ask how they did it, and they don't know how to teach you. This generation doesn't teach.' WhatsApp is the app research participants are most interested in learning because, as set out above, it addresses a concrete need, that of connecting with relatives and friends. Therefore, if smartphones open the door to digital inclusion, WhatsApp opens the door to familiarisation with smartphones. Thus, WhatsApp is the first app whose interface challenges their sense of reasoning, which is based on a linear way of thinking. Take Tereza's case. In her eighties, she started the WhatsApp course three times: 'It took me a long time to understand how this worked. I thought this technology was not for me, but I persisted nonetheless.' Now she uses WhatsApp to communicate with her employers and to ask her nephew to bring her an umbrella when the rain takes her by surprise. Despite all her progress, Tereza plans to do the course once more so as not to forget what she has learned. Vania would like to continue learning how to use WhatsApp too, but at a higher level, as she now feels ready to expand her skills. Unfortunately, she says, there are no intermediate or advanced courses for the third age, as if older people were not supposed to go beyond the basics.

Basic, but not simple

Even if they are restricted to teaching tasks at a basic user level, WhatsApp courses targeted at older people are among those most in demand in Bento. For example, at least two volunteers teach WhatsApp courses each term at one of the Catholic churches, but the current classes still do not meet local demand. For three terms, I was one of these volunteers. When I taught those classes, I found that all the students arrived with WhatsApp already installed on their smartphones (except one, Claire, to whom we will return later). The app had been installed by a relative or friend, and, as 'basic users', they knew how to send text messages and share content like pictures and videos. Yet they didn't know how to add a contact or create a group, although they were aware it was possible since they knew people who did both those things. They were at the same time excited and mistrustful. They felt too old to learn how to manage their smartphones, which they saw as designed for young users.[20] Low self-esteem was the first barrier they faced.[21] Their lack of confidence showed itself in three fears. The first was of accidentally erasing some important information, like the photos of their grandchildren singing in their school choir. Secondly, they were stressed about being charged for some service without their consent. And thirdly, they were concerned that they might 'break' the device because of their lack of ability.[22] Their devices can be a real problem. First, smartphones can turn older people into targets of robberies, cyberattacks and scams, which adds an extra layer of stress to learning and adoption. Secondly, devices can represent the very thing that makes these people's digital inclusion a nightmare.

In São Paulo city, 13 smartphones are stolen every hour,[23] and half of the streets have registered at least one occurrence per year,[24] in low-income areas as well as in higher-income ones. Consequently, it is common for people to avoid answering calls or using smartphones in public spaces, in Bento and in Brazil in general.[25] Among research participants, the most common strategy for guarding their smartphones against theft is to go inside a shopping mall or a shop if they receive a call or want to check their messages. Depending on where they are going, they may leave their smartphones at home. In chapter 3, we saw an example of this when we discussed the public squares containing gym equipment, called 'Longevity Playgrounds'. Mauro, aged 71, does this too, but he has two devices, an iPhone and a Samsung. He never travels with his iPhone in the city as he considers that that is the model thieves prefer. Another strategy is to keep the same device for as long as possible, hoping that an outdated smartphone will be less attractive to thieves. A final, more unusual, strategy is to keep a second smartphone in one's bag. This is called 'the thief's smartphone'.[26] This habit had been employed earlier in relation to handbags, especially by women who drive in the city, who may prepare bags exclusively for this possibility. These fake bags are known as 'thief's bags'. Sometimes participants combine more than one strategy to avoid having their smartphones stolen. But, even so, as Sonia, aged 59, demonstrates, they can still be taken by surprise:

> 'I rarely answer a call in the middle of the street unless I am in a group or close to police officers. If I'm out for a long time, I keep my smartphone on. But I advise close friends to send me written or voice messages through WhatsApp. I can check them in places that have a certain degree of security … a shop, a chemist's … I am always aware. However, this hasn't stopped me from getting my smartphone stolen. I was on the bus, and someone put their hand inside my bag and took it. I only noticed when I got off the bus, which was still at the bus stop. I could have gone there and talked to the driver. But my smartphone was a really old one.'

Apart from physical threats, older people have to protect themselves from scam attempts and cyberattacks circulated via fraudulent links. In the first half of 2018 alone, there were almost 26,000 attempts at virtual scams per day in Brazil.²⁷ Another report stated that up to 60.4 million Brazilians (all Android users) had been the targets of malicious links in the same year.²⁸ WhatsApp was responsible for disseminating 64.1 per cent of those links. Older people are victims of both robberies²⁹ and cyber scams (figures 5.1 and 5.2).³⁰ A man in Bento stated, 'If you have grey hair, you are already a target.' In addition, even if older people have not been victims themselves, most research participants can recount stories of violence suffered by friends, neighbours or family members.³¹ In consequence, they are always afraid.

Apart from bringing insecurity, experienced both online and offline, the device itself can be viewed as a severe barrier to learning. For example, more than half the participants carry a second-hand device they got from children, grandchildren or friends.³² Because they may be old models, they usually have memory and battery life issues. That was why Claire

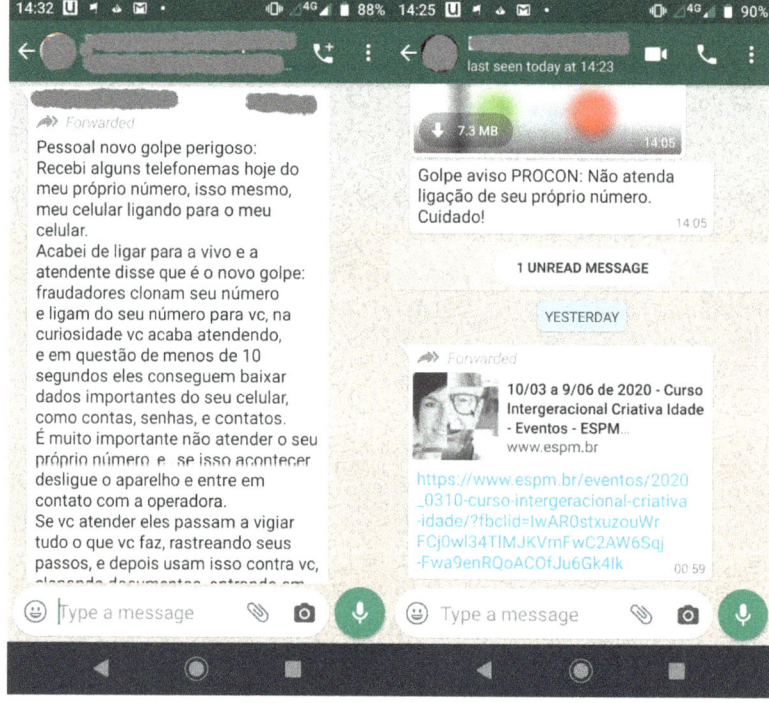

Figures 5.1 and **5.2** Messages containing alerts about new scams are constantly shared among WhatsApp groups. In both these cases the scam involves a call that appears to come from people's own phone numbers. The messages tell them never to answer the phone in those cases. Screenshots taken by © Marília Duque.

started the WhatsApp course without having the app installed onto her smartphone. She had a Mini-LG, given to her by a friend, with not enough memory left for the download. It took us three classes to erase the pictures and applications she didn't recognise before we were able to install WhatsApp. Claire had not understood that she had a very poor, outdated device. She felt it must be her that was doing something wrong, which compromised her confidence even more. Moreover, although low self-esteem can be a real constraint, together with outdated devices, interfaces generally don't recognise the natural declines related to ageing, such as the decline in motor abilities and in the capacity to process visually colours, forms, space and depth, attention, perception and memory.[33]

In other words, smartphones constantly challenge older people's motor and cognitive abilities. Among my WhatsApp students, the first difficulty often occurs when they try to tap the small space on the screen where the icon or function they want to access is. The second difficulty is understanding the difference between a tap and a long press and how the subtlety of the touch triggers different responses and shortcuts. The third difficulty is getting the brain used to the hypertextual and non-linear navigation of the smartphone. For this reason, 100 per cent of the students used pencil and paper to turn the information they receive in class into step-by-step lists. The fourth difficulty is memory. Despite having the lists, they have a problem relating their notes to the icons presented on the screen, as many of them cannot memorise the procedures which would allow them to consolidate their knowledge and expand their learning beyond WhatsApp. Finally, the fifth difficulty is understanding what smartphones are asking of them.

On the one hand, the displayed texts are confusing, the messages are long, and the letters are small. On the other hand, they hear from children and grandchildren that smartphones are intuitive, as if it were enough just to look at the device to know what to do. Therefore, overwhelmed by anxiety, they instinctively tap the screens without understanding what they are responding to. For example, during my classes, I frequently asked students to put their smartphones down and calm down while doing exercises to relax their hands and fingers. We used to laugh together as I called this practice the 'anxious finger' break (figure 5.3).

Everything on students' smartphones can be against them. Even so, with time, they gain enough confidence to recover their self-esteem. Some feel so stimulated by the sociability enabled by WhatsApp that they abandon the smartphones they got from their children, grandchildren and friends and buy, for the first time, their own smartphones. That was the case with Claire. After spending a whole semester struggling with her Mini-LG, she

Figure 5.3 Students taking notes during a WhatsApp course in Bento. © Daniel Miller.

decided to retake the Whatsapp course, but she arrived with a shiny new Samsung this time. Not all improvements are restricted to devices. Some involve upgrading one's data plan. For example, Rosangela, aged 68, thought WhatsApp was just a fashionable gimmick until she realised that the app had become the primary means of communication among her friends from school. She almost missed a celebration with them because everything was set up in their WhatsApp group. She then attended the WhatsApp course in order to join the conversation. When she started, she could only use WhatsApp when she was connected to the church's Wi-Fi. At the end of the semester, she asked her husband to buy her a mobile data plan.

Although students become more familiar with WhatsApp as the course progresses, most of them do not necessarily explore their smartphones' full potential. Therefore, as already noted, some won't do tasks like banking, searching or shopping on their smartphone because they cannot transfer their knowledge from WhatsApp to other apps. For some, their digital repertoire (the set of digital technologies they can use to meet their everyday needs, expressing their preferences, interests and skills[34]) is restricted to WhatsApp and the apps they access through links they find there. WhatsApp is also the place they might experience something close to digital literacy.[35] However, WhatsApp in itself is enough to start a revolution, both in the way users interact with family and circulate information, as we have seen in previous chapters, and in the way they engage with friends and experience the city. WhatsApp is enough to empower them as citizens, with gains in sociability, inclusion and visibility.

'WhatsApp changed my life'

Romulo, aged 68, divides his life into two periods: before and after WhatsApp. By managing multiple WhatsApp groups, he has built an intensive social life not restricted to online interactions. Through these connections, he becomes aware of many activities, courses, and events aimed at the third age in Bento. He explains that now, with WhatsApp, he has 'so many places to go, so many people to meet'. Many of his friends on WhatsApp are people he met in activities he attended in the past. As seen in Romulo's case, WhatsApp structures a feedback mechanism: from WhatsApp connections to face-to-face encounters to new WhatsApp connections. In other words, WhatsApp challenges the idea that, with age, social networks tend to become smaller[36] as older people experience events like children living home, retirement, health problems (motor limitations, for example) and the deaths of relatives and friends.[37] Instead, WhatsApp provides older people in Bento with a growing number of connections that expand their awareness and interests around opportunities for learning, self-improvement, leisure and socialising.[38]

This expanded connectivity and sociability keep research participants active in two different ways. Not only do they act as active content curators, as seen in chapter 3, selecting and sharing information they believe is relevant to their peers, but these tips also take them out of the home (or 'off the couch', as they say) to do something. With invitations popping up every day, they leave their private space to experience a city that reflects their needs and is made visible by their intense exchanges on WhatsApp. This new routine challenges the very notion of retirement. If we look closely at the etymology of the Portuguese term 'aposentado' (retired), the word means 'one who rests in a room'.[39] However, older people no longer fit this place of reclusion. Instead, and with WhatsApp as an ally, they just refuse to retire from their social and productive life.

If an invitation to a new event comes from a person they know well, even better. That was how Alice came to be in one of the WhatsApp classes at the Catholic church in Bento. She heard about the course from a neighbour, then invited a friend, who brought her sister along too. The familiar faces were the incentive she needed to overcome her fears. They started the course together and left with a new WhatsApp group. At the time of writing, two years after Alice and her two friends finished the course and more than one year after the beginning of the Covid-19 pandemic, this WhatsApp group is still active, and so are others that were started to support activities that took place during the fieldwork.

Sometimes the messages exchanged are only 'good morning, good evening and good night' visual messages, which reproduce the phatic function used to check and maintain the connection, as observed in the extended family group described in the previous chapter. However, there are groups, like the one dedicated to meditation, in which members continue to practise, but now on WhatsApp. WhatsApp challenges the term 'aposentado' again. Because of the social isolation adopted during the pandemic, participants are 'installed in a room' at home. But they are neither alone nor unproductive, as they are still interacting, acting as content curators and engaging in online activities.[40]

WhatsApp even challenges the common sense older people in Bento shared before social isolation. They were the first to reproduce discourses that claimed that smartphones cause isolation and addiction, especially in the younger generation. Olívio, aged 56, explains:

> 'You might do your shopping through your smartphone. You might do your banking. You might do a lot of things. You can use your smartphone to do everything. Did you get that? What I don't like is when someone becomes addicted. I don't stay connected 24 hours a day. But all the people, I mean the majority of people, just can't live without their smartphone. It is like they are not paying attention to the street. They don't pay attention to life. People, especially teenagers, may commit suicide if someone on social media says something about them, breaks up a relationship or does some kind of bullying. There are people who commit suicide, who do these kinds of crazy things. I think that is absurd!'

Olívio argues that his smartphone 'sleeps' and 'goes to the gym' to highlight when he is not online. He sees himself as the opposite of his 'addicted' brother, who has two smartphones and is constantly interacting with his devices. However, he is not that different. As stated in chapter 2, Olívio is 'not working at the moment', and social media (mainly WhatsApp) fills a significant part of his day. When he is not 'working' on multiple platforms to find a job, he interacts with people, many of whom are colleagues from previous jobs. By doing this, he avoids the sense that he is drifting away from work-oriented Bento. Instead, he feels he is still there working and having fun with his colleagues. He is so immersed in this routine that, even though he is unemployed, he gets confused about his smartphone's ownership; sometimes he refers to it as a corporate device given to him by his employer. Even so, what counts is that he can continue to enjoy the sociability the business environment provides.

Besides ex-colleagues from work, WhatsApp brings friends from childhood and youth back into research participants' lives, like a time machine. As we observed of the extended family in the previous chapter, these interactions, once restricted to annual events, are now embedded in everyday conversations.

Among older people in Bento smartphones are much more likely to be responsible for intensifying their social activity than to lead to isolation. However, the feeling that everything is happening on WhatsApp or is due to WhatsApp raises a different type of anxiety.[41] What happens if someone older decides to leave WhatsApp? Will this person be believed to be dead (or old)? Do they have a choice? Earlier in this chapter, we addressed how research participants looked for WhatsApp classes because they felt excluded from groups they used to get in touch with by phone or face to face only. But it is Ricardo, aged 64, who best puts these feelings into words:

> 'I started thinking a little more seriously about leaving social media. I am in a WhatsApp group with some friends. I guess there are 50 of us. We have been friends since we were kids. In the same way, there are groups where women post pictures of naked men … in groups of men … someone posted something like that, and one of my friends then asked to leave the group. I don't know – his wife might see his smartphone, who knows? Everyone insisted that he should stay. He sent us an email at the time, explaining to everyone that he doesn't like social media. I started asking myself: should I leave, too? What happens if I leave? Is there anything I could read about it? If you leave, are you off the market? Out of the world? We don't often find things to read about this. But sometimes I want to leave. Do you know what I don't like? The messages keep coming, I hear the sound alert, and I become anxious to see it. And I don't want to be a prisoner inside this.'

The attention demanded by this extended and intense social life can drive research participants to the same addiction they criticise in young people. However, this is not a contradiction but a different perspective. While younger people are labelled as addicted to the smartphone as an object, participants claim they are addicted to the people and sociability they can only experience *because* of smartphones. As argued above, they might experience anxiety, but, equally, they are entertained by the fact there is always something happening on WhatsApp (figure 5.4).

Figure 5.4 Older people in Bento have become intense users of social media, like the younger generations they criticise. Photograph taken during a social event in Bento. © Marília Duque.

Even when interactions are restricted to online exchanges, the co-presence of friends on WhatsApp makes them feel they are not alone. This can change everything, especially for those whose mobility is diminished or who need emotional support.[42] Rosana, aged 72, remembers the importance of being on WhatsApp when she was hospitalised, for example. She says, 'Knowing my friends were there was my great joy. To know what they were doing and everything that was happening to them gave me the strength to recover.' Carla, aged 62, also recognises the value of this co-presence. In the WhatsApp group that she maintains with her friends, there is always someone awake, sending messages throughout the night. She considers this important, especially for those friends who are now widows and need to be supported to adapt to a new life without their partner.

> 'I have a group with eight women friends. We used to work together, 20, maybe 30 years ago. It is funny because we are at different stages of life. One has just become a widow. Another is getting divorced. Another is single. There is this nostalgia. We have very different experiences. The one who became a widow, we followed her during the whole process. People can be lonely. Some are now widowed and live by themselves because they don't want to leave their houses. The smartphone helps in these cases. We are on WhatsApp. Even at dawn, you will find people having a "big talk" there.'

Sometimes the support provided through WhatsApp can help solve practical problems encountered in daily life. For example, Mauro, aged 71, was looking for a WhatsApp course because he wanted to learn how to create a group on WhatsApp. He had volunteered as a teacher on one of the courses aimed at the third age in Bento and needed a WhatsApp group to facilitate communication with his students. In practice, the WhatsApp group has gone well beyond this function. Mauro gets all sorts of questions and cries for help, all from his female students. He feels overwhelmed and complains that he has too many requests. However, this provides him with a sense of utility and fulfilment. He once taught a student how to file a police report after a robbery and helped another to buy a bus ticket with a seniors' discount by accompanying her to the central bus terminal. A third student had to have a medical test done and thought about doing it at one of the low-cost clinics available in Bento. But she did not know how the clinic works and was afraid to go there alone to find out. He had to accompany her. He explains that it is easier for a friend to help these female friends, because their children and husbands won't.

Mauro believes this is the main difference between young and older people. 'When young people make a mistake, they laugh at themselves. We become embarrassed.' Smartphones allow older people in Bento, embarrassed or not, to go to places and take up opportunities they have become aware of through WhatsApp. Together with WhatsApp, Uber and Google Maps are the apps that help research participants move across the city, giving them the autonomy to enjoy their freedom while allowing them to be seen as busy. Google Maps also symbolises the moment they abandon their car to discover public transport, which is now free for them. Some of them have just started to take the bus and the train for the first time. That is the case with Fernanda, who combines Google Maps with Moovit, an app for urban mobility. 'I love it! I check the app and then just leave home five minutes before the bus comes,' she says. Uber works as a complement to public transport. It is mainly used at night, extending the time in which older people can travel safely. For Mauro, this means that he doesn't accept his female friends' excuse for not going out to dance (figure 5.5), that they are afraid to go home late at night. 'Call an Uber, for Christ's sake,' he says. For Fernanda, this means that she and her husband can enjoy drinking with friends without being concerned about the 'Lei Seca' (dry law), the law that sets out Brazil's zero-tolerance approach to drinking and driving.[43]

However, the world outside WhatsApp is not always as friendly and accessible. Take Tereza, for example. She used to ask the doorman of her residential building to call her an Uber. If he was not available, she would stop someone on the street and ask for help. Mauro had a different problem. When he used the app for the first time, he selected the 'Uber Pool' option, designed for people who want to share a trip to save money. He ended up doing an extended tour through Bento with people he had never seen before, an experience that made him feel insecure. Commonly, research participants feel frustrated and embarrassed when they try a

Figure 5.5 Saturday evening in a dance club in Bento. The lady at the table brought both her smartphone and her charger to the event. © Marília Duque.

new app. The comfort they feel inside WhatsApp is then challenged. However, through arrangements with friends and relatives and with a lot of creativity, each of them will find their particular way of getting round their limitations, which we will discuss in the following sections.

Whose smartphone is this?

Downloading the apps they want and setting them up for use is one of the first barriers research participants encounter outside WhatsApp. Usually, when they get stuck, they will ask a friend for help.[44] However, it is hard for them to accept that the knowledge they have accumulated throughout their lives seems worthless when they find themselves lost in Google Play or the Apple Store.[45] Their embarrassment may worsen if they expose their lack of ability to a friend, so they set up a mutual agreement. The friend who needs help says he or she is lazy and doesn't want to learn, while the other does the downloading without questioning anything, as only good friends do. That is what happens with Rita, aged 70. She is very proud of all the books she has read, all the courses she has taken throughout her life and everything she has learned about holistic therapies, herbs, nutrition, meditation and yoga. She makes her own apple vinegar. She manages a vertical garden inside her apartment. She knows everything about composting at home. But when she wants to download an app she asks a friend, with the excuse: 'I could learn how to do it if I wanted to. But I am lazy. And I don't have the time.' The problem is that friends often think they know what is best for us. In such cases, friends will download the app they were asked to but will also install apps they believe the friend might like. This 'proactivity' explains why Eduardo, aged 59, ended up with 104 apps installed on his phone, including Transcriber, Shazam, Teamviewer, Spotify and Trivago. He hasn't a clue what those apps are for, but he doesn't care. He has a new Motorola Lenovo with plenty of memory, and he has no difficulty finding the apps he wants to use.

In some cases, however, things get out of control. Among research participants, this can mean a loss of control of their smartphones. They end up not recognising a significant proportion of the apps installed on their phone. Sometimes, the problem is pre-installed apps that come with the device. Others are apps installed by the previous owner, as many of them have second-hand devices. There are also apps that they downloaded and then abandoned because they didn't know how to set them up, apps they used once or twice in the past, and apps kept on standby because they may want to use them sometime in the future.[46] For most of them, the apps will stay precisely where they were put automatically when the download was complete. There is no organisation or priority within the smartphone screens. For example, one might expect that the most frequently used apps would be on the home screen or organised in specific folders according to their function. Luisa's phone is like this, but she is an exception. She has more than 90 apps, all organised into folders based on different categories: utilities, planners, banking apps, social media, finances, transport, music, shopping, health, lifestyle, discounts, travel, leisure, and photos and videos.

Olívio is a more typical example of the mess that research participants' smartphones can be. He doesn't know the utility of, or even recognise, 20 of the 42 apps installed on his phone. He was surprised when he realised that only three of the six apps he considers priority apps are on his home screen, as he believed that at least his home screen was under control.

> 'There are a lot of things that I don't use, but that I have used before. There are a lot of things that you don't use any more. You use it once, and then you don't use it any more. You just leave them there. I have a lot of things, but I use one-third of everything I have. I put in the front [on the home screen] the things I use the most, things that I need, that I need to access easily.'

Similarly to him, Rita recognises only five of the 10 apps she keeps on her home screen, and of these there are only two that she uses, and those only rarely. She has 45 apps installed on her iPhone, but uses only 23. But nobody can compete with Iara, aged 72. She recognises only 20 of the 55 apps she has installed on her smartphone:

> 'I don't know what this is. Many things appear out of nowhere and I don't know what they are for. So, I ignore them. I don't know what to do with this …. I tried to delete it, but I don't know what to do with it, so I ignore them.'

Eduardo, Rita and Iara have in common that they don't know how to download or uninstall their apps. The lack of ability to use certain apps results in a new kind of collaboration among relatives to solve families' practical affairs. In cases like these, apps are distributed across different smartphones according to the responsibilities allocated to each family member and taking into account the limitations of the older ones. It is as though the family personalises a smartphone for collective use but with the apps distributed across different devices. That is the case with Flávio's family. He is 72 years old, and lives with his wife, his son and his daughter. Together they manage the letting of their second apartment on Airbnb. Flávio is not familiar with the platform. So his children are in charge of managing the reservations, confirmations and payments, while he is responsible for communicating with guests on WhatsApp. Waze is another example of how apps can be 'shared' among relatives. Olívio doesn't drive, but he has Waze for the times he is 'co-piloting' with his brother.

In couples, the synergy is even greater. For example, Cesar, aged 68, is an artist whose wife has always been in charge of the couple's practical affairs. He has his bank and health insurance plan apps on his phone, but it is his wife that uses them. Paulo, aged 56, has many cases of Alzheimer's in his family. He avoids talking about it, but he likes to exercise his memory by playing the games installed on his wife's smartphone. In Carla's case, this collaborative model has resulted in extra work for her. Now aged 62, she was the first in the family after her children to have a smartphone. Her husband was reluctant to adopt the new technology, but he shared her contact details with his patients because he worked as a doctor. For two years, she managed their requests on the telephone or WhatsApp. She still handles all of the couple's accounts through her smartphone, including the finances from her husband's clinic. 'He doesn't know even the password to his bank account,' she says. The distribution of tasks may reproduce the family dynamics established before smartphones came onto the scene. That is the case with Carla. She always managed the couple's finances, even before she had a smartphone. However, sometimes dependence is established according to how comfortable each family member is with technology. Rosangela, aged 68, used her husband's email address until recently. She was never keen on technology and, as he checks his emails every day, it seemed convenient to share the same address. He would tell her if any email was addressed to her. The same thing happened with driving. Since her husband retired, he has always been available to drive her to places, so she gave up driving as she got used to getting lifts from him. Things changed when she finished her WhatsApp course. She wanted a Gmail account to manage her app downloads, including Uber. The app was previously installed on her husband's smartphone only, but she went out with a friend once and couldn't find a taxi, and he wasn't available to call her an Uber or drive her home. To avoid these constraints, she now has her own Gmail and Uber accounts. With or without adjustments like these, in the end what counts is that the family gets the job done.

That is the very essence of the relationship research participants have with their smartphones. They don't care about apps. They are interested in and excited about how smartphones can help them solve the problems they face at this stage of their lives. To achieve this kind of solutionism,[47] they will overcome their limitations relating to downloads and new apps. They will work creatively to solve all sorts of issues, using what they have to hand. As Garattini and Prendergast claim, older people don't want to be reminded of what they cannot do. Instead, they want to focus on what they can do.[48] The following section focuses on what participants do with their smartphones to achieve what they need, and what can be learned from that.

The unpredictable app

To understand how older people in Bento use their smartphones to get things done, we have first to abandon the idea of the smartphone as a repository of apps. I conducted interviews in which I asked each participant to open up their phone to me and show me all the apps they have and how they use them. During the interviews, I found that people didn't interact with any app as a whole. Nobody does. We interact with one function at a time. For example, when we say we use Facebook, we are not using Facebook in its entirety. Instead, we select one specific function which gets closer to the solution we are looking for. Let's take the birthday function to illustrate how it works. When someone wants to check on Facebook if today is someone's birthday, everything the platform provides as resources and tools will be reduced to this single function: a birthday reminder. That is how Flávio, aged 72, perceives Facebook, as he only uses the platform for this purpose. In other words, as a metaphor, it doesn't matter if Facebook is a Swiss army knife. If you have a bottle of wine to open, all you need, and will use, is a corkscrew.

By applying such selection, users go from complexity (everything an app can offer) to simplicity (the specific function they need and can manage). However, to solve everyday problems, people may combine more than one function. Most of the time, these functions are picked up from different apps. Two factors define the kind of bricolage research participants do: a technological constraint or a personal preference.[49] The term *gambiarra* can be helpful for understanding the first one. In Portuguese, *gambiarra* describes someone who fraudulently taps into the electricity supply (figure 5.6).[50] In everyday life, the word also refers to an improvised solution achieved with limited resources. This improvised solution is triggered when older people in Bento have difficulty using apps other than those they are familiar with. They often abandon the app that contains the function that could quickly solve their problem because they don't know how to use it. Instead, they go back to the apps they are familiar with and select a combination of functions that achieve the same or a similar result.

That is the case with Rita and Flávio. They do not understand how Google Calendar works on their smartphones, so they do a *gambiarra*. They organise their activities by using apps like Notes and Remember. They then use the smartphone's alarm to remind them of events as they come up. Rita loves to research on Google, and she is concerned not to lose a result she considers interesting. She could easily use Evernote, for example, to save and file these results. However, this would demand the download and set-up of a new app, something Rita struggles with, as mentioned above. Thus she opens a new window on Google Chrome every time she looks for something new, or she copies the address and saves it on her Notes app. Sandra provides another example of how older people in Bento come up with creative solutions to overcome their technological limitations. Aged 69, she uses the public health system (SUS). In São Paulo, the SUS has developed the app 'Agenda Fácil' to allow users to schedule appointments with doctors and provide them with a digital version of their SUS identification card. Sandra downloaded the app but couldn't set up her account. She came up with a *gambiarra*. Sandra used her camera to take a photo of her SUS card and saved the

Figure 5.6 Example of *gambiarra*. © Hélvio Romero.

image on Google Drive in a folder in which she now keeps a digital copy of her primary documents. When she has a doctor's appointment, she opens the picture file on her smartphone to show it to the attendant or the doctor.

What we called *gambiarra* was observed by Katrien Pype[51] during her work in Kinshasa. She describes how the idea that technology can solve everything is embedded in official discourses about smart cities in the Democratic Republic of Congo. However, far from the Congolese call for progress, the reality on the ground is that cities suffer from poor infrastructure and restricted access to the internet, which is a key resource for feeding the smartness of smart cities. She presents examples of how people create surprising solutions to bypass these constraints. Pype called this creativity 'smartness from below'. The *gambiarra* observed among research participants in Bento is the embodiment of this smartness. In other words, smartphones are not smart per se. They are smart in responding and when responding to a demand. With that in mind, it would be fair to say that smartphones don't solve problems on their own. People do. And they do so every time they put functions together, solving puzzles to improve life.

Besides overcoming limitations, the way research participants engage with multiple apps expresses their preferences. The same problem can be solved in numerous ways through a tailored process that will vary from one person to another. For example, Carla is highly organised and in charge of her family's finances. She puts all her to-do lists into her calendar on Google, including bills that have to be paid. Most of the statements come by email. When the right day comes, she accesses her bank app to make the payment. When she needs to send a proof of payment to a provider, she shares it by using her bank app's function, which includes the option of sharing it on WhatsApp. But Carla could do it all differently, as Sandra does. Sandra's main concern is not sharing receipts with providers but saving them to help her organise her monthly budget. She prefers to take a screenshot of the receipt and keep it on Google Drive, where she also keeps digital copies of her primary documents, as mentioned above. By doing that, she chooses a solution different from the one designed by the developers of her bank app (she could automatically send a copy of the proof of payment to herself by email, for example). Sandra has thus taken a 'desire line'. In urban design, 'desire lines' are the paths people create to go from point A to point B in the way they consider fastest or easiest.[52] For example, in a park it is common to see informal paths worn in the grass, which differ from the footpaths created before the space was open to the public (figure 5.7). The same kind of 'disobedience' was observed among research participants, who chose different processes and functions to go from problem A to solution B. This combination is unpredictable, as it proceeds from personal choices and preferences even if it is influenced by participants' digital skills.

Together, the *gambiarra* and 'desire lines' approaches can be combined to suggest that when research participants in Bento want to use their smartphones to solve a problem, they can make use of an 'unpredictable app'. The 'unpredictable app' is the sum of the multiple sequences of steps, functions or apps that older people put together to get things done without the help of their children, grandchildren or friends. It emerges in the moment of need and suits one's preferences. It is unique and has subjective value.[53] The 'unpredictable app' involves a set of combinations and appropriations that express a kind of smartness that can't be anticipated and may challenge the apps as developers have imagined them.[54] However, this doesn't mean they are less effective. Instead, this tactic seems to solve research participants' problems, including managing their expanded social lives, being in and experiencing the city, searching for information, and accessing health services.

Figure 5.7 Example of 'desire line'. © wetwebwork. CC BY 2.0.

In the end, good is good enough

In this chapter, we have addressed how smartphones have become a mechanism for both exclusion and inclusion for older people in Bento. Because communication with family and friends has migrated to WhatsApp, research participants have felt compelled to join the conversation even if they are afraid of adopting the new technology that they had associated with youth. Some of them had become frozen in time because they retired very early, leaving the corporate environment in which technology comes at no cost to the employee. When they found that their children and grandchildren didn't have the time or the goodwill to support them in their learning, many of them looked for professional help, joining smartphone use courses aimed at the third age in Bento. WhatsApp courses are their priority, even if they are already basic users of the app. WhatsApp has become the app responsible for promoting their first step into digital inclusion, leading to their empowerment as citizens, and expanding their social lives and their access to the city. WhatsApp makes research participants aware of the opportunities and activities they can enjoy during retirement, which will give them the feeling that they are always busy. On the one hand, as their participation in these activities is made visible on social networks, it works as a proof of productivity, which is more than welcome in work-oriented Bento. On the other hand, there are side effects to this increased social life, which demands time and attention in a way they were not used to.

Together with WhatsApp, apps related to mobility, such as Google Maps and Uber, will help older people in Bento move from the invitations they receive in their online groups to face-to-face encounters. In these events, they may make new friends and be included in new WhatsApp groups in a looping feedback mechanism. However, as well as socialising and having fun with friends, participants have to deal with practical affairs which might demand the use of new apps. The problem is that the world outside WhatsApp can be hostile to them. Every new app is a challenge, starting with its download and set-up. Some will struggle with this, but generally that does not stop them from getting things done. With a bit of help from their friends and by combining features of different apps they are getting used to, older people in Bento will find ways to unlock the smartness of their smartphones. In so doing, they create what I call an 'unpredictable app', a personalised method of putting different functions together to make their lives smarter. This bricolage challenges the way developers conceive apps, as it expresses creative responses to specific needs. It doesn't matter if there is a bespoke app that could do the same thing research participants use five apps to achieve. What matters is whether their solution worked or not. As the following chapter shows, this smartness can be a lifesaver when one is managing health and care.

Notes

1. InfoMoney 2010.
2. Guerreiro 1999.
3. Agência Senado 2021.
4. Guerreiro 1999.
5. Gomes 2013.
6. G1 2013.
7. ReclameAqui Notícias 2016.
8. Pangambam 2007.
9. Statista Research Department 2021b.
10. Kemp 2020.
11. Minha Operadora 2017.
12. Demartini 2018.
13. Panorama Mobile Time/Opinion Box 2021.
14. The outcomes of this desire to connect with friends and family can be seen in a survey conducted among Brazilians in 2018. Friendship and family were the most frequently reported group ties on WhatsApp, at 91.8 per cent and 83.6 per cent respectively (Garcia & Vivacqua 2021).
15. Cetic.br 2020.
16. National Inventors Hall of Fame 2021.
17. Brasil OnLine (BOL) is an example. The internet provider launched a free email service, with the motto 'All Brazilians deserve free email' (Karasinski 2009).
18. Morris & Murray 2018.
19. Fernanda's smartphone reflects the fact she has a child living abroad. In addition to her interest in learning a new language, she has an app for sending money abroad, which supports the argument presented in earlier chapters that parents may continue to support adult children living abroad.
20. Tetley et al. (2015) observed that in classroom-based training programmes older people fear not having the basic skills needed to learn. That fear, and the way people see technology in general, are shaped by social influences that surpass the technology itself, they claim. In Bento, this fear is associated with the belief that smartphones only suit the younger generation, a discourse associated with ageism and reinforced by children in their bargain for power while they still live with their parents, as seen in the previous chapter.
21. A Pew Research Center study shows that lack of confidence is one of the main barriers to technology adoption among older adults in the US. The same study argues that older people need help to start using a new device to go online. However, once they are online, they show a high degree of engagement with devices and content (Anderson & Perrin 2017). The same was observed during the WhatsApp courses in Bento. As older adults become more confident, they become heavy users of WhatsApp.
22. The same fear was observed by Cajita et al. (2018) among older adults; it could result in a reluctance to use mobile technology.
23. Henrique 2019.
24. Estado de S. Paulo 2018.
25. According to a Mobile Time/Opinion Box survey (2021), 83 per cent of Brazilians avoid using smartphones in public spaces because they fear being the victim of an assault. The stolen smartphones may be resold in black markets, like the one observed by Souza e Silva et al. (2019) in Rio de Janeiro. As they explain, the circulation of devices from legal to illegal to legal spheres shapes the way people use them, depending on where they are in the commodity chain.
26. Rocha 2017.

27 Kravezuk 2018.
28 Oh 2019.
29 SBT 2019.
30 A study showed that during the social isolation due to Covid-19 the number of financial scams aimed at older people in Brazil increased by 60 per cent (Melo 2020).
31 Thirty-five per cent of smartphone users in Brazil have been victims of robbery or assault at least once. Of those, 24 per cent are aged 50 or above (Mobile Time/Opinion Box 2021).
32 Among the 36 interviewed participants who answered this question, 20 received their smartphones from someone else. Among the 16 participants who had bought their own smartphones, eight don't have children. In Brazil, 14 per cent of the smartphones in use are second-hand. 23 per cent of Brazilians own a smartphone that they were given. Of these, 29 per cent are second-hand. Brazilians keep their smartphones for two years and three months on average (Mobile Time/Opinion Box 2021).
33 According to E. Rocha and Padovani (2016), some of the motor changes are located in the haptic system, affecting joints and muscles that account for the decrease in the hand's tactile sensitivity. Other changes affect the visual system, compromising the processing of space, depth, colours and shapes. In respect of cognitive changes, the authors highlight limitations in attention, perception and memory. The authors point to flaws in the design of interfaces that do not provide a sense of context or feedback on the actions performed, which may result in the disorientation of older people during their interaction with smartphones.
34 Hänninen et al. 2021.
35 Even if research participants sometimes feel lost or frustrated using WhatsApp, they apply their acquired skills to their social context as they use the platform to produce meaning and communicate. Moreover, because of their use, WhatsApp empowers them as citizens, becoming the platform on which participants are informed of the opportunities aimed at the third age in the city. Thus this set of skills can be seen as competencies, as described by Martin and Grudziecki (2006) in their review of the concept of literacy in the information society. They highlight the shift from a functional approach to a reflexive/transformative approach. The way research participants use WhatsApp and how it impacts on their social context place them in the reflexive/transformative approach, even though their digital literacy may be restricted to WhatsApp.
36 For example, in their work with older Americans Cornwell et al. (2008) found that age is negatively related to network size (although in this case network size didn't define social connectedness during the life-course).
37 Gouveia et al. 2016.
38 In his analysis of social networks, Granovetter (1973) highlighted the role weak ties play in bringing information and opportunities for interaction into communities and sharing them. In the 1990s, Rheingold (2000) made a similar observation but focused on internet communities based on shared interests. He suggested that online communities could encourage people to take up in-person activities and provide mutual support (including material support) for their members. The same dynamics are observed on older people's WhatsApp groups in Bento. The network is expanded, to include people they don't know well. Still, this diversity improves their access to information and to opportunities for in-person encounters, and to mutual support between members.
39 Houaiss et al. 2011, p.258.
40 During the pandemic, the collective that used to meet once a week to discuss work possibilities in old age developed more than a dozen weekly activities in Zoom. However, the WhatsApp group is still a place where members can find out about the group schedules (and links to Zoom's meetings) and discuss the topics they are interested in (Duque 2021). Another example is the WhatsApp group created by the Coordenação de Políticas para Pessoa Idosa (Unit for Coordinating Policies for the Elderly) within the Secretaria Municipal de Direitos Humanos e Cidadania (SMDHC; Human Rights and Citizenship Secretariat). Implemented seven days after social distancing was adopted in São Paulo, the WhatsApp group provides online activities that address physical exercise, leisure activities and mental health support for 200 participants (Gomes 2021).
41 In the networked society, Castells (1996) argues that the two dimensions that shape human practices, time and space, are transformed by a mediated communication system which results in a space of fluxes and in an always present experience of time. Harvey (1989) considers how this compression of time and space demands new forms to reflect and interact with the world. The amount of information produced and consumed by the subject can lead to an experience of disorientation. The Fear of Missing Out (FOMO) syndrome can be seen as

42 an outcome of this unbearable flux of information, leading people to remain connected online. A Brazilian survey found that the fear of missing an opportunity or of being excluded is a reason why people stay connected on WhatsApp groups, even the ones they would like to leave (Garcia & Vivacqua 2021).
42 The network formed by friends and neighbours is strongly associated with quality of life in old age (Larson et al. 1986; Gouveia et al. 2016). For research participants, their co-presence on WhatsApp groups provides what Paúl (2005) called 'perceived support', the belief that connections might be available to help in case of need. The next chapter will address the network's consequences for autonomy and access to healthcare in Bento.
43 G1 2018.
44 Relatives and friends work as 'warm experts', as opposed to 'cold experts' who provide professional IT support. Warm experts are close personal connections who support new users to navigate through technology to meet concrete demands, taking into account their backgrounds and needs (Hänninen et al. 2021).
45 Otaegui (2021), who worked on digital inclusion in Santiago, Chile, made the same observation. He pointed out that older adults who had a professional career can feel that their experience is useless when applied to smartphones. It is a new field of knowledge with new demands and skills. As one of his research participants said, it is like 'starting from square one'.
46 An example (discussed in the next chapter) is the nutritional apps that people plan to incorporate into their lives as part of their adoption of healthy behaviours with the aim of ageing well.
47 Morozov introduces 'solutionism' as a critique of the idea that every problem could and should be solved by computer technology. He argues that this ideology can simplify or ignore the complex social nature of problems and needs just to fit 'the quick-and-easy solutionist tool kit'. In addition, there is the question of what a problem is and to whom (Morozov 2013, p. 6). That 'tool kit' is what research participants challenge when they adopt an unpredictable solution to deal with the real problems they face in everyday life in Bento.
48 Garattini & Prendergast 2015.
49 This bricolage is based on the digital repertoire research participants have developed. In their study with older adults in Finland, Hänninen et al. (2021, p. 5) found that their digital repertoires are developed according to their personal interests and skills, the devices and applications available, and the support they receive from their close connections, which results in a 'set of meaningful practices' that aim to respond to their everyday needs.
50 Houaiss et al. 2001, p. 1423.
51 Pype 2017.
52 Malone 2019.
53 Value can vary as it reflects a subjective perspective (Davies 2016).
54 Certeau (2011) argues that consumers are also producers, as they transform products through their creative and unpredicted appropriation. The author calls this inventiveness the 'poetics' of everyday life.

6
Crafting health

Be healthy or leave

In 1991, Peter Laslett[1] proposed a particular way of approaching age detached from chronological age. He defined the stage of life when people are free from obligations relating to work and children as the 'third age'. The financial security provided by retirement and the availability of time for themselves would bring together the ideal conditions for older people to seek self-realisation and pleasure without judgement. In practice, as shown in previous chapters, the third age allows research participants to try almost everything. They may have their first tattoo or launch a start-up. They may deny the very notion of retirement while enjoying an intense social life that encourages them to spend time in the city. The third age is, therefore, the right to come and go ('With Uber, everything is easier'), the freedom to say what they want ('I am older, I can say this') and to pursue their wishes ('We don't only have needs, we have desires'). However, as conceived by Laslett, the third age is also a kind of conditional contract[2] as it depends upon certain things. This means that the freedom and pleasure reserved for the third age are conditional upon maintaining one's health. Once they lose their physical or mental autonomy (they are likely to have financial autonomy because of their pensions), older people no longer belong in their third age.

For these cases, the author proposed another category, the 'fourth age', which is the stage between the onset of frailties, and decline and death. As a consequence of the natural decline of ageing, losing autonomy implies the loss of governance of the self.[3] In the end, the fourth age may be subject to the will of others. That is the reason older people in Bento and in Brazil generally don't fear death.[4] Instead, they fear everything the fourth age represents. On the one hand, dependence leads to a kind of accountability, as older people may negotiate the boundaries of their freedom with their children.[5] To Lourdes, aged 64, this may mean she won't be *allowed* to undertake the facelift she wants, as her daughter thinks it is not needed or appropriate at this age. To Lúcio, aged 76, this may mean he will be *forced* to use the walking stick his daughter has bought for him, which he deliberately carries under his arm just to defy her.

On the other hand, research participants don't want to be a burden to their children (figure 6.1). First, depending on how demanding their own experience of caring for their elderly parents was, they will genuinely want to save their children from 'suffering the same fate'. Secondly, they don't want to be a distraction, an obstacle to their children's careers, whose professional achievement they value. However, as the interviews showed, the desire not to be a burden can also be a strategy to hide the fact that they believed their adult children, even those still living with them, would not take care of them at the end of their lives.

What explains this lack of reciprocity? The explanation lies in a consensus that 'times have changed', that children no longer have the obligation to take care of their parents. But there is something else. Research participants believe they should take care of themselves. This chapter addresses how the *intergenerational contract* is replaced by the construction of autonomy as a virtue[6] and how participants respond to this moral demand. It means deciding on their health and care strategies for the present and the future. As we will see, smartphones help research participants to manage their health and prolong their time in the third age. However, this doesn't necessarily mean they will comply with the participatory health system conceived by Telemedicine 2.0.[7] Instead, participants will find informal ways to achieve care and medical guidance based on their connections on WhatsApp.

The future before death

Whyte argues that Successful Ageing discourses overlap 'the intergenerational contract' in which parents take care of their children until they need their children to take care of them.[8] This agreement of reciprocity is based on moral obligations established within a cultural context. However, in the Successful Ageing perspective, the moral obligation is placed on the individual,[9] who is expected to remain healthy in order to avoid demanding resources from society. This is not the only reason that leads older people in Bento to say they don't want to be a

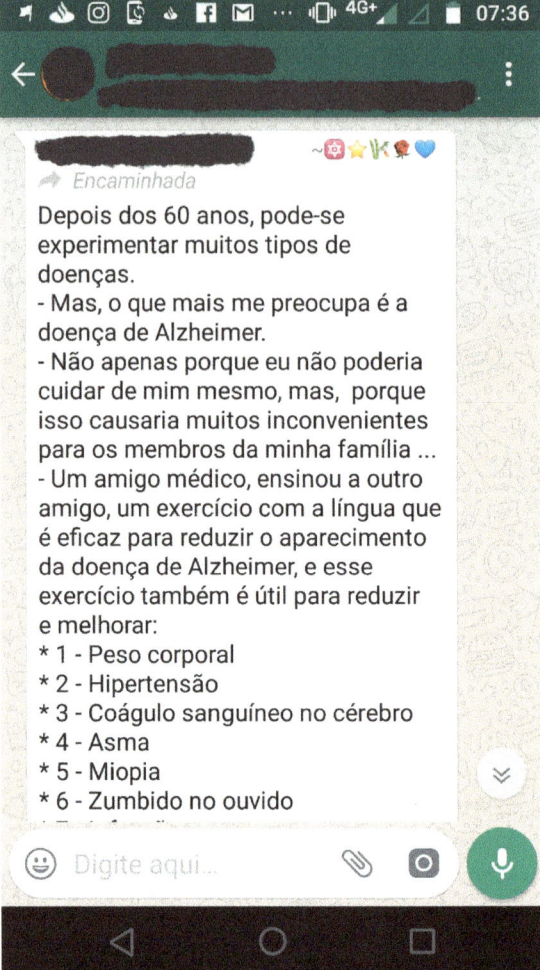

Figure 6.1 Example of a message shared on a WhatsApp group of people over 60. The message consists of guidelines attributed to a 'doctor friend' for preventing Alzheimer's. One of the reasons for taking the exercises recommended is the inconvenience Alzheimer's would bring to the family. 'After 60, we experience many kinds of diseases. However, what worries me most is Alzheimer's. It's not just because I wouldn't be able to take care of myself. It is also because it would cause a lot of inconvenience for my family members ... A doctor friend of mine taught another friend a tongue exercise which is effective in preventing Alzheimer's. This exercise is also useful for reducing and improving weight, hypertension, blood clots in the brain, asthma, myopia, ringing in the ear ....' Screenshot taken by Marília Duque.

burden to their children. As I argued in chapter 4, the idea that their children should devote themselves exclusively to work comes with the feeling that their children are likely to leave them without care. Nelson, aged 58, a father of two, explains:

> 'Our children are not worried about us. They are worried about their work, their stuff. Our children have to take care of their own lives. I take care of myself in order not to be a burden. I know there might be a time in the future when I might be a burden. Who knows? At least I do everything I can to take care of myself and be in better health. I take care of what I eat to be in better health.'

Indeed, with or without children, research participants share the same feeling: they might be on their own in the future. Couples without children, for example, joke about who is expected to die first. Amelia, aged 61, wants to die first in order not to miss her husband after his death. But she realises that her husband already depends on her, so she has changed her mind. It would therefore be 'better' for him to die first, because there will be nobody to take care of him. In the absence of children, some couples have a faint expectation that the nephews and nieces that they were close to in the past might care for them in the future. Between childless siblings, the arrangement is different. There is an expectation that the healthier one will take care of the other. However, when there is no partner or sibling, participants think about new arrangements for the later stage of their lives. Sonia, aged 59, chose to live with a friend. She now shares a house with Linda. While she feels she can still enjoy the privacy she needs, they have set up a joint bank account to facilitate their lives together. The next step is to give each other the legal power to make decisions if one of them gets seriously ill or dies.

The dream of sharing expenses and good moments with the friends of a lifetime is gaining traction among older people in Bento. The problem is that this is also the stage at which some couples break up, something that could turn that dream into a nightmare. That is what happened to Laís, aged 51. Without children, she was pretty sure she and her husband would end up living with the three couples they have spent their lives with, travelling and having fun. However, recently two of them broke up. So, she explains, 'It is complicated.' Iara, on the other hand, found a way to make the future uncomplicated. At 72, she ended up working as a supermarket cashier, despite having retired and holding a master's degree and a PhD from medical school. When asked why, she smiled and said 'To buy dollars.' She loves to travel, but feels she can't eat into her savings.

Being a widow with no children, she realised she would eventually have to pay someone to take care of her or move into a care home. She therefore took the job to pay for her trips. Her detachment from her career and her degree of planning is not, however, representative of Bento. Instead, it is more common for people to avoid thinking about the very end of their lives. That is the case with Felipe, aged 63, estranged from his siblings and children, with no prospect of retirement. He says, 'Everything I planned went wrong. So, I won't worry about this any more.' While long-term plans for the future may differ, participants share the same attitude when facing the present. They will make use of all the resources they can get to postpone dependence. But first, they will give prominence to their commitment to age well.

The will to health

The social obligation to adopt healthy habits is by no means restricted to older people. Taking care of own's health has become a form of citizenship[10] in neoliberal states, where individuals are expected to remain autonomous and productive in order to assist in the development of society. More than that, health has become a measure of success, while illness may be seen as a failure.[11] Older people are put under pressure to take responsibility for this model of a healthy nation,[12] as they are targeted as the age group that places the greatest demands on healthcare and pension systems. As we saw in chapter 2, the images and discourses that represent ageing have changed to fit this morality, supported by scientific findings[13] and public policies[14] that claim that ageing well is a matter of choice and commitment.[15] Ageing well has thus become a virtue and a duty.[16] In Bento, research participants respond to this call. However, the first thing they do is reproduce health discourses in their narratives. They can explain in detail the impacts of good nutrition and physical and cognitive activities (like learning a language or playing a brain-training game) on the quality of life in old age. These are also the topics they share most on their WhatsApp groups (figure 6.2), together with news that stresses the potential older people still have for productivity and socialising, both of which are endorsed by Successful and Active Ageing discourses.

When this awareness is given shape in their narratives and on social media, older people in Bento are practising what some authors call the 'will to health',[17] meaning the demonstration of their commitment to make healthy choices and age well. By doing this, they are crafting their identities in terms of health,[18] which works for distinction in the sense

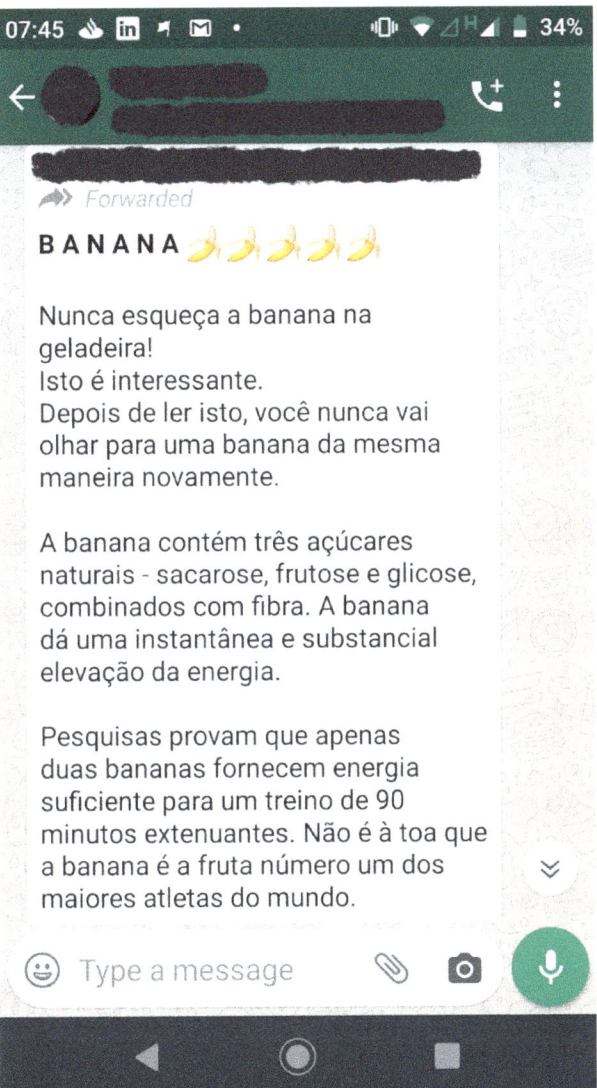

Figure 6.2 Example of nutrition tips being shared in a WhatsApp group. The text says: 'BANANA. Never leave a banana in the fridge! This is interesting. After reading this, you will never look at a banana the same way again. Bananas contain three natural sugars: sucrose, fructose and glucose. Bananas provide an instant and substantial increase in energy. Studies show that just two bananas will provide enough energy for 90 minutes of high-impact training. It is not a coincidence that the banana is the number one choice of fruit for the greatest athletes in the world.' Screenshot taken by Marília Duque.

used by Bourdieu[19] as it communicates that they are successful 'third agers'.[20] However, as mentioned above, the third age is also the stage of life reserved for pleasure, which means participants will manage conflicts between the *health-seeking lifestyles* they should adopt and the *pleasure-seeking lifestyles* they think they deserve.[21] Therefore compliance with healthy habits, whatever they are, will always be a negotiation between discourses and practices, between what becomes visible to or is hidden from others. As the sociologist Erving Goffman[22] argues, people tend to bring to the stage what is likely to please the audience the most, while the rest is kept backstage. For research participants, this means giving visibility to habits and contents associated with healthy ageing while keeping what they classify as unhealthy in the shadows.

Social media and WhatsApp groups allow participants to enjoy small indulgences without compromising their reputation as responsible citizens committed to ageing well, to avoid becoming a burden to family or society. They gain a powerful alibi by sharing their healthy consumption or acting as curators of content associated with health.[23] One man explained, 'Older people eat feijoada, but they only post photos of jelly' (figures 6.3 and 6.4). While feijoada is a typical heavy Brazilian dish made with black beans and pork, jelly is perceived as healthy as it is often made from collagen. Thus, jelly is the foodstuff chosen to be posted online.

The same dynamic was observed in previous chapters when we considered the ways in which older people in Bento give visibility to the moments they are active and productive. For them, this is also a demonstration of their will to health, as they associate being busy with remaining healthy. This association also helps them to cover up their moments of fragility. It was observed among research participants that when they struggle with a health issue they tend to opt out of their face-to-face activities while intensifying their 'work' on WhatsApp groups. By doing this, they can continue to perform their productive/healthy identities online while they gain time and privacy to recover[24] without the risk of being seen as frail or old.[25] That was what happened to Rose, aged 70. She was absent from one of the activities we had attended together for weeks, and she postponed our interview more than once during this time. She apologised to the group and to me, explaining that she was busy managing a trip while becoming more active on the WhatsApp group. However, when we finally met for our interview, she felt comfortable saying she was absent because she had a pain in her knee. By that time, she had completely recovered, and she had also started to attend her face-to-face activities again. The fact that research participants are using their smartphones to perform a healthy identity can be seen as a successful strategy in terms of reputation. But this doesn't mean they are not committed to seeking healthy lifestyles, as we will see in the following sections.

Willing to eat well

This section expands the relationship between will to health and food consumption. The choice to focus on food consumption is based on the importance research participants give to what they eat in the context of their strategies for ageing well. As illustrated above, they may use food in a performative manner. However, I want to highlight here the eating habits they adopt outside the spotlight of social media in order to understand what guides older people's searches for health information, how they evaluate it, and what choices they make in the private space of their houses. Their will to eat 'correctly' is triggered by discourses that claim that people are what they eat. By assimilating and reproducing them, participants associate the quality of their diet with the quality of life they desire to enjoy during old age. The call to eat well circulates in different spheres, from medicine to religion, also reaching WhatsApp, YouTube and Netflix. For example, in the medical school located in Bento, there is a section dedicated to studying the correlation between physical activities, cognitive maintenance and nutrition in old age. In addition to lectures given by nutritionists, the quality of food intake is measured

Figures 6.3 and **6.4**   Figure 6.3 shows 'Feijoada', a typical heavy Brazilian dish made with black beans and pork. Figure 6.4 shows jelly, often made from collagen and commonly served as a free dessert in low-cost restaurants in Bento. © Pixabay.com.

through blood samples and food assessment tools. Recently, the programme has introduced a vegetable garden, which older people maintain. The intervention aims to get them involved in growing their own food as a way of improving food choices and eating habits.

Nutritionists have a special place in the programme of lectures aimed at the third age organised by a Catholic church in Bento. At these lectures, participants receive a handbook that contains helpful information and tips on healthy diets. In religious contexts like this one, food is approached as a Foucauldian technology of the self.[26] Choosing the right food is a practice for the purification and improvement of the self and for being committed to pursuing equilibrium, plenitude and happiness (a journey that is by no means restricted to older people). This approach is also adopted by the Church of World Messianity in Bento.

On my first visit to the church, I met Rubens, in his sixties. He is prepared to provide any new visitor with a detailed explanation of the role played by good food in purifying body and spirit. His religion, founded in Japan by Mokichi Okada in 1935, has three pillars.[27] The first is 'Johrei', the divine light applied by a practitioner holding their hands over a patient's body to purify and heal. The second one is beauty. Rubens claims that his religion highlights the importance of clean and minimalist environments, which celebrate the equilibrium of forms and spaces. The fundamentals of that balanced composition are learned through 'ikebana' (the Japanese art of flower arranging) workshops which help bring to life the concept of living in beauty. On that day, it was one mini flower arrangement that led me to the church (figure 6.5). These flower arrangements are made by those on duty that day as a 'point of light' and later distributed as gifts to those who, like me, pass by on the street.

As I held my flowers in my hands, Rubens finally revealed to me the third pillar of his religion: natural food (preferably organic and grown using sustainable techniques), which is the final element of balancing the body and the mind. This was also the moment when he suddenly left our conversation. He came back with a smile and two small paper bags. One contained rice, the other salt (figure 6.6). Both had been given additional unique properties during worship that day. He indicated that both should be mixed with food prepared at home. Rubens left again. He came back carrying one more gift, an edition of the *Izunome* magazine, published by the Church of World Messianity. The editorial talks about the three pillars Rubens had explained earlier: Johrei, beauty and food. Searching online later, I found that the September 2019[28] edition places particular emphasis on food. On the cover, the headline is 'Nutrition congress unites 700 professionals'. The event, organised by the Mokichi Okada foundation,

Figure 6.5 'Point of light': mini ikebana offered as a gift at the Church of World Messianity in Bento. © Marília Duque.

was in partnership with Associação Paulista de Nutrição (APAN; the São Paulo Association of Nutrition). The article explains: 'With a scientific and spiritual approach combined with an organic and sustainable cultivation of food, this year's theme was "Food as protagonist".' Rubens went on to introduce me to 'Korin', a Brazilian company whose products are 'sustainable, organic and natural' and in line with Mokichi Okada's philosophy. The Church of World of Messianity has a partnership with the company. This close relationship means that anyone can buy Korin's products through WhatsApp and collect them on Saturdays at the church, after the service. Rubens added me to his WhatsApp group, promising to keep me updated about the church's ceremonies and activities from then on. Although he was facing some difficulties in his own life (he was searching for a job at that time), he gave me strong evidence of how his learning and practices at the church guided his choices and helped him improve himself. He had become healthier, more useful and happier.

Figure 6.6 Rice and salt enriched with special properties which they acquired during worship at the Church of World Messianity and offered to visitors with the instruction that they should be mixed into food prepared at home. © Marília Duque.

The connection between science and religion is reflected in the adjustments Eduardo, aged 59, is trying to make to his family diet. He and his wife both have fatty liver disease. When they were diagnosed, the first thing they did was look for a nutritionist and have some tests done. 'She [the nutritionist] sent me a list. A very extensive one of everything I couldn't eat and a tiny one of what I could eat. Water is allowed, right? So, now I can just have water?', he had asked her. Eduardo searched for help, approaching a friend who is a new Christian, as he is. Although they don't belong to the same church, he frequently shares experiences with this friend. Eduardo explains that at his friend's church they take care of the body by paying particular attention to food. In addition, his friend works in the healthcare sector, which makes him an authority Eduardo can trust. Thus, this friend provides him with daily recommendations of what he should or should not eat.

Eduardo also talks with friends from a third church, with whom he was able to experience, in practice, the benefits of eating good food. 'They follow this natural philosophy too, choosing to eat good and healthy food. I spent four days with them. It was very good. I felt no pain, nothing. We spent four days eating mostly vegetables, salads, beetroot, things like that,' he adds. In addition to his awareness of the importance of adopting healthy habits to age well, Eduardo is more focused on his diet now that he is retired. Food is one of the key factors impacted by retirement, as people start eating at home and have more time to prepare their meals, as we saw in chapter 3.

The imaginary of a healthy diet is built with information research participants access from different sources. The starting point is common sense, which is influenced by media coverage. An example is the association between eating less, combined with no processed food, and longevity.[29] Among research participants, common sense includes the idea that salad and vegetables, less meat and more wholefoods and organic food are healthier, together with the condemnation of bread, milk or any other food shared on social media as the villain of the day. In addition, as noted earlier, there is information provided by relatives or friends who work in the healthcare sector. This information is informal yet invested with authority. Indeed, even generic health messages shared on WhatsApp are invested with authority, as they always start by giving credit to a professional. For example, at the beginning of this chapter, we showed two messages shared on WhatsApp (see figures 6.1 and 6.2). The first message, which talks about Alzheimer's, is built on the credibility of 'a doctor friend'. The second one, which highlights the benefits of eating bananas, uses the phrase 'studies confirm' as evidence to create trust. Participants can craft their idea of a healthy diet also by reading books and participating in courses, lectures and workshops. These activities are seen as constructing more solid and formal knowledge. However, it is common to find participants searching for information about nutrition on Google, YouTube and even Netflix.

Pablo, aged 69, prefers to combine all these strategies. While studying for a master's degree in mental health in his forties, he gave up smoking and gained 20 kg. When he turned 60, he decided to end his marriage and moved in with his current wife. Since then, in what he considers the best phase of his life, he has decided to improve his health by adopting a healthy diet. He started with a book focused on natural food and ended up on a sugar- and carbohydrate-free protein diet. He celebrates the weight he lost and the fact that he can now enjoy the clothes that did not fit him in the past. He doesn't mind having more restrictions now, as he is excited about the results he achieved. His diet is not, however, only a consequence of his reading. It is the result of material gathered from Netflix, Google and YouTube, combined with the advice given by someone in the family who Pablo recognises as an authority.

'It was my second wife's son. He studied veterinary medicine, but he is a weightlifter. He knows everything. Yesterday, we were watching a Netflix series about this low-carb diet. What a spectacular idea, to fight cancer with fasting. The researchers confirmed the link and, if cancer needs sugar, if the cancerous cell needs this energy, you cut the energy, and it dies. And the studies attested to this finding. I remembered what dogs do. When they are ill, they don't eat. When an animal is ill, it will stop eating. I also researched functional food and learned about the benefits of eating papaya, avocados and bananas in moderate quantities, because bananas have too much sugar, grapes have a lot of sugar. But on the other hand, they also have some benefits. I was taking care of myself, I guess. I learnt it is time to eat right – this is it. I have already eaten everything I desired in life. Now, it is time to remain functional to avoid problems. I found another series [on Netflix]. The truth is that these are things we agree on – a natural diet, physical exercise, natural health, without drugs. [On YouTube] I also followed the advice of doctors who talk about this natural approach. But I realised there were a few things I was doing wrong.'

Research participants frequently consider the potential of a healthy diet to prevent and cure cancer in their narratives. Lúcio, aged 76, has evidence that the diet approach works. Two years ago, a biopsy revealed he had prostate cancer. A doctor from a health programme in Bento suggested he should attend a nutritional forum, which was running online. The event, whose lectures he keeps on his computer, focused on the potential of food to prevent and cure. He heard many doctors during this programme support the idea that diseases cannot thrive in alkaline environments. Lúcio changed his entire diet on the basis of what he had learned, to alter his body's pH level accordingly, including by drinking a special alkaline mineral water brand. He decided not to have the chemotherapy his doctor suggested, a decision he felt was supported by equally convincing professional knowledge. Alongside his new diet, he now sees a second doctor and has a check-up every six months. This doctor even feels that checking his prostate-specific antigen (PSA) level is no longer necessary. Lúcio complains that he keeps telling other doctors about the benefits of controlling the body's pH level, but they ignore him.

Nelson, aged 58, is adamant that doctors don't give enough importance to food. He believes doctors are too focused on diseases and not interested in finding the causes of health problems. He suffered from bad digestion and migraine for years until he found, by himself, the kinds of food that don't cause him any harm. This discovery was not made by him alone, but with the help of the 'doctors from the internet', as he calls the doctors followed by him on YouTube. One channel in particular, 'Dr Lair Ribeiro', is popular among research participants. By following him, Nelson learned how the body absorbs nutrients and how important it is to eat fresh food prepared and eaten the same day. He changed his habits to achieve a healthy diet, as one of Dr Ribeiro's arguments is that when someone is eating correctly, the body does not need any supplements. Although he is convinced of this, he enhances his diet by taking a vitamin complex that his son brings him from the United States. In addition, he practises intermittent fasting, something he learned about from another doctor on YouTube. He fasts for 16 hours a day, which helps him 'maintain his weight without being hungry'. Like Pablo and Lúcio, Nelson found that fasting can be a great ally against cancer. 'Sugar is what feeds cancer: sugar and artificial food. I came from a church [he attends the Baptist church] where I heard many cure testimonials. If one day you get cancer, start fasting,' he recommends.

As seen so far, participants' attempts to eat better, or 'correctly', creates a space for bricolage and agency, increasing their tendency to try out a wide range of new diets. With multiple opportunities to do this, and guided by the information found on social media, in books, on courses or in interactions with friends and relatives who work in healthcare and 'doctors from the internet', they combine or follow the recommendations that they judge to be the most convenient, convincing or accessible. Therefore, their everyday relationship with food leads to different strategies, all concerned with the 'good'. But are their choices good ones?

Take Felipe as an example. As mentioned above, his life is characterised by economic constraints. He is assisted by a government programme[30] that provides him with meals at a low cost. Even though he is left without much choice, he exercises his will to eat well by picking the 'diet-friendly menu'. He has no professional evidence backing this. He has chosen this menu because he considers it to be healthier. He realises he is eating less than he used to but associates the changes in his appetite with ageing. He is skinny, something he perceives as a sign of good health. Sometimes, after having his 'diet-friendly menu' for lunch, he passes the rest of the day without eating. He argues that this is due to lack of time, since he attends many courses, lectures and activities and is still searching for a job. Like Felipe, Iara has only one main meal a day. In her case, her lunch is provided at her work, the one she took in order to be able to travel without eating into her savings, as explained above. At night, she tries to satisfy her appetite by having some cheese or a small sandwich.

Celebrating her slim figure, she considers this a good deal. She saves the money she would otherwise spend on food, and is released from the obligation to cook. In their narratives, Felipe and Iara actively resignify their food choices by turning what was a constraint into a strategy for ageing well.

Participants can adjust their narratives to include extravagances they know they should avoid. In such cases, they try two different approaches. Some will try to compensate for excess, as Lourdes does. She says she can try up to 10 different flavours of ice lolly during a day at the beach, but that is okay as she will skip dinner in the evening. Others will not pay much attention to the excess, as they consider they can get back on track whenever they want. That is the case with Rita, aged 70. She believes she knows exactly what to do to keep her diabetes under control. She claims that for two years she did not have diabetes at all. Recently, she decided to introduce some self-indulgent items into her diet, like bread. Even though she realises she shouldn't do this, her discourse highlights her overall feeling that she still has control over her diet, as she knows what to do to eat 'correctly' again.[31]

We could argue that older people in Bento have become food specialists. They can even manage pleasures and constraints as calculated risk-takers. They feel they have enough information to do so. However, the agency they say they exercise over their diets is not reflected in the nutritional status of this age group in São Paulo. A survey[32] showed the proportions of underweight, overweight and obese people among older people in the city to be 20 per cent, 13.2 per cent and 21.2 per cent. There are plausible explanations for this. In the best scenario, participants have translated the knowledge they acquire into healthy behaviours and diets. If they have, they will be among the 45.6 per cent of older people with a healthy nutritional status in São Paulo. If they have not, there are three possibilities. First, what research participants say they eat differs from what they actually eat:[33] there may be a gap between what they know they should eat and what they choose to eat. Secondly, as scholars have shown, other factors are associated with nutritional status in old age apart from food choices, from economic constraints to physiological changes and declines.[34] Thirdly, despite all the information they get from multiple sources, *they are not empowered to make healthy choices regarding their diets*, which could compromise their capacity for performing essential activities for daily life[35] and increase the risk of non-communicable diseases.[36] That means that participants may, after all, end up losing their autonomy, which is the thing they were most concerned with when they tried to adopt healthy diets.

Challenging empowerment

By going beyond food and exploring everyday care practices, the following sections challenge the idea that smartphones and the internet are empowering older people in Bento to comply with the participatory health system under the telemedicine umbrella.[37] From that patient-centred perspective, focused on prevention, responsible citizens are expected to assume their role as the leading agents of their own health decisions and actions.[38] By doing so, they would be collaborating in the optimisation of health resources that are particularly challenged by rapid demographic ageing throughout the world.[39] Swan proposes that individuals could rely on three lines of defence to manage self-care and health issues.[40] First, self-tracking sensors and apps would involve them in a 'technological blanket' used for self-monitoring. Second, there is collaboration with health advisers and with peers who have similar conditions and interests, which may help them make sense of the online information. Third, and only after the two first lines of defence have been exhausted, there is the public health system, whose resources should target diagnosis and treatment. However, this empowerment depends on the development of new skills and the adoption of new attitudes towards medical authority.

Following the above, I bring in some contextual background in order to argue that older people in Bento do not achieve the level of emancipation they would need to manage self-care and health issues. To demonstrate this, I will consider the lines of defence mentioned above, starting with the 'technological blanket'. Helbostad and colleagues[41] endorse the potential of smartphones, sensors and mHealth apps to structure a new health paradigm for the elderly based on their ability to monitor, intervene in and extend their autonomy. Endorsing the premise that active and healthy ageing requires the adoption of healthy habits, the authors emphasise the always-on character and personalised real-time feedbacks of these technologies as promising for the motivation to change behaviour and sustain the changes over time. The authors argue that these technologies can work as compliance tools, which could empower older people to take charge of their health. Let's look more closely at how older people in Bento engage with these self-monitoring technologies.

Out of 38 interviewed participants, 13 have health-related apps installed on their smartphones, including self-tracking apps. Two *have never used* these apps. One of them said her daughter had installed the app for her own use, and the other said that the app was already installed when the device came into her possession. Three *have tried to use or have used a health-related app in the past*. One lost interest. One abandoned the health goal associated with the app. One didn't trust the metrics and feedbacks provided by the app. Three have *apps they haven't tried yet*. They were installed 'for the future' and all of them are diet-related.[42] The three participants *who use health-related apps* use self-tracking apps and also wear smartwatches. Two use the metrics only to gain knowledge about their bodies. The third is *the only participant* who uses the metrics and feedback provided by the app to be proactive about her health, as she is worried about remaining independent and not becoming a burden to her children in the future. This evidence shows that the empowerment associated with health-related apps in general and tracking apps in particular can be seen as an *exception* in Bento.

Older people may refuse to adopt these technologies because they would make their condition or frailty constantly visible in an inconvenient way.[43] In other words, they might be reminded that their bodies are changing and that they are inevitably getting old. In addition, as already argued, the third age is a time for balancing what is healthy and what is pleasurable, which might lead to a lack of compliance. Older people's low adherence to health-related apps is also frequently associated with general barriers to adopting new technologies and poorly designed interfaces. The main criticism is that developers ignore specific characteristics of this age group.[44] As a result, most apps aren't adapted to the cognitive, psychological, motor and sensory changes related to age. For various reasons, promotion of health-related apps for older people in Bento should take into account the same constraints participants face when they download and engage with new apps, as shown in the previous chapter. In the next section, I consider how these constraints impact how older people connect with the healthcare system, as these interactions are becoming more and more mediated by bespoke apps.[45]

Engaging with healthcare providers

Retirement is the stage of life at which older people in Bento set up new arrangements with their health providers. Some research participants lose the private health insurance provided by their last employer. Others are reviewing their health insurance policies to fit their new family budget. In those cases, some will migrate to the SUS, which is used by 73 per cent of Brazilians aged 60 or over,[46] while others will opt to downgrade their policy but remain within the private sector. In between, some will combine assistance from public and private providers. Out of 38 interviewed participants, it was found that 27 had private health insurance. Among these, one person was still working and had an employer-provided plan, and 13 people had downgraded their health insurance policy after retirement. Nine relied exclusively on the public health system and two combined the use of the SUS with sporadic use of services from low-cost clinics. This last strategy is the one adopted by Nelson. Although many low-cost clinics operate in Bento, Dr Consulta is the most popular among research participants (figures 6.7 and 6.8). Nelson is served by the SUS, but has his annual check-up at Dr Consulta. He usually opts for the 'Man 40+' package, which includes eight medical tests, with particular attention to prostate cancer prevention.[47] Dr Consulta is also used by participants when they have an emergency and don't want to wait for a medical appointment on the SUS.[48]

Among those who opted to downgrade their private insurance plans, all had chosen Prevent Senior as their new health insurance provider after retirement. Created in 1997, Prevent Senior[49] was introduced to the market as 'the first health insurance specialising in the Adult+'. Through the concept of Adult+, as their advertising campaigns showed, they aimed to create an aspirational identity addressing the older patient as one who manages to stay active and healthy in order to

Figures 6.7 and **6.8** Low-cost clinics operating in Bento, including Dr Consulta (6.8). They look like shops and one of them (6.7) is indeed inside the biggest shopping mall in Bento. © Marília Duque.

enjoy the freedom and pleasures reserved for the third age. With a focus on prevention,[50] Prevent Senior represented a paradigm shift in private health insurance policies aimed at older people in São Paulo.[51] But despite this, cost was the main reason participants chose the company, which works with its own network of doctors, clinics and hospitals. This means research participants had to abandon the doctors they were familiar with. But they don't complain, at least not to their peers. Keeping a private insurance plan in old age is seen as a mark of distinction. For that reason, they are likely to present choosing Prevent Senior as an intelligent decision, as they are healthy and don't need that much health assistance, rather than associating their choice with a downgrade.

Prevent Senior's clients are not the only ones trying new doctors in Bento. Many of the doctors who have known research participants for a lifetime have retired or died. In addition, some become unaffordable to retired people. The last case is illustrated by doctors who are not in the public health system or covered by health insurance plans. Known as 'private doctors', they are perceived as a higher category of doctors, a direct association being made between being expensive and being good. Research participants say that these doctors get to know them better, and they are primarily used in combination with the doctors covered by their health insurance. In contrast to other categories of doctors, their medical consultations don't have a limited time,[52] so they have the opportunity to talk longer. For example, one woman said that her dermatologist also works as a psychologist, so the consultation is an opportunity for her to talk about her life in general. In addition, they have a direct channel of communication with these doctors. So even after retirement, participants who used to see 'private doctors' will do their best to keep at least the one they trust the most. Women are more likely to keep their gynaecologist or dermatologist, while the cardiologist is usually the most valued specialist for men. However, such extravagance is an exception in Bento. Therefore we could say that, among interviewed participants, the SUS, Prevent Senior and Dr Consulta are the leading health providers representing the public health system, the private health insurance system and the health market respectively. Despite their differences, they have at least one thing in common. They all provide apps to optimise access to their services. However, none of them is used to its full potential by participants for the reasons presented in the previous section.[53]

By Dr Consulta's users, the app is considered complicated, and they prefer to use the company's website[54] or the phone to book an appointment. The same happens with Prevent Senior's app. In this case, the only feature research participants use is the digital identification card the app provides.

In the SUS, users in São Paulo can download the Agenda Fácil (easy scheduling) app. The application was created at the end of 2017 to make booking appointments and tests in the public health network more accessible and faster. At the same time, it aimed to reduce the number of missed appointments, as users could confirm or reschedule their appointments online. The app would also record appointments and clinical tests, from which the patient's medical records could be updated.[55] Apps like the Agenda Fácil one can fulfil the promise that technology can help healthcare providers save resources and time and lead to more people being assisted by the system.[56] However, of the 11 interviewed participants who use the SUS, only two knew the 'Agenda Fácil' app existed. Of those, Sandra, aged 69, gave up using the app in the set-up phase. Users have to go to their nearest Unidade Básica de Saúde (UBS; basic health unit) and ask for a code to validate their account in the app (figures 6.9 and 6.10). She had problems getting her code, so she left the app.

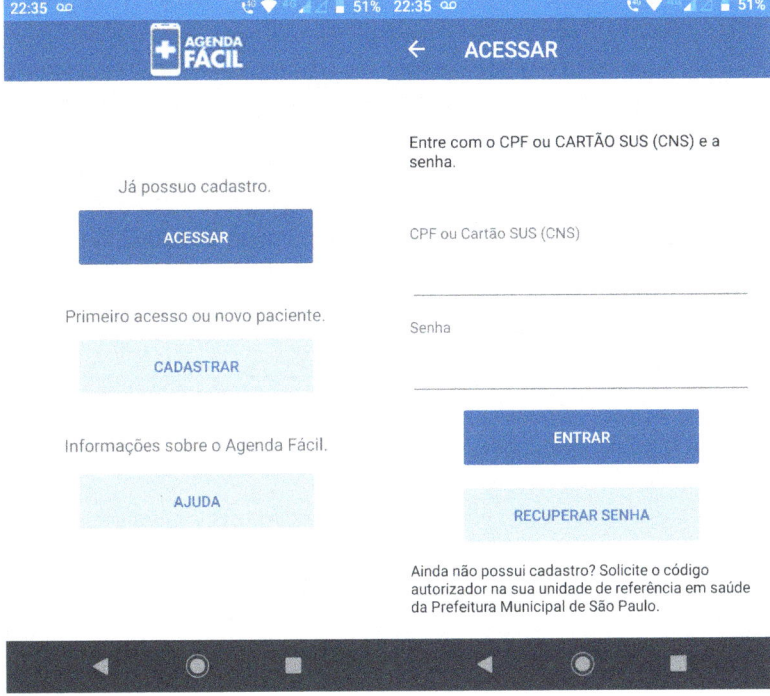

Figures 6.9 and **6.10**   Screenshots from the 'Agenda Fácil' app, in which users are advised to ask for a code at their nearest UBS. Screenshots taken by Marília Duque.

That was not true of Felipe, aged 63. He was able to get his code at his local UBS, so he can now use the 'Agenda Fácil' app on his smartphone. He has no difficulty in interacting with the app. On the contrary, he rates his experience of the app as excellent. However, he argues that the app has an administrative problem, as appointments and tests can only be booked if the UBS updates the system. If the medical request has not been uploaded to the system, or the appointment or test was at a place that is not the patient's original UBS, the app will not work. In Felipe's experience, this means overcrowded UBSes, as patients have to leave the app and go to the units in person. The last time this happened to him, he spent an hour queuing, because he was referred to another unit. He also complains that medical tests are in short supply in the app, leading to endless searching. Felipe concludes that the technology that was supposed to help him to take care of his health can be seen as demonstrating negligence on the state's part. He says:

> 'People use the word "empowerment". They keep saying they are empowering society, empowering society. ... "To empower" means "fuck you", right? Because the reality is that everything is in the hands of the state. They say they are transferring power to you because, when they empower you, they transfer power to you, right? But you depend on them. The Agenda Fácil ... how can I explain this? I went to the UBS near my house. I had an appointment with a doctor. This doctor gave me a referral to have a test done. I went to the UBS's administration. They placed my referral into the system. If they put me in the system, I can manage this through Agenda Fácil. I went through the app to choose where I can have the test done. But, as I told you, there is no test available. I can't find it. It is the same with the dentist. I usually go to a dentist in another UBS, because mine doesn't have this service. But then I can't use Agenda Fácil to book my next appointment. It is not in my hands any more. They have to do it.'

As with the apps designed for self-monitoring, the examples in this section show that technology can fail to improve the way older people in Bento connect with healthcare systems and providers. The exception is the interface with 'private doctors'. But that is not surprising, as these interactions are not supported by a bespoke app. Instead, WhatsApp is the app 'private doctors' use to connect with patients. During the ethnography, telemedicine wasn't fully regulated in Brazil. Practices like teleorientation, teleconsultation and telemonitoring were approved by the Federal Council of Medicine in March 2020 because of the Covid-19 pandemic.[57]

However, even before that, a survey of doctors conducted in the state of São Paulo in 2019 showed that 82.65 per cent had used WhatsApp to connect with patients.[58] Although this percentage is high, research participants argue that only 'private doctors' provide a channel for direct communication in case they need additional help.[59] Doctors may complain that the time spent on WhatsApp is unpaid, but this connection adds value to their services (especially for older people) and is used as a resource to win patients' loyalty. It doesn't, however, mean that research participants will use this service. On the contrary, they try not to be a burden. As the following sections show, they make use of other resources to manage their health and seek advice while reserving the connection on WhatsApp with doctors for 'real emergencies'.

Managing health information

In the light of the three lines of defence we mentioned above, participants can't fully engage with the health-related apps that were supposed to empower them to understand their bodies and manage decisions regarding their health. Nor can they benefit fully from the apps developed to mediate their connection with the healthcare system and providers. There are, however, two resources they can rely on. The 'doctors from the internet', as well as 'Doctor Google', can empower them, making up for the lack of assistance from their health providers. In addition, these resources allow research participants to avoid being seen as a burden, as they are available 24 hours a day, free. Although the guidance that participants need can be found online, educational background and literacy level[60] can result in different outcomes. Let's take Eduardo as an example. Eduardo completed the basic education level. That is not a limitation for using his smartphone for shopping and banking, but he doesn't search for medical information any more. He and his wife are both scared of the information they might find, and feel unable to identify which sources and pieces of information they should trust.

> 'The internet can be a little bit scary, right? It sends you to a wild place, with so much information that you get lost. For example, I was once looking for information about something my wife was feeling. God, it was too much information. I told myself, no. I will get out of here. I will ask the doctor directly, and he will give me the right information. I don't like it [the internet]. I did it once. It scared me more than it helped me.'

At the other end of the spectrum there is Roger, aged 61. Roger has a bachelor's degree. As one of Bento's elite, he benefits from a second pension policy and private health insurance. He sees a 'private doctor' who works as his family doctor, coordinating every decision that concerns his health. This support doesn't stop him from searching on the internet. He follows the 'Dr Drausio Varella' channel on YouTube, which he likes because Dr Drausio uses accessible language. But when Roger wants to go deeper, he searches for information on websites that share scientific articles, such as the University of São Paulo website. The way Eduardo and Roger engage with the medical information available online illustrates the impact of social inequality on the level of empowerment an individual can achieve to manage health decisions. A survey showed[61] that while 47 per cent of Brazilians use the internet to search for health information and services, the proportion of graduates who do this is 71 per cent, compared with 28 per cent of those who have had the basic level of education (9 years of schooling). The proportion among those from higher-income classes is 64 per cent against 31 per cent from lower-income classes.

Even taking into account his educational background and digital skills, Roger's level of digital health literacy[62] should be questioned. He is more likely to be seen as an informed citizen than as an empowered citizen when it comes to health issues.[63] He uses the medical information he gets online to prepare himself before his medical consultations. But he doesn't question his doctor's guidance. That is the type of behaviour shared by research participants independently of their education or income. They respect the 'old' medical authority. Even Maria, aged 70, the only person in Bento who proactively uses a health-related app to manage her health, endorses this deference. With higher education and financial security, she struggles with the medical information available online. She says, 'There is a lot of misleading information. I prefer to follow my doctor's recommendations.'

Therefore, in general, the promise that the availability of medical information on the internet could empower older people to manage their health is limited to their adopting a few habits associated with healthy lifestyles. The enthusiasm and autonomy resulting from this information are most experienced when they are deliberating about exercises (for the body and the brain) and diet, as we have seen in this chapter. However, when it comes to symptoms or diseases, internet searches are performed more to satisfy one's curiosity than to empower patients to make decisions or establish a dialogue with doctors, whose authority Google cannot yet challenge. This doesn't mean the medical gaze won't be challenged by technology. As the following section explains, older people in Bento are likely to overcome their limitations in the area of accessing healthcare support by seeking guidance among their qualified connections on WhatsApp. They will ask relatives, friends and friends of friends who work in the healthcare sector for assistance (as we have already seen in the food section of this chapter). Through these practices, they receive medical advice that is at the same time professional and informal. In the end, this guidance is mediated by technology, but not as currently conceived by the mHealth industry. Rather than a bespoke app, it is WhatsApp that facilitates participants' access to the medical information they need to manage their everyday health issues.

The social connections of health and care

It doesn't matter if it is a friend or a friend of a friend. Having a connection with a doctor or a healthcare professional on WhatsApp is perceived as a luxury among older people in Bento. WhatsApp provides the perfect conditions for them to use these friendships for medical guidance without being a burden.[64] Research participants ask their qualified connections for advice on specific issues, and these peers answer when they can. For example, Lourdes, aged 64, was unsure whether she should have the herpes zoster (shingles) vaccine. She had an appointment with her doctor in two weeks, so she didn't want to disturb him before that. Although treatment by her doctor is covered by her private health insurance plan, she has his WhatsApp contact details. As seen above, this is not the norm in Bento. In her case, this privilege is explained by the fact that she had been a patient of the doctor's father. She had to stop seeing the father when her insurance plan coverage changed. The father referred her to his son, giving her his WhatsApp contact details as a 'bonus' based on their past relationship. However, as already noted, research participants keep such connections for emergencies only. In Lourdes's words, 'I don't like to burden him.' Instead, for everyday health issues, they prefer to seek informal but professional guidance from people they know personally. Thus, Lourdes asked a friend to ask her son whether she should have the vaccine. It didn't take her long to get an answer. She explained that her friend's son wasn't just a doctor but an infectious disease specialist in one of the most respected hospitals in Bento.

Social networks are also used to bypass bureaucracy in accessing healthcare systems and for accessing preferential treatment, which can often only be achieved by going through influential connections. For example, when João, aged 64, was suffering from a rare autoimmune disease that his doctors couldn't diagnose, his wife sent a message to a friend from her church who was also a doctor. This friend asked the couple to go to the public hospital where she works, instructing them to message her as soon as they arrived. She met them at reception, let them in and introduced them to her colleague, who was a specialist in the area, saying 'This is João. He is now your patient.' João was immediately taken on as a patient and able to start his treatment without queuing, something that would be impossible without leveraging personal connections. Knowing an 'insider' can also result in privileges within the private healthcare system, as illustrated by Bia's experience. Aged 55, she had lost her father two years earlier. He had had two minor strokes, which went unnoticed by doctors, an oversight that made his medical condition worse. When her father was finally hospitalised, his situation had deteriorated. Bia's main concern then was not his death but providing him with the dignity and comfort he deserved at the end of his life. She couldn't accept that her father might die in a cubicle with no windows. She therefore contacted a friend whose husband works for her father's health insurance company. In the company's hierarchy, she explains, 'he is on a par with the Pope'. Her father was transferred to a bigger, brighter room. Bia also benefited from special support from the palliative care team, being constantly updated by the doctor in charge through WhatsApp.

The modus operandi observed in João's and Bia's cases is by no means new in Brazilian culture. The *jeitinho Brasileiro* (Brazilian way) is a social and historical practice based on the particular and creative mechanisms through which Brazilians deal with difficulties and constraints, including bureaucracies and laws. The 'Brazilian way' is based on favours performed by someone from one's social network, which often help that individual to bypass the system.[65] But though the practice exists across different social classes, the more affluent classes may benefit from it the most. Their social networks tend to be more highly qualified and influential (they may include more doctors, for example). WhatsApp extends these possibilities, especially amongst older people in Bento. As most of the activities they attend are free, their networks tend to be more diverse and inclusive. That allows Felipe, who, as mentioned above, is assisted by the state food programme, to be connected with Lúcio, who is a member of an elite club in Bento. Both attend the same activity on Mondays, when a group of older people meet to discuss new possibilities of work at their age, and are members of the WhatsApp group that supports this activity. Moreover, although the 'Brazilian way' is perceived as corruption, it doesn't necessarily result in material gains but rather in the receipt of favours in various spheres of everyday life. In João's case, he was able to receive medical treatment with the urgency he needed. In Bia's case, she achieved the comfort and support she believes her father deserved.

Because the 'Brazilian way' is rooted in favours, it creates a system of reciprocity between peers. Reciprocity is what truly empowers older people in Bento to deal with health issues. The favours they exchange go beyond the 'Brazilian way', because they are not always used just to bypass the system. On the contrary, sometimes all someone is trying to do is verify a specific piece of information, clarify a diagnosis or treatment or seek guidance. That is precisely what happened when Lourdes asked about the herpes zoster vaccine or when Eduardo asked his friend for help with improving his diet, as shown in the food section of this chapter. Reciprocity establishes a network of care based on solidarity and friendship. Research participants can support each other when they don't want to burden their children, or feel they cannot rely on them, or don't have any. For example, Martha, aged 57, has three female friends who live alone. Every morning, she sends them a 'good morning message', which provides them with some comfort and shows them that she is available if they need her. Whenever older people in Bento need someone to accompany them to a doctor's appointment, guidance on how to take an Uber or an incentive to join a new course or go out dancing on a Saturday night, they take care of each other, and this is made much easier by their connection through WhatsApp. That is another reason why research participants are committed to sharing news and opportunities they think their WhatsApp friends might like. By doing this, they remain present in the conversation while trying to be useful: one never knows when a forwarded piece of information might come in handy.

It is perhaps mainly thanks to their WhatsApp connections that research participants feel empowered to give and receive assistance with any issues they face in everyday life. Aristotle addressed the value of friendship in old age.[66] He wrote, 'Without friends no one would choose to live, though he had all other goods.' That seems to be the case in Bento and also in Rio de Janeiro, where the anthropologist Miriam Goldenberg found, for example, that older women value friendship above all, pointing to their friends as the people they rely on most in times of need.[67] Friendship networks are associated with quality of life in old age, having more positive effects than the ones formed by family connections.[68] In Bento, WhatsApp increases the number of these valuable connections and facilitates interactions between them, resulting in multiple facilities that research participants can access to overcome their daily constraints and meet their needs. Within the realm of healthcare, this is especially important if we consider how different their experiences are when it comes to navigating the results of searches for medical information, as well as their frustration when they try to use bespoke health-related apps. In addition, because they maintain a certain deference towards medical authority, their qualified connections often make up for a lack of communication with their actual doctors. WhatsApp adds a layer of efficiency to the dynamic of reciprocity. Thus, favours create debts paid with new favours, resulting in a perpetual system of care and support that has nothing to do with the kind of empowerment that technology developers and policymakers had in mind. In the end, interdependence seems to be healthier than independence.

Notes

1. Laslett 1991.
2. Law Dictionary 2021.
3. Paúl 2005.
4. Collucci & Pinto 2018.
5. In Japan, Kavedžija (2015) observed that happiness or a sense of a good life is the result of constant negotiations, which include tensions with the family. Older people showed concern about balancing freedom and autonomy against dependence on their children. The same kind of negotiation was observed in Bento, where research participants are likely to hide their frailties and decline to in order to avoid family interventions.
6. Whyte 2017.
7. Swan 2012.
8. Whyte 2017.
9. Lamb 2019.
10. Rose & Novas 2007.
11. Whyte 2009; Neff & Nafus 2016; Lamb 2019.
12. Rose (2001) argues that in a healthy nation the state treats individuals and families as partners who should accept the responsibility of managing their health and well-being. Ruckenstein and Schüll (2017, p. 265) argue that the datafication of health and the development of tracking tools contribute to individual empowerment, 'turning health care into self-care'.
13. Rowe & Kahn 1997.
14. The Active Ageing framework supports the idea that older people should extend their participation in society by adopting healthy habits in order to remain independent and productive (World Health Organization 2002). Adopted in Brazil (Batista et al. 2011), the policy contributes to what Debert (2012) called the 'reprivatisation of ageing'.
15. Lassen and Jepersen (2017) show that older people may be judged by the state. They analysed Active Ageing policies in Denmark and the resistance of subjects to being 'placed under administration'. In their ethnography, some participants stated that they don't identify with the new ideal of ageing or believe that staying active will solve the problems of ageing at the individual or the social level.
16. Whyte 2017.
17. Higgs et al. 2009.
18. Whyte 2009; Lamb 2019.
19. Bourdieu 2010.
20. Higgs et al. 2009.
21. Jallinoja et al. 2010.
22. Goffman 1990.
23. Duque 2021.

24 The capacity one has to recover health and productivity in old age is one of the milestones of the Successful Ageing paradigm (Rowe & Kahn 1997). Resilience is the measure of the individual's determination to recover, which is also seen as a virtue.
25 In her ethnography in the north of England, Degnen (2007) addressed how old age is framed by intragenerational dynamics of self-vigilance and surveillance. She observed that the 'manifestation of oldness' was subject to judgement by peers and that it results in their classification into two groups: the healthier and the old.
26 Foucault 1988.
27 Gonçalves 2009.
28 *Revista Izunome* 2019.
29 Leibing 2005.
30 Desenvolvimento Social 2020.
31 In their work with Finnish middle-aged adults, Jallinoja et al. (2010) found four patterns of negotiation between pleasurable food the subjects perceive as unhealthy and their desire to age healthily. One possibility is to revisit the unhealthy habits they abandoned in the past in a self-indulgent but controlled way, as Rita believes she does.
32 Coordenação de Epidemiologia e Informação 2017.
33 Carvalho (2018) calls this a 'décalage' (detachment) in the discourse that refers to the social strategy individuals may adopt to avoid the pressure to comply with healthy.
34 Socioeconomic factors, a decline in motor skills, the use of multiple medications and physiological changes associated with ageing are among them (Campos et al. 2000; R. J. Pereira et al. 2006).
35 Corona et al. 2014; Drumond Andrade et al. 2013.
36 Alanzi et al. 2018; Neves et al. 2020; Figueiredo et al. 2008; R. J. Pereira et al. 2006; Ministério da Saúde 2020.
37 Telemedicine's set of informational and communicational technologies distributes responsibilities and allows remote support that results in what Oudshoorn (2011, p. 26) called the 'technogeography of care'.
38 Lupton 2012.
39 Oudshoorn 2011.
40 Swan 2012.
41 Helbostad et al. 2017.
42 This can be seen as a materialisation of their intention to adopt healthy habits and diets, as discussed in the preceding sections.
43 Oudshoorn 2011.
44 Wildenbos et al. 2018; Morey et al. 2019.
45 In the Brazilian context, Libânio et al. (2021) stress the importance of making digital health services accessible and appropriate to elderly people. This process includes access to the internet and user-centred design techniques, which would allow this population to benefit from the digitisation of the SUS.
46 Ministério da Saúde 2014.
47 Dr Consulta 2021.
48 A medical appointment in primary care takes from five to 43 days, depending on the SUS unit the patient is based in (Rede Nossa São Paulo 2020).
49 Prevent Senior 2021.
50 According to Ribeiro et al. (2011), the focus on prevention results from the guidelines adopted by the Agência Nacional de Saúde Suplementar (ANS). The agency, which regulates private insurance plans in Brazil, is responsible for developing new guidelines focused on creating programmes for the promotion of health and the prevention of disease.
51 Loureiro 2019.
52 The limited time spent with doctors was among the negative factors Zitkus and Libanio (2019) identified in the SUS. Although their ethnography is a case study based on one patient diagnosed with cancer, the study brings valuable insights to how communication with doctors could be improved, including how they inform patients about treatment. They argue that doctors are likely to ignore patients' level of health literacy, compromising their compliance with and understanding of treatment.
53 As observed among research participants, downloading new apps is one of the main constraints to their adopting new technologies. Policymakers should take this into account. During the Covid-19 pandemic, for example, several apps were released to manage health information and

healthcare provision in Brazil, including the CoronavirusSUS app and the ConecteSUS app. However, as ethnography showed, older people may face difficulties accessing these resources, as they are more likely to ask relatives and friends for assistance when they want to download or try a new app. As they were isolated during the pandemic, they might have been unable to get help. Libânio et al. (2021) raised a similar point in their discussion of teleconsultation during the pandemic in Brazil. Although older people might get the most benefit from this resource, digital exclusion, which can include lack of access and digital skills, might limit its use.

54 The possibility of shifting from smartphones to websites reflects the socioeconomic background of these research participants. As a survey of internet users showed, the smartphone is the only means of access to the internet for 85 per cent of Brazilians from lower-income classes, compared with 11 per cent from higher-income classes (Cetic.br 2020).
55 Prodam 2018.
56 Oudshoorn 2011.
57 Libânio et al. 2021.
58 Collucci 2019.
59 Prevent Senior created a WhatsApp channel on which patients could connect to the medical speciality they needed. However, the contact was not with their own doctor but with the team responsible for mediating interactions on WhatsApp.
60 We should understand literacy here from a broader perspective. Literacy is a factor associated with health status, as low literacy can be a barrier to understanding, adopting and adhering to medical treatments or preventive campaigns (Kickbusch et al. 2013). In addition, the term 'health literacy' means the ability to access and process health information, which could empower the individual to make decisions about and manage their health (Kickbusch 2001).
61 Cetic.br 2020, p. 74.
62 'Digital health literacy' combines the ability to process medical information and the digital skills required to navigate and engage with technology which provides not only information but metrics, feedback and individualised plans for prevention and intervention (Dunn & Hazzard 2019).
63 Santana et al. 2011.
64 It is true that, sometimes, demands from friends can be inconvenient. This is what happened with Sandra, aged 69. When we first met, she had started to attend a homoeopathy course. The knowledge was for herself, as she had always been interested in complementary medicine. However, during the course, she started to feel uncomfortable. Relatives, neighbours, friends and friends of friends had begun to ask for diagnoses and medication through WhatsApp or by phone (sometimes at 2 a.m., she complained). This excessive demand was encroaching on the time she wished to dedicate to herself. So she left the course a few months before getting the licence that would have allowed her to prescribe homoeopathic medicines. Nevertheless, in practice, she continues to advise her friends. The difference is that, because she is not officially a professional, she believes she has no obligation to answer all requests. She shares her knowledge with others as a courtesy, which secures her place in the network of reciprocity that informally supports the care of older people in Bento.
65 Prado 2016.
66 Aristotle 2009.
67 Goldenberg 2013.
68 Webb et al. 2011; Gouveia et al. 2016.

7
Challenging sexuality at the best age

'I fantasise about you'

I heard this from a man in his seventies. He was sitting behind me in one of the events I attended during my fieldwork. He suddenly got closer and whispered the sentence in my ear. I was surprised but also curious. Before then, I hadn't stopped to think about it. What do older people in Bento fantasise about? Where do they direct their desires, including sexual ones? What turns them on? This chapter starts from there to address how research participants achieve pleasure while facing issues like the menopause and impotence. Do they experience a 'second retirement'? As we will see, this is a possibility. However, it is far from being the only one.

'I do, and I like it'

That is how Luisa answered her granddaughter when the latter asked if she still had sex at her age. Luisa, aged 72, got divorced after she turned 30. She had two daughters at the time. Like other mothers of girls in Bento, she was afraid of remarrying. A strange man could represent a threat to her little girls (from a sexual abuse perspective). However, this restriction has not stopped her from having many relationships since then, as she never intended to give up her sex life. She explains,

> 'I like sex and I have never hidden it. I am a hot person, very good in bed. I know what I like, there are few things I don't. I can get my partner to do what I like. And I can also please him. Do you know anyone good in bed? I am that person, and I am not talking about sleeping.'

Luisa also feels very comfortable when it comes to technology. She has three smart devices: her laptop, her iPhone and her latest-generation giant Smart TV. Her devices are used as technologies for seduction. Through her computer, she keeps her profile up to date on dating websites and apps, applying tactics she has learned from practice. She is an exuberant woman, and the fact that no one believes her age amuses her. Her profile says she is 66. Her choice of that age was made when she realised that if she selects a number above 66, the algorithm shows her people much older than herself. Circumventing the system, she says, means she can meet men with physical (and sexual) vigour. The conversation with potential candidates migrates from her laptop to her iPhone, where the chat gets more intimate, usually through WhatsApp or the phone itself. Over the years, Luisa has developed the skill of 'reading' people through their text messages. She has also learned how to ask the right questions to get enough information. Using these things, she can choose whether to go on a date or not. We can say that her method has a high level of accuracy, as she says that out of about a hundred dates, she was only frustrated on three or four occasions.

On the occasions when things went wrong the reason was usually that her date used a profile photo that did not match the way he looked in reality. Luisa doesn't think being attractive is essential, but she does believe that a good first impression can create the initial spark of chemistry. That is not, however, the problem at issue. To her, the fact that a man would use a photo of himself when he was younger or fitter on his dating profile indicates dishonesty (even though she lies about her own age). She recalls a time when she was flirting with a lawyer. He made appropriate but provocative conversation and got Luisa's attention. He then invited her to have dinner in a romantic restaurant and picked her up at home. But once she was in his car, the magic had vanished.

> 'He said I looked prettier in person than in my profile picture, but I couldn't pretend I was not disappointed. I told him his picture must have been taken at least 30 years ago. He was a fat, aged person. He asked me if I would rather go home, and I said yes. But apart from a few cases, the rest is just having real fun.'

When the encounters go well, she often invites dates back to her house, as her daughters have moved away. That is when her Smart TV enters the scene. She is passionate about music and has several playlists on Spotify: 'One for every occasion', she says. She selects a specific playlist for each date and syncs the Spotify app to her Smart TV. Besides having a high-quality sound, her Smart TV shows the cover of the albums selected from the playlist. She says that men are impressed because, in her view, not all men of her age can handle technology very well. In addition, there is her excellent taste in music, which sets the mood for the date. To say the least, it is hard not to be seduced by Luisa's voice, smell, confidence and hospitality. She is not just a great host. She is a delightful woman. To maintain her privacy during dates at her house, she has developed a code with her daughters. She lives alone, but one day when she was trying to change a lightbulb, she fell to the floor. She had deactivated her landline, and was unable to get to her smartphone to call for help. Since then, her daughters have had a key to her house. When she is not alone, she turns the second lock in the door. This is a sign to her daughters that they should not come inside. 'Mummy has company,' she says.

Luisa manages her sex life without inhibition. Indeed, she uses it to build her reputation as an emancipated mature woman who exercises her freedom and sexuality to achieve pleasure. As a consequence, she is the person other women look to when they want advice. One of the WhatsApp groups she is in was created for this purpose. It is a small group of women, including some who are younger than her. It is a safe place where they can talk openly. When the subject turns to sex, Luisa is so open that she has considered starting a blog on the topic. She claims, laughing, that she could even start a course to advise older women. Luisa's case is fascinating because her behaviour does not match the typical representation of the post-menopausal woman, seen in literature[1] or in Bento itself. This is visible first and foremost in the way that she (a woman in her seventies) openly shares how she feels about sex with her family, as well as with other women and men. Secondly, there is her libido, which she didn't give up on after the menopause, as other women in Bento did. On the contrary, she fought for it, challenging her doctor's authority, which is quite unusual in Bento, as seen in the previous chapter.

After 10 years of hormone replacement therapy (HRT), Luisa's gynaecologist told her she needed to stop the treatment. No longer on HRT, she noticed her libido fading, and she also got depressed. She looked to her social network for guidance (see more about this strategy in chapter 6). A dermatologist friend told her that although there is a relationship between HRT and cancer, she was not just a number (referring to the percentage of risk). Instead, she was a unique person and should be treated as a unique patient. Luisa started to research the topic. The first book to discuss the symptoms caused by oestrogen deficiency and the potential of HRT to alleviate the symptoms of the menopause was *Feminine Forever*, by Robert Wilson,[2] translated into Portuguese and published in Brazil in 1966.[3] The initial optimism about HRT and the call for women to intervene in the menopause as a matter of maintaining quality of life in old age were replaced by the publication in 2002 of a Women's Health Initiative (WHI) study,[4] which was the first to emphasise the harms caused by HRT, associating it with an increased risk of breast cancer. The WHI study undoubtedly had a long-lasting effect on the reputation of HRT all over the globe, including in Brazil.

At that time, the Brazilian newspaper *Folha de São Paulo*[5] published an article in which the Brazilian Ministry of Health proudly informed its readership that the Brazilian public health system (the SUS) was aware of the risks of recommending HRT. Since 1995, the SUS had only prescribed it in specific situations or cases (such as when women had osteoporosis). In the same article, the Women's Health Coordinator in the Brazilian Ministry of Health was quoted as saying, 'The risks are greater than the benefits. Any serious person would recommend the therapy with caution.' It is interesting to note that, in Brazil, the menopause had been included on the public health agenda in the 1980s, as part of the Programa de Assistência Integral à Saúde Mulher (PAISM; women's integral health assistance programme). The programme marked a shift in the overall approach to women's health, from an emphasis on maternity care to a more holistic approach that considered all of the stages of a woman's life and health. This can be seen as a consequence of population ageing in the country.[6]

Nowadays, the official guidance published by the Brazilian Ministry of Health, which is summarised in a document called *Manual de Atenção à Mulher no Climatério / Menopausa* (handbook of care for women in the menopause),[7] recommends physical activity and adopting a healthy diet as the primary approach to managing menopausal symptoms.[8] The same handbook encourages women to learn about the risks of HRT, so that they can decide on the type of therapy they want to have, which includes non-hormonal treatment, acupuncture and herbal medicine. That was precisely what Luisa did. Combining all the information she had, she tried to find a doctor who viewed HRT favourably. She found a doctor who is now her gynaecologist. At that time, she had a series of medical tests, and the doctor concluded that Luisa could keep having HRT on condition that she had a check-up every three months.

> 'I still have HRT. I know there is an increased risk, x per cent, of cancer incidence. I am aware of this risk. So I have my check-ups regularly. My doctor said that if I keep monitoring myself while I have HRT, I can carry on having the therapy until I die. I think I have to take responsibility for my choice and the possible consequences of it.'

Luisa celebrates the fact that she thereby quickly came out of depression, and her libido was restored. A decrease in libido is one of the symptoms associated with the menopause, along with vaginal dryness, changes to the skin, hair loss, insomnia, irritability and depression. However, hot flushes are the symptom research participants complain about the most. Some participants experienced the menopause without having enough information about it, or simply didn't have time to pay attention to the changes in their bodies because they were working too hard. For a particular generation of women, the menopause wasn't a topic their mothers talked about. It was considered a taboo, like menstruation. That was the case with Patricia, aged 65. Her mother was very Catholic and reserved. She learnt about menstruation 'on the street', and when the menopause arrived she knew nothing about it. She had hot flushes and insomnia. At that time, she was also suffering from depression, and only recently realised that this could be associated with the menopause. In addition, it was only during the interview that she remembered she had also had problems with her libido.

> 'I didn't know. At home, my mother was very reserved. I used to go to a gynaecologist, but there was not much talk. And I didn't talk about it with my friends either. I didn't have strong symptoms. My flow was decreasing, and I took note of it. I didn't realise it at that time. I regret the fact I didn't talk much about this experience, even with my cousins. Even my sister, who is 54 now. She only told me recently that she had been suffering from menopausal symptoms for three years. I never had any information about this. And I never searched for it. It was a shame. It could have been easier. Even with the gynaecologist, everything was so fast. I never found one who recommended HRT, and I never asked for the hormone. I only had an appointment with a doctor who supported HRT once, but I didn't become her patient at the time.'

In Bento, HRT is one of the therapies women use to minimise menopausal symptoms, but only when a doctor recommends it. Most of the time, women do not take the initiative, and if doctors don't introduce HRT as an option, they will not dispute this. Fernanda, aged 63, had a different experience from Patricia. She didn't suffer from any symptoms, because she had HRT as a preventive therapy. Her gynaecologist made the suggestion, and she had positive results, which include maintaining an active sex life with her husband. Because of her own experience, it is hard for her to accept the fact that her sister-in-law, who sees a different gynaecologist, is suffering because of the menopause, mainly from hot flushes. She just can't understand 'why on earth' her sister-in-law's doctor didn't recommend HRT too.

> 'I keep staring at my sister-in-law. She puts her blouse on. She takes the blouse off. She flushes. Why are you going through this? That is something I keep asking her. Her gynaecologist didn't recommend HRT. She is there, being miserable with all these symptoms. I have gone through this … it was a piece of cake. I was working, full of energy, with none of the symptoms.'

Even when their doctors back it, it is common for women on HRT to be defensive in their justification of the treatment, as if they were doing something irresponsible or immoral. 'I only did the essentials', 'I did a mini replacement', 'I only had a little bit', 'I take it, but I'm trying to stop', and 'I wish I had prepared myself better with something natural' are sentences heard regularly. This group includes Fernanda. Despite her enthusiasm about the impact of HRT on her quality of life in old age, she stresses that she no longer takes it. Her hormones are now stable, she explains. When it comes to HRT, women in Bento internalise a kind of guilt, as though taking hormones was a selfish act, an irresponsible choice when balancing its benefits against the risk of getting cancer. However, what is under scrutiny is not only the risks involved, but the women's motivation and goals. That is because HRT can be used to prevent the effects of ageing on appearance, which can be seen as an 'unnecessary' risk.[9] That was the case with Maria, aged 70. Her awareness of the 'damage' the menopause can do to women was influenced by her dermatologist. It was he who recommended she should start HRT as a preventive measure (in her case, against ageing). She entered the menopause at 50, but she had begun replacing her hormones when she was 45.

> 'I really prepared myself for this. I did replacement therapy for many years before I entered the menopause. I was always very vain. I was also very careful about my skin. One day, when I was at his clinic, my dermatologist showed me a magazine with a photo of a woman who was covered in wrinkles and overweight and told me, "See, this is the menopause. Do you want to look like her? Let's take precautions." He asked me to talk to my gynaecologist. I had a friend, you know, she was just gorgeous. She got divorced, and then she started to age. I thought the menopause might have been the cause of this. This

friend used to go to the same doctor, and he confirmed this to me. It was the menopause. It changes the body, the skin. It changes everything. I then went to see my gynaecologist. First, he said I was crazy because I had a dark spot on my breast. So we agreed to investigate it. After we did some tests, I started HRT at 45. If you leave it till later, it can be too late. I stopped having my periods the normal way. I didn't have hot flushes. I didn't have insomnia.'

The ideals of youth explored by media create a demand for older women to intervene in ageing.[10] HRT is one of the possibilities, but not for all women. At SUS, for example HRT is recommended by the SUS only in specific circumstances, such as loss of muscle mass or genital atrophy.[11] That means that, more than on motivation or choice, the use of HRT depends on access, resulting in a class divide in the country. In Rio de Janeiro,[12] for example, HRT may appear to women in high-income classes as a natural, affordable choice. However, in a low-income peripheral neighbourhood in São Paulo, doctors in the SUS avoid prescribing HRT, as women wouldn't be able to have the check-ups that are mandatory as part of the therapy but not feasible within the public health system.[13] In both cases, even when doctors recommend HRT, they make sure that these women are aware that the therapy is a risk they are expected to take responsibility for. In Bento, however, not every woman has decided to accept the risks associated with HRT even if they have the means to afford it. That is the case with Gisele, aged 60. Like Luisa, we met before, she really enjoyed her sex life and is still open to talking about sex. However, Gisele has taken the completely opposite path to Luisa's.

Gisele entered the menopause at 49. Her gynaecologist warned her about her medical record. Her mother had had breast cancer, and Gisele was a former smoker. For her, any increase in the risk of getting cancer was enough to make her mind up. She, therefore, chose hot flushes instead of hormones. She says, 'I have already had 11 years of hot flushes.' She decided to make her condition public. This makes her an exception, as Brazilian women tend to be embarrassed[14] when they flush.[15] It is not unusual to see Gisele taking her fan out of her bag as a statement of her honesty. She confesses that it hasn't always been easy. She currently delivers workshops and training to companies, and at first the men in the audiences were surprised at her attitude. Looking back, she doesn't think she had a choice. She develops ethical programmes within corporations. So, she asks, how could she not give them an example by showing transparency and character? Over the years, she has found tools other than the fan that help her manage the hot flushes, such as elastic hair bands, hair clips, tissues and a water bottle. Together they are what she calls her 'menopause kit'. With a sophisticated sense of humour, she jokes she will market it as a 'survival kit' so that other women can benefit from what she has learnt about hot flushes.

Gisele complains that keeping her bras dry is almost impossible, as she is always sweating. But that is not the most challenging thing she has to manage. As well as suffering from hot flushes, Gisele has seen her libido disappear. She remembers that she used to have a huge sex drive. She enjoyed having sex and had a lot of fun, especially during the years that followed her divorce. She never wanted to remarry and had a lot of relationships. First boyfriends, and then casual sex. Sex was an essential part of her life and, suddenly, she completely lacked any sexual appetite. It was a while before Gisele figured out who she was without sex.

> 'I am glad I enjoyed life so much. I am glad I never held myself back. I am glad because, at least today, I have something to remember. This part of me existed. Because it is hard today with no libido, zero. Where did all that go? Did I live all those things? Was it me? It was, right? It is hard to recognise myself. So, there has been a lot of therapy since then. Because everything is bizarre to me. Imagine me, without sex.'

From this crisis, a discovery emerged. Gisele realised she did not need men, as they are no longer a source of pleasure. Independent and still focused on her career, Gisele transformed her loss of libido into a kind of autonomy.[16] It was like a free pass to emancipation: she could devote her time to herself alone, without any demands from a partner. These demands were replaced by a routine of masturbation that Gisele regards as a healthy habit more than a response to sexual desire. Thus, her action reflects her concern with her functional body, reducing her pleasure to an issue she has to solve.[17]

> 'I have been alone for many years, and that is alright. If I don't stimulate myself, I don't have any sexual desire. I have to stimulate myself physically. Movies? You can play whatever you want. Nothing happens. But if I physically stimulate myself, I am alive, which is good. Besides, because I know that this is a healthy habit, I sometimes do it regularly, just going there every day to help myself with this issue. Should we put this energy into movement? Okay, let's do this. I say "sometimes" because there are also periods when I get bored. But in general, I do it almost every day. I masturbate to

feel pleasure and to feel I have achieved a good balance. I like my autonomy. With all this autonomy, I can live alone, in peace.'

Some women have taken the middle ground between Luisa, who takes HRT while conscious of the risks, and Gisele, who opted to live with the hot flushes and loss of libido instead of taking hormones. Some women in Bento try alternative and natural methods of dealing with the effects of the menopause. Blueberry tea is among the most popular remedies, together with meditation, yoga, physical exercise and a good diet. Research participants claim that these can effectively manage hot flushes, hair loss, depression and insomnia, but these interventions don't seem to work for loss of libido. The importance given to this will vary depending on the meaning women and men attribute to sex in old age in Bento.[18] Among married couples, husband and wife may have different expectations, or start a new phase in their relationship. Lourdes, aged 64, illustrates the first possibility. She is currently trying to give up the HRT by decreasing the dosage. Since her menopause started, she feels uncomfortable during sex because of vaginal dryness and decreased libido.[19] She says her husband complains that she should be more active, and that sometimes she 'looks like a nun'.

Thus far, it seems that sex among heterosexual couples in Bento is mainly determined by the menopause and its effects on women's libido. This is not the case. Some married men recognise that they are not as they were in their sexual appetite. However, they are not worried about this as they consider that this decline is natural in old age[20] (we will address erectile dysfunction and the perspective of single men later in this chapter). Thus they challenge the cultural construction of the Brazilian man, in which masculinity is defined by an insatiable sex drive and a vigorous sexual performance focused on penetration.[21] It doesn't mean they will stop having sex, but the importance of the sexual act is relativised. Like women, they are also exploring pleasures beyond sex, including new interests and activities started after retirement. When that is the case, the couple may find themselves on the same page of a book they have just started writing, whose story is based on partnership and friendship in old age. That is the case with Bia, aged 55. She says that she didn't suffer many symptoms, and her husband agrees that her menopause wasn't an issue for them. But both recognise their libido is not the same, something he attributes to age. Married for 20 years, they have managed to balance independence and partnership, so they are fine. Her focus is on developing the skills needed for her new career, while he spends his time planning the motorcycle trips they enjoy at weekends. The sex is still there but less frequent. But they are not interested in fixing that. Instead, they are investing in the quality of the moments they spend together.

> 'There is not much desire. I think that, with the menopause, things "chill out" for both women and men. Special dates are nice. We celebrate them but with no pressure from either side. And there is affection. This is very nice. It is not just sex but the rapport. Our connection is there, and that is cool. Ah! The sex has decreased. I feel lazy about it. But the affection is nice.'

The rearrangement of the couple's intimacy is not always easy. Women especially may face difficulties in communicating how they feel and what they want at this stage of life.[22] For example, a married man said he knows something is going on. He is not sure if his wife has entered the menopause or not, but he makes a guess. 'She might have. It has been two months with no sex.' Debora, aged 50, is not sure either. She has experienced hot flushes for a whole year, but she also had one or two periods during this time. As she has little information on the menopause, she wants her doctor from the SUS to confirm the diagnosis. According to her, the doctor is not sure either. She hasn't talked to her husband yet because they are in the middle of a crisis. He is distant and she complains that he is always on his smartphone, claiming to be working, which she doesn't believe. Gisele (see above) would say that Debora avoids talking to her husband because she is afraid of being rejected. Many of Gisele's married friends recall their mothers going through this experience in the past at the age they associate with the menopause now. Once, one of her friends heard from the husband, 'It is not hard to become a grandpa. What is hard is having to sleep with grandma.' In this case, the grandma figure represents the personification of an older woman that men don't fantasise about. Gisele feels sorry for her friends who cannot openly talk to their husbands about the menopause and its possible effects on their libido.

> 'We then understand every time they say they have a headache. They can't just say: I don't have any sexual desire any more. What can we do together to improve this party? It is like having a party, right? Because that is how I see it: men have problems understanding it, and women have problems admitting it. They just can't admit it.'

The woman who wasn't there

The worst part for women in Bento is not admitting that they are experiencing the menopause or a decline in sexual desire. The most significant embarrassment is admitting they have entered old age. The cultural meaning attributed to the menopause is not given. The menopause is an indicator of old age in South Africa[23] but not in Japan.[24] Apart from its symptoms and effects on health, which vary from one culture to another,[25] it can impact feminine identity and change the social expectations attributed to women.[26] It can be seen as something women are expected to take action on, by deciding whether or not to take HRT, for example,[27] or as something they accept and welcome.[28] Even within Brazil, the meaning can vary. Menopause may be seen as an act of God and as a sign that sexual activity should cease, as it is in a religious community in Paraíba, where women may be called 'dry-women' or 'non-women'.[29] In a low-income neighbourhood in São Paulo it may be seen as a 'foreign entity' or as a condition that afflicts women unexpectedly.[30] Or it may be associated with old age, for example in Rio de Janeiro.[31] By women in Bento, menopause is considered something natural, simply another stage of the cycle of female life, just as the menarche was a mark of the beginning of their reproductive life. They are okay with that. Even to those who haven't had children, the loss of fertility is not a life or death issue (some made a note of it when they were reflecting on where they were in their lives at the time, and then moved on). However, women in Bento are unanimous in reporting that the menopause is an irrefutable sign of ageing, which explains why the subject is sometimes kept from partners and even friends.

The strategies these women choose to manage menopause will vary. However, their choices should be understood in a broader perspective. These women are not approaching the menopause only, but making decisions about how they want to age, in terms of both health and beauty. The best approach to age is under dispute. On the one hand, 'natural' ageing means accepting the changes that may come with ageing.[32] On the other hand, 'normal' age is based on individual behaviour and the use of technologies to prevent decline and correct the signs of ageing, including medication and all the resources available in the anti-ageing market. However, more than as a strategy, 'normal' ageing is constructed in normative discourses as a morality, placing on individuals the expectation that they should comply with preventive and corrective measures to prolong their active and independent lives, which includes their sexual lives.³³ This morality is so embedded in the images and discourses that appear in the media that it might seem to be the only possible choice.³⁴ Although that seems to be the case in Brazil,³⁵ there is still space for 'natural' ageing in Bento when it comes to appearance.

Some women will accept ageing naturally, and will not look for any procedure or medical intervention. Instead, they will make use of other resources to feel good about themselves. They may adjust their diets and improve their exercise regime (and make-up), and make adjustments to highlight their best features. However, sometimes this is reflected not only in their appearance but also in their attitudes. In Bento, remaining active and productive can be another way for women to challenge the ageing process.³⁶ Bia invested in both her appearance and her outlook on life to craft the identity she wants to enjoy at this stage of her life. She opted not to take hormones or have any cosmetic interventions. She combines a healthy diet with a routine of exercises, together with yoga and meditation classes. With the help of a short and modern cut, she has transformed her grey hair into a key element of who she has become. She is pleased that other women stop her on the street to ask her the secret of having such beautiful hair. Her hair gives her visibility and confidence, which is reinforced by the new career she has been developing since she retired.

At first glance, all seems to be fine for Bia until the stigma of the older woman comes to the table. For example, when I invited Bia for an in-depth interview, she suggested a coffee shop near her house. I didn't know the place. When I arrived, she told me that the comfortable chairs were one reason she chose that location, because she is a 'little old lady', she explained to me, laughing. But she quickly became serious and corrected herself.

> 'I was joking about this. But it is tough to see me joking about this thing of becoming old. Do you want to know? I still skate. I don't feel old. This doesn't make sense. I think we should have good common sense, and that is all. Me, being a fifty-something woman, I won't go out wearing a mini-skirt. I have to have good common sense. There is no need for this. Some things just don't fit any more. You had your time. You had your turn. You had fun. Now it is time to find other ways to have fun.'

We could argue that by finding other ways to have fun Bia means finding another way of presenting herself as a woman. As seen above, it is partnership and friendship that make her marriage fulfilling now that 'sex has decreased' and things have 'cooled down'. However, her sex life has nothing to do with her femininity or her need to be desired and noticed by others. As for other women in Bento, what is at stake at this stage of life is her visibility and the recognition that she remains an active object of desire.[37] That is the case with Lourdes. She is not worried about her husband complaining about the lack of sex. She even acknowledges that it's her 'fault', as, after the menopause, she experienced vaginal dryness and loss of libido. However, she is still keen to be noticed and desired. The excitement she and her husband used to share as a couple is reoriented towards her social life. Within these social relationships, she keeps herself attractive, investing in beauty routines while asserting her femininity and her identity as a woman, now emancipated from sexual obligations. She still enjoys competing with other women for men's attention. 'I still have a presence,' she asserts, while resisting the invisibility experienced by older women.[38]

In addition, one could say that her husband no longer turns Lourdes on. Instead, she is focused on herself, and has discovered other things that give her pleasure in life. She enjoys spending time with her grandchildren and friends and doing little things, like travelling, with them. As with other women in Bento, this moment often coincides with retirement, when they are likely to turn their attention to themselves, enjoying freedoms they didn't have before.[39]

What comes next?

Apart from investing their time and energy in themselves, there are many reasons why women in Bento might not be focused on (or be missing out on) sexual activity. Some of them consider that sex has never played an important role in their lives. In such cases, women are likely to consider themselves to be the same person they were before. Sônia, aged 59, is an example of this. She found her libido declining during menopause, but did not consider it a problem as she had never been a 'lover'.[40] She had never been in a long-term relationship or a marriage, and she is not bothered about meeting someone. In addition, she puts her security first. She avoids going out at night, as she is concerned about her journey home.

> 'I'm a bit of a coward. I'm just like Cinderella. When the midnight bell rings, I want to be at home. And that is not an unjustified fear. We know what can happen at any time of the day. But at night, you can be caught on the street ... you have sexual abuse. People joke that older women are crazy about being caught by a guy, but it's not like that.'

In addition to this kind of fear, women in Bento are worried about their partners' 'real intentions'. For example, some financially independent women reported problems with men who demanded money from them. Among divorced women with children, the demands that might restrict new relationships were different. Some had to be fully dedicated to work in order to raise their children. In addition to this, Bete, aged 66, had to manage her ex-husband's temper, as he threatened to kill her and her daughter if she started a relationship with another man. So she never did. That was not Luisa's case. She too had had to dedicate herself to her work in order to raise her daughters. However, as we saw at the beginning of this chapter, and unlike Bete, she never gave up new relationships, but they were restricted to the spaces outside her house. She imposed this restriction to keep her daughter safe, as she was aware of cases of sexual abuse in second marriages. Like Bete and Luisa, all the divorced women who have a daughter raised this concern in interviews. Consequently, the prospect of building a stable relationship and sharing a house with a new partner was postponed or abandoned.

As well as the demands of full-time work, these women might experience demands from parents. As many of them had to go back to their parents' house after divorce, they became responsible for taking care of them too. They had to divide their time into three shifts: their job, caring for their children and caring for their elderly parents until they died. As we saw in chapter 4, culturally, women are expected to perform this role in Brazil. That was the case with Cris. Aged 63 and divorced a long time ago, she believes she lost her chance by getting married to the wrong guy. She says she has 'retired' from having a sex life and just doesn't think about it any more. The same is true of Rita. However, at 70, she remembers giving it one last shot. She didn't rest until she had met up with someone from her past that she was once passionate about. But she was disappointed when they met a few years ago. 'He was not the same person. I was not the same either. So, I decided not to think about this any more.'

This feeling that the other, the partner who was desired at a certain time in life, has become a different person is shared by married couples. In some cases, the issue is not that the woman no longer feels any sexual desire. She just doesn't desire her husband, and vice versa. This means that the quality of the affective relationship between partners can be among the reasons sexual activity decreases in old age.[41] Roland Barthes[42] considers the moment when the image of the other, the person we love and admire, is corrupted. He argues that this can be triggered by anything – a word, a gesture, anything that can transport the other to mediocrity. For women in Bento, retirement can be the thing that compromises their admiration for their partner, firstly because, as we have argued in this book, men's identities are built on their careers or professional credentials. Moreover, their position as providers is compromised, as they have to adjust the family's standard of living to their pension. If they were made redundant it is even worse: men's contribution to the family budget may be reduced to zero. In both cases, a financial crisis can compromise a husband and wife's mutual admiration and desire.[43]

That was what happened to Felipe, aged 63. He was dismissed from his workplace eight years ago. He has had a couple of informal jobs, but none of them has worked out. Two years ago, he got divorced. 'Women don't stay with an unemployed man,' he explains wryly. But he regrets saying that a minute later when he realises it is not fair to his ex-wife. He remembers everything they built together and how things went wrong after he lost his job. One day, they looked at each other. 'We could see how unhappy both of us were,' he remembers. They decided that same day to get divorced. Ricardo, aged 64, is also having a hard time. He has rows with his adult child, who still lives with them, and in addition it is difficult for his wife to understand that they can't afford to live the same life as before now that his pension is their only income. They are taking a break at the moment.

Upon retirement, some men in Bento opt to end their marriages as they feel released from their obligation to provide for the family. Like women, they can decide to invest in themselves. Pablo, aged 69, took that decision. He now lives with his second wife, with whom he has many things in common, and they have a healthy sex life. His wife talks about their sexual synchronicity, and he laughs at the fact that her children don't believe it is possible to have this at their age. Pablo's case is not an exception in Bento. However, it is also common to see couples keeping their marriage but living independent lives. This arrangement may be a consequence of social expectations or determined by material constraints. That was the case with Mauro. He realised that he and his wife had become very different people when their children were still young. She became an Evangelical Christian and lives what he calls 'an austere life', especially when it comes to her clothes and food. He, on the contrary, always liked to cook and eat everything and to enjoy an active social life. Now aged 71 and with their children grown up, he dreams of getting a divorce. The problem is that they can't agree on selling the apartment they own, where they still live together but in separate rooms. As with many couples, the flat they live in is the only property they have, and a divorce might result in a significant downgrade in their living standards. And, well, as they say, 'It is complicated.'

Iara, aged 72, doesn't have any such impediments. She is a widow who has lived in her own house for more than a decade. But that doesn't make her life less complicated. She misses the perfect sex life she had with her husband. She gave up trying to get pregnant in the past in order to continue to enjoy a sex life free of pressure. At the time, she explains, the only way to increase her chances was by calculating what time of the month she was ovulating and concentrating their sexual relations into these days. This turned their pleasure into something mechanical. So they opted to keep their 'free' sexual life the way it was and just hope for the best (this is a decision commonly made by childless couples). After her husband died, Iara had some relationships, but she found these disappointing. Although she met men keen to share a bed with her, no one respected or wanted to share her interest in dancing, the second thing that brings a sparkle to her eyes.

> 'Well, I haven't found anyone who would take me to a dance club or a dinner dance, right? I haven't found anyone like that. What I found were people wanting to come to my house, have sex and then leave, you know?'

For now, Iara has opted to be alone. It is not that she doesn't miss sex. She does. But it would be better if the sex was with someone who would join her in the activities she likes and respect her freedom. This is a complaint shared by unmarried older women in Bento. They miss having a companion to enjoy life with, but they want to preserve their independence. While they can't get everything they want, some will explore the intimacy of their smartphones to exercise their imagination or expand their possibilities. For example, there is a consensus among research participants that women consume pornography, just as men do. Yet, in both cases, this consumption is always attributed to someone else. Carla, aged 62, explains that her friends don't talk about pornography. Moreover, her friends don't talk about dating apps or about the desire to have sex. On rare occasions, someone shares a new experience related to these topics with the group. But when that opportunity arises, it elicits a chorus of 'Me too', 'Me too', 'Me too'.

During my research, even though I noticed that women are likely to keep these experiences private, I found some clues as to what happens in the privacy of their smartphones. For example, one of the divorced women who claimed she did not think about sex any more had googled 'How can women have sex using apps?' This search was saved in her Chrome app, which I accessed during our interview. Another woman I interviewed, who is married but disillusioned with her husband, has Tinder installed on her smartphone. She claimed that it was a friend who had had the idea of downloading it to find a date for her daughter. The account had not been activated. She had given up when she realised she had to provide her email address. 'You can check, you can check, it is not activated,' she says.

When it comes to men's consumption of pornography, photos and videos are often shared on their men-only WhatsApp groups. It is common for them to say that in those spaces, which they perceive as private, they just share 'bullshit' related to the male universe, including pornography and nudity. For them, 'the group' is an *entity* and at the same time an excuse. No one seems to be responsible for sharing this kind of content. It is always 'the group'. Sometimes, they are surprised when someone leaves the WhatsApp group. The exit is automatically associated with the suspicion that his wife has inspected his smartphone. In these circumstances, they will regret the person's lack of caution and male authority, which is perceived as a failure to establish limits over his property. Friends like these are known as 'those whose wives snoop on their smartphones'. Roger, aged 61, says he is not particularly interested in pornography. But 'the group' keeps sharing it. Even if he and his wife have agreed they won't spy on each other's smartphones, he deletes the most recent group conversation every night, 'just in case'.

Carla doesn't consider herself a 'wife who snoops on her husband's smartphone', but she noticed that her husband suddenly became very attached to his device. She found this quite strange, as he had not been so interested in it previously. She thought, '*Tem boi na linha*' ('There is an ox on the line'). The Brazilian expression is used when there is a communication problem, when there is noise in the conversation, expressed through the metaphor. In Carla's case, it was something other than an ox. She didn't find any pornography, but did find intimate messages exchanged with another woman. On that occasion, she intervened. Nowadays, although she still has her husband's password, she doesn't check his messages. Her lack of interest is not coincidental. She is retired now and has just started to enjoy travelling by herself, as she got tired of waiting for her husband, who keeps postponing his retirement.

In a sense, we could argue that WhatsApp groups and private conversations challenge Brazil's foundations, as proposed by the anthropologist Roberto DaMatta.[44] As discussed in chapter 4, DaMatta identifies two universes played according to different rules: 'the house' and 'the street'. The house is a moral unit, a sacred place for the family. The street, on the other hand, is the place for work, pleasure and temptation. The house counterbalances the street, and vice versa, but they remain separate, as the house is supposed to be protected from the mundane. We could say that the house is for the wife and the street – well, what happens on the street stays on the street. We could go further and say that men are supposed to know how to keep things separate in order to preserve their marriages, and women don't have to worry about what they don't know. That was what Alves found in her ethnography of older women in Rio de Janeiro.[45] Her research participants said that as long as infidelities are kept outside the relationship, there is no reason for a crisis. Although both men and women may be unfaithful, women identify men as those who 'know how to keep things separate', meaning sex and commitment. WhatsApp blurs these boundaries when it brings the issues once restricted to 'the street' inside the home. It is not just that this kind of interaction may happen in the home. Smartphones have become a place we live in,[46] a second home but possibly with some spaces where the mundane is allowed. This means we can be at the same time 'on the street' and 'at home'. As a consequence, it is not surprising that women in Bento frequently criticise smartphones. They acknowledge the gains in communication but emphasise that they facilitate the kind of conversation that can end in casual sex and betrayal. As we will see in the following section, this doesn't mean that women won't use their smartphones for that exact purpose and for their own benefit.

It's a match

While remembering the time she flirted online with an Italian who used to end their daily conversation with *'Ciao, bella!'*, Luisa reflects on what has got worse with age. Her first complaint is about her body. Her head is full of plans and ideas, and she thinks very fast, but her body can't keep up with her mind. She brags that, until a few years ago, she could outpace anyone younger than her with her limitless energy. Nowadays, however, her challenge is understanding that if she moves too fast her legs will hurt. In addition to the limitations of her body, Luisa complains about relationships. These are another thing she believes has got worse with age. In her opinion, the men she gets to know on dating apps and websites, or even at events in Bento, are all just interested in casual sex.

> 'Men are not interested in having a relationship. They haven't been for some time. I can't tell you if this happened after this online dating business took off. It has made everything so easy. There are

a lot of offers. If you want, you can meet 10 people a day. I guess men leave when they start feeling that they are getting involved, when they start thinking about a kind of commitment. They just jump off the train. I have already learned how to deal with that. But it used to hurt me. Suddenly, they just disappear.'

Felipe, who is 63 years old, has a different perception. To him, it is women that are just interested in sex. Although he considers himself to be modern rather than conservative, he didn't enjoy his experience when he tried a dating website.

'No, no, I didn't like it. Not at all. It is the same old story … I think no one should become an object. And the fact that women turned themselves into objects … that is just terrible. I never imagined women could do that. I have a lot of male friends. We are friends. Our relationship is kind of natural. You don't see us arguing. We have our opinions, we share them, but this doesn't compromise the relationship. But you women, you are visceral, you are insane, you know? Then, when you join these websites, the women give too much away. They are hunting. If a woman wants you, she wants you. Shit! That is a crazy thing. They complain men act like hunters, but they are the ones hunting! Everything they complain about in men, they do the same. But grotesquely. They don't have natural skills. So, it is grotesque. Well, at least that was my perception. I was terrified. It works something like this: you like the person, she likes you. It is a match. It seems nice, the pictures, the chat … then you set a date. Fuck! This woman was asking for sex all the time, like asking, literally. And I was there to get to know the person. That was what I wanted. I had to say, "I didn't come here for sex. That was not the idea." And what about the risks? What about diseases? There are a lot of them out there. How does it work? Who are you dating? I didn't meet her for that. I met her to chat, to get to know her. Thus, I thought everything was very aggressive. I guess I was really scared by some of the women I met.'

Luisa and Felipe have in common the fact that they do not want to remarry. However, they would like to have a good companion to enjoy this phase of their lives with. For Luisa that is why she is tired of casual sex, something she used to enjoy in the past. For Felipe the emphasis he now places on relationships is also explained by the fact that he is experiencing impotence, a consequence of his diabetes. Drugs like Viagra are not an option for him, as they are only covered by the SUS for specific conditions. As Felipe relies exclusively on the SUS, he can't access the medication, because it is restricted to specific cases, such as pulmonary hypertension and systemic sclerosis.[47] With limited resources, as he is neither retired nor employed, he can't afford it. 'It sucks,' he says. He thus tries to develop a different approach to women. He stresses that 'only a fool would think that the relationship between a man and a woman is nothing more than sex'. Although Felipe had his first experience of dating websites and apps only recently, online encounters that may lead to casual sex are not unusual for Brazilians.

In 1996, 'Universo Online' (UOL) was launched as an internet provider, but a short time later, it also became a content producer. The Bate-Papo UOL ('UOL chat') was among its most popular products. Organised by topic, the chat rooms were a space for anonymity. To enter the room, users didn't have to fill in any forms. They just needed a nickname. At the time, the rooms dedicated to topics related to sex had the most users. Everything started with the expression 'Quer TC?' ('Want to type/chat?'). The exchanges might include sexual messages and performances and sometimes led to a face-to-face meeting. Contemporary with Bate-Papo UOL, the dating website 'Par Perfeito' (perfect match) was launched in 2000, with an approach focused on relationships. In 2006, the website was acquired by the French company METIIC. At the time, 'Par Perfeito' was the biggest dating website in Brazil and is still a significant player today.[48] In 2010, METIIC and Match.com announced a partnership for Latin America, forming Match Group LatAm, a conglomerate of dating sites.[49] The holding company owns Tinder and eHarmony, another success story among Brazilians. In 2016, Match Group LatAm expanded their portfolio in Brazil, launching 'Our Time', a dating website targeting over-fifties.[50] Having operated in the US since 2011, 'Our Time' was already the company's most successful niche product, accounting for 20 per cent of users across all of the company's niche markets.[51] 'Our Time' is not alone. 'Solteiros50' is another dating site aimed at this age group, launched by Be2, another giant in the dating business. Their official page on Facebook[52] advertises the service as a dating website for 'singles at their *best age*'. This is also the approach adopted by the Brazilian website 'Coroametade',[53] which is described as 'the dating website for those who are in the *best phase* of their lives'. This section shows that the image of the 'best age' may be more a market-driven approach than an experience shared by research participants when it comes to sex and relationships.

Even though these platforms are popular among Brazilians, research participants are still getting used to them, learning how to act and how to react. Take Rose's case. She might be considered old-fashioned. A widow of 70, she was introduced to her partner by relatives. One day, a cousin realised they were both single and thought they might be a good match. When a couple don't have shared social relations, dating websites open up the possibility for older people to experience sex without the obligation to commit and without having to explain anything to anybody if they decide to end the affair and move on. For example, when Rose and her partner broke up, he had to answer her relatives' questions and cope with their judgement of him, as he had ended the relationship. However, when a match is made by a dating platform, ending things can be much more straightforward. To repeat what Luisa said, 'Suddenly, they just disappear.' This practice is known as 'ghosting', which means 'ending a relationship with someone suddenly by stopping all communication with them'.[54] The platform increases both the number and type of possible dating partners. However, among research participants, a dating pool that includes multiple generations can challenge the notion that they are living in their 'best age'.

The facilities brought by dating platforms place the 'best age' in the era of the 'liquid love'[55] proposed by Zygmunt Bauman. In this new logic, people themselves become goods, available for the ephemeral consumption of the other. In this market focused on immediate pleasures, in which everyone is disposable, people work on the best image of themselves, highlighting their best qualities (or creating ones they believe would make them more desirable) to catch others' attention and be chosen by them. These market-like values can be seen in the terms older people use to describe their seduction strategies, as observed in Rio de Janeiro[56] and also in Bento. Lúcio, for example, used the expression 'Special products have aggressive competitors. I have to show my best,' to explain to his friend all his efforts to keep his partner, who is 10 years younger than him. The orientation towards the here and now, which is a characteristic of 'liquid love', can be regarded positively, as research participants are genuinely focused on living in the present. One problem is that when they enter the 'liquid love' market, they do so with an aged body, of the kind Luisa and Felipe complained about above.

Moreover, as pointed out in chapter 2, people often feel younger than they are. They therefore tend to search for youth, which can result in mismatches. Luisa, for example, believes that men of her age only want to date younger women. So if she didn't lie about her age she would be left with those who were much older than her and lacking in vigour, as she argued earlier. The men's demand for youth may lead them to rule out women aged between 50 and 60, based on their age. As these women enter the menopause, they may be seen as old. Bianca explains how it works. Although she feels guilty that she does no physical activity and never refuses the piece of cake offered to her daily by her work colleagues, she has maintained her svelte figure. She has also invested in anti-ageing creams and has had liposuction in the past. She feels good about the fact that she doesn't look her age. She remembers that, in her forties, she was very successful when it came to younger men. She hasn't entered the menopause yet, but her friends have, which terrifies her. Her current partner, who she met on a dating website, got divorced six years ago. He complains that his then wife entered the menopause, and sex became infrequent and more difficult, which damaged their relationship. She worries that the same thing could happen to her.

> 'I don't think I'm ready for this. I want things to stay the way they are for a while. People say that sexual relations become more difficult, painful. They say the libido decreases. These aesthetic and physical changes are even more visible with the menopause. Even psychologically, it is an undeniable sign that old age has arrived. It is like there is a life before and after the menopause. The significance of this is huge. Most of my single friends have been trying to date for a while. And now, with the menopause, their chances of doing so are even slimmer. I think it is even harder to manage this. They want to have a relationship. They go out to try to meet someone, to date. But I see it is even more complicated with the menopause. Imagine, for example, meeting someone and going further until the moment you find yourself in bed … and then you need extra lubrication. God, the first time you are having sex with someone you have just met … it is complicated. It seems like a slap in the face, really complicated. Lubrication is the thing that worries me most. Even with him [her partner] being older than me. He is not a boy either. I don't know. Even so, it is complicated for men to understand this moment in women's lives. Only those who have been through this can understand what it means.'

On top of fears related to the menopause, women between 50 and 60 years old may exit the affective and sexual 'market' when they realise their bodies don't match the ideal of the desirable young body. Because they feel inadequate, some women may opt to take what Goldenberg, in her work in Rio de Janeiro, calls 'sexual retirement'.[57] However, if they stay 'in the market', women may look for men younger than themselves. What is at stake here is not necessarily the search for a youthful appearance. Women may be looking for sexual performance too. That puts men under pressure as well, especially if they start to experience impotence. As masculinity is deeply associated with erection and penetration in Brazil, impotence directly impacts men's identity,[58] just as menopause may impact women's identity. As suggested earlier in this chapter, this may not be a problem for married couples whose relationship is now focused more on friendship than on sexual activity. However, 'in the market', impotence can make men obsolete. The good news is that this issue *can be* easily fixed. More than that, it *should be* fixed, as it has become another function individuals have a moral responsibility to prevent and reverse. In support of this view, the term 'impotence' has been replaced by 'erectile dysfunction', a problem Viagra has solved.[59]

Although Viagra is likely to meet the functional/dysfunctional biosocial rationality that supports the idea that men should achieve health and well-being, as discussed by Katz and Marshall,[60] it is interesting to note how the drug was advertised in the Brazilian context.[61] Viagra ads and media coverage have explored the cultural values attributed to Brazilian men's masculinity, highlighting virility, sexual appetite and performance focused on heterosexual penetrative sex.[62] The same strategy was explored later by other competitors. 'It is time to show the capital M that is at the heart of each and every Brazilian Man' was, for example, the approach used by Helleva®, which was the first Viagra-like pill produced by a national pharmaceutical company.[63] It is possible to say that what is at stake in Brazil is not only recovering functionality but recovering the status of a Brazilian man. Erectile dysfunction should also be approached from the research participants' perspective. As argued earlier in this chapter, retirement has challenged men's identity in Bento. It is not just that they have lost their professional credentials. They also face challenges to keep their roles as providers, a status culturally attributed to men in Brazil. That means that the 'best age' might come with the decline or loss of the two central elements on which their male reputation is socially built.

As argued above, erectile dysfunction medications such as Viagra could solve one of these problems. However, the use of such medications may be restricted by financial constraints or health conditions. Men may take extreme measures in the latter case, such as having injections applied directly into the penis to produce an erection.[64] Luisa once had an experience of this kind. Her partner had a heart condition, so taking Viagra would have been a risk. But he was obsessive about penetration. He arrived at one of their dates in a state of euphoria. 'It is today!', he told her. 'Guess who had to give him the injection?', she laughs. However, it is more common for men to shift their narratives to focus on partnership and mutual support, as Felipe did at the beginning of this section. This stage of life may be the time for men to opt for 'sexual retirement'. Women with active sex lives may respond to men's 'second retirement' with resilience. In some cases, having a good partner compensates for a life without (penetrative) sex. That is the case with Rose. At 70, she explains that, on her side, 'everything is working', referring to her latest partner, who had erectile dysfunction. But she decided to express solidarity, sublimating the desire for sex and focusing on other pleasures they experienced together, like going out, dancing and travelling.

There is another possible match. Partners may find together ways of achieving sexual satisfaction by investing in a sexual life that doesn't necessarily include coital sex.[65] In addition, the performative sex may be replaced by moments that allow the enjoyment of pleasure in a more relaxed way.[66] This was how Luisa came to abandon dating websites and casual sex. Embarrassed, her current partner initially used his impotence as an excuse for not starting a relationship, but Luisa led him to new forms of excitement. As a mature woman, she has learned how to explore other areas of the body to give and achieve sexual pleasure.[67] They have been dating for a year now. Her only complaint is, again, her body. Her sleep time is compromised by the nights they spend together in intimacy. She regrets that she doesn't recover from lack of sleep as easily as she did when she was young. This is something she hasn't learned to overcome yet.

Possible happy endings

This chapter has addressed how biological, social and economic events impact sexuality in old age. It includes the menopause, libido decline, retirement, impotence, lack of rapport, divorce, demands from children and elderly parents, and the challenges the 'liquid love' market presents to the 'best age'. However, the chapter also shows there are multiple possibilities for happy endings that can result in satisfaction for research participants, whether with sex or without. The things that turn them on may change. They can be more focused on themselves. They can enjoy new freedoms, try new possibilities and discover pleasure in activities they now want to work on. As the next chapter suggests, that is why they may end up reinventing their best age.

Notes

1. Ussher et al. (2015) argue that the menopausal or post-menopausal woman popularly represented in Western culture is 'asexual, unattractive' or 'desperately attempting to hold on to youth and beauty long gone'. They claim that that is why examples like Luisa arouse fascination. Luisa embodies the contradiction between age and sexuality, remaining desirable and sexually active.
2. Wilson 1966.
3. Trench and Rosa 2008.
4. Writing Group for the Women's Health Initiative Investigators 2002.
5. *Folha de S. Paulo Cotidiano* 2002.
6. Lopes 2007.
7. Brasil, Ministério da Saúde 2008.
8. Health promotion during the menopause also includes anti-tobacco initiatives, alcohol consumption control, quality of sleep, skincare and oral health.
9. The *Manual de Atenção à Mulher no Climatério/Menopausa* ('handbook of care for women in the menopause') draws attention to the systematic use of hormones as part of the medicalisation of women's bodies. The publication stresses that menopausal women are not suffering from a disease and that HRT should only be considered when there are specific recommendations for it (Brasil, Ministério da Saúde 2008, p. 12). Among research participants, women are concerned that HRT may be seen as a beauty routine. Beauty routines, which can include cosmetic surgery, may be seen as unnecessary, especially by daughters who judge that their mothers shouldn't still be focusing on appearance. This is another sphere in which autonomy can sustain freedom, in this case financial independence. That is what allows Lourdes, aged 64, to stop her daughter's criticisms by saying, 'I like it. I want it. I can pay for it.'
10. This was observed by Brooks (2017) in her work with North American women and by Castro and Rocha (2018), Leibing (2005), Goldenberg (2010) and Edmonds (2014) in Brazil.
11. Ministério da Saúde & Instituto Sírio-Libanês de Ensino e Pesquisa 2016.
12. C. Pereira & Penalva 2014.
13. Trench & Rosa 2008.
14. Trench & Rosa 2008.
15. This was not the case in China, for example, where hot flushes were rarely associated with embarrassment (Shea 2020).
16. In their study in Sydney, Ussher et al. (2015) found that some women associate the menopause with freedom: from the risk of getting pregnant or from 'sexual urges'. The way women experience the menopause and the meanings attributed to it vary depending on the cultural context. For example, Costa & Gualda (2008) found that in a low-income community in Paraíba, Brazil, women can feel released from the risk of getting pregnant. In addition, free from menstruation, these women experience more autonomy. At the same time, however, men in this community associate the end of a woman's fertility with the end of her femininity. In Bento too, some women associate menopause with autonomy. However, this autonomy is related more to the end of the cramps, migraines and anaemia associated with menstruation than to the end of fertility. Besides, to women with no children, menstruation was seen as an onus without a bonus. For them, the end of menstruation is a positive fact when it is detached from menopausal symptoms. In some cases, this autonomy is materialised by donating the sanitary napkins they had in stock in their houses. Sisters or nieces commonly receive them. Some women, more pragmatic, will also take into account how much money the menopause saves them, as they no longer have to buy sanitary towels. As reported by some interviewed participants, the menopause can be experienced as a kind of freedom, as they are released from the burden of menstruation and now have more control over their bodies. For Chinese and Chinese American women living in the US, however, this agency can have different outcomes. Adler et al. (2020) found that the menopause is seen by some of these women as an opportunity for a second chance in life. That is not the case in Bento, where this second chance is associated with retirement.
17. By doing this, Gisele complies with the idea that individuals become responsible for their own 'preventive and rehabilitative body care' in old age (Katz & Marshall 2004, p. 67).
18. Debert (2014) observed a gender bias in her ethnography conducted in Campinas, in Brazil. Married women are more likely than unmarried women to value companionship and quality

rather than quantity when addressing their sexual life. Unmarried women approach sex as one more marital obligation they are now released from. Men, on the contrary, still see desire and sexual intercourse as central to masculinity and as a 'resistance' to becoming old.
19. As Sievert (2006, p. 123) writes, changes in interest in sex and vaginal dryness can overlap, as the latter can turn sex into a painful activity. However, she stresses that, for women, interest in sex also has emotional roots, as discussed later in this chapter.
20. The married men interviewed in Bento are not keen to restore their sexual performance. Wentzell (2013) observed the same in Cuernavaca, Mexico, where, despite all the publicity in the country on drugs such as Viagra and the discourses about successful ageing, a decline in sexual activity was seen as natural by men. Moreover, the vigorous sex of youth was seen as inappropriate at this stage of life, when home and family become more valued, with an increase in partnership between husband and wife. Even among women who claim to like sex, this change was welcomed and supported as appropriate to mature masculinity. The other way round may not be true, at least not in Pueblo, also in Mexico. Sievert (2006, p. 126) observed that married women may release men to look for sex outside the marriage when they feel their interest in sex is 'all finished'. The author adds an example of a woman who was not interested in sex because of vaginal dryness (combined with the always abusive behaviour of her husband). Her husband diminished her by saying she was 'no better than a dog underfoot', which is similar to what happened to Lourdes, in Bento, whose husband told her that she looks like a 'nun'. As set out in this chapter, married men may respond differently when the lack of desire comes from them or from their wives, and according to whether both are focused on interests other than sex.
21. DaMatta 1986; Brigeiro & Maksud 2009; Azize 2014; Faro et al. 2013.
22. Ussher et al. 2015.
23. Ramakuela et al. 1994.
24. Lock 1994.
25. In Bento, for example, hot flushes are the symptom most reported by women. However, that was not the case in China (Shea 2020) or in Japan (Lock 1994).
26. Strauss 2013; Ussher et al. 2015.
27. Murtagh & Hepworth 2003.
28. L. Hall et al. 2007.
29. Costa & Gualda 2008.
30. Trench & Rosa 2008.
31. C. Pereira & Penalva 2014.
32. Brooks 2017.
33. Higgs et al. 2009.
34. Rocha & Miné 2018.
35. Leibing 2005; Goldenberg 2010; Edmonds 2014.
36. Leibing (2005) uses the example of the Brazilian actress Fernanda Montenegro, nominated for an Oscar in her seventies, to argue that within Brazilian culture, the continuity of previous work is a way to age with integrity. In Bento, however, being seen as active is enough to achieve this sense of integrity, whether the activities women choose are attached to their previous career or not.
37. Calasanti and King (2017) argue there is a difference in the way men and women keep their gender identity. While men are focused on maintaining their ability to perform physically, women worry about losing their attractiveness and becoming invisible.
38. Women in the US, too, are struggling to deal with the invisibility they experience in old age. As Brooks (2017) found, not being perceived as physically and sexually desirable is one reason for opting for anti-ageing procedures.
39. Goldenberg 2013.
40. In the US, Thomas et al. (2014) found that higher maintenance of sexual activity in later life is associated with the importance women attributed to it in midlife.
41. Sievert 2006; Cawood & Bancroft 1996; Dennerstein et al. 2005; Osborn et al. 1988.
42. Barthes 2010.
43. In a survey conducted with adults aged 45 and over in the US, Fisher et al. (2010) also found that financial status was among the factors influencing current sexual satisfaction among couples.
44. DaMatta 1986.
45. Alves 2014, pp. 165–6.

46 Miller et al. 2021.
47 Consultoria Jurídica/Advocacia Geral da União, 2015.
48 Agência Estado 2006.
49 Match.com 2010.
50 Souza 2016.
51 Gomes 2018.
52 Solteiros50 Brasil 2021.
53 CoroaMetade 2021.
54 Cambridge Dictionary [online] 2021.
55 Bauman 2003.
56 Alves 2014, p. 169; Edmonds 2014, p. 247.
57 Goldenberg 2013.
58 Giami (2007) discusses how men's sexuality was historically focused on the penis and its performance, leading to representations of men mainly anchored in their biological and mechanical nature. Moreover, in the Brazilian scenario, Separavich and Canesqui (2013) argue that male identity was built through imagery in which men play the role of a superman who was expected to provide super-performances, including sexual ones. Therefore, men are not supposed to fail or even be ill. For this reason, the focus on the penis promotes an association between masculinity and penetration.
59 Katz & Marshall 2004.
60 Katz & Marshall 2004.
61 In Mexico too, masculinity is constructed on virility and sex drive. However, the Viagra advertising there focused also on the vigorous sex of youth. As Wentzell (2017, p. 68) stresses, youthfulness and masculinity are embedded in the discourse. She illustrates this association with a Viagra ad, in which a man is sleeping on a bed, his back bearing scratch marks from a partner, who has left, leaving a note that says 'Thanks, you were incredible! You acted like you were 20!'
62 Brigeiro & Maksud 2009; Azize 2014.
63 Faro et al. 2013.
64 Coombs et al. 2012.
65 Ussher et al. 2015.
66 Rozendo & Alves 2015.
67 Luisa's example illustrates a new gerontological approach which focuses on an attempt to eroticise and prolong sexuality in old age, as observed by Debert in Brazil. In the opposite way to the pharmaceutical market's target of erectile dysfunction correction, she writes, this new generation of gerontologists suggests that decline in sexual activity in old age can be compensated for by a 'more holistic bodily experience' in which older people can achieve a 'unique and intense sexual pleasure, based not so much on genitals' (Debert 2014, p. 238).

8
Seeking a purpose in life

If not now, then when?

'It is not that we have a short time to live but that we waste a lot of it.' The aphorism comes from the philosopher Seneca.[1] According to the Stoic, it is only near the end of one's life, when there are just a few years left, that we stop working and start living. Retirement is usually the event responsible for this shift, marking the end of obligations to others and providing the free time to contemplate life, develop self-consciousness, experience freedom and live authentically. However, Seneca raises the critical question: what guarantees do we have that we will live to retire, or live longer once we do? According to the World Health Organization,[2] 'critical gains in public health and standards of living' have allowed people to live longer, resulting in the 'worldwide triumph of population ageing'.

That was the case in Brazil, as covered in chapter 2. Moreover, before the pension reform in 2019, Brazilians could retire if they met one of two criteria: either their age, or their years of contribution to the pension system, with no minimum age.[3] In that year, the average age at retirement in the country was 54.55 years.[4] Taking an optimistic view, if we take life expectancy at birth in Bento (80.83 years[5]) and the average age at retirement in Brazil, we could argue that participants are likely to enjoy more than two decades of life after retirement. However, as shown in chapter 2, this is not a prospect for everyone, as some were made redundant before they were eligible to retire. Even so, in answer to Seneca, it is possible to say that people in Bento *do* have quite a long time to live after retirement.

Yet, as this book argues, leisure time after retirement is not entirely free from obligations. Older people in Bento may be retired, but they are still engaged in other duties, including those related to elderly parents, their children (who may be their dependants) and the maintenance of their autonomy. Ultimately, they must remain independent, as they are expected not to become a burden on the family, society or the state. However, research participants are not alone in facing this challenge. Like those in Bento, retirees from the United States[6] and Japan[7] strive to achieve a balance between freedom and duty, autonomy and dependence, pleasure and guilt, individuality and altruism. What comes after retirement can be seen as a 'moral project', in which choices are made in negotiation with cultural values, personal aspirations and social demands and updated by policies on ageing that define autonomy, health and productivity as virtues in old age.[8] In work-oriented Bento, we have already seen that participants fill their timetable with as many 'appointments' as they can. Whether these 'appointments' are related to pleasures, duties or both, being busy is a virtue in Bento. This orientation to productivity was also observed among Americans by Savishinsky,[9] who called it the 'busy ethic' of retirement. Keeping oneself busy, then, is a way of avoiding the stigma that attaches to retirees as useless to society.[10] Luborsky[11] also noticed that, with the goal of keeping busy, newly retired Americans engaged in hands-on projects in their houses and that this time helped them to avoid the 'full retiree' stigma and craft an identity that reconciles new self-images and social life after retirement.

Among older people in Bento, however, this 'identity' is still attached to their careers. As we saw in chapter 2, research participants are likely to introduce themselves by presenting their previous professional credentials, while seeking new occupations to *compensate* for them. It is true that, by engaging in these occupations, they can fulfil what ageing policies expect of them. But what is at stake here, first and foremost, is the maintenance of their identity as *citizens of São Paulo*. This means that life after retirement is not just a question of time and how to use it properly. The sense of place matters too.[12] Indeed, retirement is a life event during which one decides where one wants to age, a deliberation that can result in continuity or change (from moving away to downsizing, for example). But the point to stress here is that, for research participants, the continuation of work in old age is perceived as a condition of their permanence in Bento. But we could argue that their relationship with work has changed. If it has, as has been observed among Americans,[13] retirees will be 'free from work' as an obligation, which means they are 'free to work' in whatever activities give them pleasure and purpose. However, what seems a particularity in Bento is that, even after retirement, participants are likely to experience work in two ways, as an obligation and as a source of pleasure and purpose. This is the final balance they need to achieve if they are to maintain their citizenship and age with integrity. Thus Bento challenges Seneca's argument that life is postponed to the period after retirement. Research participants will not actually feel free to *start living* when they are released from obligations to work and to others. On the contrary, through reinventing work, they find the conditions to make life meaningful, to belong and to stay alive.[14]

Thus, we could argue that older people in Bento are less like Seneca and more like Cicero,[15] another Roman philosopher, to whom the continuation of work in old age was not just a way of developing a virtuous character but also a measure (among others) for staying healthy, active and socially connected.[16] Cicero uses himself as an example in a rhetorical argument to show that his devotion to work, applied to self-development, learning, supporting his friends or going to the Senate 'without being forced', could balance the inevitable declines of ageing and extend the sense of utility and joy in old age. In his words, 'One who is always occupied in these studies and labors is unaware when age creeps upon him. Thus one grows old gradually and unconsciously, and life is not suddenly extinguished, but closes when by the length of time it is burned out.'[17]

This chapter addresses the three main ways in which older people in Bento are crafting new forms of work in order to age with integrity and purpose, as suggested by Cicero. While they may not be formal kinds of work, they are taken seriously as showing professionalism and often reproducing working routines. The first of the three is the development of new skills, mainly to work as entrepreneurs. The second is investment in self-knowledge and autonomy. The third is volunteering. It may not be a coincidence that these forms of work are closely related to the three ways in which character is shaped in society, as proposed by Sennett.[18] He argues that people can show character and win respect by developing abilities and skills (self-development), by remaining self-sufficient (care of the self), or by giving back to others (altruism). As we will see, gaining respect and a sense of belonging as a senior citizen of São Paulo may become the purpose of life in old age. By working towards this, research participants reshape the representation of old age in Bento, expanding their permissions and freedoms as a kind of activism, as will be addressed in the conclusion. However, before embracing work, they will take a deep breath and face their past to know what they have achieved so far.

Settling a score with the past

By recalling their past, older people can evaluate their actions and experiences. This accountability results in self-awareness and narratives that vindicate their existence, accomplishments and character.[19] In other words, they may go through a crisis, like anyone who faces the challenge of reflecting on life.[20] But it is true, as we will see in this section, that old age creates the conditions that push older people further in the direction of introspection. First, there is the time they spend by themselves after retirement. Secondly, there is the awareness that death is closer than before, especially when they experience the loss of some of their loved ones.

Under these conditions, older people may look back and evaluate the life they have lived so far. They may achieve a sense of integrity if the past is considered positive and successful, and so gain serenity and wisdom. However, if that is not the case, they may experience disillusionment or regret.[21] Maybe the idea that, in the end, life can be judged good or bad, satisfactory or not, is not enough. Older people may be very satisfied with their family, for example, but frustrated with their working life. One of these things may compensate for the other, or it may not, depending on the importance attributed to each. What seems to be relevant here is finding some evidence that life is worth it. Often, this evidence is taken as a legacy or something that deserves some continuity or raises issues of succession.[22] Indeed, this something may be anything that denotes that they have left a 'mark on the earth'.[23]

A possible outcome of this drawing up of the balance sheet is that a career characterised by dedication, discipline and passion has the potential to leave behind a legacy strong enough to bring a positive sense of balance into one's life. However, as we saw in chapter 2, retirement has challenged research participants' sense of usefulness and, in some cases, the emotional attachment they had to work. Some retired because of rumours of an imminent reform to the national pension system. In contrast, others were made redundant or included in compulsory retirement programmes as their employers no longer valued their experience. In both cases, retirement was unexpected, undesired or unfair. The note on which each of them ended their working life may define their overall perception of it. However, it is possible to say that, in Bento, this generation shares the feeling that the working life they were devoted to was interrupted. They feel they still had work to do, and they enjoyed doing it. That was how Roberta felt. Today, at 69, she remembers that suddenly, after retirement, there was nothing, only emptiness. 'I was really, really, really angry. I just couldn't deal with my retirement with all that useless time. It was a tough time,' she says. Felipe, aged 63, also shows how traumatic this 'exit' can be:

> 'I used to be in what I considered to be a valued role in the senior management of the bank. When another company bought the bank, as my supervisor liked me she did what she could to keep me there, but in a different department. Then everything changed. My responsibilities were very different, and so was the company culture. Before I left, I was also harassed by my new colleagues.'

Because of ruptures like the ones experienced by Roberta and Felipe, not all research participants can romanticise their past at work or retain the memories which could contribute to a positive perception of life in retirement. In such cases, their families may compensate for the loss of work, providing them with alternative memories to support the feeling that they have lived a good life. Feeling proud of a marriage lasting for many decades, having successful children or grandchildren and having evidence that these have inherited their values may be enough to give research participants the sense of having lived worthwhile lives, leading to a sense of dignity, resilience and wisdom. Indeed, some marriages are celebrated as a significant accomplishment. However, as we saw in the previous chapter, not all couples have reached this stage of life in a cherished partnership. Indeed, quite often, the time at which older people are rethinking their lives is also the time when they are facing a crisis in their marriage. Rosangela, for example, gets sad when she looks back. Recently, she has started to question the foundations of her marriage, as now, aged 68, she realises that her husband was never really in love with her. Juliana, aged 66, is more focused on the important things she and her husband have achieved in life, but her present experience is making her memories fade away. As she puts it, 'Before, he used to invite me to do things with him. Now, when I look for him, he has already gone.'

Apart from marriage, children, where present, could make their parents' lives worthwhile. As we saw in chapter 4, on retirement parents lose their professional status. From this moment onwards, they appropriate their children's achievements as their social capital. Sometimes they consider themselves to have sacrificed their own achievements for their children's education. Thus the children's success is used to compensate for what they couldn't achieve themselves. That is the case with Bete, aged 66. She worked hard her entire life as a hairdresser to give her child a good education. She couldn't become a bilingual secretary as she wanted. But her daughter compensates for that with her PhD degree and a successful international career. Juliana shares this feeling. She says she doesn't have to accomplish anything else in life. Like her father, she considers education the best 'inheritance' she could leave to her children. Although their children's education plays a significant role in how they evaluate their lives, it is not enough to give research participants a sense of purpose after retirement, as they consider that they have already achieved their primary goal, of offering their children a better future. Instead of receiving expressions of gratitude from their children, research participants are likely to realise that their children have no time or patience for anything and do not value their knowledge and advice, as they are likely to be seen as 'outdated'.

Even if the memories they cherish of their time in their careers or spent with their family make them look back on life fondly, the sense of integrity these memories provide is only enough to make them feel happy about their past. But what about the future? At this point, research participants are likely to share a feeling of incompleteness triggered by the experience of loss when they face the death of someone close to them. They don't fear death itself. Religion, spirituality and faith give them comfort and security concerning the afterlife. It doesn't matter if they believe in resurrection or reincarnation, or go to church or the temple or follow Umbanda (an Afro-Brazilian religion practised in Brazil). They share the belief that theirs is just one life in the journey of existence. Death is not the end but a sort of rebirth perceived as renovation. The death of the ones they love, however, has a different weight. It creates awareness of the years left to live. And that is how, suddenly, they find the urgency to fill, with purpose, the time they have left. In other words, life after retirement can come with 'the intimidations of mortality'.[24] Rose, aged 70, explains what this means. Since her father died, she has been thinking about the years left. 'You have to think about death every day to live well, to turn every single day into a special one,' she says.

Research participants have also learned from their elderly parents that 'real' death can come earlier when someone becomes ill or frail. Thus, the 'first' death they face is dependence. That makes the call to live in the present even more urgent. Even for those who ended with a positive retrospective view of their life, this is the moment when they stop contemplating the past and reorient their attention to the present, to live every moment in a meaningful way.[25] Reflections on the purpose of life are replaced by the desire to live life with purpose.[26] This desire drives older people in Bento back to work. This work can itself represent a project, as proposed by Simone de Beauvoir[27] and discussed by the

Brazilian anthropologist Miriam Goldenberg[28] as a way of rescuing those who have reached old age from emptiness and invisibility. In Bento, despite giving a purpose to everyday life, this project can come with a bonus, especially when approached as a full-time job. Research participants can recover the social life they lost on retirement while solving the problem of inactivity so widely condemned in their community. In addition, even when it is not oriented to those ends, working on a project can keep research participants healthy, as they identify being busy with being healthy. The following section discusses how older people in Bento are reinventing the possibilities of work after retirement, mainly through becoming entrepreneurs.

A new type of work for older people

A new commercial role is not usually an option for older people in Bento. First, the market, for the most part, no longer values their experience. Secondly, they recognise that their physical abilities may no longer be compatible with the demands of regular working hours, which are now extended by the internet and smartphones. Thirdly, they don't want to be stuck in corporations whose values they don't admire. As mentioned above, they may already have become disillusioned with these companies, when they retired or were made redundant. Instead, they are building new narratives based on their own values. Generally, research participants don't want to work for other people. They want to work *with* other people, for themselves. By doing so, they hope to achieve a healthy old age, one in which they are useful and productive and enjoy the city they live in. In other words, they hope they can spend their time working and having pleasure while doing something meaningful. They may well make some money. If they do not, they may instead make gains in dignity, a social life and self-realisation. This was what made Beto seek change.

> 'I was a benchmark on the market. I owned one of the first internet providers in Brazil. Then other players came, and everything changed. Today, 500,000 guys are doing the same things I used to do but with more infrastructure, so I wanted to leave. When I turned 50, I started thinking about what I was going to do with my life. I started feeling really, really, really old. A male midlife crisis, maybe. I don't know. You realise that life is finite, that it is approaching the end. At the time, I thought about death. My father died when he was 47. He went from being healthy to dying within a month due to

aggressive cancer. So at 50 I thought I might die too. Now I think about doing something meaningful. I have never worried about taking care of myself, but for some reason I started thinking that I still have some important things to do in this life. I then started thinking about something that I enjoy doing. I wanted to use my expertise to do something for myself. Also, I was always unsociable, but suddenly this changed too. I just left my bubble. I started a website focused on content production, targeting people who were more or less my age. I started attending many events and got to know everybody. I don't expect to become rich. What I consider nice now is doing something useful to others.'

Now aged 58, Beto is an entrepreneur. In addition to his website, he has developed other initiatives aimed at older people and their needs. Because their needs are also his needs, his actions made him feel he is living his life with a purpose. He turned his experience in the technology sector into a portfolio of courses and workshops that promote digital inclusion among older people. The courses tackle subjects like blockchain, artificial intelligence and chatbots, as he believes older people need to be knowledgeable about these things in order to join the conversation with the new generation. In addition, he gives support to older people who want to become entrepreneurs themselves. He teaches them how they can start a blog or an online business, for example. His ventures are among the most popular initiatives aimed at the third age in Bento, and he was recently selected to join a start-up trainee programme at Google.

As opposed to working for corporations, entrepreneurship seems to be a perfect alternative for research participants. As Casaqui[29] explains, the entrepreneurship culture is also a communicational phenomenon, with an affective-prescriptive logic, in which the entrepreneur represents a kind of hero whose journey is used to inspire others in neoliberal economies. Entrepreneurs are self-made, authentic and committed to making the world a better place. Their narratives are based on resilience and willpower, which means entrepreneurship is a meritocracy. For research participants, this means that, through entrepreneurship, they can rewrite the end of their working lives. As entrepreneurs, they rise from the ashes like the legendary phoenix. They are back in the game with a new professional credential that attests that they remain productive and useful, as any citizen of São Paulo should be. In addition, they find purpose in what they are doing. And if they take the risk of starting a business project that offers no guarantees, they do so because they understand that they are working for themselves, motivated by their beliefs. Thus, research participants who became entrepreneurs are in charge of many initiatives that end up benefiting older people.

Vera, 62 years old, is an example. When she turned 60, she realised that she still has many years left to live. She started to think about how to prepare for the second half of her productive life. She took a course that helped her map her abilities and purpose in life. This process of gaining self-awareness resulted in a co-housing start-up founded with friends and based on a platform that matches people who want to live and grow old in shared houses. An alternative to care homes, co-housing is gaining the attention and interest of older people in Bento, Brazil,[30] and worldwide.[31] Co-housing meets the needs of older people in different ways. It can improve social lives, prolong independence of family and help older people reduce their living costs, as many expenses are shared.

Airbnb is another entrepreneurial possibility for participants. The management of properties and rooms is taken on as a new kind of work, lighter, informal and with immediate payback. For example, after the death of her husband, when her children had already left home, Diana, aged 69, decided to let three rooms in her house through Airbnb. Many of her guests are frequent returners, and one of them rented a room for an extended stay. She doesn't think his presence disturbs her privacy. Instead, they have become friends, and because of him she is no longer alone. Now there is always someone at home to talk to, other than her dog. In addition to the extra income and the social contact that comes with it, dealing with Airbnb helps her fill her free time, as she manages other tasks like the laundry and cleaning. To Diana, her work as a host doesn't necessarily represent additional housework. Instead, she sees it as a pleasant occupation that makes her feel useful and busy.

Flávio, aged 72, has similar feelings. As we saw in chapter 5, his family uses Airbnb to let a second flat they own in the building they live in. The flat can accommodate up to eight guests and the demand for accommodation in this area is enormous. Because Bento is a hub for medical services and education, people come here from different parts of Brazil and abroad to study and for medical treatments. Flávio has not worked out how to use the platform but is responsible for interacting with guests. Whether via WhatsApp or in person, this task is responsible for a large part of Flávio's sociality. The guests may compensate for the loss of a time when neighbours knew each other and had lunch together on Sundays. 'The new ones don't want to talk. They are not friendly at all,' he complains. They can also compensate for the social life he lost when he retired. In addition, Flávio now has an occupation. A house cleaner helps him, but he is in charge of doing the laundry and managing any issues that come up. His work as host has restored his self-esteem, as he can end his day feeling he has spent his time with a purpose.

Becoming a host or founding a start-up can be very different experiences, but both can be retold through entrepreneurship narratives. These narratives inspire others, as they demonstrate that finding a meaningful and pleasant occupation in old age is possible. Entrepreneurs are heroes who succeed in reconciling work, pleasure and purpose. The senior person in charge of a start-up that teaches older people how to write computer games, the personal stylist, the trip adviser and the digital influencer are just a few examples of the trajectories of older people who share this crusade. However, there is no prescribed way of getting on this boat. The idea of what to do doesn't come in a eureka moment. On the contrary, finding an occupation that can give a purpose to life demands some work. Thus, the search can become an occupation in itself. In other words, before committing themselves to a pleasant occupation they value, older people in Bento have to find what they value and what pleases them. That can be a problem.

Some of the research participants had never found a vocation in life, even when they were young. Others are just seeking a change, whatever it may be. They are different people now, so they want to come up with something different and meaningful. Moreover, they are under pressure. The clock is ticking and their social networks are full of posts and articles about entrepreneurs who have succeeded at their age. As argued earlier, this success is not necessarily measured in financial gains but is based on older people's attitudes and the impact they can have on the experience of ageing. That impact is what puts Beto and Vera frequently in the press, and their articles and interviews are shared and celebrated on research participants' social media. They are proof that older people can reinvent themselves to remain productive and do work that matters. The entrepreneur's image is aligned with the representation of old age in Bento as active, healthy and autonomous, as discussed in chapter 2. That causes more anxiety, first because not everyone wants to play the role of entrepreneur and secondly because not everybody fits the new representation (and demands) of old age.

For example, Patricia was never sure what she wanted to do, and she went through her professional life with a certain degree of passivity. She first thought about becoming a psychologist, but a vocational test showed that she got too involved in other people's problems. She ended up studying cinema. Her choice was influenced by friends who, at the time, also took this course. She worked at the film library in Bento, but she never made a film herself. In addition, she has always enjoyed studying languages and has taken English, French, German and Japanese classes. She started teaching French when her friend invited her to do so, thinking that this would help her overcome her shyness. She built a new career in one of the most respected French schools in Bento. She worked there for many years until she was made redundant a few years before she reached retirement age.

The older generation of teachers, her colleagues, were dismissed before her, because they tended to express their opinions freely, which was seen as inconvenient.[32] For most of her life, she was the kind of person who never complained. But before she was fired, Patricia noticed that she was changing, as she started to express her thoughts at work more openly too. A few years ago, through Facebook, she reconnected with her classmates from college. It wasn't long before they decided to meet in person. They organised an event, but Patricia was seriously considering not joining them. 'I was going to meet people who had succeeded, who did stuff in life, but I have done nothing,' she said. Today, at 65, Patricia has joined many groups and attended many events focused on developing new forms of work and entrepreneurship aimed at the third age in Bento. Although she gets involved and makes contributions to her new friends' ideas, she has no idea what she will do. She knows she has to do something, but she feels lost and anxious. Embarrassed, she says, 'I have to reinvent myself.'

Professional reinvention in old age is not just a self-awareness journey. It is a call for older people to play their roles as protagonists of their ageing, which means it is their responsibility to find an occupation that provides them with happiness and fulfilment, as well as physical, mental and financial autonomy. While research participants discuss their possibilities through courses, events and groups, a complex market is developing to prescribe and manage the kind of 'reinvention' they are supposed to engage in.[33] The Empreendedorismo Sênior ('senior entrepreneurship') programme, for example, focuses on the skills people older than 50 need to develop in order to become entrepreneurs. On their website,[34] they explain what they can deliver:

> Here, we are not concerned with teaching magic formulas for you to become a millionaire. Instead, we will help you to find your path, so that you can perform an activity which gives you pleasure while making you feel useful, productive and valued, leading to healthy longevity.

The promise that staying active can lead to healthy longevity has gained prominence among the public policies promoting active ageing in Bento.

For example, the Hospital do Coração (HCor; heart hospital) hosted a free course aimed at people in the third age and focused on entrepreneurship. The event was in partnership with the Serviço Brasileiro de Apoio às Micro e Pequenas Empresas (Sebrae; Brazilian service for the support of micro and small businesses), the Conselho Estadual do Idoso (state council for the elderly) and the Secretaria do Desenvolvimento Social (social development secretariat).[35] Although there are many options for those who want to become entrepreneurs, the Programa Reinvente-se (reinvent yourself programme) is the most popular initiative among research participants. They remember with enthusiasm the moment they received an email from the programme. Without questioning how the initiative got their data, they refer to this email as 'a call', as though they have finally got an answer to what they want and need. For them, the programme was a life-changing experience. Through the process, they could develop self-awareness, find a purpose for the second half of their lives and receive training to start their journeys as entrepreneurs. In July 2019, it was my turn to receive an email from the Programa Reinvente-se:

> What is the Reinvent-Yourself Programme?
> To help you on your journey of transition and transformation, we have developed a programme that considers, in a practical way, the possibilities that open up for each individual to develop the second half of their life. Experiences take place in organisations with a social impact, in welcoming environments chosen to facilitate each individual's immersion in the Reinvention process. In a practical way, it is an immersion in specific contemporary challenges.
>
> Carried out in an environment of collective growth, which respects individuality, it allows each person to be supported by a network of transdisciplinary professionals who will help us identify the skills we have built throughout our lives and try to rearticulate them for the challenges we face in the next 20, 40, 60 years of life. In São Paulo alone, 200+ people have already gone through the Programme and developed their awareness of the 60+ Reinvention of Work, designing new possibilities for civic participation, work and self-realisation!

Lis, aged 51, was influenced by the testimonials of friends who attended the Programa Reinvente-se. But in the end she undertook her professional reinvention with the support of another initiative. She follows a course that involves weekly meetings. Her first challenge was to write a short paragraph about her purpose in life. Next, they helped her create a map of her competencies. These competencies were detached from her professional experience. It did not matter, for example, whether she had had a career as a sales manager. There are not many jobs in sales management for someone her age. Thus, she needed to create a map of her talents, such as her ability to manage deadlines, budgets and people, and her talent for being empathetic towards and communicating with people. With a list of her talents as the starting point, she was advised to create a portfolio. The difference between the portfolio and an ordinary CV is that the latter would be organised around her past professional roles. Instead, the portfolio focuses on the three types of work she imagines herself doing in the future. These potential roles or projects, as stressed earlier, aim to reconcile pleasure and self-realisation. However, in Lis's case, they should ideally also lead to financial gains, as she is not retired yet.

Lis is not alone. A Google report[36] shows that from 2002 to 2014 the number of entrepreneurs in Brazil aged 50 to 59 and above 60 increased by 57 per cent and 56 per cent respectively. Another survey[37] assessed their motivation for becoming entrepreneurs. Among Brazilians aged 50 or above, 49.7 per cent are considering starting a business to supplement their income, 21.2 per cent to stay busy after retirement, and 21 per cent to continue to provide for their families. In Bento, the decision to become an entrepreneur after retirement is mainly motivated by older people's desire to keep themselves busy. But there is something else. They want to 'reinvent' their social lives. That is why, in some cases, being with friends who are working together on a new business project is as important as starting the business itself. Some projects will be put into practice, while others will remain ideas. But in the end, both will fill the time and keep research participants stimulated and busy, partly because of the creative and challenging process these projects represent, and partly because of the social contact they promote, which is based on peer collaboration.

As shown in this section, becoming an entrepreneur demands what some participants call 'the reinvention of themselves'. For this group, their past professional credentials are about to be replaced by a new one, full of promises. At this point, with or without the support of experienced coaches, they may ask themselves questions like who they are, what they are good at, which activity may provide them with a purpose in life, how they can contribute to others, how they can make an impact on the world. Developing new skills to support the project they envisage for the second half of their lives is a learning process that provides them with respect and a sense of belonging. In addition, by creating paths to go back to work, participants are coping with the demand to remain active and participate in society. However, if they are taking the risk of working as entrepreneurs, at least they will pursue initiatives that celebrate their values, the ones that are worth working for.

Working on a better self

In the previous section, we saw that the shift from being an employee to becoming an entrepreneur is a process in which research participants pursue greater awareness of their skills, strengths and purpose. Sometimes, however, their cultivation of self-awareness and self-development is an end in itself. In such cases, the self will be the object of their work, time and effort. This is the case with Juliana. Retired from her work as a doctor, and with two children, she has never had time for herself. Now, things have changed. She herself has become the object of her main occupation. 'My friends keep asking me whether I will go back to work. I don't have the time. My time now is for myself,' she explains. Juliana combines beauty routines, physical activities, and a succession of courses that keep her busy studying things she is interested in.

Although learning something can become a hobby or an activity that gives purpose to life,[38] knowledge applied to self-care is valued among research participants as proof that they are committed to maintaining their autonomy and avoiding becoming a burden to others. As mentioned above, Sennett[39] argues that such activities demonstrate their character and gain them respect as people who are committed to self-preservation. Self-preservation practices may also reorient older people in Bento towards the past. The reason is the belief that diseases in old age are the result of unresolved matters or emotional issues carried throughout life, or even the legacy of some traumatic or stressful experience in the past. Consequently, it is not uncommon to find research participants devoted to learning from their past in order to live in the present without sorrows or regrets. In cases like this, developing consciousness of what can hurt them and the techniques to fix it may be seen as a preventive health measure, or even become a life project.

Therefore, to avoid health problems[40] in the future, some participants look for tools that help them manage these feelings and move on. This doesn't necessarily mean resolving the issue with the other person involved in it. Instead, their efforts are towards healing their souls by overcoming the sorrows or regrets inside themselves. With this job done, they can go back to what matters: the present. Messages that spread awareness of the relationship between body and soul are constantly shared by research participants in their WhatsApp groups. More than reminders, they are calls to action. In many cases, a message is signed by or attributed to a doctor, like the one below written by a geriatrician.[41] A doctor's authority validates this type of content, and participants tend to trust their recommendations most.

> * When everything hurts, the pain is not physical *
> When I was still in academia, I heard something from a teacher that I will always remember. 'When everything hurts, the pain is not physical.' Maybe at that time I didn't realise the importance of what he said. Today, as a geriatrician, helping my patients with their daily routines, I see how this approach has helped me understand them when they arrive with a complaint about physical pain but sometimes not even knowing how to begin to describe this pain or how it started. I listen to them carefully as they tell me about their stomach pain, muscle pain, pain in their bones, palpitations, nausea and itches. I then ask just one question: 'What is really going on with you?' After a moment of hesitation and even surprise, most of them end up crying, quite compulsively and with visible pain. I let this restorative crying happen. Then, instead of physical complaints, I start listening to them talk about the end of relationships, the loss of loved ones, financial problems, fears, anguish and anxieties. It is then that I remember the saying, 'When everything hurts, the pain is not physical.' Indeed it is not. It is a pain in the soul. Everything that has hurt us and that we have held on to as a defence mechanism will come out somehow, maybe in the form of a disease. It is our physical body screaming for us to rescue our soul. It is our body confronting us with ourselves. It is our body showing us what is not right. It is our body saying, 'Look inside yourself.'[42]

The ways in which research participants answer this call to 'look inside themselves' will depend on their purchasing power. They can engage in therapies provided by professionals (who charge for the service) or by volunteers, or they can try to heal themselves through praying or reciting mantras. The 'Ho'oponopono' is an example of the latter. This traditional Hawaiian practice is an exercise for healing the soul. It consists of re-establishing balance in interpersonal relationships, which should bring healing. In Hawaii, the 'Ho'oponopono' is being tested as a health intervention.[43] In Bento, the 'Ho'oponopono' is one of the more popular self-help tools available to older people. Sandra, aged 69, practises the 'Ho'oponopono' every day by repeating the words 'I am sorry. Please forgive me. Thank you. I love you.' She, and others who engage in the practice, consider it a lifesaver, a measure to prevent diseases associated with sadness. The 'Ho'oponopono' is a free, accessible intervention that can be performed anywhere, just by repeating the words or following any of the hundreds of videos with the mantra available on YouTube. Moreover, it helps that this healing process doesn't require the presence of the person that caused the suffering or was hurt in the past. This cure is a task one can perform for oneself.

When it comes to avoiding new misfortunes in the present, research participants believe that they are better prepared to manage their relationships with others than they were in their youth. As they age, they say, they can set aside differences and manage conflicts better than they could before. However, some of them are still struggling to manage themselves and their feelings, especially after retirement. They might have gained some wisdom or self-control, but there is still much about themselves that they may not understand. Yet what has changed with retirement is that now they have time to figure it out. At this point, some will start a self-awareness journey that is more practical than philosophical, as they are aware that they don't have time to waste. For example, they may use a short course of therapy, as such practices are perceived as an effective resource that can provide insights to help them understand their behaviour and make rapid changes. This is the case with Luisa, aged 72. As we saw in the previous chapter, she got tired of having casual relationships. She dedicated time and effort to investigating why she had started having casual relationships in the first place. She opted for family constellation therapy, a therapeutic method in which individuals role-play as family members in order to bring to light hidden interpersonal dynamics and structures.[44] In one session, she was able to identify that her behaviour was a consequence of an unresolved issue with her ex-husband, who had passed away a few years earlier. Because these insights led to knowledge about herself, she could make a change that had a beneficial effect on her current long-term relationship.

However, some research participants are not in such a hurry as Luisa. Instead, they are enjoying the journey. For them, what counts is their commitment to themselves and their self-development process. For this reason, it is long-term techniques such as meditation and mindfulness that provide an ongoing process, which might function as a life project as well. Lúcio, aged 76, is an example. He started meditating to understand how stressed he had become when he retired. It was hard for him to manage all the free time he had. He attends a meditation group in Bento, and practises daily at home. Through this routine, he endeavours to know himself better every day so that he can recognise moments of anger or anxiety. He considers meditation a helpful tool which he is still learning how to use in order to attain more self-control, which he identifies as one of his priorities in life. He explains: 'I have been practising meditation for 25 years, even if I still don't do it properly. But I can assure you, when I am stressed, oops! … let's stop … and I change.'

Of the many groups and courses aimed at the third age in Bento, meditation seems to match research participants' need to overcome the past in order to enjoy the present. Keeping one's mind on the present is both a benefit and a challenge during meditation. Not letting the mind be distracted by thoughts, and resisting the temptation to follow them, require training and self-discipline. Among research participants, these intrusive thoughts often lead them to reflect on their lives and achievements, resulting in anxiety, depression, insomnia and irritability. This kind of reflection is exactly what some want to avoid.[45] They can't change the past. Thus, it is healthier to let it go by keeping the mind in the present moment. A woman who regularly practises meditation explains: 'People keep revisiting the past, thinking about what happened or didn't happen. The present is the best moment in life. That is the reason I focus on the present.'

So far, we have seen how research participants can choose to work on a better self, turning it into a self-development project that can give life a purpose. In addition, their routines produce proof of character, first because their practices keep them busy, and secondly because they show that they are committed to self-preservation. There are some, however, who will skip part of this process. They don't have to find out who they are, what hurts them or what would make them happier at this stage of their life. Their faith has provided them with the most valued answer, namely how God expects them to act. For them, and this was observed particularly among Evangelical Christians, being a better person is a matter of doing what is right. This gives them a practical orientation towards the present, as they don't have to pursue the purpose of life. Instead, they focus on living everyday life in the best way according to the guidance provided by their religion.

Debora, aged 51, illustrates this shift. She has a little grocery shop in the house she shares with her husband and her son. She talks with fortitude about her lack of prospects for retirement and her disillusionment with marriage. Despite all her worries, her faith helps her focus on the present. She remains a devoted wife and mother. She wakes up early in the morning to get her child ready for school. She opens the garage door early in the morning every day to receive the first customers into her grocery shop. Debora combines discipline with resilience. She is anchored in the present, as she doesn't have to worry about the future. That is God's decision. For her, what matters is continuing to do what is right. She explains: 'Although sometimes we think He isn't, God is always a step ahead. His plan is perfect.'

Nelson, aged 58, also tries to live his life doing what is right, according to the rules of his religion. He honours his wife and plays his role as the family provider because he believes that scripture clearly defines the roles of a husband and a wife within a marriage. 'A wife should be loved, a husband should be respected,' he asserts. Even after retirement, he works with his wife in a business located in their house. This routine gives him peace of mind, and at the same time it keeps him busy. He takes care of his body so as to age well and avoid being a burden with the same discipline with which he manages the couple's finances. He is constantly improving on the knowledge he needs to achieve these goals. For example, by following doctors' advice on YouTube, he has found a way to restore their sex life as a couple and regain his 'functions as a husband'.

Moreover, he has recently attended a domestic finance course at his church. He learned that 'If everything is shared, you cannot succeed', an aphorism that endorses his view that he should remain in charge of the couple's money. This is how he finds the guidance to do what he believes a husband is expected to do. By putting his beliefs into practice, Nelson can live in the present and with purpose. While he uses this knowledge to improve his own family's life, many others in Bento apply what they know to help others. In such cases, the logic is the opposite. The more they share, the more they get in return.

Working for respect

Volunteering is another type of work that allows research participants to live in the present with purpose. It may be the kind of occupation that brings the most benefits to older people in Bento. Volunteering keeps them busy while showing them to be good people who, exercising reciprocity, give back what they have accumulated throughout their lives.[46] This can mean sharing knowledge or time. As volunteers, they can work for a cause and recover their usefulness and gain visibility as active and productive citizens. In other words, they can win respect.[47] Indeed, working as a volunteer can be a lifesaver in terms of self-esteem in Bento. For example, even with no income, since he has no job or pension, Felipe, aged 63, donates the only resource he has. He uses his free time to organise a library in a low-income community so that people can find comfort in reading books about spirituality. By doing this, he can focus on the collective need rather than on his own uncertain future, thereby achieving a sense of purpose that helps restore his dignity.

> 'When you are excluded from formal employment, when you are in … let's use the term "limbo", because limbo is exactly what it is. When you are out of the market, you become unproductive. And then you enter that delicate stage that is old age. Practically speaking, you don't have much support. You don't have anything to hold on to. I am still searching, in my battle, to find something new, to create something new … I can't do something just for myself because, wherever I go, I observe my surroundings, and they worry me. I am worried about other people's situations, and if I can't help them … well, it is true that I can't even help myself at the moment, but if I can't help them, I will not feel complete.'

Beyond the social recognition, volunteers feel nourished by the gratitude of those who have benefited from their actions. Cris, aged 63, explains: 'When you volunteer, you think you will give something to others. But, in the end, it is always you who gains something.' Cris is devoted to a saint in whose church her daughter got married. She made a vow at the time. As she had been diagnosed with cancer, she asked the saint to let her live to see her daughter's wedding. She achieved more than that. She has completely recovered, and now spends her time as a volunteer, supporting families in a cancer centre in Bento and coordinating the courses aimed at the third age at her beloved Catholic church. These courses are given by other volunteers, most of them retired. Course instructors enjoy a high status in the community. They are seen as benevolent people who share their knowledge and time in the interest of others. So students express their gratitude with chocolates, greeting cards, and money delivered in a communal envelope on special occasions like the instructor's birthday, Christmas, and the annual party celebrating Teacher's Day. This gratitude may be more significant in old age. As we saw earlier, some research participants had been fired because their companies no longer valued their knowledge. Others are considered out of date by their children, who no longer ask for their advice. However, their students recognise their value and respect the knowledge they have accumulated throughout their lives, which helps restore their dignity.

At this church, there are many roles open to volunteers. Some positions involve dealing with administrative and financial issues or organising events and the logistics around the courses. Other volunteers manage the WhatsApp groups created to support the Christmas bazaar, a charity fashion show or an informal second-hand market in which sales take place on the messaging app. In addition, every course needs a coordinator and sometimes a sub-coordinator, both students who volunteer for the job. Positions like these can provide new professional-style credentials, replacing the ones lost on retirement. Thus, it is no surprise that these volunteers do their 'jobs' with an impressive level of professionalism. For example, when Romulo, aged 68, became the coordinator for one of the French classes, he decided to manage the group as if the members were work colleagues. He made all the students wear a badge with their names and emergency contact details on the back, as there had been incidents with older people in the past (some had felt ill during the class). In addition, he placed his desk at the entrance to the room. At the beginning of each class, he was there with a printed list he had prepared in Excel so that students could 'clock in'. When the class was over, he was in charge of moderating the content of and interactions on the WhatsApp group created to support the students.

Sometimes, the kind of commitment Romulo showed is the reason research participants decide to retire from their careers as volunteers. In such cases, the demands of 'the job' can become incompatible with the idea of retirement as a phase of life oriented to themselves. However, unlike their first retirement, this one can be presented as a success story in which research participants met their obligations to society. And in this case, retirement is their own decision, and they can always go back to 'work' if they want to. Lúcio is among those who decided to retire from volunteering. He got tired of the 'job' obligations, and he believes he has already done enough. Like others, he gives volunteering the same status as a formal job. This allows him to say, for example, that his 20 years of work as a volunteer are included in his 'employment record book'.

> 'I worked at a vocational school I helped to build. As an electrical engineer, I worked there for 20 years. I organised booklets. I gave classes. The classes were on Sundays, once a month, from eight in the morning till noon. I did this for 20 years. I have 20 years of volunteering in my employment record book. At least for now, I don't want to do it. There were always a lot of appointments and demands coming from here and there. It was overwhelming. I started to get tired of so many obligations. You are a volunteer until you start doing the job. Once you start, it isn't volunteering any more. It is an obligation. So I stopped doing it.'

Balancing the pros and cons of volunteering depends on what research participants are searching for.[48] As well as providing an opportunity to do good, volunteering creates new opportunities for improving social life after retirement. Amelia benefits from this. Aged 61 and retired for a couple of years, she feels she deserves some time to herself, as she started working very young. She confesses that she enjoys being at home: 'For now, I just want to do nothing.' All the same, every Sunday she wears her impeccable white coat and stands at the altar at one of the main churches in Bento, helping at the Eucharistic ritual. She and her husband have always enjoyed the social life associated with the church. They attended couples' meetings at another Catholic church for many years before moving to Bento. The church they attend now doesn't organise couples' meetings. However, volunteering at the church gives her the best of both worlds: access to social activities and the community's respect.

For two years she was also in charge of wine sales at the annual church party. She celebrates the fact that, under her 'administration', the revenue increased year by year. She manages resources and people (also volunteers) with the same professionalism as other volunteers in Bento. She combines an Excel spreadsheet with a WhatsApp group in which she coordinates shifts and cheers people up. This creates another opportunity for interaction. After the party, the people who worked on it discuss the event and assess how well it went. It is at this social event that her performance gains visibility and results in reputation and respect. Amelia ends the day with two professional-style credentials: as well as being an extraordinary minister of Holy Communion she is recognised as 'Amelia in charge of the wine'.

The visibility and reputation achieved by volunteers don't depend on a large audience. Actions can happen within a small group that takes a more low-profile approach. For example, Carla, aged 62, uses WhatsApp to organise the efforts of her friends, who help homeless people in Bento. She manages the donations and assigns responsibilities, so that, together, they can deliver *cestas básicas* to those in need. *Cesta básica* is a Brazilian term for the minimum food provision to sustain an adult worker for a month.[49] Lourdes, aged 64, is another example. She is the coordinator of a group of women who get together once a week to do hand embroidery. Their pieces of embroidery are donated to and sold through philanthropic projects in Bento. Their work doesn't have the same visibility as the work Amelia does. Nevertheless, it can be seen by those who matter. Their friends know what Carla and Lourdes do for the community (and for their social lives, as they have put the group together), and that is enough to build their reputations and win them respect. As well as these two, we have seen other examples in this chapter of how participants engage in various causes in order to live in the present, with purpose, through volunteering. However, the most significant impact volunteering has is on older people's *own* experience of ageing. Their work expands the portfolio of activities and courses aimed at the third age in Bento and supports the events that contribute to the social life of their community. And so they are, once again, working for themselves.

The work that really matters

This chapter started with Seneca's premise that it is only after retirement, when one has free time and has been released from work obligations, that one can contemplate life and start to live authentically. For the Stoic philosopher there is a crucial difference between time wasted (dedicated to work or to others) and free time (dedicated to oneself). As we have seen, older people in Bento also experience this shift. After retirement, they will reorient their attention towards themselves, engaging with activities that please them and celebrate their values. However, participants are likely to turn these activities into new forms of work so that they can treat their free time as if it was working hours. Re-creating a working routine shows they are busy, which is proof of character in work-oriented Bento. These new forms of work do not necessarily represent a return to 'conventional' work, but they are activities people *work on*. That is the trait that unites all the examples addressed in this chapter. Through entrepreneurship, self-development and volunteering, research participants can achieve the feeling that they are living their life with a purpose, because they are spending their time meaningfully. In addition, they can acquire new professional-style credentials that allow them to be recognised as respectable citizens of São Paulo. They are alive and working. More than that, they are alive *because* they are working.

By making their busy schedule of activities visible, without noticing it research participants are working on something else. Together, they are changing how old age is represented in Bento. As set out in chapter 2, following Bourdieu,[50] age is not a number that tells us who is young or old but a classificatory system for permissions and privileges. This cultural construction defines who is expected to do what and who can access which opportunities and places. By 'going back to work', older people in Bento challenge the stigma of the retiree in Brazilian society,[51] historically seen as inactive and useless and expected to be confined to their home. That is where research participants refuse to be. Instead, they are increasing their visibility, presence in the city, and opportunities to participate in society.⁵² With great help from WhatsApp, they are informally turning São Paulo into a smart city for older people.⁵³ That means turning the city into a participative and responsive city, which can be game-changing in the experience of ageing in Bento.

As argued earlier, by doing this they are also delivering what the family, society and the state now expect from older people, as those who should remain active in order to postpone their dependence.⁵⁴ As protagonists of their ageing, research participants craft ways of meeting their needs and desires. They are working for themselves and with their peers, creating, expanding or engaging in activities that combine pleasure and purpose. As a consequence, they may leave a legacy of freedoms, dignity and respect. This legacy will not necessarily be inherited by their children or grandchildren, but by the succeeding generations of older people. As a man in his sixties put it, 'Our biggest challenge is to take older people out of the home. And there is no way back. It is from here to infinity and beyond. We want to leave a legacy for those who will come after us.' Not everyone shares this awareness. Some older people are just busy living their own lives with purpose, without noticing that they are also contributing to the reinvention of the image of old age in Bento. In the end, the construction of old age and the subjective experience of ageing are works in progress, just as life is.

Notes

1. Seneca 2005.
2. World Health Organization 2002, p. 4.
3. Estado de S. Paulo 2019.
4. Costanzi 2020.
5. Cidade de São Paulo Direitos Humanos e Cidadania 2020.
6. Savishinsky 2000.
7. Kavedžija 2015.
8. Whyte 2017; Willcox et al. 2007; Lamb 2019.
9. Savishinsky 2000.
10. Luborsky 1994; Willcox et al. 2007; Debert 2012.
11. Luborsky 1994.
12. Savishinsky 2000.
13. Savishinsky 2000.
14. As Luborsky and LeBlanc (2003) assert, the concept of retirement varies depending on the culture. Their review shows that, away from Western societies, there are cultures in which retirement is impossible or unacceptable. This happens where there is no social identity other than the continuation of the activities that define adulthood. That is not the case in Brazil, where retirement is a constitutional right. However, participants share the feeling that remaining productive and busy is a condition for ageing as citizens of São Paulo.
15. Cicero 1884.
16. Gianakos 2007.
17. Cicero 1884, p. 29.

18 Sennett 2004.
19 Setiya 2017; Savishinsky 2000; Kavedžija 2015.
20 Butler 1963.
21 Erikson 1982.
22 Savishinsky 2000.
23 Luborsky 1994.
24 Savishinsky 2000, p. 148.
25 An orientation to the present was a strategy for stopping time adopted by older people in a beach community in Jaffa, in the south of Tel Aviv. Lieblich (2014, p. 74) said that members of this community refused to tell her their life stories, as they considering dwelling in the past useless. Instead, she noted, they were committed to 'living the now'.
26 Luborsky (1994) observed the same in his work with newly retired men in America. He explains that his efforts to persuade his informants into philosophical reflections on life were in vain. Instead, they preferred to talk about the special projects they had engaged in after they retired, which helped them to craft new self-images and make the transition to this next stage of life.
27 Beauvoir 1972.
28 Goldenberg 2013.
29 Casaqui 2018.
30 Valente 2019; Triboni 2021; Cidade de São Paulo Habitação 2007.
31 Brualla 2020; Pedersen 2015; Glass 2012.
32 Sennett (2006) observed that in the US older people are more likely to speak out when they disagree with the decisions taken by the corporation they believed they had helped build, while younger employees tend to exercise their discontent by leaving their jobs. Sennett's observation dialogues with the work of the political economist Albert Hirschman (2004). Hirschman proposed that there are three mechanisms by which people can deal with institutions, as members of those institutions or as, for example, dissatisfied customers. Voice (speaking out) and exit (leaving) are two of them.
33 In a book first published in 2000, Savishinsky addressed the emergence of this new market in the United States, where consultancies specialise in helping older people to develop opportunities and occupations for life after retirement.
34 Empreendedorismo Sênior 2021.
35 HCor 2009.
36 Calixto & Maceira 2019.
37 Sebrae 2017.
38 Savishinsky 2000.
39 Sennett 2004.
40 Among diseases, cancer is the one participants are most likely to consider to be a manifestation of unresolved feelings of sadness. The association between accumulated emotions and the risk of cancer was also observed by Gibbon (2017, p. 185) in her ethnography of cancer patients in urban areas of southern Brazil.
41 This text circulated in research participants' WhatsApp groups during fieldwork. It is attributed to the geriatrician Roberta França.
42 See https://www.enfoquems.com.br/artigo-quando-tudo-doi-a-dor-nao-e-fisica/.
43 Ka'Opua 2003.
44 In 2018, Constelação familiar ('family constellation') was included in the integrative therapies supported by the SUS (*Diário Oficial da União* 2018).
45 Kavedžija (2015, p. 151) observed that some of her interlocutors in Japan resisted thinking about their past or using it for life narrativisation. For some of them, focusing on the present and avoiding comparison with the past is a way of achieving a successful life free from regrets.
46 As observed also in the United States, retirees in Bento experience volunteering as one way of responding to the 'moral obligation to use their talents to some end' (Savishinsky 2000, p. 150).
47 Sennett 2004.
48 As argued earlier, life after retirement is a matter of balancing altruism and self-realisation, as Savishinsky (2000) and Kavedžija (2015) observed in the United States and Japan respectively.
49 Teixeira et al. 2019.
50 Bourdieu 1993.
51 Debert 1997; Leibing 2005; Correa 2009.
52 Rancière (2006) doesn't address the classificatory system of age. However, he develops an equivalent approach which considers how society distributes roles and identities, shapes the

experience of time and space, and defines which forms of sensibility gain visibility and to whom. This aesthetic regime is political, as it defines at the same time what is shared and what is exclusive in a community. Moreover, he argues, the distribution of the sensible (what can be seen, heard, felt) takes into account one's occupation within the structure of society. Hence it is possible to establish a parallel with older people in Bento, as what they can say, see and experience can also change depending on their status as retirees only or as active citizens of São Paulo.

53 M. D. E. S. Pereira & Oliveira 2019.
54 Willcox et al. 2007; Debert 2012; Whyte 2017; Lamb 2019.

9
Conclusions

Pandora's box

One of the questions this book has aimed to answer is 'What role do smartphones play in the experience of ageing in Bento?' As we have seen, smartphones expand social contact with family and friends, give access to health guidance, coordinate care and improve mobility. They organise research participants' routines in Bento, providing access to an extensive portfolio of activities aimed at the third age and shared through WhatsApp groups. In other words, smartphones bind older people together in their challenge to be productive, postpone dependence and live in the present with purpose. However, before they can benefit from the positive aspects of being part of this powerful network, they face the challenges of adopting a new technology. Smartphones impose a new logic that changes the way older people experience time and space. Smartphones also demand plenty of work from them, as they have to deal with a huge influx of information and social relationships that they were not formerly used to.

    I would like to use the Pandora's box metaphor to draw some conclusions about the process research participants go through when they decide to adopt the smartphone and its impacts on age in Bento. Pandora[1] was part of a revenge plan. Prometheus stole fire from the gods and gave it to mortals. He was punished for this by being chained to the Caucasus Mountains, where every day an eagle ate his liver, which grew back overnight. But that was not enough. Zeus wanted to punish humankind for accepting his gift. He created Pandora, the first woman. Zeus offered Pandora to Prometheus's brother, who succumbed to her charms and married her. Pandora received a box as a wedding present together with the warning she should never open it. However, motivated by curiosity, she did open the box, releasing all kinds of plagues and devils. She quickly closed the box, but it was too late. Since then, humankind has had to deal with greed, envy, hatred, pain, illness, hunger, poverty, war and death. The narrative associated with Pandora's myth could be observed when older people in Bento turned their first smartphone on.

At first, participants are wary about using smartphones. As they had associated this technology with youth, they believe smartphones are not for them (mortals) but for the younger generation (gods). The contradiction here is that their first smartphones are not stolen but usually offered by young people themselves as gifts. Indeed, as ethnography showed, research participants' first smartphones are often given them by their children. At the same time, these young people claim that smartphones are intuitive and older people are expected to learn how to use this technology by themselves. Although they are slightly apprehensive, research participants are strongly motivated by curiosity and the desire to join WhatsApp, as the conversations of their friends, transnational and extended families are now on the app.[2] This desire drives older people to try this technology[3] borrowed from the youngsters. Suddenly, the gift takes on multiple properties. They now have a camera, a calendar, a radio, a television, a computer and a telephone, all of which they can hold in their hands.[4] However, together with the potential represented by these functions, they find that their smartphones have released some 'plagues and devils', just as Pandora's box did. As seen in chapters 3 and 5, smartphones also unlock fear and anxiety.

Fear is the first thing research participants experience when they turn on their smartphones. They fear breaking the device, being charged for something they were not aware of, and deleting something important, like the pictures of their grandchildren living abroad. That is the moment when they see their self-esteem diminish.[5] At this stage of their lives, all the professional experience they have accumulated seems useless.[6] However, the evidence from chapter 5 shows that their digital skills have less to do with age than with the time of retirement. As noted, many older people in Bento left their jobs in the middle of the internet revolution, just as email accounts were starting to spread, which event was followed by the emergence of social media.[7] They left the working environment, where technology tends to be adopted earlier and in applied tasks that would facilitate learning. Retirement also challenged their place within their families, as children don't recognise their authority any more, even though many of them still live in their parents' houses. In Bento, smartphones will be, then, a new arena for disputes about power, with children taking advantage of their knowledge to control their parents. To the degree that they fail to teach their parents how to overcome their limitations and adopt technology, children will subtly sustain this dependence. That is why many research participants looked for professional help, becoming students on the courses aimed at the third age in Bento.

With time, however, students become confident. Some will explore their smartphones and engage with other apps, such as the ones that deal with mobility and learning. Others will continue to use mainly WhatsApp. This app in itself is enough to promote a true revolution in older people's lives in Bento. Through WhatsApp groups, they receive information related to pensions, benefits they are entitled to, scams they should watch out for, diets they could follow, and health-related information. This is also the space in which they share new opportunities for courses, events and activities aimed at the third age in Bento. These opportunities usually lead to new WhatsApp groups being created to support these activities. Thus, their networks keep growing, in number and diversity. That is when the anxiety begins. They now have to manage an always-on connection with friends and relatives.

Moreover, smartphones blur the boundaries between 'the house' and 'the street'. As the anthropologist Roberto DaMatta[8] argued, these are distinct universes used to organise private and public lives in Brazil. While 'the house' is a moral unit run according to family rules, 'the street' is the space for the mundane, including work, pleasure and temptations. For research participants, this means that, whether lying in bed or waiting for a bus, they are learning to manage a digital life full of 'temptations'. Thus, they must be aware of what content they are sending to whom, as what belongs to 'the house' and what belongs 'to the street' can be swapped with one click.

Managing this digital life can become an activity itself, as shown in chapter 2. As content curators, research participants compete to share the most helpful information with peers. This competition can lead to social capital, but also to reputational damage if they share fake news. Even so, the messages keep coming. Thus, people can be overwhelmed and frustrated, as they can't keep up to date. Instead, they feel they are missing something. As curators, they collaborate in the spread of new images and representations of ageing in Brazil,[9] which endorse active and successful ways of ageing. In doing so, they can also gain a reputation, as these images communicate their awareness of the importance of ageing well.[10] Thus while WhatsApp promotes opportunities for older people in Bento to be active, it also provides proof that they are committed to, and sometimes successful at, turning ageing into a stage of life that is happy, productive, healthy and full of purpose. As suggested in chapter 8, this combination of productivity and purpose may create more anxiety, as this balance does not follow a predetermined formula for everyone.

Just as humankind did after Pandora opened her box, older people in Bento are finding ways of dealing with life after the advent of smartphones. This is the last parallel I will make with Pandora's myth: Pandora opened her box once more and found one last thing there. It was hope, which, having finally been released, has helped humankind deal with all of its troubles since then. The following section will address how, motivated by hope, research participants use their smartphones to manage problems related to ageing. However, before that, I want to look more closely at hope itself. Swedberg[11] suggests that hope can be understood as 'the wish for something to come true'. His concept highlights the social dimension of hope, as the 'something' one wishes for is influenced by society, group membership and culture. At the same time, he continues, the possibility of turning this 'something' into reality depends on the social, cultural and economic capital one holds, together with economic opportunities, structures and resources. So the first question is what older people in Bento wish for and how they came to wish for this and not for something else.

We observed that research participants wish to remain busy, extending their productivity and utility into old age. They are also concerned about autonomy, as they don't want to become a burden to anyone. And, in remaining busy, they dream of the possibility of spending their time with purpose, enjoying freedom and respect. They may feel that their hopes are unique and express their own life projects in old age. But this is not the case. Their hopes are grounded in a shared time, space and culture. Research participants made their lives in Bento as citizens of São Paulo, where they learned that work is what binds people together, organises the city, and shapes identity and character.[12] Work is sacred, so they don't want to become a burden to other workers, especially when they are their own children. Work is also how they recognise themselves. They want to go back to work even after retirement so that they can feel busy and alive. This attitude may also explain why, as described in chapter 3, participants are concerned with maintaining physical condition while some older people, in Rio de Janeiro for example, may focus on body appearance.[13]

However, Bento is not an island. Neither is São Paulo, nor Brazil. Older people around the world also wish for independence, autonomy, participation and productivity after retirement.[14] Normative discourses and images taught them they should want to age that way.[15] More than that, they learned that they are expected to work hard to turn this normativity into their reality.[16] Yet this expectation of autonomy is not restricted to older people. Old age has indeed been constructed as a global problem since the 1980s, as the ageing population worldwide was identified as a risk factor to development and the economy.[17] But the moral obligation to take care of oneself, to stay healthy and active, is extended to everyone in neoliberal societies.[18] With that in mind, I argue that local and global values influence research participants' hopes.

On the one hand, older people in Bento hope to remain as productive and busy as any citizen of São Paulo should be. On the other, they hope to succeed as virtuous citizens responsible for their autonomy.[19] Finally, they hope to reconcile their duties with their commitment to live with a purpose in old age. That is the 'something' that older people in Bento hope for. But what resources do they have to 'make it come true'? This is when smartphones arrive on the scene as a powerful tool that helps research participants to change their realities in accordance with their 'duties' and wishes.

Turning wishes into action

Smartphones can expand older people's possibilities for action by offering them abilities that result in a smarter ageing experience in Bento. First and foremost, smartphones allowed research participants to build a network of solidarity and care. By exchanging favours and providing mutual support on WhatsApp, friends become allies in research participants' hope not to become a burden to their families. The same connections can be used to access medical guidance. In such cases, friends who work or have worked in the healthcare sector will be their preferred choice. These qualified friends can provide the information they trust, in contrast to the information they find on Google, for example. Through this chain of favours and reciprocity, they can avoid burdening the few doctors they 'officially' rely on. Even when they have their contact details on WhatsApp, they are more likely to ask friends for informal guidance, hoping to reserve these connections for real emergencies. In addition, friends' social capital can become a resource for bypassing the bureaucracies of both the private and public health sectors. In these cases, participants make use of the *jeitinho brasileiro* ('Brazilian way'), the cultural practice of using personal influence to make things happen.[20]

The same network turns Bento into a smart place for older people. WhatsApp groups are where participants share the resources and activities available to them in the neighbourhood and in São Paulo. As in a forum, they discuss their rights and organise themselves around opportunities that match their desire to stay busy and useful. In other words, WhatsApp is a space for hope but also for action. Whatever they decide to do, research participants embrace as many activities as possible, so that they can claim they 'don't have time', which is a virtue in São Paulo.[21] If they engage in projects that can provide them with new professional-style credentials, that is even better: they can replace the ones they lost when they retired. As we saw in chapters 2, 3 and 8, smartphones help research participants to become digital influencers, chefs, trip advisers, entrepreneurs or volunteers. These 'new jobs' allow them to regain their status as citizens of São Paulo. If they don't have jobs like these, social media can help them give visibility to their busy agenda, compensating for the lack of these credentials. From English classes to pompoir workshops, everything can be used as proof of character, including registers of past and planned activities.[22] Whatever these activities are, they demonstrate that research participants are busy living with purpose while showing the commitment and professionalism associated with the jobs they had before they retired.

For all these reasons, smartphones are deeply associated with a sense of utility in Bento. Smartphones can always be turned into an activity. As shown in chapter 3, even when research participants have a free slot in their timetable, they can still feel they are doing something. Smartphones can be used to read a book, watch a video, play a brain-training game, take a language quiz, search for a cake recipe, follow a tutorial for a new hobby or manage their domestic routines by coordinating tasks with their family. Even the time spent watching TV gains a layer of productivity, as they are commonly simultaneously chatting with friends on WhatsApp or going through their Facebook feeds. These multiple possibilities are what Miller et al.[23] called 'perpetual opportunism', the intrinsic characteristic smartphones have of being capable of providing opportunities to connect with other people or to do things at any time. This can be both a solution in work-oriented Bento and a 'plague', as research participants complain that they are experiencing addiction to their smartphones. They are addicted to the possibilities offered by the purposeful activities that smartphones facilitate, the ones that help participants to recover their identity as busy persons.

Smartphones help older people in Bento to solve everyday life issues. For example, they can stay out late at night as they can call an Uber, save time they would formerly have spent queuing at a bank or manage the letting of a property on Airbnb in a couple of clicks. However, the smartphone is not smart per se. Among research participants, its smartness is unlocked and perceived when the smartphone actually provides a solution to a problem. This solution is not always predictable or ready for use. Research participants may choose to solve a problem in multiple ways, by combining different functions and by coordinating the simultaneous use of different apps. This bricolage is a consequence of two factors. First, it may be associated with digital skills. Secondly, it may express personal preferences.

Participants' digital skills may restrict the number of apps available to them. Once again, friends will be crucial in such cases. They may request their help if they struggle to download the apps they are interested in. However, some also struggle to use those apps for the first time, as they may not understand how they work. In these cases, research participants are likely to go back to the apps they are more familiar with. I have discussed some examples, such as the app offered by the SUS in São Paulo (which provided a digital ID to be presented at appointments) that was replaced by a combination of the use of the camera and Google Drive (the user created his own digital ID by taking a picture of the hard copy of his ID). I called this bricolage a *gambiarra* (see chapter 5). Research participants can express their preferences for getting something done. Some will save their invoices to their Google Drive; some will email them to themselves; some will take a screenshot to archive them in the Gallery or Google Photos. I used the concept of 'desire paths' from urban design to describe how participants can choose to go from problem A to solution B using multiple apps, which are not necessarily the ones developed for this purpose.

Research participants showed impressive creativity in unlocking the smartness of their smartphones, or, to be more precise, in unlocking the smartness that makes sense for them. The anthropologist Katrien Pype, who works in the Democratic Republic of Congo (DRC), has called this creativity 'smartness from below'. In her work, she highlighted the strategies people from the DRC have developed to bypass constraints like cost and access to engage with the technological imaginary of smart cities. Chapter 5 showed that, even when the technological constraints experienced by older people in Bento are not related to cost and access,[24] research participants use similar 'smartness from below' when using their smartphones to achieve the solutions they need. They do so by constantly combining functions they take from the apps they feel comfortable with. This puzzle challenges developers' concepts and prototypes, as this kind of appropriation is always unpredictable.[25] Even though they may combine five different apps when one could have solved their problem, research participants can get things done in their own way. This creativity is what truly empowers them. Sometimes, however, smartphones are used not for empowerment but to cover up the issues older people in Bento can't solve.

Between whispers and silence

At the beginning of her essay on old age, Simone de Beauvoir[26] denounces the conspiracy of silence surrounding ageing. As an inconvenient event of life, she argues, getting older is a topic no one is interested in. Speaking about it would serve as a reminder of our mortality and the inevitable period of decline that precedes death. Moreover, older people are likely to be seen as a burden to family and society. If they are regarded in this way, their experience and wisdom can't compensate for the fact that they have become dependent and unproductive. She gives plenty of examples of how life in different societies can end as an experience with no respect or dignity. She challenges the idea that retirement is the time for freedom and pleasure. Instead, she stresses the miserable conditions reserved for elderly people in the later stages of life. Bringing more visibility to these conditions might lead society to confront their beliefs. If the outcomes of life in society were poverty and abandonment in old age, this precarity would be irrefutable proof that society has failed as a project.

Fifty years after the publication of the Beauvoir essay, we could say the silence surrounding old age has vanished. As argued throughout this book, ageing has become a topic of interest globally; policies and discourses frame ageing societies as a social and economic problem. The Active Ageing framework developed by the WHO and adopted in Brazil is an example. Moreover, we have seen a shift in the representation of ageing, supported by the production of images that emphasise activity, pleasure, freedom and consumption.[27] In Bento, we observed how research participants engaged with this new imaginary after retirement by using their smartphones to produce and circulate their own images of active ageing. While there is more openness about old age, this openness exposes other ways in which practices continue to confirm the points raised by Beauvoir. Older people are still seen as a potential burden to family and society. Furthermore, they are now seen as responsible for solving this problem. They are confronted with the duty to remain healthy and productive in order to avoid or postpone the dependency associated with the frailties and decline of the ageing body.[28]

So, the silences surrounding old age haven't been completely banished from Bento, even if they have changed. The first thing about which the silence remains is the material conditions of ageing. As chapter 2 showed, retirement is not a stage of financial security for everyone. An income comprising only a pension can be a constraint. The demands of adult children on elderly parents may add expenses to the family budget after retirement. Moreover, there are plenty of examples of people who cannot retire and live in 'limbo', too young for retirement and too old for the labour market. This scenario can be expanded to Brazil in general if we consider that almost 65 per cent of state pensions paid in Brazil are equivalent to the national minimum wage.[29] In 2021, this is R$ 1,100 per month (approximately £153.37).[30] In addition, of the 71.3 million households in Brazil, 12.9 million depend exclusively on older people's incomes. In these cases, 63.9 per cent of incomes are from state pensions.[31] However, this is not the picture circulated in the discourses that present ageing as a stage for self-realisation and pleasure. Instead, this precarity is silenced.

The same occurs with the natural physical changes associated with ageing. Older people can't stop growing older. Nobody can. However, while the performance of the healthy autonomous body gains visibility, the natural decline of the ageing body is hidden in the shadows, as older people are expected to intervene and correct it so as not to become a burden to family and society. This morality creates one more space for inequalities. The quality of life one enjoys in old age is now attributed to one's will to make healthy choices.[32] Ageing is thus constructed as a meritocracy. However, Rowe and Kahn[33] show that, even within the Successful Ageing findings, the nature of the work done in adult life and the years of education in childhood may be associated with quality of life in old age. These findings imply that the resources older people have, including their backgrounds, can lead to very different experiences of ageing.

Lamb raised the same point in her research with older Americans.[34] On the one hand, the elite can afford to adopt 'correct' lifestyles while feeling empowered to manage their health and enjoy ageing free from decline and dependency. Lower-income seniors, on the other hand, often feel unable to achieve healthy ageing, and they experience this as a lack of agency over themselves. However, as Lamb stresses, what is at issue here is not individual motivation but different socioeconomic contexts. Lower socioeconomic conditions may lead to illness and death at earlier ages. She stresses that a lack of access to healthy food or healthcare, and type of working environment and residence, can be external obstacles to healthy ageing. The same inequalities occur in Bento. Among the research participants we saw that one man could afford to drink a special brand of mineral water to increase his alkaline level and so protect his body against cancer, while another had just one main meal a day, supported by a government food programme.[35] In addition, I observed that some of those whose work had included an activity that demanded physical strength now live with a condition or pain that they attribute to their past jobs. With regard to the impact of education on health literacy, it is unfair to insist that managing health is a possibility for everyone when, in the city of São Paulo, the number of illiterate people aged 60 or over varies from 1.23 per cent in Bento's district to 26.96 per cent in the Marsilac District.[36]

There is silence about the inequalities of ageing, while dependence is represented as a moral failure. In Bento, as we have argued before, dependence means disturbing the children, who are supposed to be working and investing in their careers. That is why research participants are likely to manage their health problems themselves or rely on close friends. Their concerns about not becoming a burden are contradictory, as most participants don't believe their children will take care of them anyway. But that is not something they share with others. Saying such a thing could compromise their children's reputation, and even their own, as the lack of reciprocity could raise questions about the kind of parents they were. There is, however, something else they are hiding. Dependence in old age might represent a loss of agency over oneself. That is why dependence is the real death that research participants want to avoid. During my fieldwork I observed that their children are the people from whom participants try hardest to hide their frailties and needs. Some of them believe that a sign of weakness might allow children to interfere in their lives, including in areas or matters they believe they are perfectly able to manage.[37] This results in silence, but also in a kind of self-surveillance in which they give visibility only to the positive aspects of ageing.

This performance may also be a strategy for avoiding judgement from their peers.[38] As argued in chapters 2 and 3, ageing is experienced through the eyes of others. As no one wants to be seen as 'the old', frailties and pains are hidden in social relations. Smartphones can offer older people the opportunity to lower their guard. When they have physical issues that make it impossible for them to perform healthy ageing, they confine themselves to their social media. While they hide their conditions from view, their online presence can prove that they are still active, protecting their reputation and working towards a positive image of old age. Digital spaces thus provide a place of safety but also a time for recovery. That is when they ask friends for help, but only close ones and via private messages.

However, it is not the case that older people in Bento don't address health issues openly with friends. On WhatsApp groups and social media, they exchange tips about diets and share information on living a healthy life and postponing physical and mental dependency. They also address the frailties that commonly come with age. But when they do, they use humour and sarcasm, mainly by sharing memes. Deafness and loss of memory are their favourite topics. Their caricature-based jokes reveal an awareness of the decline related to ageing and give visibility to the 'zone' they wish to avoid entering. As pointed out in chapter 6, frailties are associated with the fourth age, while freedom is associated with the third age.[39] Even so, almost every participant interviewed reported living with some physical pain or having a condition that demands daily care. Although they keep this information private, hiding the natural decline of ageing can become difficult over time. This is something else this long-term ethnography has shown. Sixteen months was long enough for me to observe some signs of decline among research participants, including the start of essential tremor (ET), involuntary shaking movements associated with becoming elderly and with memory loss. However, no one talks about these.

Silence is a strategy that older people in Bento may use to avoid conflict or to make a point about how unsatisfied they are. As discussed in chapter 2, when they think their needs are not being considered or respected by service providers, they usually don't complain. Instead, they will simply avoid the provider in question. If a supermarket doesn't use price tags in a size they can read, for example, participants are likely just to take their business elsewhere. Silence is also used (see chapter 3) in relation to physical activity. When instructors push them to overcome the limitations participants consider appropriate to their age, they don't argue. They simply leave the course or change class. Another complaint is made about the way people talk to them: shouting, or speaking very slowly. In such cases, participants stress how disrespected they feel when they are treated as if they were two years old or had a cognitive disability. Again, they tend to avoid exchanges like this. Instead, they end the conversation and leave as soon as they can.

Finally, research participants keep silent about habits and food choices that may be seen as unhealthy. They don't want to damage their identity as responsible citizens embracing active ageing. Just as with their physical frailties, smartphones work as alibis. While research participants confine these practices to private spaces, they may continue to post whatever indicates that they are committed to ageing well in order to avoid becoming a burden to others. What is at issue here is their negotiation between pleasure-oriented life choices and health-directed ones.[40] In other words, smartphones help them give visibility to the lifestyle they are supposed to have while they carry on enjoying what pleases them, celebrating the best part of the third age as the stage of life reserved for pleasure and freedom.

All things considered, it seems that the silence surrounding old age in Bento has become a paradox. On the one hand, images of ageing, showing healthy, productive, independent and happy people, have gained visibility and established a norm. On the other hand, this normativity is the very thing that drives participants' frailties, decline, pains, needs and some desires into the shadows. Silence helps older people to comply with this normativity. While their busy timetable, including their healthy habits, is made public and signifies the morally desirable way of ageing, their silence is what keeps 'failures' and 'deviations' private. Managing the shift between the public and private spheres is among the activities they reconcile while they continue to search for ways to make old age meaningful.

Towards happiness

One of the main criticisms of policies on health and ageing is that they can harm people. Sarah Lamb[41] edited an entire book on how approaches to successful ageing may be inadequate and unfair if the cultural context of an individual society is not taken into account. Castro and Singer[42] edited a volume on international health policies and how they can end up being unhealthy for the populations they are supposed to help. On the basis of the ethnographic analysis presented in this book, I want to conclude by asking a final question: do the health and ageing policies followed in Brazil make older people in Bento happier? I choose to approach this topic through the concept of happiness because I believe happiness can be an appropriate measure of well-being, especially in old age. And I am not alone in my choice. Mathews and Izquierdo[43] have edited a book that considers the relationship between well-being and happiness and sets out a holistic and culturally sensitive approach to them. But what is happiness?

Aristotle[44] argues that happiness is an end in itself. Moreover, it is the end that should be pursued by every good man. Happiness is measured by a virtuous life, in which one should do good and do it well. By doing good, one experiences the good. However, the virtuous life should consider the common good, which means considering others and, most of all, life in the polis. Thus, happiness is always accountably achieved through actions. From Aristotle's perspective, this means that a virtuous life lived in the past can't provide happiness in the future, as happiness is an ongoing balance. As seen in the previous chapter, this can also explain why the past is not enough to fulfil the future in Bento, where older people are likely to orient their actions towards the present.

Moreover, we could argue that research participants have captured the essence of happiness, as they replace the purpose of life with the choice to live life with purpose. Happiness is pursued through daily actions, which lead to a virtuous life. But how? Virtue is always achieved by balancing two vices, namely lack and excess. This middle ground is what Aristotle called the 'golden mean', the balance between pleasures and fears. This 'in-between' is not given by mathematics. It is a personal deliberation through which one can make a balanced virtuous choice that reveals character and creates the path to happiness. This thoughtful choice can be our starting point for approaching the health and ageing policies that shape old age in Bento.

As argued throughout this book, older people in Bento are trying to balance two 'vices'. On one side, there is excess, represented by all the pleasures saved up for the stage of life that finally allows them to dedicate time to themselves. It is also the time to cast aside social norms (to end a marriage and try casual sex, for example, as seen in chapter 7) or become self-indulgent. On the other side, there are the restrictions represented by all the information they receive and share about what they should be doing or avoiding. In addition (chapter 2) there are all the images and advice that make healthy and active ageing the norm. However, in Aristotle's view, even when others and society are taken into account, the individual should be the one that deliberates on these extremes in order to achieve the balance between them. That is how one demonstrates character and acquires the virtue that leads to happiness. It is also why policies focused on prevention and autonomy may become unfair. When this balance becomes a framework, the *virtuous* action, which may lead to happiness, is replaced by a prescription, constructed as morality, with no space for individual deliberation (and sometimes without taking into consideration the particularities of the society where it is applied). Furthermore, what becomes morally expected can be impossible to achieve even if one is concerned with making the 'right' choices. This is the case when one finds oneself with no means of complying with the lifestyles established as morality. (In this chapter, we challenged the concept of ageing as a meritocracy when we observed that social and economic background could determine very different experiences of ageing in Brazil.)

That is the case with policies such as Successful and Active Ageing. A 'responsible older person' can try to do the right thing, even when facing constraints and inequalities. They can make an effort to eat well, exercise and adopt healthy habits within their capacities. By so doing, they may succeed in postponing the dependence that compromises the economy, especially when the relationship between productive and unproductive populations is taken into account. But no one can choose not to age. Thus, when these policies treat the decline and frailties associated with ageing as a personal failure, we have a problem. So the question to be asked at this point is: for how long one can remain active and autonomous? Until death?

Maybe it is because they fear becoming a burden to others, which they would see as a failure, that older people in Bento wish to die before dependence comes. Alternatively, as posited above, they develop strategies of silence, relying on close friends in order to hide their frailties from their children and their broader circle of friends and acquaintances. Frailty may be seen as indicating a lack of character, because it is an undeniable sign that a person has become 'old', triggering the stigma of uselessness and dependence associated with the fourth age. In addition, they may be punished when frailty becomes evident, as they may be put under family administration whose rules may restrict their freedom. We should ask two more questions. Is there a degree of decline that would be acceptable, taking into account that older people do comply with the requirements of healthy ageing? And who is going to determine this 'golden mean'? These questions raise a sensitive issue about Active Ageing policies, as they are conceived as a global framework, with standards to be 'adopted' locally. For example, Pike argues that there is no evidence to support a universal level of activity in old age. Nevertheless, the same guidelines are used to evaluate whether older people are 'sufficiently active', which leads to parameters for the 'right' and 'wrong' ways to age that privilege some over others.[45] From this perspective, global frameworks should consider the particularities of each population. It is not just about their health profiles and the material conditions in which older people are expected to regulate their habits.[46] Local values should also be taken into account. If they are not, if a global framework is applied as though it were a universal measure of what a virtuous life should be, some populations may become healthier but unhappy.

Even though it is not related to ageing per se, Izquierdo's work[47] illustrates why local values matter. She argues that, despite the significant improvement in health rates and infrastructure brought about by natural gas explorers, international organisations and missionaries, the Matsigenka people of the Peruvian Amazon had the perception that their quality of life had got worse. On the one hand, the community was objectively 'healthier': blood sampling proved it. On the other hand, the Matsigenka people experienced domestic violence, alcohol consumption, family deterioration, laziness and anxiety for the first time. Their insertion into a hybrid cultural context had brought about an identity crisis. Therefore, rather than seeing themselves as 'healthy', they were suffering a deterioration in their own ideal of well-being.

In the Active Ageing framework, the concept of health is based on the adoption of healthy habits and the maintenance of autonomy, which would allow older people to continue to participate in society without becoming a burden to others. In other words, a 'healthy' person is one who succeeds in extending independence into old age. In Bento, however, research participants consider that being healthy is not the condition that will allow them to remain active, autonomous and useful to society. On the contrary, they believe that continuing to work is what will keep them healthy as they age. It is true that, for some, maintaining a full timetable is enough to compensate for retirement. For these people, the lack of idle time is proof of a virtuous productive life, which is a measure of health. For these people, the Active Ageing framework as adopted in Brazil will fit like a glove, providing a portfolio of activities through which they can achieve happiness. For others, happiness means finding a way to return to the workforce. Work is addressed by the Active Ageing policy as a way of extending older people's participation in society. But, in the framework, work in old age is conceived as a contribution, a donation to society. Thus, older people's work is oriented to informal or unpaid kinds of work, mainly taking care of relatives or volunteering.

On the one hand, as we have seen, volunteering is well accepted in Bento. It gives life a purpose. It provides new professional-style credentials. It wins respect and dignity. On the other, for some participants volunteering is a way of giving back to society, but it is not the kind of work they hope to do in the second half of their lives. This is when they start their process of self-reinvention and become entrepreneurs. In one way or another, these examples show that health has a specific meaning in the cultural context of Bento, where it is measured by productivity. As one man put it, people have two options in life: 'Either you stop working and get ill and die, or you keep working and die but without getting ill.' Maybe, for people like these, developing alternatives to work (besides working as caregivers or volunteers) should be the focus of health policies on ageing. That way, older people in Bento would have more chance of ending up healthier and happier, as remaining productive is likely to be the most effective route to achieve *their* 'golden mean', which will always tend to a *lack of idle time*, as this is how they demonstrate character as citizens of São Paulo.

For someone outside Brazil to appreciate this conclusion, a change in perspective is required, as proposed in the introduction of this book. São Paulo is not a festive tropical paradise in which beaches and carnivals are at the same time the icons and events that organise life in the city.[48] Also, the connection people in São Paulo have with work has nothing to do with obligation or punishment.[49] Instead, the identity of the city is built on the glorification of work. Productivity is what historically promoted the integration of those born in the city or who moved there in order to make a living and succeed. It is a form of belonging and a source of citizenship.[50] This explains why older people in Bento would refuse to retire if they could, as they make a profound association between work, dignity, virtue, character and identity. However, a whole generation did retire, and at an early age. Some were motivated by the widely disseminated rumours of an imminent reform to the pension system. Some retired to avoid ageism after being treated as old or obsolete by corporations, while others didn't have this option and are thus neither retired nor employed. To fill this moral gap, older people in Bento take every opportunity to feel busy again. By re-creating their work routines as entrepreneurs or volunteers, or focusing on self-development, they can find a familiar environment that allows them to practise the kind of virtuous actions they know best and associate themselves with. At this stage of life, as in the past, it is above all through work that they can do good and experience the good as they know it, both practices being conducive to happiness.

Hannah Arendt[51] would say that this is not a peculiarity of Bento or of São Paulo, but a consequence of modernity. She would criticise this kind of happiness, and she did it by using the same term, 'active'. She calls *vita activa* the practices through which humans produce the vital and material conditions for their existence and the actions through which they became historical and political subjects. In labouring societies, however, the *vita activa* is reduced to a state of simply doing things in which people would be alienated from their work, emerging as *animal laborans*. Productivity would then be the measure of their value. Because they are unproductive, both the contemplative and the political lives would become impractical, and happiness would become more likely to be experienced through consumption. Thus, work would become a proof of utility, a human condition for not being discarded from society. Under such conditions, it is not hard to imagine that this labouring society would become the 'burnout society' theorised by Byung-Chul Hun,[52] which boosts the medicalisation of fatigue and depression, resulting in the 'happiness industry' presented by William Davies.[53]

This is not the story told by research participants. Work is rooted in the memories they carry of their parents, grandparents and ancestors. It is the value they taught to their children. It is the virtuous activity that provided for their families. It is the routine that shaped who they are and the practice that conferred citizenship on them. Participants have always lived under the conditions of what Arendt called a labouring regime. We could, then, argue that their affective connection to work is simply a sign of their alienation. Instead, this ethnography has shown how this connection was built through time and how it became a local value and the basis of their culture.[54] Over several generations, work has become the measure of the *good* and the *right* choice to be made in Bento. Thus, it doesn't matter if a contemplative life free from work obligations or material constraints finds a place in Aristotle's philosophy or in Seneca's (as seen in the previous chapter). That is not the kind of life that would give older people in Bento a sense of happiness.

On the contrary, their excitement about retirement vanishes after one or two years, to be replaced by a feeling of emptiness.[55] That is when they start their search. They don't want to find the fountain of eternal youth. Rather, they miss the fountain where they used to find joy, energy, purpose and respect. They miss working, as work is the thing that makes them feel young, healthy and alive. They don't want to just sit down and contemplate the past. What would be the purpose of living longer then? That is why they work on the opportunities they have to reproduce their working routines and, if they are lucky, to reinvent their working lives. And they will do this last project together. Connected with their friends on WhatsApp, they will resist becoming a burden while having pleasure and demonstrating character. They will spend their time with purpose and for their own interests and legacy. They will ignore the future while working on the present. That is what happiness in Bento is about.

Notes

1. Menezes 1985.
2. WhatsApp is installed on 98 per cent of the smartphones in Brazil, and 86 per cent of Brazilians use it every day (Mobile Time Opinion Box 2021).
3. Gonzalez & Katz 2016.
4. Miller et. al. 2021.
5. As Anderson and Perrin (2017) observed among older adults in the US, low self-esteem is the main barrier to the adoption of new technologies.
6. Otaegui (2021) noticed the same when older adults in Santiago, Chile, start learning how to use smartphones.
7. This conclusion should take into account that most of the participants have a high level of education and are from the middle class. In Brazil both class and education correlate strongly with internet usage (Cetic.br 2020). First, 57 per cent of Brazilians from lower-income classes

have access to the internet, against 95 per cent from higher-income classes. The proportions of those with basic (nine years of schooling) and higher education are 60 per cent and 97 per cent respectively. Secondly, there is inequality when it comes to solving problems through the internet, which can be seen as an indicator of digital literacy. For example, the proportion of Brazilians searching online for medical information ranges from 28 per cent of those with a basic education to 71 per cent of those with higher education. Brazilians aged 60 and over are indeed the age group with less internet access (34 per cent) and who make fewer searches for medical information (39 per cent). Even so, these numbers can't be isolated from socioeconomic background.

8   DaMatta 1986.
9   Debert 1997; Leibing 2005.
10 Duque 2021.
11 Swedberg 2016, p. 43.
12 Queiroz 1992; Moura 1994; Marins 1999.
13 C. Pereira & Penalva 2014.
14 Savishinsky 2000; Kavedžija 2015; Luborsky 1994; Lassen & Jespersen 2017; Willcox et al. 2007.
15 Higgs et al. 2009.
16 Lamb 2019.
17 United Nations 1983, 2002; World Health Organization 2002.
18 Rose 2001.
19 Rose & Novas 2007.
20 Prado 2016.
21 Moura 1994.
22 The desire to remain productive was also observed in North Americans by Luborsky (1994) and Savishinsky (2000) as a way of refusing the stigma of being 'fully' retired and useless. From engaging in personal projects to continuing to work or volunteering, all activities can be used to craft an identity that recovers utility after retirement.
23 Miller et. al. 2021.
24 Among research participants, cost and access were not crucial issues. All of them were smartphone users, and they all had a data package by the end of my fieldwork. In addition, Bento has many free Wi-Fi spots. The cost of the devices, however, can be a constraint. With battery and memory issues, their second-hand devices can restrict their usage, especially the possibility of downloading new apps. Even so, participants tend to invest in a new device when they feel their skill level justifies it.
25 As Garattini and Prendergast (2015) argue, older people are not interested in what they can't do but focus on what they can. Thus, developers and public policymakers should learn what older people can do and how they do it by adopting an empathetic approach when planning solutions to improve their lives. If they don't, they may exclude this age group from crucial resources for life in society. An example was what happened during the Covid-19 pandemic in Brazil. The government choice was for the development of apps to manage the situation, including an app to allow Brazilians to receive financial support, and the apps created to manage health provision and information, such as the CoronavirusSUS and ConecteSUS apps. This implies that older people would have to adopt apps they were not familiar with. In addition, as ethnography showed, research participants are likely to ask friends to do their new downloads. However, during social isolation, this help was unavailable. Consequently, some of them might have struggled to benefit from these initiatives.
26 Beauvoir 1972.
27 Debert 1997, 2012; Leibing 2005; Featherstone & Hepworth 2005.
28 Debert 2012; Whyte 2017; Lamb 2019; Lassen & Jespersen 2017; Pike 2011.
29 Mota 2019.
30 Conversion as at 28 July 2021.
31 Camarano 2020.
32 Whyte 2017; Lamb 2019.
33 Rowe & Kahn 1997.
34 Lamb 2019.
35 Both of these participants had had higher education. However, the first receives a state pension which is complemented by a private one and the second is neither retired nor employed.
36 Secretaria Municipal de Direitos Humanos e Cidadania 2019.

37 The Brazilian judge Andréa Pachá (2018) raised the same issue in her book *Velhos são os outros* ('Old are the others'). Although it is fictional, it draws on hearings in the family court in Rio de Janeiro, where she works.
38 Degnen (2007) observed that older people in the north of England monitor signs of ageing in their peers. As in Bento, signs of decline and frailties are used to classify the 'real' old as distinct from those who are ageing actively and healthily.
39 Laslett 1991.
40 Jallinoja et al. 2010.
41 Lamb 2017.
42 Castro & Singer 2004.
43 Mathews & Izquierdo 2009.
44 Aristotle 2009.
45 Pike 2011, p. 220.
46 Lieblich (2014) points out that promoting healthy behaviour by making older people believe they have the capacity to remain healthy and control their bodies by managing their habits can result in stress rather than resilience.
47 Izquierdo 2009.
48 Goldenberg 2010.
49 DaMatta 1986.
50 Queiroz 1992; Moura 1994.
51 Arendt 1998.
52 Han 2017.
53 Davies 2016.
54 Although the demands for productivity claimed by Arendt (1998) may reinforce the desire in Bento to keep working, chapter 2 showed that, as well as non-industrial societies, there are work-oriented cultures in which retirement is not acceptable, as people have no social identity other than that associated with labour (Luborsky & LeBlanc 2003).
55 The desire to engage in some project or activity after retirement is not a particularity of Bento; it has also been observed in the US by Luborsky (1994) and Savishinsky (2000).

Bibliography

Acervo Estadão. 2020. https://acervo.estadao.com.br/. Accessed 20 November 2021.
Adler, S. R., J. R. Fosket, M. Kagawa-Singer, S. A. McGraw, E. Wong-Kim, E. Gold and B. Sternfeld. 2000. 'Conceptualizing menopause and midlife: Chinese American and Chinese women in the US'. *Maturitas*, 35(1), 11–23. https://doi.org/10.1016/S0378-5122(00)00090-6.
Agência Estado. 2006. 'Site de relacionamentos Meetic compra brasileiro ParPerfeito'. *Estadão*, 4 May. https://www.estadao.com.br/noticias/geral,site-de-relacionamentos-meetic-compra-brasileiro-parperfeito,20060504p71366. Accessed 20 November 2021.
Agência IBGE. 2020. 'Summary of social indicators: In 2019, proportion of poor people falls to 24.7% but extreme poverty still reaches 6.5% of the population'. *Notícias*, 12 November. https://agenciadenoticias.ibge.gov.br/en/agencia-press-room/2185-news-agency/releases-en/29439-sintese-de-indicadores-sociais-em-2019-proporcao-de-pobres-cai-para-24-7-e-extrema-pobreza-se-mantem-em-6-5-da-populacao-2. Accessed 24 November 2021.
Agência IBGE Notícias. 2018. 'Projeção da População 2018: Número de habitantes do país deve parar de crescer em 2047'. *Estatísticas Sociais*, 27 July. https://agenciadenoticias.ibge.gov.br/agencia-sala-de-imprensa/2013-agencia-de-noticias/releases/21837-projecao-da-populacao-2018-numero-de-habitantes-do-pais-deve-parar-de-crescer-em-2047. Accessed 21 November 2021.
Agência IBGE Notícias. 2020. 'Em 2019, expectativa de vida era de 76,6 anos'. Estatísticas Sociais, 26 November. https://agenciadenoticias.ibge.gov.br/agencia-sala-de-imprensa/2013-agencia-de-noticias/releases/29502-em-2019-expectativa-de-vida-era-de-76-6-anos. Accessed 21 November 2021.
Agência Senado. 2021. 'Rodrigo Pacheco promulga lei do salário mínimo de R$ 1,1 mil'. *Senado Notícias*, 4 June. https://www12.senado.leg.br/noticias/materias/2021/06/04/rodrigo-pacheco-promulga-lei-do-salario-minimo-de-r-1-1-mil. Accessed 20 November 2021.
Ahlin, T. 2018. 'Only near is dear? Doing elderly care with everyday ICTs in Indian transnational families'. *Medical Anthropology Quarterly*, 32(1), 85–102. https://doi.org/10.1111/maq.12404.
Alanzi, T., S. Bah, S. Alzahrani, S. Alshammari, and F. Almunsef. 2018. 'Evaluation of a mobile social networking application for improving diabetes Type 2 knowledge: An intervention study using WhatsApp'. *Journal of Comparative Effectiveness Research* 7(9), 891–9. https://doi.org/10.2217/cer-2018-0028.
Alegretti, L. 2020. 'Coronavírus: Por que pandemia está acelerando saída de idosos do mercado de trabalho'. *BBC News Brasil*, 24 June. https://www.bbc.com/portuguese/brasil-53109747?at_custom4=E861C4A6-B616-11EA-BD3A-A0E8923C408C&at_custom1=%5Bpost+type%5D&at_campaign=64&at_custom2=facebook_page&at_custom3=BBC+Brasil&at_medium=custom7&fbclid=IwAR1EKEPF7ZPgnCSZZM7VxqdfRPK_jPrklKxJQLJHwPiqFu8pEi5u9EUAP1g. Accessed 17 December 2021.
Alves, A. M. 2014. 'Gerações em perspectiva: Os sentidos da sexualidade feminina na velhice e na vida adulta'. In M. Goldenberg (ed.), *Corpo, Envelhecimento e Felicidade* (2nd edn), pp. 159–80. Rio de Janeiro: Civilização Brasileira.
Amossy, R. 2011. 'Introdução'. In R. Amossy (ed.), *Imagens de Si no Discurso: A construção do ethos* (2nd edn), pp. 9–21. São Paulo: Editora Contexto.
Anderson, M. and A. Perrin. 2017. 'Tech adoption climbs among older adults'. Pew Research Center. https://www.pewresearch.org/internet/wp-content/uploads/sites/9/2017/05/PI_2017.05.17_Older-Americans-Tech_FINAL.pdf. Accessed 20 November 2021.

Arendt, H. 1998. *The Human Condition* (2nd edn). Chicago, IL: University of Chicago Press.
Aristotle. 2009. *The Nicomachean Ethics* (trans. D. Ross and L. Brown). Oxford: Oxford University Press.
Arquivo Público do Estado de São Paulo. 2009. 'Imigração em São Paulo'. http://www.arquivoestado.sp.gov.br/imigracao/estatisticas.php. Accessed 22 November 2021.
Augé, M. 2016. *Everyone Dies Young: Time without age* (trans. Jody Gladding). New York: Columbia University Press.
Azize, R. L. 2014. 'A "evolução da saúde masculina": Virilidade e fragilidade no marketing da disfunção erétil e da andropausa'. In M. Goldenberg (ed.), *Corpo, Envelhecimento e Felicidade* (2nd edn), pp. 181–98. Rio de Janeiro: Civilização Brasileira.
Baldassar, L., C. V. Baldock and R. Wilding. 2007. *Families Caring across Borders: Migration, ageing, and transnational caregiving*. Basingstoke: Palgrave Macmillan.
Barthes, R. 2010. *A Lover's Discourse: Fragments* (trans. R. Howard and W. Koestenbaum). New York: Hill and Wang.
Batista, M. P. P., M. H. M. de Almeida and S. Lancman. 2011. 'Politicas públicas para a população idosa: Uma revisão com ênfase nas ações de saúde' (Public policies for the elderly population: A review with emphasis on healthcare action). *Revista de Terapia Ocupacional da Universidade de São Paulo*, 22(3), 200–7. https://doi.org/10.11606/issn.2238-6149.v22i3p200-207.
Bauman, Z. 2003. *Liquid Love: On the frailty of human bonds*. Cambridge: Polity.
Beaumont, J. G. and P. M. Kenealy. 2004. 'Quality of life perceptions and social comparisons in healthy old age'. *Ageing and Society*, 24(5), 755–69. https://doi.org/10.1017/S0144686X04002399.
Beauvoir, S. de. 1972. *Old Age* (trans. Patrick O'Brian). London: Deutsch, and Weidenfeld and Nicolson.
Boni, A. P. 2019. 'Idosos reinventam carreira como influenciadores digitais'. *Radar do emprego*, 14 April. *Estadão*. https://economia.estadao.com.br/blogs/radar-do-emprego/idoso-reinventa-carreira-como-influenciador-digital/. Accessed 20 November 2021.
Bourdieu, P. 1993. *Sociology in Question* (trans. Richard Nice). London: Sage.
Bourdieu, P. 2010. *Distinction: A social critique of the judgement of taste* (trans. Richard Nice). London: Routledge.
Brashier, N. M. and D. L. Schacter. 2020. 'Aging in an era of fake news'. *Current Directions in Psychological Science*, 29(3), 316–23. https://doi.org/10.1177/0963721420915872.
Brasil, Ministério da Saúde. 2008. *Manual de Atenção à Mulher no Climatério/Menopausa*. Brasilia: Editora do Ministério da Saúde.
Brasil, Ministério da Saúde. 2013. *Estatuto do Idoso* (3rd edn). Brasilia: Ministério da Saúde.
Brazilian Report. 2020. 'Slavery in Brazil'. *Think Brazil*, 13 May. https://www.wilsoncenter.org/blog-post/slavery-brazil.
Brigeiro, M. and I. Maksud. 2009. 'Aparição do Viagra na cena pública brasileira: Discursos sobre corpo, gênero e sexualidade na mídia'. *Revista Estudos Feministas*, 17(1), 71–88. https://doi.org/10.1590/S0104-026X2009000100005.
Brooks, A. T. 2017. 'Opting in or opting out? North American women share strategies for aging successfully with (and without) cosmetic intervention'. In S. Lamb (ed.), *Successful Aging as a Contemporary Obsession: Global perspectives*, pp. 41–54. New Brunswick, NJ: Rutgers University Press. www.jstor.org/stable/j.ctt1q1cqw5.7.
Brualla, A. 2020. 'Cohousing: La solución residencial para los mayores que crece en España'. ElEconomista.es, 5 February. https://www.eleconomista.es/empresas-finanzas/noticias/10338783/02/20/Cohousing-la-solucion-residencial-para-los-mayores-que-crece-en-Espana.html. Accessed 20 November 2021.
Butler, R. N. 1963. 'The life review: An interpretation of reminiscence in the aged'. *Psychiatry*, 26(1), 65–76. https://doi.org/10.1080/00332747.1963.11023339.
Cajita, M. I., N. A. Hodgson, K. W. Lam, S. Yoo, and H.-R. Han. 2018. 'Facilitators of and barriers to mHealth adoption in older adults with heart failure'. *CIN: Computers, Informatics, Nursing*, 36(8), 376–82. https://doi.org/10.1097/CIN.0000000000000442.
Calasanti, T. and N. King. 2017. 'Successful aging, ageism, and the maintenance of age and gender relations'. In S. Lamb (ed.), *Successful Aging as a Contemporary Obsession: Global perspectives*, pp. 27–40. New Brunswick, NJ: Rutgers University Press. www.jstor.org/stable/j.ctt1q1cqw5.6.
Calixto, N. and R. Maceira. 2019. '*É hora de aposentar seu conceito de "velho": Dados e insights sobre os sêniores do Brasil*'. Think with Google, March, 5 pp. https://www.thinkwithgoogle.com/_qs/documents/7274/twg_seniors.pdf. Accessed 20 November 2021.

Câmara dos Deputados. 2018. PL 10282/2018. 22 May. https://www.camara.leg.br/proposicoesWeb/fichadetramitacao?idProposicao=2176182. Accessed 23 November 2021.

Câmara Municipal de São Paulo. 2019. 'Em tramitação PL 830/2017: Regras para adequar São Paulo ao conceito de cidade inteligente são tema de projeto'. *Notícias*, 17 July. https://www.saopaulo.sp.leg.br/blog/regras-para-adequar-sao-paulo-ao-conceito-de-cidade-inteligente-sao-tema-de-projeto/. Accessed 21 November 2021.

Camarano, A. A. 2020. 'Os dependentes da renda dos idosos e o coronavírus: Órfãos ou novos pobres?' Disoc (Diretoria de Estudos e Políticas Sociais), Technical Note no. 81, 20 pp. Ipea. https://www.ipea.gov.br/portal/images/stories/PDFs/nota_tecnica/200724_nt_disoc_n_81_web.pdf. Accessed 20 November 2021.

Camarano, A. A. and D. F. Carvalho. 2015. 'O que estão fazendo os homens maduros que não trabalham, não procuram trabalho e não são aposentados?'. *Ciência & Saúde Coletiva*, 20(9), 2757–64. https://doi.org/10.1590/1413-81232015209.00642015.

Cambridge Dictionary [online]. 2021. 'Ghosting'. https://dictionary.cambridge.org/dictionary/english/ghosting.

Campos, M. T. F. de S., J. B. R. Monteiro and A. P. R. de C. Ornelas. 2000. 'Fatores que afetam o consumo alimentar e a nutrição do idoso'. *Revista de Nutrição*, 13(3), 157–65. https://doi.org/10.1590/S1415-52732000000300002.

Cancian, N. and L. Alegretti. 2018. 'Total de idosos que vivem em abrigos público sobe 33% em cinco anos'. *Folha de S. Paulo*, 2 July. https://www1.folha.uol.com.br/cotidiano/2018/07/total-de-idosos-que-vivem-em-abrigos-publicos-sobe-33-em-cinco-anos.shtml. Accessed 20 November 2021.

Caradec, V. 2014. 'Sexagenários e octogenários diante do envelhecimento do corpo'. In M. Goldenberg (ed.), *Corpo, Envelhecimento e Felicidade* (2nd edn), pp. 21–44. Rio de Janeiro: Civilização Brasileira.

Cardoso, W. 2017. 'Idosos viram motoristas do Uber por grana e vida ativa'. *Agora*, 18 June. https://www.pressreader.com/article/281719794575836. Accessed 20 November 2021.

Carvalho, M. C. V. S. 2018. 'Aspectos públicos e privados de escolhas alimentares em práticas virtuais de comunicação e consumo'. In L. Peres-Neto and J. B. Corral (eds), *Éticas em Redes: Políticas de privacidade e moralidades públicas* (2nd edn), pp. 34–68. São Paulo: Estação das Letras e Cores.

Casaqui, V. 2018. 'Estudos da cultura empreendedora no campo da comunicação: Macroproposições, narrativas, inspiração'. *Galáxia (São Paulo)*, 37, 55–65. https://doi.org/10.1590/1982-2554132741.

Castells, M. 1996. *The Rise of the Network Society*. Oxford: Blackwell.

Castro, A. and M. Singer (eds). 2004. *Unhealthy Health Policy: A critical anthropological examination*. Walnut Creek, CA: AltaMira Press.

Castro, G. G. S. and J. A. da Rocha. 2018. 'Cosmética pró-idade: Astúcias das retóricas do consumo em tempos de longevidade'. In G. G. S. Castro (ed.), *Os Velhos na Propaganda: Atualizando o debate*, pp. 136–69. Pimenta Cultural. https://doi.org/10.31560/pimentacultural/2018.884.136-169.

Cawood, E. H. H. and J. Bancroft. 1996. 'Steroid hormones, the menopause, sexuality and well-being of women'. *Psychological Medicine*, 26(5), 925–36. https://doi.org/10.1017/S0033291700035261.

Certeau, M. de. 2011. *The Practice of Everyday Life* (trans. Steven Rendall). Berkeley: University of California Press.

Cetic.br. 2020 *Pesquisa sobre o uso das Tecnologias de Informação e Comunicação nos domicílios brasileiros – TIC Domicílios 2019/Survey on the Use of Information and Communication Technologies in Brazilian Households: ICT Households 2019*. São Paulo: Comitê Gestor da Internet no Brasil. https://cetic.br/media/docs/publicacoes/2/20201123121817/tic_dom_2019_livro_eletronico.pdf. Accessed 20 December 2021.

Cicero. 1884. *De senectute (On old age)* (trans. A. P. Peabody). Boston, MA: Little, Brown, and Company.

Cidade de São Paulo. 2021. 'Razões para visitar'. https://cidadedesaopaulo.com/pqsp/razoes-para-visitar/. Accessed 23 November 2021.

Cidade de São Paulo, Direitos Humanos e Cidadania. 2019. 'Programa São Paulo Amigo do Idoso'. 22 January. https://www.prefeitura.sp.gov.br/cidade/secretarias/direitos_humanos/idosos/programas_e_projetos/index.php?p=270237. Accessed 23 November 2021.

Cidade de São Paulo, Direitos Humanos e Cidadania. 2020. 'Indicadores sociodemográficos da população idosa residente na cidade de São Paulo', 52 pp. https://www.prefeitura.sp.gov.

br/cidade/secretarias/upload/direitos_humanos/IDOSO/PUBLICACOES/Indicadores%20sociais%20(2).pdf. Accessed 22 November 2021.

Cidade de São Paulo, Habitação. 2007. 'Vila dos Idosos: Secretaria de Habitação e COHAB entregam Vila dos Idosos', 20 August. https://www.prefeitura.sp.gov.br/cidade/secretarias/habitacao/noticias/?p=4101. Accessed 24 November 2021.

Cidade de São Paulo, Subprefeitura Vila Mariana. 2019. 'Histórico', 20 March. https://www.prefeitura.sp.gov.br/cidade/secretarias/subprefeituras/vila_mariana/historico/index.php?p=416. Accessed 22 November 2021.

Collucci, C. 2019. 'Mais de 80% dos médicos de SP dizem que já usam tecnologias para atender pacientes'. *Folha de S. Paulo Uol*, 4 April. https://www1.folha.uol.com.br/equilibrioesaude/2019/04/mais-de-80-dos-medicos-de-sp-dizem-que-ja-usam-tecnologias-para-atender-pacientes.shtml. Accessed 20 November 2021.

Collucci, C. and A. E. de S. Pinto. 2018. 'Brasileiros não temem a morte, mas a dependência, mostra Datafolha'. *Folha de S. Paulo*, 29 January. https://www1.folha.uol.com.br/equilibrioesaude/2018/01/1953745-brasileiros-nao-temem-a-morte-mas-a-dependencia-mostra-datafolha.shtml. Accessed 17 December 2021.

Consultoria Jurídica/Advocacia Geral da União. 2015. Technical Note no. 333/2014. Ministério da Saúde. https://www.gov.br/saude/pt-br/composicao/conjur/demandas-judiciais/notas-tecnicas/notas-tecnicas-medicamentos/notas-tecnicas/s/sildenafila.pdf. Accessed 27 February 2022.

Coombs, P. G., M. Heck, P. Guhring, J. Narus and J. P. Mulhall. 2012. 'A review of outcomes of an intracavernosal injection therapy programme'. *BJU International*, 110(11), 1787–91. https://doi.org/10.1111/j.1464-410X.2012.11080.x.

Coordenação de Epidemiologia e Informação. 2017. 'Estado nutricional da população da cidade de São Paulo'. *Boletim ISA Capital* 2015, no. 6, 83 pp. Secretaria Municipal da Saúde de São Paulo. https://www.prefeitura.sp.gov.br/cidade/secretarias/upload/saude/arquivos/publicacoes/ISA_2015_EN.pdf. Accessed 29 December 2021.

Cornwell, B., E. O. Laumann and L. P. Schumm. 2008. 'The social connectedness of older adults: A national profile'. *American Sociological Review*, 73(2), 185–203.

CoroaMetade. 2021. 'O site de relacionamento para quem está na melhor fase da vida'. https://www.coroametade.com.br/. Accessed 23 November 2021.

Corona, L. P., T. R. Pereira de Brito, D. P. Nunes, T. da Silva Alexandre, J. L. Ferreira Santos, Y. A. de Oliveira Duarte and M. L. Lebrão. 2014. 'Nutritional status and risk for disability in instrumental activities of daily living in older Brazilians'. *Public Health Nutrition*, 17(2), 390–5. https://doi.org/10.1017/S1368980012005319.

Correa, M. R. 2009. *Cartografias do envelhecimento na contemporaneidade: Velhice e terceira idade*. São Paulo: Cultura Acadêmica.

Costa, D. 2018. 'Terceira idade é o grupo que mais cresce em rede social'. *O Globo*, 3 November. https://oglobo.globo.com/economia/terceira-idade-e-o-grupo-que-mais-cresce-em-rede-social-23208824. Accessed 5 December 2021.

Costa, G. M. C. and D. M. R. Gualda. 2008. 'Conhecimento e significado culturalda menopausa para um grupo de mulheres' *Revista da Escola de Enfermagem da USP*, 42(1), 81–9. https://doi.org/10.1590/s0080-62342008000100011.

Costanzi, R. N. 2020. 'Análise das concessões de benefícios previdenciários no período de Janeiro a Outubro de 2020'. *Informações Fipe*, 483, 17–22.

DaMatta, R. 1986. *O que faz o brasil, Brasil?* Rio de Janeiro: Rocco.

DataSenado. 2019. 'Redes sociais, notícias falsas e privacidade de dados na internet', 113 pp. https://www12.senado.leg.br/institucional/datasenado/arquivos/mais-de-80-dos-brasileiros-acreditam-que-redes-sociais-influenciam-muito-a-opiniao-das-pessoas. Accessed 24 November 2021.

Davidson, J. 2016. 'What really happens when a singing voice gets old'. *Vulture*, 6 October. https://www.vulture.com/2016/10/mysteries-of-the-aging-voice.html. Accessed 20 November 2021.

Davies, W. 2016. *The Happiness Industry: How the government and big business sold us well-being*. London: Verso.

Debert, G. G. 1997. 'A invenção da terceira idade e a rearticulação de formas de consumo e demandas políticas'. *Revista Brasileira de Ciências Sociais*, 12(34), 39–56.

Debert, G. G. 2003. 'O velho na propaganda'. *Cadernos Pagu*, 21, 133–55. https://doi.org/10.1590/S0104-83332003000200007.

Debert, G. G. 2012. *A Reinvenção da Velhice: Socialização e processos de reprivatização do envelhecimento*. São Paulo: Editora da Universidade de São Paulo/FAPESP.

Debert, G. G. 2014. 'Aging, gender and sexuality in Brazilian society'. *Anthropology & Aging Quarterly*, 34(4), 238–45. https://doi.org/10.5195/aa.2014.4.

Degnen, C. 2007. 'Minding the gap: The construction of old age and oldness amongst peers'. *Journal of Aging Studies*, 21(1), 69–80. https://doi.org/10.1016/j.jaging.2006.02.001.

Demartini, F. 2018. 'Vivo libera WhatsApp gratuitamente em planos pré-pagos e Controle'. *Canaltech*, 11 July. https://canaltech.com.br/apps/whatsapp-de-graca-vivo-117672/. Accessed 8 January 2022.

Dennerstein, L., P. Lehert, H. Burger and J. Guthrie 2005. 'Sexuality'. *American Journal of Medicine*, 118(12), Suppl. 2, 59–63. https://doi.org/10.1016/j.amjmed.2005.09.034.

Desenvolvimento Social. 2020. 'Infográfico dos 20 anos do Bom Prato'. 1 December. https://www.desenvolvimentosocial.sp.gov.br/infografico-bom-prato/. Accessed 22 November 2021.

Diário Oficial da União. 2018. 'Portaria No. 702, de 21 de Março de 2018'. https://www.in.gov.br/web/guest/materia/-/asset_publisher/Kujrw0TZC2Mb/content/id/7526450/do1-2018-03-22-portaria-n-702-de-21-de-marco-de-2018-7526446. Accessed 20 November 2021.

Dias, E. N. and J. L. Pais-Ribeiro. 2018. 'Evolução das políticas públicas á pessoa idosa no Brasil'. *Enfermagem Brasil*, 17(4), 413–20. https://doi.org/10.33233/eb.v17i4.860.

Dória, C. A. 2012. 'Flexionando o gênero: A subsunção do feminino no discurso moderno sobre o trabalho culinário'. *Cadernos Pagu*, 30, 251–71. https://doi.org/10.1590/S0104-83332012000200009.

Dr Consulta. 2021. 'Check-up do Homem 40+'. https://drconsulta.com/servicos/checkups/check-up-do-homem-40. Accessed 17 December 2021.

Drumond Andrade, F. C., A. I. N. Mohd Nazan, M. L. Lebrão and Y. A. de Oliveira Duarte. 2013. 'The impact of body mass index and weight changes on disability transitions and mortality in Brazilian older adults'. *Journal of Aging Research*, 2013, art. no. 905094, 1–11. https://doi.org/10.1155/2013/905094.

Dunn, P. and E. Hazzard. 2019. 'Technology approaches to digital health literacy'. *International Journal of Cardiology*, 293, 294–6. https://doi.org/10.1016/j.ijcard.2019.06.039.

Duque, M. 2021. 'Performing healthy ageing through images: From broadcasting to silence'. *Global Media and China*, 6(3), 303–24. https://doi.org/10.1177/2059436420975221.

Edmonds, A. 2014. 'Surgery-for-life: Aging, sexual fitness and self-management in Brazil'. *Anthropology & Aging Quarterly*, 34(4), 246–59. https://doi.org/10.5195/aa.2014.3.

Empreendedorismo Sênior. 2021. 'Porque fazer parte do nosso programa?' https://empreendedorismosenior.com.br/conheca-o-programa/. Accessed 23 November 2021.

Erikson, E. H. 1982. *The Life Cycle Completed: A review*. New York: Norton.

Escola Paulista de Medicina. 2019. 'A Escola Paulista de Medicina', 23 October. Universidade Federal de São Paulo. https://sp.unifesp.br/epm/sobre/a-escola#historia. Accessed 19 November 2021.

Estado de S. Paulo. 2018. 'Roubos de celular atingem metade das ruas de São Paulo'. *Estadão*, 23 October. https://sao-paulo.estadao.com.br/noticias/geral,roubos-de-celular-atingem-metade-das-ruas-de-sao-paulo,70002022457. Accessed 23 November 2021.

Estado de S. Paulo. 2019. 'Reforma da Previdência: Veja o que muda na aposentadoria'. *Estadão: Economia & Negócios*. 22 October. https://economia.estadao.com.br/noticias/geral,como-fica-minha-aposentadoria-com-a-reforma-da-previdencia-aprovada-no-congresso,70003059742. Accessed 24 November 2021.

Exame Invest. 2018. 'Reajustes altos afastam 3 milhões de brasileiros dos planos de saúde'. Minhas Finanças, 23 April. https://invest.exame.com/mf/preco-de-planos-de-saude-explode-e-afasta-milhoes-de-usuarios. Accessed 24 November 2021.

Faro, L., L. Krakowski Chazan, F. Rohden and J. Russo. 2013. 'Homem com "H": ideais de masculinidade (re)construídos no marketing farmacêutico. *Cadernos Pagu*, 40, 287–321. https://doi.org/10.1590/S0104-83332013000100009. Trans. Elena Calvo Gonzalez and Phillip Villani as 'Man with a capital "M": Ideas of masculinity (re)constructed in pharmaceutical marketing'. https://www.scielo.br/j/cpa/a/jKWDsWTW6ddqLd4CPdRgy4r/?format=pdf&lang=en. Accessed 22 November 2021.

Featherstone, M. and M. Hepworth. 1991. 'The mask of ageing and the postmodern life course'. In M. Featherstone, M. Hepworth and B. Turner, *The Body: Social Process and Cultural Theory*, pp. 371–89. London: SAGE. https://doi.org/10.4135/9781446280546.n15.

Featherstone, M. and M. Hepworth. 2005. 'Images of ageing: Cultural representations of later life'. In M. L. Johnson, V. L. Bengtson, P. G. Coleman and T. B. L. Kirkwood (eds), *The Cambridge Handbook of Age and Ageing*, pp. 354–62. Cambridge: Cambridge University Press. https://doi.org/10.1017/CBO9780511610714.036.

FecomercioSP. 2016. 'Especialistas apresentam soluções para a Reforma da Previdência Social brasileira'. 7 March. https://www.fecomercio.com.br/noticia/especialistas-apresentam-solucoes-para-a-reforma-da-previdencia-social-brasileira. Accessed 21 November 2021.

Figueiredo, I. C. R., P. C. Jaime and C. A. Monteiro. 2008. 'Fatores associados ao consumo de frutas, legumes e verduras em adultos da cidade de São Paulo'. *Revista de Saúde Pública*, 42(5), 777–85. https://doi.org/10.1590/S0034-89102008005000049.

Fisher, L., G. O. Anderson, M. Chapagain, X. Mentenegro, J. Smoot and A. Takalkar. 2010. *Sex, Romance, and Relationships: AARP survey of midlife and older adults*. AARP Research. https://doi.org/10.26419/res.00063.001.

Folha de S. Paulo. 2008. 'Vila Mariana nasceu em um matadouro'. 10 August. https://www1.folha.uol.com.br/fsp/especial/fj1008200822.htm. Accessed 24 November 2021.

Folha de S. Paulo Cotidiano. 2002. 'SUS limitava terapia hormonal desde 95'. *Folha S. Paulo*, 12 July. https://www1.folha.uol.com.br/fsp/cotidian/ff1207200215.htm. Accessed 10 January 2022.

Foucault, M. 1988. *Technologies of the Self: A seminar with Michel Foucault* (ed. L. H. Martin, H. Gutman and P. H. Hutton). Amherst: University of Massachusetts Press.

Freitas, A. 2017. 'Vinte coisas que só quem mora na Vila Mariana vai entender'. *Veja São Paulo*, 1 June. https://vejasp.abril.com.br/cidades/vinte-coisas-que-so-quem-mora-na-vila-mariana-vai-entender/. Accessed 22 November 2021.

G1. 2013. 'Brasil tem o minuto de celular mais caro do mundo, diz relatório da ONU'. *Tecnologia e Games*, 7 October. http://g1.globo.com/tecnologia/noticia/2013/10/brasil-tem-o-minuto-de-celular-mais-caro-do-mundo-diz-relatorio-da-onu.html. Accessed 20 November 2021.

G1 2015. 'Haddad sanciona lei que permite transporte de animais em ônibus'. 2015. *G1 São Paulo*, 11 March. http://g1.globo.com/sao-paulo/noticia/2015/03/haddad-sanciona-lei-que-permite-transporte-de-animais-em-onibus.html. Accessed 22 November 2021.

G1. 2018. 'Lei Seca ficou mais rígida nos últimos anos; veja o que pode e o que não pode'. *Auto Esporte*, 18 June. https://autoesporte.globo.com/videos/noticia/2018/06/lei-seca-ficou-mais-rigida-nos-ultimos-anos-veja-o-que-pode-e-o-que-nao-pode.ghtml. Accessed 22 November 2021.

Garattini, C. and D. Prendergast. 2015. 'Critical reflections on ageing and technology in the twenty-first century'. In D. Prendergast and C. Garattini (eds), *Aging and the Digital Life Course*, pp. 1–19. New York and Oxford: Berghahn Books.

Garcia, A. C. B. and A. Vivacqua. 2021. 'Should I stay or should I go? Managing Brazilian WhatsApp groups'. *First Monday*, 26(2). https://doi.org/10.5210/fm.v26i2.10641.

Garvey, P. and D. Miller. 2021. *Ageing with Smartphones in Ireland: When life becomes craft*. London: UCL Press. https://discovery.ucl.ac.uk/id/eprint/10126928/1/Ageing-with-Smartphones-in-Ireland.pdf. Accessed 11 January 2022.

Giami, A. 2007. 'Permanência das representações do gênero em sexologia: As inovações científica e médica comprometidas pelos estereótipos de gênero'. *Physis: Revista de Saúde Coletiva*, 17(2), 301–20. https://doi.org/10.1590/S0103-73312007000200006.

Gianakos, D. 2007. 'Cicero and healthy aging'. *American Journal of Medicine*, 120(12), 1097. https://doi.org/10.1016/j.amjmed.2007.10.001.

Gibbon, S. 2017. 'Entangled local biologies: Genetic risk, bodies and inequities in Brazilian cancer genetics'. *Anthropology & Medicine*, 24(2), 174–88. https://doi.org/10.1080/13648470.2017.1326756.

Glass, A. P. 2012. 'Elder co-housing in the United States: Three case studies'. *Built Environment*, 38(3), 345–63. https://doi.org/10.2148/benv.38.3.345.

Goffman, E. 1990. *The Presentation of Self in Everyday Life* (reprint). New York: Doubleday.

Goldenberg, M. 2010. 'The body as capital: Understanding Brazilian culture'. *Vibrant: Virtual Brazilian Anthropology*, 7(1), 220–38.

Goldenberg, M. 2013. *A bela velhice*. Rio de Janeiro: Editora Record.

Gomes, H. S. 2013. 'Pela 1ª vez, maioria das casas do Brasil usa apenas celular, diz Pnad'. *Tecnologia e Games*, 27 September. http://g1.globo.com/tecnologia/noticia/2013/09/pela-1-vez-maioria-das-casas-do-brasil-usa-apenas-celular-diz-pnad.html. Accessed 22 November 2021.

Gomes, H. S. 2018. 'Brasil é 2º maior mercado do "Império do amor", empresa que fatura US$ 1,1 bilhão com relacionamento online'. *G1 Economia*, 12 July. https://g1.globo.com/economia/

tecnologia/noticia/brasil-e-2o-maior-mercado-do-imperio-do-amor-empresa-que-fatura-us-11-bilhao-com-relacionamento-online.ghtml. Accessed 22 November 2021.

Gomes, S. R. 2021. 'WhatsApp Solidário! Exemplo exitoso de políticas públicas em SP'. *Portal do Envelhecimento e Longeviver*, 4 May. https://www.portaldoenvelhecimento.com.br/whatsapp-solidario-exemplo-exitoso-de-politicas-publicas-em-sp/. Accessed 22 November 2021.

Gonçalves, A. de F. and M. T. Maeda. 2017. 'IDH E a dinâmica Intraurbana na Cidade de São Paulo'. In B. O. Marguti, M. A. Costa and C. V. da Silva Pinto (eds), *Territórios em números: Insumos para políticas públicas a partir da análise do IDHM e do IVS de UDHs e regiões metropolitanas brasileiras*, vol. 2, pp. 171–91. Rio de Janeiro: IPEA.

Gonçalves, H. R. 2009. 'Alimentação e agricultura natural na Igreja Messiânica Mundial do Brasil e suas dissidências'. *Revista Nures*, 9(September/December). https://www.pucsp.br/revistanures/Revista13/goncalves.pdf. Accessed 22 November 2021.

Gonzalez, C. and V. S. Katz. 2016. 'Transnational family communication as a driver of technology adoption'. *International Journal of Communication*, 10, 2683–703.

Gouveia, O. M. R., A. D. Matos and M. J. Schouten. 2016. 'Social networks and quality of life of elderly persons: A review and critical analysis of literature'. *Revista Brasileira de Geriatria e Gerontologia*, 19(6), 1030–40. https://doi.org/10.1590/1981-22562016019.160017.

Governo do Estado de São Paulo. 2021. 'Migrantes'. https://www.saopaulo.sp.gov.br/conhecasp/nossa-gente/migrantes/. Accessed 23 November 2021.

Granovetter, Mark. S. 1973. 'The strength of weak ties'. *American Journal of Sociology*, 78(6), 1360–80.

Guell, C., G. Shefer, S. Griffin and D. Ogilvie. 2016. '"Keeping your body and mind active": An ethnographic study of aspirations for healthy ageing'. *BMJ Open*, 6(1), art. no. e009973. https://doi.org/10.1136/bmjopen-2015-009973.

Guerreiro, R. N. 1999. 'A nova fase das telecomunicações'. *Folha de S. Paulo*, 10 September. https://www1.folha.uol.com.br/fsp/opiniao/fz10099909.htm.

Guess, A., J. Nagler and J. Tucker. 2019. 'Less than you think: Prevalence and predictors of fake news dissemination on Facebook'. *Science Advances*, 5(1), art. no. eaau4586. https://doi.org/10.1126/sciadv.aau4586.

Hall, L., L. C. Callister, J. A. Berry and G. Matsumura. 2007. 'Meanings of menopause: Cultural influences on perception and management of menopause'. *Journal of Holistic Nursing*, 25(2), 106–18. https://doi.org/10.1177/0898010107299432.

Hall, M. M. 1969. 'The origins of mass immigration in Brazil, 1871–1914'. PhD dissertation, Columbia University. https://www.proquest.com/openview/9ddc31cbd2d6d001556fb66a20675dca/1.pdf?pq-origsite=gscholar&cbl=18750&diss=y. Accessed 22 November 2021.

Han, B.-C. 2017. *Sociedade do Cansaço*. Petrópolis: Vozes.

Hänninen, R., L. Pajula, V. Korpela and S. Taipale. 2021. 'Individual and shared digital repertoires: Older adults managing digital services'. *Information, Communication & Society*. https://doi.org/10.1080/1369118X.2021.1954976.

Harvey, D. 1989. *The Condition of Postmodernity: An enquiry into the origins of cultural change*. Oxford: Blackwell.

HCor. 'HCor promove curso gratuito de empreendedorismo para idosos no Sebrae'. 2009. https://www.hcor.com.br/imprensa/noticias/hcor-promove-curso-gratuito-de-empreendedorismo-para-idosos-no-sebrae/. Accessed 22 November 2021.

Helbostad, J. L., B. Vereijken, C. Becker, C. Todd, K. Taraldsen, M. Pijnappels, K. Aminian and S. Mellone. 2017. 'Mobile health applications to promote active and healthy ageing'. *Sensors*, 17(3), art. no. 622. https://doi.org/10.3390/s17030622.

Henrique, A. 2019. 'Cidade de São Paulo tem 13 celulares roubados por hora'. *Agora São Paulo*, 7 June. https://agora.folha.uol.com.br/sao-paulo/2019/06/cidade-de-sao-paulo-tem-13-celulares-roubados-por-hora.shtml.

Higgs, P., M. Leontowitsch, F. Stevenson and I. R. Jones. 2009. 'Not just old and sick: The "will to health" in later life'. *Ageing and Society*, 29(5), 687–707. https://doi.org/10.1017/S0144686X08008271.

Hirschman, A. O. 2004. *Exit, Voice, and Loyalty: Responses to decline in firms, organizations, and states*. Cambridge, MA: Harvard University Press.

Houaiss, A., M. de S. Villar and F. M. de M. Franco. 2001. *Dicionário Houaiss da Língua Portuguesa*. Rio de Janeiro: Objetiva.

IBGE. 2017. Brasil, São Paulo, Panorama. https://cidades.ibge.gov.br/brasil/sp/sao-paulo/panorama. Accessed 20 November 2021.

IBGE. 2020a. 'PNAD: Educação 2019' (Pesquisa Nacional por Amostra de Domicílios Contínua). IBGE. https://biblioteca.ibge.gov.br/visualizacao/livros/liv101736_informativo.pdf. Accessed 22 November 2021.

IBGE. 2020b. 'Síntese de indicadores sociais: Uma análise das condições de vida da população brasileira'. Estudos & Pesquisas, Informação Demográfica e Socioeconômica, no. 43, 148 pp. IBGE. https://biblioteca.ibge.gov.br/visualizacao/livros/liv101760.pdf. Accessed 22 November 2021.

IBGE. 2020c. 'Tábua completa de mortalidade para o Brasil – 2019: Breve análise da evolução da mortalidade no Brasil', 28 pp. IBGE. https://biblioteca.ibge.gov.br/visualizacao/periodicos/3097/tcmb_2019.pdf. Accessed 22 November 2021.

IBGE. 2021. 'Produto interno bruto – PIB'. IBGE. https://www.ibge.gov.br/explica/pib.php. Accessed 23 November 2021.

InfoMoney. 2010. 'Celular completa 20 anos de sua chegada ao Brasil nesta quinta-feira'. *UOL Economia*, 30 December. https://economia.uol.com.br/noticias/infomoney/2010/12/30/celular-completa-20-anos-de-sua-chegada-ao-brasil-nesta-quinta-feira.htm. Accessed 22 November 2021.

Instituto Nacional do Seguro Social (INSS). 2017. 'Breve histórico'. Gov.br, 15 December. https://www.gov.br/inss/pt-br/acesso-a-informacao/institucional/breve-historico. Accessed 22 November 2021.

International Monetary Fund. 2019. *Brazil*. IMF Country Report No. 19/242, 70 pp. https://www.imf.org/~/media/Files/Publications/CR/2019/1BRAEA2019001.ashx. Accessed 20 November 2021.

Izquierdo, C. 2009. 'Well-being among the Matsigenka of the Peruvian Amazon: Health, missions, oil, and "progress"'. In G. Mathews and C. Izquierdo (eds), *Pursuits of Happiness: Well-being in anthropological perspective*, pp. 67–87. New York and Oxford: Berghahn Books.

Jallinoja, P., P. Pajari and P. Absetz. 2010. 'Negotiated pleasures in health-seeking lifestyles of participants of a health promoting intervention'. *Health: An interdisciplinary journal for the social study of health, illness and medicine*, 14(2), 115–30. https://doi.org/10.1177/1363459309353292.

Ka'Opua, L. S. I. 2003. 'Training community practitioners in a research intervention: Practice examples at the intersection of cancer, Western science, and Native Hawaiian healing'. *Cancer Control*, 10(5_suppl), 5–12. https://doi.org/10.1177/107327480301005s02.

Karadağ, E., Ş. B. Tosuntaş, E. Erzen, P. Duru, N. Bostan, B. M. Şahin, İ. Çulha and B. Babadağ. 2015. 'Determinants of phubbing, which is the sum of many virtual addictions: A structural equation model'. *Journal of Behavioral Addictions*, 4(2), 60–74. https://doi.org/10.1556/2006.4.2015.005.

Karasinski, Edgar. 2009. 'A história do email'. *Tecmundo*, 21 September. https://www.tecmundo.com.br/web/2763-a-historia-do-email.htm. Accessed 19 November 2021.

Katz, S. and B. L. Marshall. 2004. 'Is the functional "normal"? Aging, sexuality and the biomarking of successful living'. *History of the Human Sciences*, 17(1), 53–75. https://doi.org/10.1177/0952695104043584.

Kavedžija, I. 2015. 'The good life in balance: Insights from aging Japan'. *HAU: Journal of Ethnographic Theory*, 5(3), 135–56. https://doi.org/10.14318/hau5.3.008.

Kemp, S. 2020. *Digital 2020: Global digital overview*. We are Social/Hootsuite. 247 pp. https://wearesocial.com/digital-2020. Accessed 22 November 2021.

Kickbusch, I. S. 2001. 'Health literacy: Addressing the health and education divide'. *Health Promotion International*, 16(3), 289–97. https://doi.org/10.1093/heapro/16.3.289.

Kickbusch, I., J. M. Pelikan, F. Apfel and A. D. Tsouros (eds). 2013. *Health Literacy: The solid facts*. Copenhagen: World Health Organization Regional Office for Europe.

Kravezuk, T. 2018. 'Brasil soma quase 26 mil tentativas de golpes virtuais por dia'. *R7 Economia*, 29 July. https://noticias.r7.com/economia/brasil-soma-quase-26-mil-tentativas-de-golpes-virtuais-por-dia-29072018. Accessed 23 November 2021.

Kublikowski, I. and C. M. Rodrigues. 2016. '"Kangaroo generations": New contexts, new experiences'. *Estudos de Psicologia (Campinas)*, 33(3), 535–42. https://doi.org/10.1590/1982-02752016000300016.

Küchemann, B. A. 2012. 'Envelhecimento populacional, cuidado e cidadania: Velhos dilemas e novos desafios'. *Revista Sociedade e Estado*, 27(1), 165–80. https://doi.org/10.1590/S0102-69922012000100010.

Lamb, S. (ed.). 2017. *Successful Aging as a Contemporary Obsession: Global perspectives*. New Brunswick, NJ: Rutgers University Press.

Lamb, S. 2019. 'Interrogating healthy/successful aging: An anthropologist's lens'. *Bulletin of the General Anthropology Division*, 26(2), 1, 7–9. https://doi.org/10.1111/gena.12059.

Laplantine, F. 2010. *Antropologia da Doença* (4th edn). São Paulo: Martins Fontes.

Larson, R., R. Mannell and J. Zuzanek. 1986. 'Daily well-being of older adults with friends and family'. *Psychology and Aging*, 1(2), 117–26. https://doi.org/10.1037/0882-7974.1.2.117.

Laslett, P. 1991. *A Fresh Map of Life: The emergence of the third age*. Cambridge, MA: Harvard University Press.

Lassen, A. J. and A. P. Jespersen. 2017. 'Getting old and keeping going: The motivation technologies of active aging in Denmark'. In S. Lamb (ed.), *Successful Aging as a Contemporary Obsession: Global perspectives*, pp. 141–53. New Brunswick, NJ: Rutgers University Press.

Law Dictionary, The. 2021. 'What is conditional contract?'. https://thelawdictionary.org/conditional-contract/. Accessed 24 November 2021.

Leibing, A. 2005. 'The old lady from Ipanema: Changing notions of old age in Brazil'. *Journal of Aging Studies*, 19(1), 15–31. https://doi.org/10.1016/j.jaging.2004.03.010.

Leibing, A. 2017. 'Successful selves? Heroic tales of Alzheimer's disease and personhood in Brazil'. In S. Lamb (ed.), *Successful Aging as a Contemporary Obsession: Global perspectives*, pp. 203–17. New Brunswick, NJ: Rutgers University Press.

Lemos, V. 2018. 'Mochileiras depois dos 60: As mulheres que, na terceira idade, foram conhecer o mundo'. *BBC News Brasil*, 27 May. https://www.bbc.com/portuguese/geral-44177612?fbclid=IwAR1i2_ThxwjXFqn_dj9Ol7CyTlXYb-4WAs2zrPXs1yTOgEhmZRVFlSTTs4A. Accessed 23 November 2021.

Levmore, S. 2017. 'Must we retire?'. In M. C. Nussbaum and S. Levmore, *Aging Thoughtfully: Conversations about retirement, romance, wrinkles, and regrets*, pp. 39–53. New York: Oxford University Press.

Libânio, C. de S., E. Zitkus and A. Pimenta. 2021. 'Case Study 4: Brazil: Public healthcare access for older people: Accessibility of the public healthcare services to the Brazilian elderly population during the COVID-19 pandemic'. In E. Tsekleves et al. (eds), *The Little Book of Global Health. Volume 1: Design & Covid-19*, pp. 29–31. Lancaster: ImaginationLancaster.

Lieblich, A. 2014. *Narratives of Positive Aging: Seaside stories*. New York: Oxford University Press.

Lins, I. L. and L. V. R. Andrade. 2018. 'A feminização da velhice: Representação e silenciamento de demandas nos processos conferencistas de mulheres e pessoas idosas'. *Mediação: Revista de Ciências Sociais*, 23(3), 436–65.

Lippmann, W. 2010. *Public Opinion*. New York: Greenbook Publications.

Lock, M. 1994. 'Menopause in cultural context'. *Experimental Gerontology*, 29(3–4), 307–17. https://doi.org/10.1016/0531-5565(94)90011-6.

Lopes, C. G. 2007. *Integridade na Saúde da Mulher: A questão do climatério*. Fiocruz: Fundação Oswaldo Cruz. https://www.arca.fiocruz.br/bitstream/icict/5359/2/903.pdf. Accessed 23 November 2021.

Lorenz, T. 2017. 'The Facebook Wall is dead – and Facebook is struggling to get personal again'. *MIC*, 10 May. https://www.mic.com/articles/176599/the-facebook-wall-is-dead-social-network-struggles-to-get-personal-again. Accessed 23 November 2021.

Loureiro, M. 2019. 'Prevent Senior resulta de um plano que ficou maduro em 20 anos'. *Exame*, 23 October. https://exame.com/revista-exame/um-plano-que-ficou-maduro-em-20-anos/. Accessed 23 November 2021.

Luborsky, M. R. 1994. 'The retirement process: Making the person and cultural meanings malleable'. *Medical Anthropology Quarterly*, 8(4), 411–29. https://doi.org/10.1525/maq.1994.8.4.02a00050.

Luborsky, M. R. and I. M. LeBlanc. 2003. 'Cross-cultural perspectives on the concept of retirement: An analytic redefinition'. *Journal of Cross-Cultural Gerontology*, 18(4), 251–71. https://doi.org/10.1023/B:JCCG.0000004898.24738.7b.

Lupton, D. 2012. 'M-health and health promotion: The digital cyborg and surveillance society'. *Social Theory & Health*, 10(3), 229–44. https://doi.org/10.1057/sth.2012.6.

Maele. 2021. 'Maele persona'. https://www.amigaeletronica.com.br/botao-de-emergencia-para-idosos-maele-persona/. Accessed 23 November 2021.

Malone, L. 2019. *Desire Lines: A guide to community participation in designing place*. London: RIBA Publishing. https://doi.org/10.4324/9780429345913.

Marins, P. C. G. 1999. 'O Parque do Ibirapuera e a construção da identidade paulista'. *Anais do Museu Paulista: História e Cultura Material*, 6–7(1), 9–36. https://doi.org/10.1590/S0101-47141999000100002.

Marquioni, C. E. and C. C. de Oliveira. 2015. 'Para além da competição: Consumindo afetos como cultura material no programa *MasterChef*: Análises e reflexões iniciais'. *Conexão – Comunicação e Cultura (UCS)*, 14(28), 73–97.

Martin, A. and J. Grudziecki. 2006. 'DigEuLit: Concepts and tools for digital literacy development'. *Innovation in Teaching and Learning in Information and Computer Sciences*, 5(4), 249–67. https://doi.org/10.11120/ital.2006.05040249.

Martines, G. 2015. *Envelhescência* [Documentary, 74 min]. https://youtu.be/i4cLyLdK5EA.

Match.com. 2010. 'Match.com and Meetic announce Latin America partnership'. PRNewswire, 4 February. https://match.mediaroom.com/news-releases?item=94864. Accessed 10 January 2022.

Mathews, G. and C. Izquierdo. 2009. *Pursuits of Happiness: Well-being in anthropological perspective*. New York and Oxford: Berghahn Books.

McPhee, J. S., D. P. French, D. Jackson, J. Nazroo, N. Pendleton and H. Degens. 2016. 'Physical activity in older age: Perspectives for healthy ageing and frailty'. *Biogerontology*, 17(3), 567–80. https://doi.org/10.1007/s10522-016-9641-0.

Melo, K. 2020. 'Golpes financeiros contra idosos cresceram 60%, diz Febraban'. *AgênciaBrasil*, 2 September. https://agenciabrasil.ebc.com.br/economia/noticia/2020-09/golpes-financeiros-contra-idosos-cresceram-60-diz-febraban. Accessed 23 November 2021.

Mendonça, H. 2017. 'Geração canguru, os jovens que escolheram não sair da casa dos pais'. *El País Brasil*, 23 June. https://brasil.elpais.com/brasil/2017/06/05/politica/1496687911_980154.html. Accessed 23 November 2021.

Menezes, E. D. B. de. l985. 'Prometeu e Pandora entre o espelho e a máscara ou Fantasia, ordem e mistério no moinho do sentido (Notas sobre Mito e Ideologia)'. *Revista de História*, 118, 97–156. https://doi.org/10.11606/issn.2316-9141.v0i118p97-156.

Miller, D., E. Costa, N. Haynes, T. McDonald, R. Nicolescu, J. Sinanan, J. Spyer, S. Venkatraman and X. Wang. 2016. *How the World Changed Social Media*. London: UCL Press.

Miller, D., L. A. Rabho, P. Awondo, M. de Vries, M. Duque, P. Garvey, L. Haapio-Kirk, C. Hawkins, A. Otaegui, S. Walton and X. Wang. 2021. *The Global Smartphone: Beyond a youth technology*. London: UCL Press.

MindMiners and Hype60+. 2018. *Hábitos dos 50+: Um estudo sobre como os maduros consomem*. http://bit.ly/or-maduros-download2. Accessed 23 November 2021.

Minha Operadora. 2017. 'Claro vai deixar de cobrar por ligações em todos os planos pós-pagos'. *Redação Minha Operadora*, 23 April. https://www.minhaoperadora.com.br/2017/04/claro-vai-deixar-de-cobrar-por-ligacoes.html. Accessed 20 November 2021.

Ministério da Saúde. 2014. 'Diretrizes para o cuidado das pessoas idosas no SUS: Proposta de modelo de atenção integral: XXX Congresso Nacional de Secretarias Municipais de Saúde'. https://bvsms.saude.gov.br/bvs/publicacoes/diretrizes_cuidado_pessoa_idosa_sus.pdf. Accessed 23 November 2021.

Ministério da Saúde. 2020. 'Situação alimentar e nutricional no Brasil: Excesso de peso e obesidade da população adulta na Atenção Primária à Saúde', 17 pp.

Ministério da Saúde and Instituto Sírio-Libanês de Ensino e Pesquisa. 2016. *Protocolos da Atenção Básica: Saúde das mulheres*. Brasília: Ministério da Saúde. https://bvsms.saude.gov.br/bvs/publicacoes/protocolos_atencao_basica_saude_mulheres.pdf. Accessed 10 January 2022.

Mitnitski, A. B., J. E. Graham, A. J. Mogilner and K. Rockwood. 2002. 'Frailty, fitness and late-life mortality in relation to chronological and biological age'. *BMC Geriatrics*, 2, art. no. 1. https://doi.org/10.1186/1471-2318-2-1.

Mobile Time/Opinion Box. 2021. 'O brasileiro e seu smartphone' (Panorama, 14 pp.).

Moré, C. L. O. O. 2015. 'A "entrevista em profundidade" ou "semiestruturada", no contexto da saúde: Dilemas epistemológicos e desafios de sua construção e aplicação'. *Atas CIAIQ*, 3, 126–31.

Morey, S. A., R. E. Stuck, A. W. Chong, L. H. Barg-Walkow, T. L. Mitzner and W. A. Rogers. 2019. 'Mobile health apps: Improving usability for older adult users'. *Ergonomics in Design: The quarterly of human factors applications*, 27(4), 4–13. https://doi.org/10.1177/1064804619840731.

Morozov, E. 2013. *To Save Everything, Click Here: The folly of technological solutionism*. New York: PublicAffairs.

Morris, J. W. and S. Murray (eds). 2018. *Appified: Culture in the age of apps*. Ann Arbor: University of Michigan Press.

Mota, C. V. 2019. 'Reforma da Previdência: Um retrato das aposentadorias no Brasil em 6 fatos'. *BBC News Brasil*, 22 January. https://www.bbc.com/portuguese/brasil-46866691. Accessed 23 November 2021.

Moura, E. B. B. de. 1994. 'Bandeirantes do progresso: Imagens do trabalho e do trabalhador na cidade em festa. São Paulo, 25 de janeiro de 1954'. *Revista Brasileira de História*, 14(28), 231–46.

Murtagh, M. J. and J. Hepworth. 2003. 'Feminist ethics and menopause: Autonomy and decision-making in primary medical care'. *Social Science & Medicine*, 56(8), 1643–52. https://doi.org/10.1016/S0277-9536(02)00172-7.

Natalini, G. 2018. 'São Paulo conta com mais de 2000 academias ao ar livre para a população idosa'. *Vereador Gilberto Natalini*, 30 July. https://natalini.com.br/sao-paulo-conta-com-mais-de-2000-academias-ao-ar-livre-para-a-populacao-idosa/. Accessed 23 November 2021.

National Inventors Hall of Fame. 2021. 'Robert E. Kahn: Transmission Control Protocol/Internet Protocol'. https://www.invent.org/inductees/robert-e-kahn#:~:text=Robert%20Kahn%20and%20Vinton%20Cerf,IP%20that%20implements%20the%20architecture.&text=In%202004%2C%20Kahn%20received%20the,pioneering%20work%20on%20the%20Internet. Accessed 24 November 2021.

Nedelcu, M. 2017. 'Transnational grandparenting in the digital age: Mediated co-presence and childcare in the case of Romanian migrants in Switzerland and Canada'. *European Journal of Ageing*, 14(4), 375–83. https://doi.org/10.1007/s10433-017-0436-1.

Neff, G. and D. Nafus. 2016. *Self-tracking*. Cambridge, MA: MIT Press.

Neves, F. J., L. Y. Tomita, A. S. L. W. Liu, S. Andreoni and L. R. Ramos. 2020. 'Educational interventions on nutrition among older adults: A systematic review and meta-analysis of randomized clinical trials'. *Maturitas*, 136, 13–21. https://doi.org/10.1016/j.maturitas.2020.03.003.

Nissenbaum, H. 2011. 'A contextual approach to privacy online'. *Daedalus*, 140(4), 32–48. https://doi.org/10.1162/DAED_a_00113.

Nogueira, A. 2016. 'Vila Mariana concentra templos para todo tipo de fé'. *Folha de S. Paulo Especial Morar*, 20 March. http://especial.folha.uol.com.br/2016/morar/campo-belo-vila-mariana/2016/03/1751762-bairro-da-vila-mariana-agrupa-templos-de-todos-os-santos.shtml. Accessed 23 November 2021.

Oh, S. H. 2019. 'Estudo revela que 60,4 milhões de brasileiros foram alvos de cibercrime em 2018'. *Canaltech*, 14 March. https://canaltech.com.br/hacker/estudo-revela-que-604-milhoes-de-brasileiros-foram-alvos-de-cibercrime-em-2018-134841/. Accessed 9 January 2022.

Oliveira, A. and T. Iwata. 2016. 'Os meus, os seus, os nossos'. *psico.usp*, 2(3), 76–95.

Osborn, M., K. Hawton and D. Gath. 1988. 'Sexual dysfunction among middle aged women in the community'. *British Medical Journal*, 296, 959–62.

Otaegui, A. 2021. 'An older adult and the smartphone: Starting over at the age of 80'. Anthropology of Smartphones and Smart Ageing blog, 7 June. https://blogs.ucl.ac.uk/assa/category/chile/page/2/. Accessed 23 November 2021.

Oudshoorn, N. 2011. *Telecare Technologies and the Transformation of Healthcare*. Basingstoke: Palgrave Macmillan.

Pachá, A. 2018. *Velhos são os outros*. Rio de Janeiro: Intrínseca.

Pangambam, S. 2007. 'Steve Jobs iPhone 2007 presentation (full transcript)'. *Singju Post*, 4 July. https://singjupost.com/steve-jobs-iphone-2007-presentation-full-transcript/. Accessed 23 November 2021.

Panorama Mobile Time/Opinion Box. 2021. *Mensageria no Brasil*, February, 16 pp. https://silo.tips/download/mensageria-no-brasil-infobip. Accessed 11 January 2022.

Paúl, C. 2005. 'Envelhecimento activo e redes de suporte social'. *Sociologia: Revista da Faculdade de Letras da Universidade do Porto*, 15. https://ojs.letras.up.pt/index.php/Sociologia/article/view/2392. Accessed 23 November 2021.

Paula, J. J. de, L. Bertola, R. T. de Ávila, L. de O. Assis, M. Albuquerque, M. A. Bicalho, E. N. de Moraes, R. Nicolato and L. F. Malloy-Diniz. 2014. 'Development, validity, and reliability of the General Activities of Daily Living Scale: A multidimensional measure of activities of daily living for older people'. *Revista Brasileira de Psiquiatria*, 36(2), 143–52. https://doi.org/10.1590/1516-4446-2012-1003.

Pedersen, M. 2015. 'Senior co-housing communities in Denmark'. *Journal of Housing for the Elderly*, 29(1–2), 126–45. https://doi.org/10.1080/02763893.2015.989770.

Pereira, C. and G. Penalva. 2014. '"Mulher-Madonna" e outras mulheres: Um estudo antropológico sobre a juventude aos 50 anos'. In M. Goldenberg (ed.), *Corpo, Envelhecimento e Felicidade* (2nd edn), pp. 133–58. Rio de Janeiro: Civilização Brasileira.

Pereira, L. T. S., G. J. de Novaes, L. de Moraes, C. J. Borges, M. R. de Souza, L. A. da Silva and P. de S. Barros. 2017. 'Um olhar sobre a saúde das mulheres cuidadoras de idosos: Desafios e possibilidades'. *Revista Kairós Gerontologia*, 20(1), 277–97. https://doi.org/10.23925/2176-901X.2017v20i1p277-297.

Pereira, M. D. E. S. and A. L. de Oliveira. 2019. '"Compartilha no Whats": Como o WhatsApp está transformando São Paulo em uma cidade inteligente para os idosos'. X Seminário ALAIC 2019: Diálogos desde el sur: comunicación + comunidad + alternatividad, Universidade Federal Fluminense (UFF), Rio de Janeiro, 24–5 October. https://drive.google.com/file/d/16ngEwtQCfjUJ9KdXlB6Vt50sbCYCqF1T/view. Accessed 23 November 2021.

Pereira, R. J., R. M. M. Cotta and S. do C. C. Franceschini 2006. 'Fatores associados ao estado nutricional no envelhecimento' ('Factors associated with nutritional status in the elderly'). *RMMG: Revista Médica de Minas Gerais*, 16(3), 160–4.

Petruccelli, J. L. and A. L. Saboia (eds). 2013. *Características Étnico-raciais da População: Classificações e identidades*. Rio de Janeiro: Instituto Brasileiro de Geografia e Estatística – IBGE.

Pew Research Center. 2014. 'Religion in Latin America: Widespread change in a historically Catholic region', 13 November. https://www.pewforum.org/2014/11/13/religion-in-latin-america/. Accessed 24 November 2021.

Pike, E. C. J. 2011. 'The Active Aging agenda, old folk devils and a new moral panic'. *Sociology of Sport Journal*, 28(2), 209–25. https://doi.org/10.1123/ssj.28.2.209.

Plaza, D. and L. Plaza. 2019. 'Facebook and WhatsApp as elements in transnational care chains for the Trinidadian diaspora'. In Philip Q. Yang (ed.), *Transnationalism and Genealogy*, special issue of *Genealogy*, 3(2), art. no. 15. https://doi.org/10.3390/genealogy3020015. (Printed edition Basel: MDPI, 2020, pp. 55–74.)

Pols, J. 2012. *Care at a Distance: On the closeness of technology*. Amsterdam: Amsterdam University Press.

PopulationPyramid.net. 2019. 'Lista de países ordenados pelo tamanho da população'. https://www.populationpyramid.net/pt/popula%C3%A7%C3%A3o/2020/. Accessed 23 November 2021.

Porter, E. 2017. 'How care for elders, not children, denies women a paycheck'. *New York Times*, 19 December. https://www.nytimes.com/2017/12/19/business/economy/women-work-eldercare.html. Accessed 17 December 2021.

Prado, A. M. 2016. 'O jeitinho Brasileiro: Uma revisão bibliográfica'. *Horizonte Científico*, 10(1). http://www.seer.ufu.br/index.php/horizontecientifico/article/view/33308. Accessed 11 January 2022.

Prefeitura de São Paulo, Desenvolvimento Urbano. 2019. 'Retrato da pessoa idosa na cidade de São Paulo'. *Informes Urbanos*, 37, 9 pp. https://www.prefeitura.sp.gov.br/cidade/secretarias/upload/Informes_Urbanos/IU_Idoso_2019_REV_Final.pdf. Accessed 23 November 2021.

Prevent Senior. 2021. 'Quem somos'. https://preventsenior.com.br/quemsomos.php. Accessed 23 November 2021.

PricewaterhouseCoopers Brasil and EAESP-FGV. 2013. 'Envelhecimento da força de trabalho no Brasil', 40 pp. https://www.pwc.com.br/pt/publicacoes/servicos/assets/consultoria-negocios/pesq-env-pwc-fgv-13e.pdf. Accessed 11 January 2022.

Prodam. 2018. 'Aplicativo Agenda Fácil completa três meses de operação'. 8 February. https://www.prefeitura.sp.gov.br/cidade/secretarias/inovacao/prodam/noticias/?p=249550. Accessed 20 November 2021.

Pype, K. 2017. 'Smartness from below: Variations on technology and creativity in contemporary Kinshasa'. In C. C. Mavhunga (ed.), *What do Science, Technology, and Innovation Mean from Africa?*, pp. 97–115. Cambridge, MA: MIT Press.

Queiroz, M. I. P. de. 1992. 'Ufanismo paulista: Vicissitudes de um imaginário'. *Revista USP*, 13, 78–87. https://doi.org/10.11606/issn.2316-9036.v0i13p78-87.

Ramakuela, N. J., H. A. Akinsola, L. B. Khoza, R. T. Lebese and A. Tugli, A. 2014. 'Perceptions of menopause and aging in rural villages of Limpopo Province, South Africa'. *Health SA Gesondheid*, 19(1), art. no. 771. https://doi.org/10.4102/hsag.v19i1.771.

Rancière, J. 2006. *The Politics of Aesthetics: The distribution of the sensible* (trans. Gabriel Rockhill). London: Continuum.

ReclameAqui Notícias. 2016. 'Você ainda usa celular com dois chips? Brasileiro muda hábitos'. 12 December. https://noticias.reclameaqui.com.br/noticias/voce-ainda-usa-celular-com-dois-chips-brasileiro-muda-habito_2596/. Accessed 8 January 2022.

Rede Nossa São Paulo. 2020. 'Mapa da desigualdade 2020'. https://www.nossasaopaulo.org.br/wp-content/uploads/2020/10/Mapa-da-Desigualdade-2020-MAPAS-site-1.pdf. Accessed 23 November 2021.

Revista Izunome. 2019. 'Congresso de Nutrição discute sobre "o alimento como protagonista"'. 140 (September), 34–5.

Rheingold, H. 2000. *The Virtual Community: Homesteading on the electronic frontier* (rev. edn). Cambridge, MA: MIT Press.

Ribeiro, C. D. M., T. B. Franco, A. G. da Silva Júnior, R. de C. D. Lima and C. S. Andrade (eds). 2011. *Saúde Suplementar, Biopolítica e Promoção da Saúde*. São Paulo: Hucitec.

Rocha, C. 2017. '"Celular de bandido": Organizando direitinho todo mundo rouba todo mundo'. *O Globo: Panorama Carioca*, 8 January. https://blogs.oglobo.globo.com/panorama-carioca/post/celular-de-bandido-organizando-direitinho-todo-mundo-rouba-todo-mundo.html. Accessed 24 November 2021.

Rocha, E. and S. Padovani. 2016. 'Usabilidade e acessibilidade em smartphones: Identificação de características do envelhecimento e suas implicações para o design de interface de smartphones'. *Revista ErgodesignHCI*, 4(Especial), 58–66. https://doi.org/10.22570/ergodesignhci.v4iEspecial.119.

Rocha, J. A. da and T. Z. Miné. 2018. 'A imagem do idoso bem-sucedido na publicidade brasileira'. In G. G. S. Castro (ed.), *Os Velhos na Propaganda: Atualizando o debate*, pp. 203–26. São Paulo: Pimenta Cultural. https://doi.org/10.31560/pimentacultural/2018.884.203-226. Accessed 24 November 2021.

Rodrigues, L. de S. and G. A. Soares. 2006. 'Velho, idosos e terceira idade na sociedade contemporânea'. *Revista Ágora*, 4, 1–29. https://periodicos.ufes.br/agora/article/view/1901. Accessed 24 November 2021.

Rose, N. 2001. 'The politics of life itself'. *Theory, Culture & Society*, 18(6), 1–30. https://doi.org/10.1177/02632760122052020.

Rose, N. and C. Novas. 2007. 'Biological citizenship'. In A. Ong and S. J. Collier (eds), *Global Assemblages: Technology, politics, and ethics as anthropological problems*, pp. 439–63. Malden, MA: Blackwell. https://doi.org/10.1002/9780470696569.ch23.

Rossi, A. 2018. 'Navios portugueses e brasileiros fizeram mais de 9 mil viagens com africanos escravizados'. *BBC News Brasil*, 7 August. https://www.bbc.com/portuguese/brasil-45092235. Accessed 24 November 2021.

Rowe, J. W. and R. L. Kahn. 1997. 'Successful aging'. *The Gerontologist*, 37(4), 433–40. https://doi.org/10.1093/geront/37.4.433.

Rozendo, A. da S. and J. M. Alves. 2015. 'Sexualidade na terceira idade: Tabus e realidade'. *Revista Kairós Gerontologia*, 18(3), 95–107. https://doi.org/10.23925/2176-901X.2015v18i3p95-107.

Ruckenstein, M. and N. D. Schüll. 2017. 'The datafication of health'. *Annual Review of Anthropology*, 46, 261–78. https://doi.org/10.1146/annurev-anthro-102116-041244.

Santana, S., B. Lausen, M. Bujnowska-Fedak, C. E. Chronaki, H. U. Prokosch and R. Wynn. 2011. 'Informed citizen and empowered citizen in health: Results from an European survey'. *BMC Family Practice*, 12, art. no. 20. https://doi.org/10.1186/1471-2296-12-20.

Sartori, A. C. R. and M. L. Zilberman. 2009. 'Revisitando o conceito de síndrome do ninho vazio' *Revista de Psiquiatría Clínica*, 36(3), 112–21. https://doi.org/10.1590/S0101-60832009000300005.

Savishinsky, J. S. 2000. *Breaking the Watch: The meanings of retirement in America*. Ithaca, NY: Cornell University Press.

SBT. 2019. 'Idosos sãos alvos preferido de ladrões no Estado de São Paulo'. 2019. *SBT Brasil*, 25 May. https://www.youtube.com/watch?v=XdZYpCX3iL0. Accessed 22 November 2021.

Schneider, R. H. and T. Q. Irigaray. 2008. 'O envelhecimento na atualidade: Aspectos cronológicos, biológicos, psicológicos e sociais'. *Estudos de Psicologia (Campinas)*, 25(4), 585–93. https://doi.org/10.1590/S0103-166X2008000400013.

Sebrae. 2017. 'Perfil do potencial empreendedor aposentado', 66 pp. https://www.sebrae.com.br/Sebrae/Portal%20Sebrae/Anexos/Apresenta%C3%A7%C3%A3o%20Potencial%20Empreendedor%20aposentado%20vf.pdf. Accessed 23 November 2021.

Secretaria Municipal de Direitos Humanos e Cidadania. 2019. 'Indicadores sociodemográficos da população idosa na cidade de São Paulo, 100 pp. https://www.prefeitura.sp.gov.br/

cidade/secretarias/upload/direitos_humanos/IDOSO/PUBLICACOES/Indicadores%20 sociais_10_02_2020%20(3).pdf. Accessed 24 November 2021.
Senado Federal. 2018. 'Símbolo para identificação de idoso não pode ser pejorativo, prevê projeto aprovado na CDH'. *Senado Notícias*, 25 April. https://www12.senado.leg.br/noticias/materias/2018/04/25/simbolo-para-identificacao-de-idoso-nao-pode-ser-pejorativo-preve-projeto-aprovado-na-cdh. Accessed 24 November 2021.
Seneca, L. A. 2005. *On the Shortness of Life* (trans. C. D. N. Costa). London: Penguin.
Sennett, R. 2004. *Respect: The formation of character in an age of inequality*. London: Penguin.
Sennett, R. 2006. *The Culture of the New Capitalism*. New Haven, CT: Yale University Press.
Separavich, M. A. and A. M. Canesqui. 2013. 'Saúde do homem e masculinidades na Política Nacional de Atenção Integral à Saúde do Homem: Uma revisão bibliográfica'. *Saúde e Sociedade*, 22(2), 415–28. https://doi.org/10.1590/S0104-12902013000200013
Setiya, K. 2017. *Midlife: A philosophical guide*. Princeton, NJ: Princeton University Press.
Shea, J. L. 2020. 'Menopause and midlife aging in cross-cultural perspective: Findings from ethnographic research in China'. *Journal of Cross-Cultural Gerontology*, 35(4), 367–88. https://doi.org/10.1007/s10823-020-09408-6.
Shirky, C. 2011. *A Cultura da Participação: Criatividade e generosidade no mundo conectado*. Rio de Janeiro: Zahar.
Sievert, L. L. 2006. *Menopause: A biocultural perspective*. New Brunswick, NJ: Rutgers University Press.
Silveira, P. G. and A. Wagner. 2006. 'Ninho cheio: A permanência do adulto jovem em sua família de origem'. *Estudos de Psicologia (Campinas)*, 23(4), 441–53. https://doi.org/10.1590/S0103-166X2006000400012.
Simson, O. R. de M. von, A. L. Neri and M. Cachioni (eds). 2003. *As Múltiplas Faces da Velhice no Brasil*. Campinas: Alínea Editora.
Solteiros50 Brasil. n.d. Home: About. Facebook. https://www.facebook.com/Solteiros50Brasil/. Accessed 24 November 2021.
Souza, B., F. Cymbaluk, M. J. Marques, M. Bezerra and T. Pronin. 2016. 'É grave, doutor?' *UOL Notícias*. https://www.uol/noticias/especiais/sus.htm#igualdade-deigual. Accessed 24 November 2021.
Souza, R. de. 2016. 'OurTime: Novo site de encontros foca em internautas com mais de 50 anos'. *Tecmundo*, 31 October. https://www.tecmundo.com.br/novidade/111181-ourtime-novo-site-encontros-foca-internautas-50-anos.htm. Accessed 10 January 2022.
Souza e Silva, A. de, C. S. Damasceno and D. Bueno. 2019. 'Generic phones in context: The circulation and social practices of mobile devices in Rio de Janeiro'. In R. Wilken, G. Goggin and H. A. Horst (eds), *Location Technologies in International Context*, pp. 158–72. Abingdon: Routledge.
Spyer, Juliano. 2018. *Mídias Sociais no Brasil Emergente: Coma a internet afeta a mobilidade social* (trans. Julia Martins Barbosa). London: UCL Press.
Stafford, P. B. 2018. 'Introduction: Theorizing and practicing age-friendly development'. In P. B. Stafford (ed.), *The Global Age-Friendly Community Movement: A critical appraisal*, pp. 1–12. New York: Berghahn Books.
Statista Research Department. 2021a. 'Cities with the highest number of museums worldwide as of May 2019'. *Statista*, 9 March. https://www.statista.com/statistics/1064544/top-cities-museums-worldwide/. Accessed 24 November 2021.
Statista Research Department. 2021b. 'Most popular global mobile messaging apps 2021'. *Statista*, 2 August. https://www.statista.com/statistics/258749/most-popular-global-mobile-messenger-apps/.
Strauss, J. R. 2013. 'The baby boomers meet menopause: Fertility, attractiveness, and affective response to the menopausal transition'. *Sex Roles*, 68(1–2), 77–90. https://doi.org/10.1007/s11199-011-0002-9.
Swan, M. 2012 'Health 2050: The realization of personalized medicine through crowdsourcing, the quantified self, and the participatory biocitizen'. *Journal of Personalized Medicine*, 2(3), 93–118. https://doi.org/10.3390/jpm2030093.
Swedberg, R. 2016. 'A sociological approach to hope in the economy'. In H. Miyazaki and R. Swedberg (eds), *The Economy of Hope*, pp. 37–50. Philadelphia: University of Pennsylvania Press.
Taipale, S. and M. Farinosi. 2018. 'The big meaning of small messages: The use of WhatsApp in intergenerational family communication'. In J. Zhou and G. Salvendy (eds), *Human Aspects of*

IT for the Aged Population: Acceptance, communication and participation, pp. 532–46. Cham: Springer. https://doi.org/10.1007/978-3-319-92034-4_40.

Taipale, S., T.-A. Petrovčič and V. Dolničar. 2018. 'Intergenerational solidarity and ICT usage: Empirical insights from Finnish and Slovenian families'. In S. Taipale, T.-A. Wilska and C. Gilleard (eds), *Digital Technologies and Generational Identity: ICT usage across the life course*, pp. 69–86. New York: Routledge.

Tajra, A. 2020. '7 em cada 10 brasileiros dependem do SUS para tratamento, diz IBGE'. *UOL Notícias*, 4 September. https://noticias.uol.com.br/saude/ultimas-noticias/redacao/2020/09/04/7-em-cada-10-brasileiros-dependem-do-sus-para-tratamento-diz-ibge.htm. Accessed 24 November 2021.

Tassara, E. T. de O. and E. P. Rabinovich. 2007. 'Movimentos migratórios na metrópole de São Paulo no século XXI: Um estudo qualitativo'. *Psicologia para América Latina*, 10. http://pepsic.bvsalud.org/scielo.php?script=sci_arttext&pid=S1870-350X2007000200013&lng=pt&tlng=pt. Accessed 24 November 2021.

Teixeira, L. da S., L. C. da S. Palos and W. Simões. 2019. 'Cesta básica'. Câmara dos Deputados. https://bd.camara.leg.br/bd/bitstream/handle/bdcamara/37787/cesta_basica_teixeira_palos_simoes.pdf?sequence=1. Accessed 24 November 2021.

Temóteo, A., H. de Andrade and G. Mazieiro. 2019. 'Congresso promulga reforma da Previdência'. *UOL Economia*, 12 November. https://economia.uol.com.br/noticias/redacao/2019/11/12/congresso-promulga-reforma-da-previdencia.htm. Accessed 24 November 2021.

Tetley, J., C. Holland, V. Waights, J. Hughes, S. Holland and S. Warren. 2015. 'Exploring new technologies through playful peer-to-peer engagement in informal learning'. In D. Prendergast and C. Garattini (eds), *Aging and the Digital Life Course*, pp. 39–62. New York and London: Berghahn Books.

Thomas, H. N., C.-C. H. Chang, S. Dillon and R. Hess. 2014. 'Sexual activity in midlife women: Importance of sex matters'. *JAMA Internal Medicine*, 174(4), 631–3. https://doi.org/10.1001/jamainternmed.2013.14402.

Trench, B. and T. E. da C. Rosa. 2008. 'Menopausa, hormônios, envelhecimento: Discursos de mulheres que vivem em um bairro na periferia da cidade de São Paulo, estado de São Paulo, Brasil'. *Revista Brasileira de Saúde Materno Infantil*, 8(2), 207–16. https://doi.org/10.1590/S1519-38292008000200008.

Triboni, S. 2021. 'Cohousing é o novo jeito de morar e viver em comunidade'. *Maturi*, 3 June. https://www.maturi.com.br/comunidade/cohousing-e-o-novo-jeito-de-morar-e-viver-em-comunidade/. Accessed 11 January 2022.

Trindade, E. 2018. 'Disputa Bolsonaro x Haddad acirra ânimos em grupos de família no WhatsApp'. *Folha de S. Paulo*, 10 October. https://www1.folha.uol.com.br/colunas/redesocial/2018/10/grupos-no-whatsapp-revelam-clima-de-odio-com-polarizacao-pt-x-bolsonaro.shtml. Accessed 20 December 2021.

United Nations. 1983. 'Vienna International Plan of Action on Aging'. United Nations. https://generationen.oehunigraz.at/files/2012/07/Wiener-Aktionsplan-zur-Frage-des-Alterns-1982.pdf.

United Nations. 2002. *Political Declarations and Madrid International Plan of Action on Ageing*. https://www.un.org/esa/socdev/documents/ageing/MIPAA/political-declaration-en.pdf. Accessed 24 November 2021.

United Nations. 2021. 'Outcomes on Ageing'. https://www.un.org/en/development/devagenda/ageing.shtml. Accessed 23 November 2021.

United Nations, Department of Economic and Social Affairs. 2018. *World Urbanization Prospects 2018: Highlights* (ST/ESA/SER.A/421; 38 pp.). https://population.un.org/wup/Publications/Files/WUP2018-Highlights.pdf. Accessed 24 November 2021.

United Nations, Department of Economic and Social Affairs. 2019. *World Population Ageing 2019: Highlights* (ST/ESA/SER.A/430; 46 pp.). https://www.un.org/en/development/desa/population/publications/pdf/ageing/WorldPopulationAgeing2019-Highlights.pdf. Accessed 24 November 2021.

Ussher, J. M., J. Perz and C. Parton. 2015. 'Sex and the menopausal woman: A critical review and analysis'. *Feminism & Psychology*, 25(4), 449–68. https://doi.org/10.1177/0959353515579735.

Valente, L. 2019. 'Modelo de habitação cohousing sênior cai no gosto de quem quer uma velhice independente e tranquila'. *Saúde Plena*, 11 February. https://www.uai.com.br/app/noticia/

saude/2019/02/11/noticias-saude,241377/modelo-de-habitacao-cohousing-senior-cai-no-gosto-de-quem-quer-uma-vel.shtml. Accessed 24 November 2021.

Veras, R. P. and M. Oliveira. 2018. 'Envelhecer no Brasil: A construção de um modelo de cuidado'. *Ciência & Saúde Coletiva*, 23(6), 1929–36. https://doi.org/10.1590/1413-81232018236.04722018.

Wagner, P., Y. P. Duan, R. Zhang, H. Wulff and W. Brehm. 2020. 'Association of psychosocial and perceived environmental factors with park-based physical activity among elderly in two cities in China and Germany'. *BMC Public Health*, 20, art. no. 55. https://doi.org/10.1186/s12889-019-8140-z.

Walton, S. M. 2021. *Ageing with Smartphones in Urban Italy: Care and community in Milan and beyond*. London: UCL Press. https://discovery.ucl.ac.uk/id/eprint/10126968/1/Ageing-with-Smartphones-in-Urban-Italy.pdf (accessed 5 January 2022).

Watson, E. A. and J. Mears. 2019. *Women, Work and Care of the Elderly*. Abingdon: Routledge.

Webb, E., D. Blane, A. McMunn and G. Netuveli. 2011. 'Proximal predictors of change in quality of life at older ages'. *Journal of Epidemiology & Community Health*, 65(6), 542–7. https://doi.org/10.1136/jech.2009.101758.

Webb, L. M. 2015. 'Research on technology and the family: From misconceptions to more accurate understandings'. In C. J. Bruess (ed.), *Family Communication in the Age of Digital and Social Media*, pp. 3–31. Peter Lang.

Wejsa, S. and J. Lesser. 2018. 'Migration in Brazil: The making of a multicultural society'. *Migration Information Source*, 29 March. Migration Policy Institute. https://www.migrationpolicy.org/article/migration-brazil-making-multicultural-society. Accessed 24 November 2021.

Wentzell, E. 2013. 'Aging respectably by rejecting medicalization: Mexican men's reasons for not using erectile dysfunction drugs'. *Medical Anthropology Quarterly*, 27(1), 3–22. https://doi.org/10.1111/maq.l2013.

Wentzell, E. 2017. 'Dysfunction as successful aging in Mexico'. In S. Lamb (ed.), *Successful Aging as a Contemporary Obsession: Global perspectives*, pp. 68–82. New Brunswick, NJ: Rutgers University Press. https://doi.org/10.36019/9780813585369-007.

Westin, R. 2019. 'Primeira lei da Previdência, de 1923, permitia aposentadoria aos 50 anos', 3 June. Senado Federal. https://www12.senado.leg.br/noticias/especiais/arquivo-s/primeira-lei-da-previdencia-de-1923-permitia-aposentadoria-aos-50-anos. Accessed 24 November 2021.

Whyte, S. R. 2009. 'Health identities and subjectivities: The ethnographic challenge'. *Medical Anthropology Quarterly*, 23(1), 6–15. https://doi.org/10.1111/j.1548-1387.2009.01034.x.

Whyte, S. R. 2017. 'Epilogue: Successful aging and desired interdependence'. In S. Lamb (ed.), *Successful Aging as a Contemporary Obsession: Global perspectives*, pp. 243–8. Rutgers University Press. www.jstor.org/stable/j.ctt1q1cqw5.21.

Wildenbos, G. A., L. Peute and M. Jaspers. 2018. 'Aging barriers influencing mobile health usability for older adults: A literature based framework (MOLD-US)'. *International Journal of Medical Informatics*, 114, 66–75. https://doi.org/10.1016/j.ijmedinf.2018.03.012.

Wilding, R., L. Baldassar, S. Gamage, S. Worrell and S. Mohamud. 2020. 'Digital media and the affective economies of transnational families'. *International Journal of Cultural Studies*, 23(5), 639–55. https://doi.org/10.1177/1367877920920278.

Willcox, D. C., B. J. Willcox, J. Sokolovsky and S. Sakihara. 2007. 'The cultural context of "successful aging" among older women weavers in a northern Okinawan village: The role of productive activity'. *Journal of Cross-Cultural Gerontology*, 22(2), 137–65. https://doi.org/10.1007/s10823-006-9032-0.

Wilson, R. A. 1966. *Feminine Forever*. New York: M. Evans.

World Health Organization. 2002. 'Active ageing: A policy framework'. https://apps.who.int/iris/bitstream/handle/10665/67215/WHO_NMH_NPH_02.8.pdf;jsessionid=9A418B629755E58207E0C0FF1D6531C6?sequence=1. Accessed 24 November 2021.

World Health Organization. 2005. *Envelhecimento ativo: Uma política de saúde* (trans. S. Gontijo). Pan-Americana Saúde. https://bibliotecadigital.mdh.gov.br/jspui/bitstream/192/401/1/WORLD_envelhecimento_2005.pdf. Accessed 20 December 2021.

World Health Organization (ed.). 2007. *Global Age-Friendly Cities: A guide*. World Health Organization. https://apps.who.int/iris/bitstream/handle/10665/43755/9789241547307_eng.pdf;jsessionid=4FF9C55D3142695B51B845EF749A7FAD?sequence=1. Accessed 24 November 2021.

Writing Group for the Women's Health Initiative Investigators. 2002. 'Risks and benefits of estrogen plus progestin in healthy postmenopausal women: Principal results from the Women's Health

Initiative randomized controlled trial'. *JAMA: Journal of the American Medical Association*, 288(3), 321–33. https://doi.org/10.1001/jama.288.3.321.

Zago, A. V. and A. S. da Silva. 2003. 'Dançando com a Terceira Idade'. *A Terceira Idade*, 14(28), 54–73. https://www.sescsp.org.br/files/edicao_revista/11169179-524a-409a-bf8b-efa2c6e42bd7.pdf. Accessed 24 November 2021.

Zhai, Y., K. Li and J. Liu. 2018. 'A conceptual guideline to age-friendly outdoor space development in China: How do Chinese seniors use the urban comprehensive park? A focus on time, place, and activities'. *Sustainability*, 10(10), art. no. 3678. https://doi.org/10.3390/su10103678.

Zitkus, E. and C. Libanio. 2019. 'User experience of Brazilian Public Healthcare System: A case study on the accessibility of the information provided'. *The Design Journal*, 22(sup1), 707–21. https://doi.org/10.1080/14606925.2019.1595449.

Index

abandonment
   of children, elderly parents, 52, 99, 103, 240
Active Ageing discourse, framework, policy, 5, 15, 20, 26–7, 31, 57, 64–7, 92, 156, 240, 245–7
activism, 4, 210
addiction
   caused by smartphones, social media, 92, 136–7, 238
adult children, 53, 107, 153, 195, 241
Adventists, 18
African(s), 7, 30
ageing
   as a conditional contract, 152
   decline associated with ageing, 29, 39, 41, 152, 210, 243
   discourses about decf, 30, 39, 42, 153, 156, 236, 240–1
   as global problem, 237
   and grey hair, 36, 132, 192
   images of 2, 35, 37–40, 57, 85, 156, 235–6, 240, 244–5
   nation, 5
   natural ageing (as opposed to normal ageing), 191–2
   normal ageing (as opposed to natural ageing), 191
   policies, 2, 5, 65, 209, 244–6
   population, worldwide, 65, 237 (*see also* Brazil)
   reinvention of, 37
   representation of, 4, 39, 210, 217, 235, 240
   reprivatisation of, 39
   as social construct, 35, 70, 229
   societies, 240
   and sorrow, 19, 22
   successful, 30, 39, 85, 153, 241, 244
ageism, 2, 48, 55, 128, 248
age-friendly, 9, 11, 13, 65, 88
agenda/schedule, busy, 3, 25, 63, 94, 229, 238
Agenda Fácil SUS (app), 145, 171, 172
Ahlin, Tanya, 109
Airbnb (app), 143, 216, 238
algorithm, 182
alienation, 249
altruism, 209–10
Alzheimer's, 43, 62, 74, 100, 102, 143, 154, 163
animal laborans, 248
anti-ageing, 191, 202
anxiety, 24, 48, 50–1, 92, 126, 133, 137, 217–8, 222, 224, 234–6, 245
apps (*see also* under names of individual apps)
   banking, 43, 129, 142
   bespoke, 4, 149, 168, 172, 175, 178
   dating (and platforms, websites), 4, 182, 196, 198–202, 204
   downloading, 133, 141–2, 145, 148, 169, 171, 197, 239
   relating to health, 167–8, 173–4,
   training the brain game, 75, 156, 238
   unpredictable, 144, 147–8
Arendt, Hannah, 248–9
Argentina, 6
Aristotle, 177, 244–5, 249
autonomy
   financial, 6, 44, 152, 218 (*see also* crisis)
   mental, 74, 152, 218 (*see also* mental dependence)
   physical, 44, 94, 152, 218
   as a virtue, 153

babysitting, 110–12
backstage, of the performance, 158
Bandeirantes (colonial conquerors), 8, 45
banking, 134, 136, 173
Baptist church, 18, 165
Baptists, 28
Basic Health Unit (UBS), 171–2
Bauman, Zygmunt, 201
Beauvoir, Simone de, 30, 213, 240
belonging, sense of, 4, 25, 35, 45, 51, 82, 210, 221
best age, 2, 4, 42, 181, 200–1, 203–4
biosocial rationality, 203
blog
   starting one, 42, 183, 215
blood ties, 20 (*see also* kin)
boss
   and support of women at work, 99
body
   ageing, 25, 36, 53, 64, 72, 111, 201, 240–1
   appearance of, 64, 236
   Brazilian, 63
   functional, 64, 188
   healthy, 63, 241
   limits of, 38–9, 71–4, 111
   as social capital, 63–4
   sculpted, 63
   young, 202
Bourdieu, Pierre, 40, 158, 229
brain, 133, 154
   exercising the, 24, 62, 74, 76, 174
   smartphones as second brains, 75
Brazil
   ageing population in, 5, 48, 184 (*see also* ageing)
   budgetary deficit in, 48
   diversity in, 5, 7, 103
   and Federal Council of Medicine, 172
   and Gross Domestic Product (GDP), 33

income distribution in, 6, 33
inequality in, 5–7, 10, 46, 250
macro-regions in, 6
minimum wage in, 127, 241
National Health Policy for Elderly Persons in, 23
national pension system in, 2, 6, 48, 54–5, 128, 211 (*see also* pension)
official language in, 5
population in, 5
and Public Health System (SUS), 5, 33, 145, 167, 169–70, 184, 187
society in, 64, 230
and Statute for Elderly People, 5
telecommunication sector in, 126–7
and Women's Integral Health Assistance Program (PAISM), 184
Brazilian way, 176–7, 237
bricolage, 144, 148, 165, 239
bullying, 47, 136
burden, 29, 29, 43, 115, 249
  on children, family, 6, 25, 29, 43, 62–3, 72, 94, 101, 153, 155, 158, 168, 177, 209, 221, 225, 236–7, 240–3, 246–7
  on doctors, 173, 175
  as failure, 246
  on friends, 175
  on society, 2, 6, 64, 158, 209, 240–1
  on state, 2, 209
bureaucracy, 175–6, 237
burnout society, 248

Calvinist tradition, 8
cancer 25, 215, 226, 242
  breast, 71, 184, 187
  and diet, 164–5
  and HRT (Hormone Replacement Therapy), 183–4, 186–7
  prostate, 164, 169
Caradec, Vincent, 64
cardiologists, 170
care
  at a distance, 109–10
  geographies of, 109
  home, 100–1, 156, 216
  as obligation, 63, 99, 104, 153
  and reciprocity, 4, 63, 98, 106, 109, 115, 153, 177–8, 237, 242
  as unpaid work, 99
caregivers 102
  grandchildren as, 102
  as heroes, 102
  women as, 99
carnival, 8, 71, 248
Catholic, 8, 104, 185
Catholicism, Roman Catholic foundation, 8, 28
Catholic church (in Bento), 15, 17–21, 24, 56, 75, 92, 101, 128, 130, 135, 160, 226, 228
character (demonstration/proof of) 2, 8, 25, 35, 46, 56, 102, 107, 187, 210–1, 222, 224, 229, 236, 238, 245–9
check-up, 164, 169, 184, 187 (*see also* low-cost clinics)
chef, de cuisine, 78–9
Chile, 6, 111

China, 42, 65
Christian 18, 109, 162
  Evangelical, 195, 224
  new, 162
chronic disease, 5, 40
chronological age, 36, 42, 44, 152
Church of World Messianity, 18, 28, 160–2
Cicero, 210
citizenship 4, 8, 45, 100, 156, 210, 248–9
clothing, 11, 35–37, 63, 106–7, 163, 195
coffee culture, plantation, 7, 8, 45
co-housing, 216
colonial times and expeditions, 8, 45
compliance (with ageing policies, with healthy habits), 39, 158, 167–8
computer (device), 47, 56, 128–9, 164, 182, 234
conditional contract (ageing as a), 152
Dr Consulta, 28, 169-70 (*see also* low-cost clinics)
consumption, 36, 38, 158–9, 196–7, 201, 215, 240, 248, 247 (*see also* food)
contemplative life, 248–9
content curators, 3, 89, 135–6, 235
conviviality, 98, 117
cook/cooking, 56, 78–9, 106–7, 166, 195
co-presence, 3, 110, 113, 117, 122, 138
Coroametade (dating website), 200
corporate device, 136
corporations, corporate environment 46–7, 55, 128, 148, 187, 214–5, 248
corporative surname, 46
cost 5, 39, 53, 128, 148, 170
  of communication (device, calls, landline, mobile phone), 127, 239
  of living, 100, 106, 216
counseling, 108
Covid-19 pandemic, 24, 27, 135, 172
co-working, 78, 82
creativity, 126, 141, 146, 239–40
crisis, 101, 108, 211
  financial, economic, 106, 195 (*see also* autonomy)
  identity, 51, 63, 247
  marital, 79, 190, 198, 212
  midlife, 214
cultural
  capital, 9, 236
  context or background, 8, 18, 31, 51, 153, 205, 244, 247
  construct, 189, 229
  cross-cultural, 44
  diversity, 7
  programmes and events in Bento, 20, 40
  values (references, meaning and practices), 191, 203, 209, 237
cyberattacks, 131

DaMatta, Roberto, 8, 197, 235
dating
  act of, 199, 201, 204
  profile, 182
death
  age at, 10
  dependency as a form of, 43, 213, 242,
  of personhood, 43

as rebirth and renovation, 213
Debert, Guita Grin, 5, 38–9, 71
dementia, 74, 104
demographic change, 5, 167
Dependency Ratio, 6 (*see also* Old-age Dependency Ratio)
depression, 24, 55, 108, 183, 185, 189, 224, 248
dermatologist, 170, 183, 186
desire lines/paths, 146–17, 239
developers, 126, 146–7, 148, 168, 178, 239
diabetes, 184, 199
diet, 30, 89, 159–60, 162–6, 168, 174, 177, 184, 189, 192, 235, 243
digital identification card (digital ID), 170, 239
digital
 health literacy, 174
 inclusion, 3, 22, 88, 92, 126, 128, 130–1, 148, 215
 influencer, 37, 87, 217, 238
 life, 54, 83, 235
 literacy, 134 (*see also* illiterate)
 skills, 3, 43, 108, 147, 174, 234, 239
dignity, 1–2, 4, 8, 25, 31, 176, 212, 214, 226, 230, 240, 247–8
disease, 5, 33, 40, 43, 100, 162, 164, 166, 174, 176, 205, 221–3
distinction, 63, 72, 75, 107, 109, 157, 170
divorce (and being divorced), 110, 116, 139, 181, 186, 188, 194–6, 202, 204
doctors
 authority of, 174, 183, 222,
 from the internet, 165, 173
 private, 170, 172–4
 and WhatsApp, 173, 178, 237
 on YouTube, 4, 164–5, 174, 225
'Doctor Google', 173
domestic
 affairs, 77, 113
 arrangements, dynamics of, 106, 122, 238
 crisis and tension, 109
 life, 77
 space, 77
 violence, 247
Doriana family, 102–4
downgrade, 47, 168–70, 195
downsizing, 209
Dr Dráusio Varella (on Youtube), 174
'dry-women' (post-menopausal women), 191
Duolingo (app), 42, 62, 75

eating
 habits, 159-60
 at home, 163
economic recession, 106
Edmonds, Alexander, 63–4
education
 children, 212–3
 level of, 107, 174
elderly (parents), 3, 98, 101–3, 106, 109, 115, 153, 194, 204, 209, 213, 241
emergencies (managing), 4, 109, 115, 127, 173, 175, 237
emojis, 120
employment
 formal, 53, 99, 108, 226–7
 informal, 52
empowerment, 2, 37, 42, 114, 134, 148, 166–8, 172–4, 177–8, 240–1
empty nest, 106
enslaved Africans, 7
entrepreneur, 61, 215, 217, 220–1
entrepreneurship, 4, 8, 215, 217–9
epidemiological transition, 5
erectile dysfunction, 189, 203–4
essential tremor, 243
Europe, European, 30, 110
evangelicals, 18, 195, 224
everydayness, sense of, 113

face-to-face
 activities, 75, 82, 89, 158, 200
 conversation, 31
 encounters, 101, 118, 135, 148
 family interactions, 124
 rituals, 117
Facebook (app), 23–4, 31, 42, 54, 62, 79–81, 83–9, 101, 105, 113, 129, 144, 200, 218, 238
 Messenger (app), 31
facelifts, 153
failure
 dependence as, 63
 frailties and illness as, 156, 246
fake news, 32, 90–3, 235
family
 bonds, 120, 122
 budget, 107, 168, 195, 241
 constellation therapy, 223
 extended, 3, 117, 120, 122, 136, 137
 finances of, 146
 income of, 106
 nuclear, 103
 obligations, 98
 as the primary institution responsible for elderly care, 103
 standard of living of, 55, 195
 transnational, 109, 114, 122
 under the administration of, 43, 246
fashion industry, 37
fasting, intermittent, 165

Featherstone, Mike, 35, 38
Feminine Forever, 183
femininity, 193
fertility, 191 (*see also* maternity)
food
 artificial, 165
 choice, 160, 166, 243
 consumption, 159
 natural, 160, 163
football, 1, 73, 120
Fourth Age, 1, 73, 120
frailty, 25, 29, 30, 36, 38, 40, 42–4, 85, 99, 101, 109, 152, 158, 213, 240, 242–4, 246
free time, 2, 24–5, 35, 44, 55, 81, 89, 106–8, 120, 208, 216, 224, 226, 229
friendship, 4, 42, 122, 175, 177, 189, 192, 203

'gambiarra' (bricolage of apps), 144–7, 164, 147, 239
gender, 23, 55
generation
    kangaroo, 106
    latest (devices), 182
    older (participant), 2, 36, 46, 84, 110, 118, 120, 185, 215, 218, 248
    younger (children, grandchildren), 106–8, 112, 120, 129–30, 136, 234
geriatrician, 222
ghosting, 201
gifts (giving, receiving), 62, 113, 126, 160–1, 233–4
God, gods, 74, 173, 191, 202, 224–5, 233–4
Goffman, Erving, 158
Goldenberg, Miriam, 63–4, 177, 202
golden mean (Aristotle), 245–6
Google, 4, 80, 92–3, 129, 145, 163, 174, 215, 220, 237
    Calendar, 145–6
    Chrome, 145, 196
    Drive, 43, 54, 146, 239
    doctor from, 173
    Gmail, 54, 143
    Maps, 3, 42, 75, 80, 139, 148
    Maps Street View, 100
    Photos, 239
    Play, 141
governance of self (loss of), 152
government food programme, 176, 242
grandparenting, 110–14
gratitude, 82, 99, 213, 226
guidance
    from doctors, 174
    health, 233
    medical, 4, 28, 153, 175, 237
    religious, 18, 224
    seeking, 82, 173, 175, 177, 183–4, 225
gym, 12, 22–3, 56, 70–2, 78, 86, 115–6, 131, 136
gynaecologist, 170, 183–7

happiness 224, 244–5, 247–9
    industry, 248
happy ending, 4, 204
health
    and ageing, 18, 38–9, 65, 158, 167, 241–2, 246
    choices relating to, 166, 241, 156
    diet and, 160, 163–6, 184, 192
    and habits, 27, 39, 62, 70, 73–4, 76, 92, 156, 158, 163, 167, 188, 244, 246–7
    and identity, 158
    information concerning, 4, 159, 173–4, 235
    insurance and, 143, 168–9, 174–6
    of nation, 156
    policies, 3, 5, 244, 247
    and routines, 63
healthcare
    providers, 168–73
    system, 39, 168, 172–3, 175–6
Hepworth, Mike, 35, 38
heroes
    caregivers as, 102

    entrepreneurs as, 215, 217
herpes zoster, 175, 177
heterosexual, 4, 30, 189, 203
higher-income class, 131, 174
Ho'oponopono, 222–3
hobbies, 61, 73, 79–83, 221, 238
homeless people, 65, 228
hope, 31, 196, 214, 236–8, 247
Hormone Replacement Therapy (HRT), 183–7, 189, 191
hospital, 11, 15–6, 20, 24, 28, 52, 67, 73, 92, 99–100, 105, 108, 170, 175–6, 219
housework, 77–8, 100, 107, 216
house ownership, 6, 108

ICTs, 109
identity
    crisis, 51, 63, 247
    embodied, 35
    feminine, 191
    men, 203
    of São Paulo, 2, 8, 45
    women, 203
illiterate, 242
    digitally, 129 (*see also* digital literacy)
illness, 24, 156, 234, 241
immigrants, migrants, 7–9, 11, 45
inclusive, 103, 120, 176
incompleteness, feeling of, 49, 213
independence, 3, 5, 39, 65, 106, 109, 178, 189, 196, 216, 236, 247
industrialization, 8, 45
inequality, 5–7, 35, 46, 174
infrastructure, 6, 146, 214, 246
inheritance, 5, 11, 54, 74, 82, 96, 105, 110, 212–3, 230
inner self, 35
insomnia, 185, 187, 189, 224
instructor, 19–20, 38–9, 49, 71–2, 226, 243
interdependence, 39, 178
interface (smartphone, interface, technology), 128, 130, 133, 168, 172
intergenerational
    collaboration, 24
    contract, 63, 153
    issue, 106
internet
    access to, 22, 128, 146
    revolution, 234
intimacy, 4, 18, 190, 196, 204
invisibility, 193, 214 (*see also* visibility)
iPad, 112
iPhone, 127, 131, 142, 182
Italians (immigrants, descendants of), 7, 11, 198

Japan, 45, 160, 191, 209
Japanese immigrants, descendants of, 7, 11

Kahn, Robert L., 241
kangaroo generation, 106
Katz, Stephen, 203

labour market, 2, 24, 55, 241
lack of reciprocity, 106, 153, 242
Lamb, Sarah, 241, 244

landline, 127–8, 183
laptop, notebooks, 20, 182
Laslett, Peter, 152
Latin America, 6, 9, 200
lazy (being or being labelled as), 44, 71, 99, 128, 141, 190
learning
　as a double gain, 74
　how to manage a digital life, 235
　a new language, 75, 156
　smartphones, 129, 131–2,
　WhatsApp, 3, 20, 22, 126, 130, 133
legacy, 4, 110, 211, 221, 230
Leibing, Annette 38, 64, 102
leisure activities, 64
libido, 183, 185, 188–90, 193, 202, 204
life expectancy, 11, 38
　at birth, 36, 208
life project, 221, 223, 236
limbo (living in), 2, 27, 53, 56, 226, 241
LinkedIn (app), 31, 54, 61
'liquid love', 201, 204
longevity, 163, 218
Longevity Playground, 65–70, 92, 131 (see also open-air gyms)
low-cost clinics, 28, 139, 169 (see also check-ups)
low-income, 52, 187, 191, 226
loyalty, 47, 173
Luborsky, Mark R., 44, 77, 209

make a 21 (Embratel's motto), 126, 128
marriage, 4, 44, 55, 77, 104–5, 114, 163, 192–3, 195, 212, 224–5, 245
　second, 194
Marshall, Barbara L., 203
masculinity, 189, 203
mass (Catholic), 25, 101, 103
masturbation, 188
material conditions, 241, 246, 248
maternity, 184 (see also fertility)
mature woman, 37, 183, 204
media coverage, 24, 48, 54, 59, 64, 91, 102, 163, 187, 192, 203
medical
　advice, 175
　authority, 4, 167, 174, 178
　gaze, 174
　guidance, 4, 28, 153, 175, 237
　referral, 28, 172, 219
　school, 11, 13, 24, 155, 159
medicalization, 248
meditation, 24, 62, 109, 141, 189, 192, 223–4
memes, 85, 243
memory
　decline associated with ageing, 36, 74–6, 133, 243
　exercising the, 2, 74, 76–7, 143
　games, 24, 76
　and mobile devices, 132–3, 141
　and smartphones, 75
menarche, 191
menopause, 4, 181, 183–7, 189–91, 193, 202–4
　and hot flushes, 185–90
menstruation, 185

mental dependence, 43, 243 (see also autonomy)
meritocracy, ageing as, 215, 241, 245
messages
　good morning, 136, 177
　phatic function, 120, 125, 136
　texts, 121, 130, 182
　visual, 120, 136
　voice, 131
metrics, provided by apps, 168
mhealth
　apps, 167
　industry, 175
migraine, 164
migration, 7–9, 11, 30, 45, 109
mindfulness, 24, 223
mini-LG (device), 133–4
mobility, 3, 27, 138, 140, 148, 233, 235
Moovit (mobility app), 42, 140
moral
　expectation, 2
　failure, 2, 30, 242
　gap, 248
　obligation, 63, 153, 237
morality, 2, 31, 39, 63, 156, 191–2, 241, 245
mortality, the intimidations of, 213, 240
Motorola Lenovo (device), 141
mutual support, 204, 237

'neither, nors' (neither working, nor retired), 55–6
Netflix (streaming), 55, 159, 163–4
network
　of favours, 4
　of solidarity, 237
new career, after retirement, 78, 115, 189, 192, 218
night (going out at), 42, 140, 193, 238
normativity, 2, 57, 63, 237, 244
North America, 38–9, 205
nutrition, 141, 156–7, 159, 160–1, 163
nutritionists, 92, 159–60, 162

obese, 166
Old-age Dependency Ratio (OADR), 6 (see also Dependency Ratio)
open-air gyms, 65 (see also Longevity Playground)
'Our Time' (dating platform), 200
outpatient
　care centre, 92
　service, 13
overweight, 166, 186

palliative care, 176
Pandora's box, 233–4, 236
Par Perfeito (perfect match, dating platform), 200
parents' house
　as a safe place for adult children, 106
　as a house-within-a-house cohabitation, 109
participatory culture, 89
patience (lack of, from children), 3, 20, 129, 213
'Paulistas' (born in São Paulo), 8–9

INDEX　　**273**

peers, 3, 20, 32, 63, 91–2, 121, 126, 135, 167, 170, 175, 177, 220, 235, 242
pension
    reform, 46, 48, 55, 208, 248
    scheme, 6
    from the state, 6, 106, 241
    system, 6, 46–7, 52, 208 (*see also* Brazilian national pension system)
PhD, 82, 155, 213
physical activity, 2, 24, 64–5, 70, 73–4, 76, 83, 92, 159, 184, 202, 221, 243
Pilates, 23, 38, 49, 51, 56, 62, 71, 74–5
plastic surgery, 63–4
policymakers, 178
pornography, 4, 196-7
portfolio of activities (aimed at the third age), 15, 18, 44, 56, 229, 233, 247
postmenopausal women, 183
poverty, 234, 240
Prevent Senior (health insurance plan), 169, 170
prevention, 3, 5, 13, 27, 39, 64, 167, 169–70, 245
priority seat paradox, 40
privacy, 29, 31, 109, 113, 116, 155, 158, 183, 196, 216
productive life, 49, 135, 216, 247
professional credentials, 4, 45, 51, 63, 79–80, 86, 107, 195, 203, 209, 215, 220, 227–9, 238, 247
profile picture, 182
protagonists (older people as), 42, 44, 218, 230
Protestantism 8
psychologist, 29, 52, 82, 170, 217
public transport, 10, 15, 40–1, 139–40
Pype, Katrien 146, 239

quality of life, 10, 100, 156, 159, 177, 184, 186, 241, 246

reciprocity
    lack of, 106, 153, 242
    system of, 177
regrets, 99, 120, 185, 195, 197, 204, 211, 221
reinventing work (in older age), 210, 214
Reinvent Yourself Programme, 219
religion, 18, 28, 74, 120, 159–60, 162, 213, 224–25
resilience, 72, 204, 212, 215, 225
respect, 37, 41, 57, 72, 121, 150, 174, 196, 210, 220–1, 225–6, 228–30, 236, 240, 247, 249
retirement
    age at, 208
    and hands-on projects, 209
    compulsory, 1, 47, 211
    institutionalisation of, 39
    sexual, 203–4
    statutory age, 6
    second, 181, 204
Dr Lair Ribeiro (on Youtube), 165
Rio de Janeiro, 45, 63–4, 177, 187, 191, 198
Rowe, John L., 241

Samsung (device), 62, 131, 134

São Paulo
    citizen of, 8–9, 46, 64, 210, 215, 237
    districts of, 10, 11, 27, 36, 242
    Gross Domestic Product (GDP) in, 7
    identity, 2, 8, 45
    outskirts of, 24
    population, 9
savings, 155, 165
Savishinsky, Joel S. 209
scams, 89, 131–2, 235
second-hand devices, 132, 141, 250
self-esteem, 3, 64, 74, 79, 82, 130, 133, 217, 225, 234
self-help, 233
self-monitoring, 167, 172
self-surveillance, 29, 109, 242 (*see also* surveillance)
self-care, 25, 56, 63, 94, 98, 167, 221
Seneca, 208, 210
Sennett, Richard, 210, 221
sensors (self-tracking), 167
sex
    casual, 4, 188, 198–200, 204, 245
    drive, 188–9
    life, 181, 183, 185, 187, 192, 194–6, 204, 225
sexual abuse, 181, 193–5
sexual performance, 189, 203
sexuality, 4, 18, 181, 183, 204
siblings, 62, 79, 103, 109, 115, 155–6
silence (surrounding age), 30–1, 44, 240–4, 246
SIM card, 127
slavery, 7, 45
smart city, 146, 230, 239
smart TV, 182–3
smartwatch, 73, 68
smartness from below, 239
smartphones
    adoption of, 129, 131
    as alibis, 18, 243
    as allies, 18, 75
    as family albums, 114
    as game-changers, 2
    as a house-within-a-house, 109, 122
    and intuition, 133, 234
    ownership of, 136
    as a place we live in, 198
    as repositories of emotions, 114
    as second brains, 75
    snooping on, 197
    as a space for intimacy, 4
    thief and, 131
    use in public spaces, 67, 131, 149
social
    capital, 63–4, 91, 212, 235, 237
    contract, 216, 220, 233
    expectations, 2, 18, 35, 38, 191, 195
    inclusion, 70
    isolation, 136
    life, 3, 135, 137, 148, 152, 193, 195, 209, 214, 216, 228–9
    recognition, 89, 226
social media, 4, 39–40, 56, 80, 82–3, 88, 91, 102, 109, 112–3, 120, 136–8, 142, 156, 158–9, 163, 165, 217, 234, 238, 242–3

polarization on, 120
social network, 31, 62, 79, 81, 83, 91, 107, 135, 148, 175–6, 183, 217
societies, labouring, 248, 249
solutionism, 144
South Africa, 191
South America, 5
South India, 109
spirituality, 27, 213, 226
Spotify (app), 62, 76, 82, 141, 182
staying active and keeping fit, 2, 44–5, 54, 72, 169
stereotypes, 36, 39, 102, 121
stickers, 76, 115–6, 120–1
stigma, 20, 29, 39–40, 44, 47, 91, 126, 192, 209, 230, 146
'the street' (in opposition to 'the house' in Brazil), 197–8, 235
succession, 221
supervisors (supporting women at work), 212
supplements (vitamin complex), 165
surveillance, 62, 71, 179 (see also self-surveillance)

taboo, 120, 185
technological blanket, 167
technological constraint, 144, 239
technology
　adoption of, 20, 55
　of the self, 160
telemedicine, 76, 153, 167, 172
therapies (integrative, holistic), 141
therapist, 92, 101
third age, 3–4, 15, 18, 20, 24, 29, 35, 42, 44, 56, 64–5, 70–1, 73, 75, 89, 92, 94, 98, 106, 122, 126, 130, 135, 139, 148, 152–3, 158, 160, 168, 170, 215, 218–9, 224, 226, 229, 233, 235, 243–4
third agers, 158
Tinder (app), 42, 197, 200
tourism, 37, 49
tracking apps, 167–8, 178
travelling, 55, 62, 75, 78, 80, 104, 155, 193, 197, 204
trust, 4, 32, 91, 113, 162–3, 168, 170, 173, 222, 237
tutorials (on YouTube), 79–80

Uber (app), 3, 42, 53–54, 61, 107, 139–140, 143, 148, 152, 177, 238
Umbanda (religion), 18–19, 28, 213
underweight, 166
unemployment, 44, 106
United States (USA), 165, 209
Uruguay, 6
usefulness, sense of, 2, 61, 211
utility, sense of, 49, 78, 86, 139, 210, 238

vaginal dryness, 185, 189, 193
Viagra, 199, 203–4
virtue, 156, 245, 248
　autonomy as, 153
　being busy as, 209, 239
　self-care as, 63
　work as, 4, 56
virtuous life, 224, 245–6

visibility, 3, 31, 37, 63, 92, 98, 102, 134, 158, 192–3, 225, 228, 230, 238, 240–4 (see also invisibility)
volunteering, 4, 25, 64, 210, 225, 227–9, 247

Waze (app), 75, 143
WhatsApp course, 20, 107, 128–130, 133–5, 137, 139, 143
WhatsApp groups
　family group, 117–9, 120–1, 136
　as a feedback mechanism, 3, 135, 148
　for managing care, 62, 115
　as a network of favours, 4
　as source of information, 89, 91, 94
　stickers, 76, 115–6, 120–1
　supporting an activity, 20, 24, 51, 89, 135, 139, 158, 161, 176, 227–8
　when to leave, 197, 121
Whyte, Susan R., 153
Wi-Fi, 109, 134
widow, 100–1, 139, 156, 196, 201
will to health, 156, 158–9
wisdom, 211–12, 223, 240
Women's Health Initiative (WHI), 184
work
　abroad, 109, 117
　as character, 2, 8, 25, 35, 46, 56, 102, 107, 167, 187, 210, 224, 229, 236, 238, 245, 248
　environment, 234, 241
　glorification of, 248
　informal, 216, 247
　life, 1, 36, 44, 47–8, 57
　as punishment, 8, 248
　as a source of citizenship, 4, 8, 45, 248–9
　routine, 49, 56, 87, 111, 210, 229, 249
　unpaid, 99, 173, 247
　and not working, 56, 108, 136
work-oriented
　Bento, 31, 42, 45, 56, 109, 136, 148, 209, 229, 238
　Community, 2
　São Paulo, 9, 63
workshops, 74, 82, 92, 160, 163, 187, 215, 238
World Health Organization (WHO), 64, 208

yoga, 23, 50, 62, 70–1, 116, 141, 189, 192
youth, 38, 40, 57, 63–4, 73, 137, 148, 187, 201–2, 223, 234, 249
YouTube (app), 4, 52, 79–80, 82, 89, 105, 159, 163–5, 174

Zoom (app), 24

Lightning Source UK Ltd.
Milton Keynes UK
UKHW050353230422
401908UK00012B/89